Competency	Chapter
Professional Identity	
Practice Behavior Examples...	
Serve as representatives of the profession, its mission, and its core values.	
Know the profession's history.	6, 9
Commit themselves to the profession's enhancement and to their own professional conduct and growth.	
Advocate for client access to the services of social work.	1, 8
Practice personal reflection and self-correction to assure continual professional development.	12
Attend to professional roles and boundaries.	
Demonstrate professional demeanor in behavior, appearance, and communication.	
Engage in career-long learning.	
Use supervision and consultation.	
Ethical Practice	
Practice Behavior Examples...	
Obligation to conduct themselves ethically and engage in ethical decision-making.	
Know about the value base of the profession, its ethical standards, and relevant law.	
Recognize and manage personal values in a way that allows professional values to guide practice.	1
Make ethical decisions by applying standards of the National Association of Social Workers Code of Ethics and, as applicable, of the International Federation of Social Workers/International Association of Schools of Social Work Ethics in Social Work, Statement of Principles.	7
Tolerate ambiguity in resolving ethical conflicts.	5, 11
Apply strategies of ethical reasoning to arrive at principled decisions.	
Critical Thinking	
Practice Behavior Examples...	
Know about the principles of logic, scientific inquiry, and reasoned discernment.	
Use critical thinking augmented by creativity and curiosity.	3, 9
Requires the synthesis and communication of relevant information.	
Distinguish, appraise, and integrate multiple sources of knowledge, including research-based knowledge and practice wisdom.	5, 7, 12
Analyze models of assessment, prevention, intervention, and evaluation.	
Demonstrate effective oral and written communication in working with individuals, families, groups, organizations, communities, and colleagues.	

CSWE's Core Competencies and Practice Behavior Examples in this Text

Competency	Chapter
Diversity in Practice	
Practice Behavior Examples...	
Understand how diversity characterizes and shapes the human experience and is critical to the formation of identity.	
Understand the dimensions of diversity as the intersectionality of multiple factors including age, class, color, culture, disability, ethnicity, gender, gender identity and expression, immigration status, political ideology, race, religion, sex, and sexual orientation.	9
Appreciate that, as a consequence of difference, a person's life experiences may include oppression, poverty, marginalization, and alienation as well as privilege, power, and acclaim.	2, 5
Recognize the extent to which a culture's structures and values may oppress, marginalize, alienate, or create or enhance privilege and power.	3
Gain sufficient self-awareness to eliminate the influence of personal biases and values in working with diverse groups.	
Recognize and communicate their understanding of the importance of difference in shaping life experiences.	
View themselves as learners and engage those with whom they work as informants.	
Human Rights and Justice	
Practice Behavior Examples...	
Understand that each person, regardless of position in society, has basic human rights, such as freedom, safety, privacy, an adequate standard of living, health care, and education.	4
Recognize the global interconnections of oppression and be knowledgeable about theories of justice and strategies to promote human and civil rights.	6
Incorporate social justice practices in organizations, institutions, and society to ensure that these basic human rights are distributed equitably and without prejudice.	2, 9
Understand the forms and mechanisms of oppression and discrimination.	10
Advocate for human rights and social and economic justice.	
Engage in practices that advance social and economic justice.	
Research-Based Practice	
Practice Behavior Examples...	
Use practice experience to inform research, employ evidence-based interventions, evaluate their own practice, and use research findings to improve practice, policy, and social service delivery.	
Comprehend quantitative and qualitative research and understand scientific and ethical approaches to building knowledge.	11-12
Use practice experience to inform scientific inquiry.	4
Use research evidence to inform practice.	1, 7

Competency	Chapter
Human Behavior	
Practice Behavior Examples...	
Know about human behavior across the life course, the range of social systems in which people live, and the ways social systems promote or deter people in maintaining or achieving health and well-being.	1, 3, 8, 10-11
Apply theories and knowledge from the liberal arts to understand biological, social, cultural, psychological, and spiritual development.	
Utilize conceptual frameworks to guide the processes of assessment, intervention, and evaluation.	
Critique and apply knowledge to understand person and environment.	
Policy Practice	
Practice Behavior Examples...	
Understand that policy affects service delivery and actively engage in policy practice.	8
Know the history and current structures of social policies and services, the role of policy in service delivery, and the role of practice in policy development.	2, 5
Analyze, formulate, and advocate for policies that advance social well-being.	4
Collaborate with colleagues and clients for effective policy action.	6, 12
Practice Contexts	
Practice Behavior Examples...	
Keep informed, resourceful, and proactive in responding to evolving organizational, community, and societal contexts at all levels of practice.	7
Recognize that the context of practice is dynamic, and use knowledge and skill to respond proactively.	
Continuously discover, appraise, and attend to changing locales, populations, scientific and technological developments, and emerging societal trends to provide relevant services.	2-3, 10, 11
Provide leadership in promoting sustainable changes in service delivery and practice to improve the quality of social services.	

Competency	Chapter
Engage, Assess, Intervene, Evaluate	
Practice Behavior Examples...	
Identify, analyze, and implement evidence-based interventions designed to achieve client goals.	
Use research and technological advances.	
Evaluate program outcomes and practice effectiveness.	
Develop, analyze, advocate, and provide leadership for policies and services.	4, 8
Promote social and economic justice.	
A) ENGAGEMENT	
Substantively and effectively prepare for action with individuals, families, groups, organizations, and communities.	
Use empathy and other interpersonal skills.	
Develop a mutually agreed-on focus of work and desired outcomes.	6
B) ASSESSMENT	
Collect, organize, and interpret client data.	
Assess client strengths and limitations.	
Develop mutually agreed-on intervention goals and objectives.	
Select appropriate intervention strategies.	
C) INTERVENTION	
Initiate actions to achieve organizational goals.	
Implement prevention interventions that enhance client capacities.	10
Help clients resolve problems.	
Negotiate, mediate, and advocate for clients.	
Facilitate transitions and endings.	
D) EVALUATION	
Critically analyze, monitor, and evaluate interventions.	

Engaging Social Welfare

An Introduction to Policy Analysis

Mark J. Stern
University of Pennsylvania

PEARSON

Boston Columbus Indianapolis New York San Francisco Upper Saddle River
Amsterdam Cape Town Dubai London Madrid Milan Munich Paris Montréal Toronto
Delhi Mexico City São Paulo Sydney Hong Kong Seoul Singapore Taipei Tokyo

Editor in Chief: Ashley Dodge
Editorial Assistant: Amandria Guadalupe
Managing Editor: Denise Forlow
Program Manager: Carly Czech
Editorial Project Manager: Alverne Ball, Integra Software Services Pvt. Ltd.
Executive Marketing Manager: Kelly May
Marketing Coordinator: Jessica Warren
Senior Operations Supervisor: Mary Fischer
Operations Specialist: Eileen Corallo

Art Director: Jayne Conte
Cover Designer: Karen Salzbach
Cover Art: Shutterstock.com/Linda Webb
Digital Media Director: Brian Hyland
Digital Media Project Manager: Tina Gagliostro
Full-Service Project Management: Integra Software Services, Ltd./Shiny Rajesh
Composition: Integra Software Services Pvt. Ltd.
Printer/Binder: RR Donnelley BAR/Harrisonburg
Cover Printer: RR Donnelley BAR/Harrisonburg

Credits and acknowledgments borrowed from other sources and reproduced, with permission, in this textbook appear on appropriate page within text.

Many of the designations by manufacturers and seller to distinguish their products are claimed as trademarks. Where those designations appear in this book, and the publisher was aware of a trademark claim, the designations have been printed in initial caps or all caps.

Library of Congress Cataloging-in-Publication Data

Stern, Mark J.
  Engaging social welfare : an introduction to policy analysis / Mark J. Stern, University of Pennsylvania.
    pages cm
  ISBN-13: 978-0-205-73067-4 (alk. paper)
  ISBN-10: 0-205-73067-1 (alk. paper)
  1. Social service—United States.   2. Social planning—United States.   3. United States—Social policy—Evaluation.   I. Title.
  HV91.S6494 2015
  361.6'10973—dc23

2013033983

9

ISBN-10: 0-205-73067-1
ISBN-13: 978-0-205-73067-4

Contents

PART II: ADDRESSING HUMAN NEEDS

7. Physical and Behavioral Health 152

8. Employment, Public Assistance, and Job Training 177

PART III: ADDRESSING THE NEEDS OF SPECIAL POPULATIONS

Preface

To Michael Katz

Social workers are policymakers. This truth, however, often escapes them.

For many social work students, policy happens on the distant horizon. They may read about a new law or Congressional hearing in the newspaper or online. Their supervisor may mention that a budget cut has changed their agency's procedures. It's not hard to convince them that *social workers are influenced by policy.*

This text makes a more ambitious argument: *social workers influence policy.* Obviously, when social workers sign a petition, join a demonstration or protest, or lobby a local official, they make a contribution to shifting policy. But again, these are relatively rare events that are often not central to their professional duties.

Social workers influence policies in ways that may not feel like policymaking. When they figure out how best to reduce the impact of a stupid law on their clients, they make policy. When they discuss with their colleagues whether an agency regulation hurts the people the agency serves, they make policy. When they figure out a more efficient and effective way to deliver a service, they make policy. Policy is a blanket that engulfs professional practice.

I wrote this text with the conviction that every social worker is a policymaker and that they need a body of knowledge and a set of competencies to fulfill that role. More importantly, perhaps, it looks at a variety of policies from the standpoint of a practitioner. What forces constrain our actions? Where are there opportunities for innovation? Who do we need to join forces with? These are the types of questions we need to ask if we are to translate the phrase *policy practice* into meaningful action.

Features

There are many features of this text to enhance your experience, however, they are only as useful as you make them. By engaging with this text and its resources, you'll gain a variety of skills-based outcomes including

- **The ability to understand the political and economic forces that drive social welfare policy.** By using a *policy-in-environment* framework to see social welfare policies as a product of political and economic forces, you'll learn how the historical development of *ideas* and *institutions* frame the policy choices Americans have made. In particular, it demonstrates that we need to understand how politics and economics influence one another rather than treating them as two separate fields.

- **The ability to analyze the role of social justice and social oppression in the development of social welfare policy.** Through the years, social workers have contributed to these struggles through innovative tactics—like the use of neighborhood surveys as discussed in Chapter 6 (Housing and Community Development)—and civil disobedience. The struggles of the twenty-first century are more complex. They cross national boundaries—like migrants who must live a shadowy existence—and move beyond straightforward civil rights movements. The book allows students to analyze the role of professional ethics in engaging social justice movements.

- **The ability to explain how recent changes in family, community, and social life are influencing social welfare policies.** Human behavior and the social environment provide part of the social context within which policies are created and implemented. Whether we're speaking of a Social Security system created for the "breadwinner" family of "mom, dad, and the kids" or an approach to older Americans' services that assumes that we all will have a daughter or son to provide services as we age, the tension between rigid social welfare policies and flexible personal lives continues to undermine Americans' social well-being. The book gives students the ability to apply knowledge to understand person and environment and their changing relationship.

- **The ability to critically assess recent changes in social welfare policy, including the Affordable Care Act of 2010.** I began writing this text before the Affordable Care Act became law and needed to revise its description after the Supreme Court ruled on its constitutionality in 2012. It was completed on the eve of its full implementation in 2014. The book helps students understand how these changes in policy affect service delivery.

Learning Outcomes

Students will be able to achieve a variety of learning outcomes by using this text and its resources including

- **Critical thinking skills**—Students can develop their critical thinking skills by reviewing the competency boxes (indicated by the Core Competencies series icon) and engaging with the multimedia resources highlighted in blue boxes throughout the chapter.

- **Oral communication skills**—Students can develop their oral communication skills by engaging with others in and out of class to discuss their comprehension of the chapter based on the chapter's learning objectives.

- **Assessment and writing skills**—Students can develop their assessment and writing skills in preparation for future licensing exams by completing topic-based and chapter review assessments for each chapter.

- **CSWE core competencies**—Students can develop their comprehension and application of CSWE's core competencies and practice behaviors by discussing the competency box critical-thinking questions.

Acknowledgments

This text represents more than three decades spent trying to make sense of social welfare policy. Many teachers and colleagues have aided me in this quest. Michael Katz taught me the methods and approach of historians and how to meld critical judgments with a commitment to social justice. Two senior colleagues when I first began teaching—Hal Levin and June Axinn—provided my initial orientation to the field. Many of my current colleagues helped me understand specific fields, including Dennis Culhane (homelessness), Phyllis Solomon and Yin-Ling Irene Wong (mental health services), Domenic Vitiello (food systems and immigration), Elaine Simon (education), and Ira Goldstein (housing and community development). Richard Gelles and I agree about almost nothing, but his work required me to clarify my own thinking about domestic violence and asset-based social policies. My research collaborator and spouse, Susan Seifert, learned more about social welfare policy over the past few years than she expected and made important conceptual and editorial contributions to the text.

This is the first edition of this text. In covering so many topics and fields, it is inevitable that I've sometimes fallen short in some of my explanations and analyses. Indeed, simply keeping abreast of recent economic and political changes is a challenge. I welcome instructors' and students' comments and suggestions about how future editions of the book could be more effective. Please email me at engagingsocialwelfare@gmail.com.

This text is available in a variety of formats—digital and print. To learn more about our programs, pricing options, and customization, visit **http://www.pearsonhighered.com**.

1

An Approach to Policy Practice

POLICY IS PRACTICE

Social work is a practice profession. From its beginnings, the focus
has been on developing effective methods for intervening in social
processes to improve the quality of life of members of our society.
As the NASW Code of Ethics begins,

> A historic and defining feature of social work is the profes-
> sion's focus on individual well-being in a social context and the
> well-being of society. Fundamental to social work is attention
> to the environmental forces that create, contribute to, and
> address problems in living.[1]

For many social workers, this mission statement means that
they should sharpen their clinical skills to better address their clients'
personal issues. Policy often seems far removed from their everyday
concerns. Yet, increasingly, members of the profession have come
to see that this is shortsighted. The rise of managed care during the
1990s had a direct and profound impact on how social workers did
their jobs. The increased visibility of concentrated poverty in urban
neighborhoods changed the context in which social workers did
their work. And the economic recessions of the first decade of the
twenty-first century—culminating in the mass unemployment and
underemployment of 2009–12—aggravated old problems and created new ones while local and state governments and social agencies
saw their resources dry up.

In short, the past decade taught social workers that social welfare policy is an integral dimension of their practice. Some aspects

---

[1]"Code of Ethics of the National Association of Social Workers," *NASW,* http://
www.socialworkers.org/pubs/code/code.asp

1

of policymaking—backroom legislative deals, international monetary agreements—seem very distant from social workers' immediate professional concerns, but the effects of those distant decisions have a clear impact. Less obvious, however, is a second connection between social workers' experience and this distant world of policy: how the social environment influences the nature of social policy. Indeed, social work and other helping professions have frontline experience with many of the environments—disadvantaged neighborhoods, behavioral and physical health agencies, the child welfare system—that are the objects of social welfare policy. Social workers do not just feel the effects of social policy; they are critical to shaping the context in which policy is developed and implemented.

Many social workers use a person-in-environment approach in their clinical practice. In contrast to a purely psychological perspective that focuses on internal cognitive processes, this approach typically incorporates information about a client's social environment into assessment and intervention strategies. Depression or stress may call for different types of interventions depending on whether one's client lives in a well-off or a poor community or whether the client is broadly connected or socially isolated. In most social work programs, the teaching of human behavior and its relationship to the social environment is based on some variant of this perspective.[2]

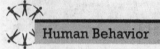

Human Behavior

Practice Behavior Example: Know about human behavior across the life course, the range of social systems in which people live, and the ways social systems promote or deter people in maintaining or achieving health and well-being.

Critical Thinking Question: How might clinical depression present itself differently between a client living in an affluent community and a client living in a poor community? What services and support might be available in each setting?

THE POLICY-IN-ENVIRONMENT MODEL

Assess your comprehension of "The Policy-in-Environment Model" by completing this quiz.

The model presented here builds on the person-in-environment approach. However, instead of a focus on individual functioning, it examines the internal decision-making of policymakers and analysts in hammering out specific programs as well as examining the broader environmental factors that influence social policy outcomes.[3]

The policy-in-environment model is based on the interaction between two interdependent systems. On the one hand, there is the immediate world of policy formulation. This "little world" is populated by decision makers—presidents, legislators, judges, lobbyists, and others—who devote most of their time to developing and formulating social policies. This world is governed by a variety of processes through which problems are identified; alternative approaches are debated; and a policy is adopted, implemented, and evaluated.

On the other hand, the little world of policy development—a world where powerful people sit around tables and make decisions—does not operate in a vacuum. It occurs in a force field dominated by political economy, that is, the interaction of decisions about the distribution of material goods and social power. Three important factors join political and economic decisions:

- *institutional arrangements* that define routine patterns of behavior
- *ideas* that rationalize or legitimate these institutional arrangements
- *social movements* that challenge and sometimes supplant dominant institutions and world views

---

[2]Mary E. Kondrat, "Person-in-Environment," in *Encyclopedia of Social Work*, 20th ed., online version, eds. Terry Mizrahi and Larry E. Davis (Oxford: Oxford University Press, 2008).

[3]Kondrat, "Person-in-Environment."

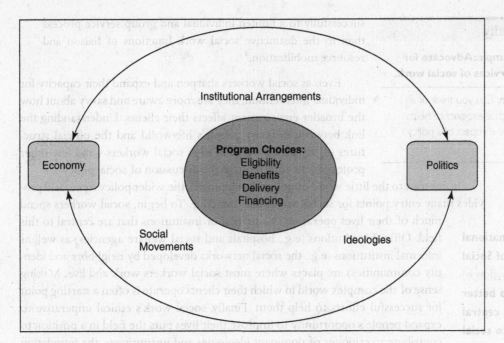

Figure 1.1
The Policy-in-Environment Model
The political and economic environment influences decisions about social welfare policy. Social workers and other professionals can play a role in influencing that environment.

Much of the discussion of policy practice in the social work profession has been devoted to exerting influence on the little world of policy development. Lobbying, giving testimony, and advocating for particular changes in laws are the typical behaviors that come to mind when we speak about policy practice.[4]

Yet, if we define policy narrowly as just the world of policymaking, social workers are at a distinct disadvantage. First, most social workers do not have time to immerse themselves fully in this world. Policy development is dominated by individuals who spend most of their work lives doing little else. In contrast, social workers typically come to policy as practitioners engaged in improving the "real world" circumstances of ordinary people. If policy is only about deciding on a set of regulations or the wording of a particular legislative bill, many groups other than social workers are better positioned to make a difference.

Second, a narrow definition of policy practice threatens to lure social workers away from the strength they bring to the policy world. During my years of teaching, I frequently encountered MSW students who said they were "into policy" but were dismissive of their classmates who focused primarily on helping people, families, and communities. Yet, it is precisely their practice experience that is social workers' contribution to the world of public policy. As Roy Lubove noted in *The Professional Altruist,*

> Yet if social work could claim any distinctive function in an atomized urban society with serious problems of group communication and mass deprivation, it was not individual therapy but liaison between groups and the stimulation of social legislation and institutional change. Since no other occupational group presumes as does social work a generalized mandate to perform these indispensible functions, the preeminence of the therapeutic role created a vacuum which remains unfilled. Professionalization—the machinery of altruism—was adapted far more

---

[4]Bruce Jansson, *Becoming an Effective Policy Advocate* (Belmont, CA: Brooks/Cole, 2010).

Read the International Federation of Social Workers' Definition of Social Work, **to better understand how central policy is to social work's mission.**

successfully to a limited individual and group service process than to the distinctive social work functions of liaison and resource mobilization.[5]

Even as social workers sharpen and expand their capacity for individual intervention, they are more aware and savvy about how the broader environment affects their clients. Understanding the link between ordinary people's life-world and the official structures of the policy world is what social workers—and few other professionals—can bring to the discussion of social policy.

In contrast to the little world of policy development, the wider policy force field provides many entry points for social work policy practice. To begin, social workers spend much of their lives operating in a myriad of institutions that are central to this field. Official institutions (e.g., hospitals and social welfare agencies) as well as informal institutions (e.g., the social networks developed by neighbors and identity communities) are places where most social workers work and live. Making sense of the complex world in which their clients operate is often a starting point for successful efforts to help them. Finally, social work's ethical imperative to expand people's opportunity to improve their lives puts the field in a position to contribute to critiques of dominant ideologies and institutions—the foundation of any social movement.

A policy-in-environment approach, therefore, can change policy practice from an activity that seems distant and even alien to one that is central to the daily experience of social workers. Certainly, political advocacy—like lobbying legislators for increased funding for domestic abuse programs, organizing a letter campaign in support of a ballot initiative, or working on a political campaign—is an important dimension of policy practice. But many less distant aspects of social work practice—like questioning the "standard operating procedures" of your agency when they are unresponsive to client needs, challenging a moralistic definition of a client's behavior by a physician or other colleague, or joining a social movement in support of your clients (even if it doesn't promise to lead directly to a policy change)—are also policy practice. Proactive social work practice also contributes to shifting the institutional and ideological context within which the little world of policy development operates.

Chapter 1 explores the "little world" of policy development with a particular focus on the types of choices that inform social welfare programs. In Chapter 2, we widen our lens to examine the nature of the force field within which policymaking occurs.

WHAT IS SOCIAL WELFARE POLICY?

Assess your comprehension of "What is Social Welfare Policy?" **by completing this quiz.**

Social work is in the midst of a redefinition of what policy means for the profession. In recent years, the concept of policy practice has gained new prominence as a way of making an important point: social workers and other professionals contribute to policy through activities that are an integral part of their professional lives.

Unfortunately, we have not yet fully caught up to the implications of this new idea. Typically, the term policy practice implies a separate set of activities that a practitioner might

---

[5]Roy Lubove, *Professional Altruist: The Emergence of Social Work As a Career 1880–1930* (Cambridge: Harvard University Press, 1965), 220–221.

undertake to influence public policy—such as participating in a demonstration, giving testimony before a legislative body, or writing a letter to a congressperson. While such actions are certainly a component, they do not capture the full range of ways that social workers influence policy every day. The following diagram helps clarify the scope of policy practice.

In this book we define policy as *an institutional arrangement that guides action*. This very general and broad definition is useful in two ways. First, it doesn't require that a policy be a formal decision, like the passage of a law. Second, while it specifies that the arrangement is institutional, it doesn't require that the institution is formal.

We first want to distinguish between *policy* and *public policy*. A number of authors view policy as synonymous with public policy. That is, policy implies that government is the institution in which the decisions (or nondecisions) take place. By contrast, this book addresses many situations in which private decision-making is at the core of policy.

There is good reason to restrict our attention to public policy. After all, the etymology of the word "policy" comes from the ancient Greek word *polis*, which referred both to a self-governing city-state and to the collective of citizens of that city-state. But for the Greeks, not everything that was public was governmental. The *agora*, where citizens met to speak their minds and to trade, was an essential part of the polis, even though these activities were not governmental.

The financial crisis of 2008–09 provides an example of how restricting one's attention to public policy may obscure some important parts of the story. Since the 1930s, the federal government has regulated the securities industry. The Glass-Steagall Act of 1933 and subsequent bills sought to insulate commercial banks from the more speculative

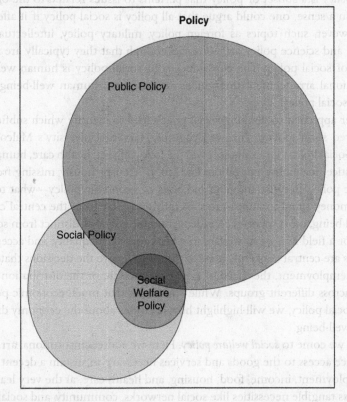

Figure 1.2
Different Types of Policies
Social welfare policy is part of a larger system of policies and focuses on actions that influence the immediate well-being of people.

parts of the financial services industry. In 1999, Congress and the president repealed parts of this structure, allowing for the proliferation of institutions that included a bank, an investment firm, and an insurance company. This is all public policy.

But public policy was only the beginning. Given its new lack of constraints, the financial services industry then made countless individual decisions—developing derivatives that sliced and diced other securities to make new ones, expanding a predatory lending industry to generate new securities, and many others—that in aggregate became the world's guiding policies for financial services.

Private decisions have a significant impact on social welfare's guiding principles, that is, on social welfare policy. To take just one example, a large share of the people in our society who need regular help performing routine tasks—moving around, feeding themselves, personal care and hygiene—get that care from family and friends. If, for some reason, all of those caretakers decided to stop doing these tasks, a huge increase in the personal social service budgets of government would be required. Thus, while we need to pay attention to public policy decisions—for example, those governing home health care—we must also follow the policy decisions being made by individuals who consent to take care of others.

Even if we restrict our attention to public policy, we are often concerned with more than just governmental action. As we'll see in several chapters, nongovernmental organizations (NGOs)—what in the United States we usually call nonprofits—play an increasing role in many social welfare activities. While not government agencies, nonprofit organizations are central both in the formulation and implementation of policy.

Social policy is a subset of policy that pertains to issues related to the organization of society. In a sense, one could argue that all policy is social policy if it affects human beings. However, such topics as foreign policy, military policy, intellectual property, technology, and science policy are nonsocial enough that they typically are not considered fields of social policy. The core concern of social policy is human well-being, so any institutional arrangement that guides actions about human well-being should be considered social policy.

Another approach to defining social policy tries to identify which subfields should be considered social policy. The web page of Harvard University's Malcolm Weiner Center for Social Policy, for example, gives the following list: health care, human services, criminal justice, inequality, education, and labor.[6] Conspicuously missing from this list is economic policy. Because the nuts and bolts of economic policy—what to do about issues like money supply, interest rates, or tariffs—are far from the central concerns of human well-being, most scholars consider economic policy as distinct from social policy. However, for a field like social welfare in which poverty, inequality, and access to goods and services are central concerns, it is hazardous to ignore the decisions that determine levels of unemployment, the speed of economic growth, or the distribution of income and assets across different groups. While we concur that much economic policy is not central to social policy, we will highlight how decisions about the economy directly bear on human well-being.

Finally, we come to *social welfare policy*. Here we address institutional arrangements that influence access to the goods and services necessary to sustain a decent life. These include employment, income, food, housing, and health care, at the very least, but also touch on less tangible necessities like social networks, community, and social inclusion.

---

[6]"Malcolm Weiner Center for Social Policy," Harvard Kennedy School, accessed January 11, 2013, www. hks.harvard.edu/centers/wiener/about-us.

A FRAMEWORK FOR THINKING ABOUT SOCIAL WELFARE PROGRAMS

A number of years ago, two important social welfare policy analysts— Neil Gilbert and Harry Specht—proposed a framework for analyzing choices in social welfare program design.[7] They, in turn, credited Eveline Burns for developing the framework in her book on Social Security.[8] In three decades of teaching, I have never come across a better structure for allowing students to understand how social welfare programs work. The Gilbert, Specht, and Terrell framework is based on four questions:

Assess your comprehension of "A Framework for Thinking about Social Welfare Programs" by completing this quiz.

1. Who should be eligible to receive a particular benefit?
2. What types of benefits should be available?
3. How should the benefit be administered?
4. How should the benefit be financed?

In this section we provide a brief summary of the framework, which we then use throughout the book to look at social programs. In Chapter 2, we place this model within its broader social environment. These two frameworks are complementary, the one explaining what choices must be made and the other what factors influence those choices.

Eligibility: Who Should Be Eligible to Receive a Benefit?

On the face of it, eligibility should be an easy question to decide. We set up a program to address a particular problem. In that case, those people who suffer from that problem should be eligible to receive the benefit. What could be simpler?

Only when we attempt to move beyond this general principle do things get complicated. Let's use a common problem as an example: unemployment. When a worker loses her job, it can be devastating for her and for her family. While there are many emotional and psychological aspects to unemployment, the biggest problem faced by an unemployed worker is loss of income. So we want a program that helps replace the lost income of unemployed workers. So far, so good.

Who is an unemployed worker? Again, the answer seems straightforward—someone without a job! Really, is this so complicated?

Well, yes. After all, not all of the unemployed are the same. Some are members of families with other employed members, some are the sole support for their families, and some have to support only themselves. So, in fact, the first question is whether we should target benefits to the financially needy. Should we give aid only to those with incomes below a certain level—determined by means of an *income test*—or should all of the unemployed receive benefits?

This question is at the heart of determining eligibility. Programs without an income test are called *universal* programs, while those with an income test are called *selective* programs. The choice of universal or selective eligibility carries a number of important

---

[7]Neil Gilbert and Harry Specht, *Dimensions of Social Welfare* Policy (Englewood Cliffs, NJ: Prentice-Hall, 1974). In 2002, Paul Terrell became a coauthor.

[8]Eveline M. Burns, *Social Security and Public Policy* (New York: McGraw-Hill, 1956).

Moral Hazard

Moral hazard refers to the risk created by security. Simply speaking, if one has any sort of insurance against a particular risk, one is less likely to take actions to prevent that risk. Take a practical example. I recently bought a cell phone for my daughter and agreed to purchase a service contract on the phone; if it is dropped, lost, or stolen, the phone company will replace it. If I hadn't purchased insurance, I would tell her that if her phone is stolen, she'll have to go back to using her "old" phone—which is now (horror!) two years old. The lack of insurance would have provided an incentive for her to take care of her phone. With the insurance, however, she knows she'll always get a new phone if something happens to hers. Because the insurance is providing an incentive for bad behavior (not taking care of her phone), it is a moral hazard.

In the late 2000s, America was awash in moral hazard. The recession that began in 2008 can be blamed in part on a finance bubble that was fed by people avoiding the risk of their own behavior. Predatory lenders were willing to offer risky mortgages because they were able to sell them before they went bad. Investment bankers were willing to buy those mortgages, repackage them, and sell them again for the same reason. When the day of reckoning came in the fall of 2008, several of these financial institutions were "bailed out" by the federal government because they were "too big to fail," thereby creating even more incentive for their employees to take risks.

Health care presents another case of potential moral hazard. For many of us, health care is "free" in the sense that we have health insurance and therefore only pay a small share of the cost. If I wake up in the morning and my back hurts, I might call my doctor who tells me to come into the office. After examining me, she sends me for an MRI and a set of blood tests to rule out anything serious. She then tells me to come back in two weeks for another visit. By then, my back feels better!

If I had to pay the actual cost of the doctor visits and tests—which would come to several thousand dollars—I might have simply waited a week to see if I felt better. Because I had insurance, however, I decided to have it checked out. In this case, I decided on a high-cost set of actions because I didn't have to pay the cost. That's a moral hazard.

Of course, the story could have a different ending. The MRI or blood test could have saved my life by alerting the doctor to a serious condition that was easily cured because of early intervention. If my health care plan had been structured to reduce unnecessary care, I might have skipped going to the doctor.

The bottom line is that moral hazard is always an issue when we try to protect people from risks. First, social policy analysts must weigh the potential of the actual risk against the potential for moral hazard. This is an issue of evaluation. Second, we must pay attention to how program design features—eligibility, benefits, and administration—either encourage or discourage moral hazard.

implications. First of all, if we require an income test, we need to specify what that income level is and a method of determining whether someone meets that standard.

The choice of an eligibility level for income-tested benefits leads us directly into the problem of moral hazard (see textbox entitled "Moral Hazard"). If we set benefits too high—it is argued—workers might "choose" to remain unemployed and collect benefits rather than accept a lower-paying job. But if we set the income level too high, the program will fail to reach people who need the aid.

In fact, when dealing with a program for people who can work, we face a more acute problem that has been called the "notch effect." Suppose we decide our unemployment system is going to have an income test. Only people who earn less than $3,000 a month will be eligible for benefits. Suppose that the benefit is worth $500 per month. Let's think through what a family's income might be with different combinations of work and aid.

Notice what happened? A family that earned one dollar over the eligibility level actually had lower income than a family with two dollars less in earnings. We might say that we're rewarding the lower-income family for not working so hard. More practically, we might put the higher-income family in a dilemma. If they keep track of such things, the

Chart 1.1   Example of Notch Effect in Hypothetical Program

Family earnings ($)	Unemployment aid ($)	Total family income ($)
2,000	500	2,500
2,200	500	2,700
2,500	500	3,000
2,700	500	3,200
2,999	500	3,499
3,000	0	3,000
3,200	0	3,200
3,500	0	3,500

earners in this family might choose to take a week of unpaid vacation so as not to lose their benefits. Either way, we've built unfairness into the system.

There are many ways of handling this difficulty, but the bottom line is that any selective social welfare program runs the risk of creating a moral hazard and an inequitable distribution of benefits.

"Okay," you say, "let's avoid the problem by not including an income test. Universal programs must be simpler." In some respects, you would be right; at the same time, if a benefit is universal, then—unless we really want everyone to get it—we need to set specific eligibility standards to distinguish the "truly" unemployed from other individuals. In order to qualify for benefits, for example, you might want to require that a recipient worked a certain number of weeks during the past year or earned a certain amount from employment.

Have you noticed something? When we were working on a selective, income-tested program, we worried about people earning too much to qualify. If we construct a universal, non-income-tested program, we worry about recipients earning too little.

One final point about eligibility. Our simple example leads us directly to the heart of the entire social welfare system. In the United States and many other countries, governments have designed a welfare system with both selective and universal components. For example, we have an unemployment compensation system that is universal and has relatively stringent tests for weeks worked and earnings. However, in most states, if you don't qualify for unemployment compensation, you'd have to rely on public assistance, an income-tested program.

This program design leads to an important feature of our social welfare system—its dualism. Programs have developed along two distinct lines: one universal and the other selective. Because the benefits of the universal programs are so much better than those for the selective programs, the social welfare system has become an important element of social stratification. In a sense, the welfare system contributes to social inequality by creating two distinct populations of recipients who receive very different benefits.

But we're getting ahead of ourselves; let's talk about benefits.

Benefits: What Should People Receive?

Decisions about eligibility have implications for benefits as well. Essentially, we have two sets of choices: the type of benefit the eligible population should receive and the amount each person receives.

Types of benefits

We differentiate four types of benefits:

- cash
- cash-like
- in-kind goods
- services

A good deal of the American social welfare system is about sending out checks or (increasingly) making electronic transfers to recipients' bank accounts. The greatest strength of cash is that it is fungible, that is, it can be used to buy anything. Our unemployed person might be short of food, need to pay her rent, or go to school to retrain for a new job. If she receives cash, she gets to make the decisions about how best (and hopefully most effectively) to use the benefit.

Of course, fungibility is exactly what worries some policymakers. Many who design and administer welfare programs want to direct how benefits are used. Sometimes this directedness is a result of their distrust of recipients. Because administrators often see poor people as incompetent, they think we have to limit the use of a benefit so that it won't be used for the "wrong" purpose.

Another reason for not giving out cash may be an inadequate supply of some needed good. For example, it would make little sense for the government to distribute money for people to buy an influenza shot unless there were enough doses available. As a result, the government may focus on giving out the shots rather than cash.

Finally, sometimes circumstances other than the well-being of the recipient influence social welfare programs. For example, real estate developers and construction workers are two relatively powerful lobbies that find common ground around building projects. There have been programs through the years—public housing is one example—that this alliance has advocated for its own good as much as to address the housing needs of low-income people.

For these reasons, program designers often turn to other forms of benefits. If they aren't worried about the supply of the good and don't have some other issue, very often a cash-like benefit is the choice. In these cases, beneficiaries receive a voucher that entitles them to receive the benefit. Food stamps or SNAP (Supplementary Nutritional Assistance Program) are the most common cash-like benefit. Beneficiaries typically receive a credit on their electronic benefits card that they can use to buy only qualified food products. The

Ronald Reagan on Food Stamps

Ronald Reagan, during his first term as president, used to tell a story about how the poor used food stamps.

3/1/82
Senator Bob Packwood (R-OR) claims President Reagan frequently offers up transparent fictional anecdotes as if they were real. "We've got a $120 billion deficit coming," says Packwood, "and the president says, 'You know, a young man went into a grocery store and he had an orange in one hand and a bottle of vodka in the other, and he paid for the orange with food stamps and he took the change and paid for the vodka. That's what's wrong.' And we just shake our heads."

Of course, a few days later it was pointed out that food stamp recipients never received more than 99 cents in cash as change for their stamps, but the intent of the story was to underline that the poor would use their money to buy the wrong goods.

Source: http://www.quickchange.com/reagan/1982.html, accessed October 30, 2009.

other most common voucher is associated with housing subsidies. Section 8 vouchers, for example, are one of several ways that the government provides housing assistance to eligible individuals and families.

The question of vouchers has often become caught in battles over political ideology. Conservatives often believe that markets work and that if there is demand for a good, the market will produce the supply. They see vouchers as a way of increasing the consumer choice of the population. Liberals also believe that markets work, but they are also sensitive to occasions when markets fail.

Housing is an example of a good—like a vaccine—that may not always be available in sufficient supply to meet the demand. As we discuss in Chapter 5, for a number of reasons, the cost of housing has increased more rapidly than that of most other necessities. As a result, the supply of affordable housing has declined. Put another way, many low-income families now have to risk homelessness or spend much more of their income on housing than has historically been the case.

If there is a shortage of affordable housing, you can address the problem in one of two ways: you can subsidize consumers (to increase demand) or you can increase the supply. The housing voucher program focuses on increasing the amount a consumer can afford for housing. Imagine that we think a family should spend no more than 40 percent of its income on housing. If a family is making $2,000 a month and can't find an apartment for less than $1,000, it would be facing a housing crisis. However, if the voucher is worth $200, the thousand-dollar apartment is now affordable.

Income	Ideal housing cost	Actual housing cost	Amount of subsidy
2,000	800	1,000	200

But housing solutions aren't always that simple. One can't move a house across town if that's where the demand is, and the interests of housing developers don't always mesh with the needs of low-income families. In addition, many communities don't want to become home for low-income residents, so they pass zoning requirements to keep out affordable housing. As a result, government has often provided housing as an in-kind good. The most common example is public housing. In this case, the government provides funding so that local housing authorities can build housing and then provides the housing authority with subsidies so that it can rent the units to families at affordable prices.

The final type of benefit is a service. This is particularly important for social workers. In most cases, services are the type of good they have to offer. Of course, social work services are only one of a crowded field of social services. Over the past several decades, other types of programs—like job training, child care and development, and child protective services—have attracted more attention than general social casework.

The same logic that applies to in-kind goods applies to social services. Because it's unlikely that the market economy would provide enough of these services to meet actual need, the government decides to provide them directly (or indirectly) as a way to ensure that they exist.

The provision of services often poses a value conflict for social workers. On the one hand, social workers as professionals believe that they have the expertise to make the best decision about the types of services most appropriate for a client. On the other hand, social workers believe in client autonomy. As we discuss in Chapter 9, the disability rights movement was in part a response to the perceived paternalism of case workers in providing services to people with disabilities.

Benefit levels

The decision of how much of a benefit an individual should receive involves a number of choices. Often these decisions raise the issue of moral hazard because generous benefits will discourage people from seeking alternatives.

The first question to answer is whether everyone who is eligible for a benefit should have a right to receive it. This may strike you as a silly question. "Well, if you're eligible for something, of course you should receive it!" If this is your reaction, get ready for a shock. Most of the benefits discussed in this book don't meet this test. If a person has a legal right to receive a particular benefit, it is called an *entitlement*. If you qualify for a program with an entitlement, the government is legally obligated to provide you with that benefit, even if it had not planned the expenditures.

Among entitlement programs, there are still many decisions to make. Going back to our unemployment example, decisions about eligibility have implications for benefit levels. Generally speaking, universal programs are preoccupied with reducing the damage of income loss, so they tie benefits to one's previous income; while selective programs focus on providing a minimum across the board, so they provide a flat benefit. Flat-benefit programs often base benefits on the size of one's family rather than one's previous income. For example, under the TANF program, a family of three living in Pennsylvania would receive a benefit of $421 in 2009 (Chapter 8).

Later in the book, we'll be looking at income support programs for a wide range of populations. An issue that influences both eligibility and benefit levels is whether a particular population is expected to work. If an individual is not expected to work—for example, because she is retired or suffers from a disability that prevents her from working—there is no moral hazard (or at least not a severe one), so benefits can be based on a notion of a decent standard of living. In contrast, if an individual is expected to work, the fear is that offering a decent level of benefit would make her so comfortable that she wouldn't have sufficient incentive to move from social welfare to the workforce. So we have to tailor benefits to be in a sweet spot where they keep families from going under but don't make them too comfortable.

One way to keep families from becoming too comfortable is by imposing time limits on benefits. The logic of time limits is based on aid being transitional. If a person needs help only for a short period while shifting from one situation to another (for example, from an old to a new job), then we don't have to worry about support over a long period of time. In the United States, for example, basic unemployment benefits last only six months, a transitional period to allay immediate economic distress.

The logic of time limits gained new popularity during the 1990s and served as one of the major elements of welfare reform. Whether the ideology of temporary assistance matched the reality of low-income families is a question we shall come back to when we examine public assistance programs.

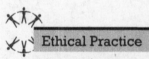

Ethical Practice

Practice Behavior Example: Recognize and manage personal values in a way that allows professional values to guide practice.

Critical Thinking Question: What role should professional discretion play in assessing a family's need for "transitional" aid?

Let's get back to our unemployed worker. So far, we've discussed only her income needs, but are there other types of benefits that we might want to offer? What about health insurance? Because US health care is centered on employment-based programs, an unemployed worker is likely to lose access to health care. Should we address this issue by using a cash, cash-like, or service model? With the cash approach we would increase the unemployed worker's benefits and let her go out and buy health insurance. Or, if we're worried that she would use the money for something else, we could give her a voucher to buy health care.

Finally, we could actually offer her and her family access to a program that provides health care outside of the private system. In fact, the US system taps each of these models, a complex story that we address later in the book.

The other obvious need of unemployed workers is the means to get back into the labor force. They may require training or a degree they don't have—such as a college degree, post-secondary training, or a GED if they haven't finished high school. Finally, we have had ongoing debate about whether we should help the unemployed set themselves up in a small business. Again, we'd need to make a set of choices about whether such benefits should be provided as cash, vouchers, or direct services.

Adequacy

The final issue to consider about benefits is their adequacy, a topic we will examine in detail in later chapters. As a starting point, we can consider program adequacy to have two elements: one that relates to eligibility and one that relates to benefits.

If a program reaches most of the people who need a particular kind of help, we speak of it as *horizontally adequate*. Horizontal adequacy is a function of eligibility requirements. For example, if we require individuals to work for a long time before they qualify for unemployment benefits, the program may fail to cover many of the unemployed. It is horizontally inadequate.

Horizontal adequacy can be influenced by another factor: uptake. Not everyone who is eligible for a program actually applies and receives the benefits. Sometimes this is a result of the social stigma involved. Sometimes it is a function of the administrative requirements of applying for a benefit. Sometimes people who are eligible may simply not know about a program.

Vertical adequacy refers to the extent to which the benefits received from a program actually relieve the conditions that they were designed to address. Health insurance is vertically adequate if it results in people having access to decent health care. A social service is vertically adequate if it actually improves the functioning of the individual receiving the service.

Because many social welfare programs are directed at redressing inadequate income, the vertical adequacy of these programs is measured by their ability to get people out of poverty. If a person who qualifies for a benefit escapes poverty as a result of receiving the benefit, it is vertically adequate. If she remains in poverty, it is not.

One simple way researchers measure vertical adequacy is to compare the poverty rate for a group with what it would have been if they had not received income from the program. We call this a measure of *pre-transfer poverty* because it is what their poverty rate would be without government aid. If a group has a pre-transfer poverty rate of 40 percent and an actual poverty rate of 20 percent, we'd say that the effectiveness rate of the program is 50 percent $[(40 - 20)/40 = 50\%]$. If the pre-transfer poverty rate is 40 percent and the actual poverty rate is 30 percent, the effectiveness rate would be 25 percent $[(40 - 30)/40 = 25\%]$ because only one in four recipients escaped poverty because of the program.[9]

Research-Based Practice

Practice Behavior Example: Use research evidence to inform practice.

Critical Thinking Question: What indicators of horizontal and vertical adequacy could you develop from your practice experience?

---

[9]This measure has some problems. Because the availability of benefits influences people's behavior, the difference between pre-transfer and official poverty tends to overstate the effectiveness of a program. For example, the rise in Social Security benefits in the 1960s and 1970s led to a drop in the number of older Americans who worked. This led to a rise in their pre-transfer poverty rate and an increase in the effectiveness measure. If benefits hadn't increased, more older Americans would have remained at work, so their pre-transfer poverty rate would not have been as high.

Delivery: How Should Benefits Be Delivered?

Once we've decided who should benefit and what they receive, we have a set of decisions to make about how those benefits should be delivered. While program designers have a degree of freedom in making these choices, methods of delivery are often constrained by history and earlier decisions. For example, if states or localities already have organizations for certifying eligibility and providing benefits, we are more likely to build on these systems than create entirely new ones.

The oldest of the existing systems is the American system of *federalism*. Federalism refers to the fact that our Constitution established a system of shared responsibilities between the federal government and the states. As with any situation of shared responsibility—roommates, business partnerships—there has always been controversy about where the line between federal and state responsibility should be drawn.

The controversy goes back to the Constitution itself. In Article I, the Constitution includes what is called an "elastic" clause (because it can be stretched to authorize federal responsibility in many situations). The clause states that Congress has the right

> To make all laws which shall be necessary and proper for carrying into execution the
> foregoing powers, and all other powers vested by this Constitution in the government
> of the United States, or in any department or officer thereof.

Almost immediately, however, this expansive statement of federal power was countered by a limitation of the national government in the Bill of Rights:

> Amendment X. The powers not delegated to the United States by the Constitution,
> nor prohibited by it to the states, are reserved to the states respectively, or to the people.

Until the 1930s, social welfare was usually left to the states to worry about. The passage of the Social Security Act in 1935 expanded the federal government's role, but it was not until 1937 that the Supreme Court ruled that the federal government could enter the field of social welfare. However, as a latecomer, the federal government has typically shown reserve in pushing aside states' role in the field.

Still, between the 1930s and the 1970s, the federal government tended to take on more and more responsibility for social welfare programs, with the "federalizing" of cash assistance programs for the elderly and people with disabilities (Supplemental Security Income or SSI) marking the high point of federal expansion.

Since the late 1970s, the general trend of federal-state relations has been less steady. A belief in devolution—moving decisions from central to decentralized authorities—has motivated a variety of reform movements, although the fiscal condition of the states often leads to the federal government acquiring new financial responsibilities for funding social welfare. In 2012, the Supreme Court decision on the Affordable Care Act imposed new limits on the federal government's ability to require states to expand Medicaid. That decision may have broader implications in the future.

As a result, we find a variety of combinations of federal and state responsibilities for social welfare. To begin, a few programs are purely federal. In these cases, the federal government takes full responsibility for structuring, funding, and administering the program. Old Age, Survivors, and Disability Insurance (OASDI) under Social Security is the preeminent "pure" federal program. Supplemental Security Income (SSI) too is primarily a federal program, although states provide supplements to the basic federal benefit. In addition, programs for Native Americans bypass the states and are based on connections between the federal government and Indian tribes.

Individual Versus State Entitlements

You'll notice that we just used the term entitlement for the second time in this chapter. In fact, *entitlement* is used in ways that confuse students...and often their professors.

First, there is a concept of *individual* entitlement—an issue of eligibility. If a program is an entitlement, government is legally obligated to provide the benefit to anyone who meets the eligibility requirements. Not all programs are like this. For some programs, government can say to a potential recipient: "You do qualify for this program, but—sorry—we've used up all the money, so we can't include you." For example, states often run out of low-income heating and energy assistance (LIHEAP) before the end of the winter. This shortfall isn't possible for an entitlement program.

The second usage has to do with the delivery and financing of benefits. Here a *state* entitlement refers to the obligation of the federal government to pay a share of state spending on a particular program. For example, under Title IV-E of the Social Security Act, the federal government must provide three-to-one matching funds for foster care services provided by the states.

Individual entitlement and state entitlements often overlap. Medicaid, for example, is an individual entitlement (many low-income people have a legal right to receive it) and a state entitlement (the federal government must pay half the cost of state programs). But there are many individual entitlements (Social Security, Medicare) that have nothing to do with states, and many state entitlements are more concerned with state spending on services rather than programs for individuals.

The confusion about entitlements was particularly intense during the debate over welfare reform in the 1990s. The old AFDC program was both a state and an individual entitlement, although states had always found administrative ways of restricting the individual entitlement. The new TANF program abolished both entitlements, although the ending of the state entitlement to matching funds probably was more important than the formal abolition of the individual entitlement. We'll discuss this more in Chapter 8.

The most common way of delivering benefits is through joint federal-state action. Although there is a dizzying array of forms, the two most common are block grants and grants-in-aid.

Grants-in-aid provide funding to states for a specific purpose. Historically, the federal government has used grants-in-aid as an incentive for states to do something that they have not been inclined to do on their own. As a result, grants-in-aid tend to be narrow in focus and include relatively open-ended funding mechanisms. For example, for many years the federal government provided three dollars for every one dollar that the states spent on social services. The broadest form of grant-in-aid is an entitlement program that obligates the federal government to provide funding no matter how much a state spends.

The other common form of joint federal-state delivery is a *block grant*. Block grants typically provide a pot of money to the state for a general purpose. In 1981, for example, Congress combined approximately 50 grants-in-aid programs into nine block grant programs. In combining these programs, Congress also reduced funding for them, applying the logic that the states would use the money more efficiently.[10]

Another argument in favor of block grants is that they strengthen the federal system by giving substantial policymaking power back to the states. In fact, many of the grants-in-aid of the 1960s and 1970s went directly from the federal government to either localities or special authorities, deliberately bypassing state government. In particular, programs with an urban focus, like Community Development Block Grants (CDBG), are allocated directly to urban communities because state governments are seen as less responsive to cities than to the needs of rural and suburban areas.

---

[10]US General Accounting Office, *"Block Grants: Characteristics, Experience, and Lessons Learned,"* (Washington, DC: Government Printing Office, 1995), http://www.gao.gov/assets/230/220911.pdf.

Nonprofit and for-profit companies

Except for purely federal programs, states typically have responsibility for figuring out how to deliver benefits. With 50 states, we have many different models.

Some states run pure public systems where everyone involved is a state employee. Other states use public systems, but devolve their responsibility down to local government, often to counties. Still other states rely heavily on nongovernmental organizations through contracting out or *purchase of service agreements*. More recently, for-profit companies have gained a greater share of the delivery system. A number of states have turned over a large share of their prison system to private companies. The 1996 welfare reform law opened up many areas of service delivery—which were historically restricted to nonprofit organizations—to private for-profit firms.

We have no authoritative way of determining if some of these systems are better than others. Using the example of child welfare services, we have found wide-ranging failure in systems across the nation—with pure state, state-local, and contracting-out systems all providing examples of failure. What we do know is that once nonprofits and for-profit firms are established in a particular area of social welfare, it is difficult to remove them. Without clear criteria for judging quality, decisions about service delivery often turn on historical precedent and political or ideological concerns.[11]

Mandates

A final means of administering a program is to require government or business to undertake particular functions. The most important social welfare examples are corporate health and pension systems. Since the 1970s, rather than expand the Social Security system, Congress has encouraged private employers and individuals to provide larger pensions. Similarly, with the exception of seniors and the poor, a majority of Americans receive their health coverage through an employer.

Government has two ways of getting business to take on these social welfare functions. It can either pass laws that require employers to do certain things or it can provide tax breaks to encourage employers to provide benefits. For example, employers are not required to offer pension programs for their employees; however, if they do, they are required to meet certain requirements and to pay into an insurance fund that protects these pensions if the company fails.

The health care debate of 2009 was notable as an attempt to shift employer-provided health care from a discretionary, tax incentive to a mandate. Currently, employers are encouraged to offer health coverage for their employees through generous tax incentives (see discussion of tax exemptions below). The Affordable Care Act will eventually mandate companies above a certain size to offer their employees health insurance or pay a penalty, and it sets minimum standards for the coverage.

Financing: Who Pays the Bill?

The final aspect of program analysis has to do with financing benefits. Here the basic choices are few, although the variations on them are practically limitless. In essence, the basic choice comes down to using tax revenue to pay for benefits or having individuals or companies pay for them. But even that division is misleading because the government pays a large share of privately provided benefits.

---

[11]Jane Waldfogel, *What Children Need* (Cambridge: Harvard University Press, 2006).

Public money: Earmarked, general revenue, and tax expenditures

Taxes are easy to understand, although few of us enjoy paying them. The government collects money from us and then uses it to provide the services we need. But once you get beyond this simple cycle of collect and spend, the role of taxation in social welfare becomes more complicated.

At its core, social welfare is about addressing human needs, with particular attention to reducing the difficulty that modest- and low-income people have in doing so. Thus the issue of distribution of resources and sacrifices is fundamental for social welfare. So we must pay attention to who gets taxed and how much they get taxed as much as to who receives benefits from social welfare. These questions, in turn, are associated with the fiscal capacity of different levels of government.

Types of taxation

Choices about what to tax have implications for social justice. If we tax low-income people more than high-income people, it may lead to a less equal society, even if we use the funding to pay for social welfare.

The basic distinction in the distribution of taxation across the population is between progressive and regressive taxes. A *progressive tax* is one in which the prosperous pay a higher proportion of taxes than do the poor. A *regressive tax* is one in which low-income people pay a higher tax rate than high-income people. Two things determine the progressiveness or regressiveness of taxes: what is taxed and the tax rate. Below is a list of typical items that are taxed:

- *Income*—Both the federal government and most states collect taxes on people's total income.
- *Earnings*—In contrast to income (which includes all the ways that people get money), earnings refer only to wages and salaries. Taxes on earnings are often called payroll or wage taxes. A number of federal programs rely on these.
- *Corporate profits*—When companies earn a profit, they usually must pay a tax to both the federal government and to the states.
- *Capital gains*—This is a hard one. People who possess wealth (stocks, savings in the bank, productive assets like a coal mine or oil well) receive income from the increase in the value of these assets—that is, their capital gains in value. Sometimes government treats capital gains like other income, but at other times it has a different tax rate.

Taxation and the Supply-Side Dream

Notice that the question here is one of *proportion* of income paid, not whether the rich pay more of the total amount of taxes paid. This issue has been muddied over the past several decades because two things have happened simultaneously: the basic tax system has become less progressive and inequality has exploded. Some advocates of *supply-side economics* have argued that by cutting taxes on the rich, you inspire them to work harder, earn more, and pay more taxes. As a result, they believe, cutting taxes can increase the amount of taxes collected.

The supply-side dream is just that—a dream. When the federal government has cut taxes for rich people significantly—first in the 1980s and then again early in the twenty-first century—it has resulted in major declines in the amount of revenue collected. However, because these policies happened as the overall distribution of income became more unequal, the proportion of all taxes collected from the rich increased.

- *Value-added or consumption taxes*—The broadest consumption tax is a sales tax levied on all goods purchased. In the United States this is typically a state tax (sometimes supplemented by a local tax). Narrower versions include "sin" taxes on cigarettes, alcohol, or gambling; "hospitality" taxes on car rentals, restaurants, or hotel rooms; and excise taxes on the production and sale of specific goods such as gasoline.
- *Property*—Property owners typically pay an amount based on the value of their property. Local government usually collects this tax.

As the following table shows, the federal and state and local governments have different sources of taxes. The federal government receives more than 90 percent of its revenue from three sources: personal income taxes, corporate income taxes, and payroll taxes. State and local governments receive about two-thirds of their revenue from sales taxes and property taxes, with personal income tax the third most important source.

Generally speaking, state and local taxes are more regressive than federal taxes. Both the sales and property taxes are focused on necessities—food, clothing, and housing—that are likely to disproportionately affect lower-income people. Moreover, many state income taxes are based on a fixed tax rate, so low-income people pay the same percentage as high-income people.

The federal tax structure is generally more progressive. The federal personal income tax rate increases with one's income. Marginal tax rates rise from 10 percent for families with incomes under $16,700 to 35 percent for families with incomes over $373,000. However, because of various deductions and credits, few families earning less than $20,000 have any federal income tax liability.

The federal payroll taxes, on the face of it, are regressive because higher-income people pay a lower rate. The story is more complicated, however, because federal retirement benefits are tied to these taxes, and the structure of these benefits is highly progressive.

Although sales and property taxes tend to be regressive and income taxes tend to be progressive, there are many ways to alter these tendencies. In Pennsylvania—to take one example—food and clothing are exempt from the sales tax, which makes it less regressive. Similarly, the special lower rate on capital gains by the federal income tax makes it more regressive.

Chart 1.2   Sources of Revenue by Percentage, Federal and State and Local Governments, 2007

Type of tax	Federal	State and local
Personal income	45.3	22.7
Corporate income	14.4	4.9
Payroll tax	33.9	
Sales tax		33.2
Excise tax	2.5	
Property		30.1
Other	3.9	9.1
Total	100.0	100.0

Source: Adapted from Statistical Abstract of the United States 2009, Tables 413 and 457, http://www.census.gov/compendia/statab/cats/federal_govt_finances_employment.html.

Yet, there is a lesson here on the connection between the administration and financing of social welfare. *Devolution*—the shift of responsibility from the federal to state and local government—means that we transfer responsibility from a more progressive to a more regressive tax environment. Devolution's promise to increase local control of decision-making may sound appealing, but the price one pays for local control is a more regressive way of financing benefits.

Earmarked taxes versus general revenue

As we've noted, the federal payroll tax is reserved for a particular purpose: paying old age, survivors, disability, and health insurance. When a tax can be used only for a particular purpose, we refer to it as an *earmarked tax*. The chief benefit of earmarked taxes is that the revenue collected is kept separate from a government's general revenue, so policymakers cannot use the money for some other purpose. At the local level, many cities have established business improvement districts in which a special tax on businesses can be used only for maintenance and improvement of the district.[12]

Usually, an earmarked tax is deposited in a trust fund as a means of assuring that it can be drawn upon for a particular purpose only. For example, the federal gasoline excise tax is placed in a trust fund for funding transportation-related projects. We'll have more to say about trust funds when we discuss the Social Security system.

In recent decades, earmarked taxes have become more popular because politicians fear a strong public reaction to tax increases. By tying a particular tax to a particular purpose, politicians hope that they will get credit for the good produced by government spending without the opprobrium associated with raising taxes. On a more practical level, when government begins cutting its budget, earmarked taxes and the spending they support are typically off the table.

Tax expenditures

Much government social welfare spending is paid for using money that the government never sees. Government sometimes provides individuals and companies with a tax break if they spend money for a particular purpose. We call these *tax expenditures*. The economics of tax expenditures are the same as those of government taxing and spending, but the politics of tax expenditures is entirely different.

Take the most common example, the deduction on home mortgage interest. If an individual or couple buys a house, they are entitled to deduct the interest payments on their mortgage from their income tax. For example, if a homeowner has a mortgage of $100,000 and pays $700 per month of interest on the mortgage, she can deduct $8,400 from total income when filing income tax forms in April. In addition, homeowners are allowed to deduct property taxes on their homes and any profit they make on the sale of the property if they use the money to buy another house. If these tax deductions did not exist, the government would have collected $100 billion more in 2008 than it did. It could have used that money to fund programs to encourage home ownership and other policies to improve housing options for all Americans.

The appeal of tax expenditures is that they blur one of the fundamental divides in American politics, the divide between liberals who want to encourage active government policies and conservatives who want to reduce the size of government. For a liberal, a

[12]Jerry Mitchell, "Business Improvement Districts and the 'New' Revitalization of Downtown," *Economic Development Quarterly* 15, no. 2 (May 2001): 1115–123.

tax expenditure is an expenditure; it's government taking an active role in American life. For a conservative, a tax expenditure is a tax cut; it's allowing people to "keep their own money" rather than turning it over to the government. Thus, where one could never gain consensus for a vast expansion of housing programs, Congress has refused to limit the mortgage interest deduction—even though its cost has soared.

Tax expenditures thus have an almost magical quality of producing consensus on issues that often divide political parties and the public. However, though they sometimes seem like a "free lunch," they aren't. When we discuss retirement security, we'll examine how the expansion of tax expenditures has introduced new elements of inequality into American social welfare policy.

CONCLUSION: SOCIAL INSURANCE AND PUBLIC ASSISTANCE

The four elements of social welfare programs that we have discussed—eligibility, benefits, delivery, and financing—are often closely related to one another. Major social welfare programs tend to cluster in one of two groups that we call *social insurance* and *public assistance*.

Social insurance programs tend to be universal (that is, they have no income test); are restricted to people who have worked a minimum amount of time; are more likely to have a strong federal role; and are financed through earmarked taxes, often called a contribution. Public assistance programs are selective (that is, they have an income test), are not tied to work history, tend to be delivered at the state or local level, and are financed through general revenue. The tables at the end of this chapter summarize the core social insurance and public assistance programs and their features.

This chapter has focused on these four basic elements of the little world of policy development. Beginning in Chapter 5, we'll use this framework to describe a variety of social welfare programs and assess how effective they are. Before we get to programs, however, we first need to address some broader issues, including the wider political and economic environment in which social welfare policy occurs (Chapter 2), how history influences social welfare development (Chapter 3), and the nature of poverty (Chapter 4).

Assess your analysis and evaluation of the chapter's content by completing the Chapter Review.

Chart 1.3 Overview of Major *Universal* (i.e., not income-tested) Social Insurance Programs

Program	Population served	Special eligibility	Type of benefit	Adequacy of benefits	How financed	How administered
Old Age and Survivors Insurance	Elderly population & survivors (spouse and children)	Worker must have paid into system (usually for 10 years)	Cash based on income & contributions	Very good, raises large share of recipients above poverty line	Earmarked payroll taxes	Federal government
Disability Insurance	People with disabilities	Worker must have paid into system	Same as above	Same as above, although younger workers may not have enough work experience to qualify	Same as above	Same as above
Unemployment Compensation	People with a job who are actively seeking work	Must have worked in recent months	Cash based on most recent salary	Most unemployed not covered	Earmarked tax on employers	States. Fed. Trust fund loans money to states during high employment periods
Workers Compensation	Workers injured on job	Need to document injury—often contested by employer	Cash award based on severity of injury and loss of wages	Decline in coverage, major object of "reform" by employers	Employers either buy private insurance or pay into state fund	States
Medicare	Elderly and people with disabilities	Must qualify for OASI or DI	Health insurance	Incremental declines in adequacy of coverage	Payroll taxes, premiums paid by recipients	Federal

21

Chart 1.4 Overview of Major *Selective* Public Assistance Programs that Express a *Residual* Approach to Social Welfare

Program	Population served	Special eligibility	Type of benefit	Adequacy of benefit	How financed	How administered
Supplemental Security Income	Aged, people with disabilities	Income tested	Cash, adjusted down for earnings	Yes, if combined with OASDI	General revenue	Federal govt., some states supplement
Food Stamps (Supplemental Nutrition Assistance Program SNAP)	Individuals & families with low income	Income test, "mild" work test	Vouchers for food	Provides supplement to food budget, effected by decline in number of welfare recipients	General revenue	Federal/state
TANF	Families	Income test, work test, drug felon test, etc.	Cash	Inadequate benefit levels, decline in "uptake"	General revenue, block grant	States with plan approved by feds.
Medicaid (MA)	Typically public assistance recipients, nursing home residents	Income test	Medical care (either through third-party reimbursement or HMO)	Expanded by Affordable Care Act (if states agree)	General revenue	Federal /state
Earned Income Tax Credit	Working families	Income test	Refundable tax credit	Provides significant income to those eligible; 1993 changes significantly expanded eligible population	General revenue	Federal, through IRS

2

Politics and Economics

The Institutional Structure of Social Welfare

INTRODUCTION

In the last chapter, we proposed a broad framework for understanding social policy: the policy-in-environment model. Central to that model is the idea that politics and economics establish a force field within which policy is formulated and implemented. Furthermore, the model highlights three important connectors that link politics and the economy: institutions, ideas, and social movements.

This chapter focuses on the role of politics and the economy in the structure of American social welfare. First, we examine American social welfare in global perspective. A half-century ago, Wilensky and Lebeaux argued that the United States had an "incomplete" welfare state that created some programs similar to those of European welfare states but not others.[1] In recent years, this assertion has been challenged from several perspectives. Some scholars have argued that we can't simply measure a welfare state *quantitatively*—from more complete to less complete. Rather, if we look at the world, there are several distinct types of welfare regimes, each with a distinctive character. Furthermore, although the United States spends less than many nations on direct social welfare programs, if we include tax benefits, the level of American social welfare spending doesn't make it appear so "incomplete".

---

[1]Harold L. Wilensky and Charles N Lebeaux, *Industrial Society and Social Welfare: The Impact of Industrialization on the Supply and Organization of Social Welfare Services in the United States* (New York: Russell Sage Foundation, 1958).

Next, we examine the institutional structure of the economy. The idea that the market is *natural* and *self-regulating* is part of American folk wisdom. In fact, government is very involved in the workings of the economy. What is confusing, perhaps, is that much of this intervention is not for the *public interest* but rather for the benefit of powerful business interests. After an overview of the current structure of the economy—the role of "big business" and the changing importance of different industries—we examine the role of stock markets and investors and changes in the ideas that influence their behavior. We then turn to changing ideas about economic regulation and their institutional consequences. Here we discuss the decline of *Keynesianism* with its focus on fiscal policy and the rise of *monetarism* with its focus on monetary policy; we will discuss how this shift increased the importance of the Federal Reserve System in assuring economic growth and restraining inflation. This section ends with a description of *neoliberalism* as an international phenomenon and its implications for social welfare.

The chapter then examines the institutional structure of politics. We describe several models for analyzing policy and politics and the importance of *social problem definition* in these processes. This is followed by an analysis of the federal system, including the role of the federal government and the states, how laws are passed, and the role of the executive and judicial branches in implementing and limiting laws.

THE AMERICAN SOCIAL WELFARE SYSTEM IN GLOBAL PERSPECTIVE

Assess your comprehension of "The American Social Welfare System in Global Perspective" **by completing this quiz.**

"[T]he world's two big organizing institutions are indeed state and market."[2]

Political science and economics—the study of states and the study of markets—have developed as separate academic fields. This divide has made things difficult for those who wish to make sense of either one. Much of political science treats the economy as something that happens "out there" (what social scientists call an *exogenous* force). Government may take this or that action, but the basic economic order operates outside their purview. Economists have a similar problem. Having *assumed* an idealized market system in which people operate by making cost/benefit decisions based on their own individual *tastes and preferences*, the poor economists constantly need to rejigger their system to explain why people make so many "irrational" decisions. A classic example is Mancur Olson's *The Logic of Collective Action* (1971) in which the author demonstrates that joining labor unions is "irrational" and then must explain why, in spite of this irrationality, so many people actually join unions.[3]

Treating politics and economics as separate is a particular problem for social welfare. Much of social welfare is about using politics to change the condition of people in the economy. Yet, people's economic status influences their interest in social welfare. We need to treat the *political economy* as a single system.

---

[2]Charles E. Lindblom, *Politics and Markets: The World's Political Economic Systems* (New York: Basic Books, 1977), 11.

[3]Mancur Olson, *The Logic of Collective Action: Public Goods and the Theory of Groups* (New York: Schocken Books, 1965), 3.

ESPING-ANDERSEN: THREE WORLDS OF WELFARE CAPITALISM

Many analysts have viewed the expansion of welfare programs (or the welfare state) as a natural evolution. In his classic formulation, T. H. Marshall viewed history as the steady expansion of rights—from civil to political to economic—and argued that although the speed of this progression might vary from country to country, most nations would eventually follow the same path.[4]

Yet, the rapid expansion of social welfare during the 1970s and then its rapid retrenchment during the 1980s and 1990s challenged this evolutionary story. Increasingly, scholars began to focus on the distinctiveness of welfare states' development rather than their similarity. Swedish political scientist Gosta Esping-Andersen's work has been particularly influential in this regard.

For Esping-Andersen, the key difference among welfare states is not the amount they spend on different types of welfare programs. Because so much of welfare spending is directed at individuals and families that have moderate incomes, the total amount spent can be misleading. Focusing rather on the relationship of markets and government, Esping-Andersen believes what distinguishes different *welfare regimes* is the extent to which they allow individuals and families to make decisions about their lives without regard to their labor market status—a concept he calls *decommodification*.[5]

Esping-Andersen differentiates three types of welfare regimes:

- conservative
- liberal
- social democratic

Each of these regimes has a distinctive relationship to the labor market. Conservative regimes—like Germany and France—are based on a concern that market relations will undermine traditional hierarchical relationships. They provide a high level of support to families, but tie support to traditional social hierarchies. For example, Germany's pension programs help preserve traditional systems of social prestige by creating separate programs for different occupational groups. Social democratic regimes—like Sweden and Norway—provide a high level of support as well; however, in contrast to conservative regimes, they use it to increase social equality across lines of social class and gender. Thus while both regimes offer generous programs, they do so for very different reasons.

Liberal welfare regimes—like the United States and the United Kingdom—use welfare programs to improve the functioning of the labor market, not to insulate families from it. You might think that if the goal were to improve the labor market, you would eliminate rather than promote welfare programs, but this is not always the case. Some welfare programs, like education and training, are designed to improve people's ability to work. Others provide common solutions to problems that individuals cannot solve on their own—old age pensions, for example. However, as you might expect,

---

Practice Contexts

Practice Behavior Example:
Continuously discover, appraise, and attend to changing locales, populations, scientific and technological developments, and emerging societal trends to provide relevant services.

Critical Thinking Question: Explain how a dualistic welfare system might increase the stigmatization of poor people over time.

---

[4]T. H. Marshall, *Class, Citizenship, and Social Development: Essays* (Garden City, NY: Doubleday, 1964).

[5]Gosta Esping-Andersen, *The Three Worlds of Welfare Capitalism* (Princeton: Princeton University Press, 1990). The key feature of capitalism as an economic system is that most of the population must sell its labor in order to survive. In other words, capitalism *commodifies* labor. For Esping-Andersen, a successful welfare state would allow individuals and families to escape this imperative; hence, it would *decommodify* labor.

liberal welfare regimes offer low benefits to the "able-bodied," who are expected to work to support themselves. Liberal welfare states tend to offer lower benefits, but their key rationale is to increase the efficiency of the economy not to free people from the discipline of the labor market.

Esping-Andersen's analysis of the historical development of different welfare regimes identifies some distinctive features of *liberal* welfare states, like the United States, that are helpful for our analysis.

First, because liberal welfare states are interested in promoting work among the able-bodied *and* increasing economic efficiency by keeping individuals who aren't expected to work out of the labor market, they tend to develop a *dualistic structure.*[6] In other words, liberal welfare systems often have two distinct tiers: one that offers relatively generous benefits to those whom the system wants to protect and another that offers meager benefits to those expected to work. The distinction noted in Chapter 1 between social insurance and public assistance represents this dualistic feature of the American welfare state.

Second, liberal welfare states tend to be associated with political systems in which business has played a dominant role.[7] In social democratic regimes, a strong labor movement has been able to form political coalitions first with farmers and later with white-collar workers to constrain the role of business. In conservative regimes, the Catholic Church has often been influential in forging political alliances between workers, farmers, and the middle class in support of policies that maintain traditional social hierarchies. But in liberal welfare states, organized labor tends either to be weak (as in the United States) or to have difficulty forming strong alliances with other social groups (as in Canada and the United Kingdom). Instead, in liberal countries, business is able to convince other groups—like farmers and white-collar workers—that "What's good for General Motors is good for the USA."[8]

Liberal welfare states appear to have had a surprising impact on gender inequality. Conservative regimes tend to promote the traditional family, so it is not surprising that women remain second-class workers in these countries. Social democracies, although committed to gender equality, give women (and men) the freedom to stay out of the labor force to raise children. Because women are more likely to use this freedom, however, they have made less progress in achieving equity in many sectors of the labor force. Indeed, it appears that the *occupational segregation* of women in traditional jobs (like child care and social work) is greater in social democracies than in liberal welfare states.[9] In contrast, liberal states appear to have achieved higher levels of gender equity, although they still have a long way to go.

Liberal welfare states—even in areas where government is active, like pensions—are likely to have a large private sector that provides a significant share of benefits. For example, in the United

Diversity in Practice

Practice Behavior Example: Appreciate that, as a consequence of difference, a person's life experiences may include oppression, poverty, marginalization, and alienation as well as privilege, power, and acclaim.

Critical Thinking Question: In social democratic societies, women and men sometimes use increasing flexibility to choose traditional gender roles. In what context might increasing people's choices in the United States serve to preserve racial, ethnic, or gender inequality?

[6]Esping-Andersen, *Three Worlds*, 24.
[7]Esping-Andersen, *Three Worlds*, 16–17.
[8]The phrase is often attributed to Charles Wilson, head of General Motors and Secretary of Defense during the 1940s and 1950s. "Wilson made a comment that was widely misquoted and was to dog him throughout his governmental years. According to the press, Wilson told the senators: 'What's good for General Motors is good for the country.' What he actually said was: 'For years I thought that what was good for our country was good for General Motors, and vice versa.'" *Time* Friday, October 6, 1961, accessed February 12, 2010, http://www.time.com/time/magazine/article/0,9171,827790,00.html.
[9]Esping-Andersen, *Three Worlds*, 144–161.

States, in contrast to other countries, the private sector plays a particularly important role in the provision of workers' compensation and old age pensions.

The tendency of liberal welfare states to develop public/private welfare schemes has become more pronounced in the past several decades. Older tax expenditures—like those for corporate contributions to health care—have expanded rapidly. At the same time, new tax breaks—like those for Individual Retirement Accounts and other *defined-contribution* pension plans—are currently among the largest tax expenditures.

As a result, two surprising patterns now characterize American social welfare spending compared to that of other nations. First, in total dollar amounts, the United States is no longer a "welfare laggard." According to Hacker, in 1995 the United States spent much less than social democratic or corporatist nations on public welfare benefits—16 percent of GDP in the United States versus 25 percent in social democracies and 23 percent in conservative welfare states. However, practically the entire gap was closed when after-tax private expenditures were included; the US share of GDP (8 percent) far exceeded that of the social democracies (1 percent) or conservative welfare states (2 percent).[10] Taken together, the US total social spending of 24 percent was less than 2 percent below the social democratic systems and less than 1 percent below the conservative total.

Hacker's analysis supports Esping-Andersen's conclusions. Although the United States may spend nearly as much on social programs as other welfare states, the distribution and impact of these expenditures is quite different. Low-income groups are likely to be dependent on public programs, while private pension plans—supported by tax breaks—benefit higher-income groups.

The United States has a distinctive approach to social welfare, a consequence of the political and economic climate in which it has developed. In contrast to many nations, no durable coalition ever evolved that could consistently constrain the role of business in the development of welfare programs. As a result, those programs that emerged have generally served, rather than challenged, private business.

The welfare programs in the United States have, however, influenced the development of the economy, sometimes in unexpected ways. In contrast to other nations, the United States' approach to social welfare has expanded what economists call "labor flexibility"—the ability of employers to hire or dismiss workers as they wish. The lack of welfare alternatives has also served to accelerate the growth of low-wage jobs in the American economy, resulting in the rapid growth of sectors that could make use of low-skill, low-wage employees. The expansion of the hospitality industries—recreation and leisure, eating and drinking, lodging and tourism, and gambling—is one of the consequences of the "liberal" character of American social spending.[11]

THE INSTITUTIONAL STRUCTURE OF THE ECONOMY

Why should a social worker or other human service worker care about the structure of the economy? First, economic structures influence the availability of work and the wages and salaries of most of the population. It is impossible to understand *need* without understanding how individuals and families use the labor market, private resources, or public funds to provide for themselves.

Assess your comprehension of "The Institutional Structure of the Economy" by completing this quiz.

---

[10]Jacob Hacker, *The Divided Welfare State: The Battle Over Public and Private Social Benefits in the United States* (New York: Cambridge University Press, 2002), 19.

[11]Esping-Andersen, *Three Worlds*, 191–220.

Human Rights and Justice

Practice Behavior Example: Incorporate social justice practices in organizations, institutions, and society to ensure that these basic human rights are distributed equitably and without prejudice.

Critical Thinking Question: What theories of social justice are consistent with high levels of social and economic inequality?

Second, people's economic position influences the *types of social policies they support.* The connections of "big business" to small business, relations between business and labor, how consumers influence economic decision-making—all of these relationships influence the types of laws that are passed and how they are implemented.

Finally, economic relations carry their own assumptions about *social justice.* In an ideal market, people make decisions about what they want to buy with their resources, and the "laws of supply and demand" ensure that we all end up as happy as possible. Although there is good reason to be skeptical about this vision of social harmony and fairness, it is a good starting point for comparing ideal with real issues of justice.

Who Owns the Economy?

The American economy is much like a funhouse mirror. What we see of it bears some similarity to its reality, but the distortions can be confusing, misleading, and ugly. In particular, there is a large gap between how the economy looks from the standpoint of dollars and how it looks from the standpoint of people.

Most business establishments in the United States are small. Nearly 9 in 10 establishments have less than 10 employees. From this perspective, America remains a country dominated by small entrepreneurs pursuing profit. Yet, this view can be misleading. While dominating the number of establishments, these very small businesses don't matter much to the overall economy, accounting for only 11 percent of all employees, 10 percent of payrolls, and 12 percent of total sales. Rather, very large firms—those with over 10,000 employees, which make up only 2 percent of establishments—account for more than a third (36 percent) of total sales.[12]

This pattern has many implications for social policy. First, most businesspeople run small businesses, but most employees work for large businesses. On issues in which large and small businesses share a common position, business can mobilize at both a national level—through the power of larger corporations and the lobbying of small business associations like the National Federation of Independent Business (NFIB)—and at the grassroots level through small businesses representatives.

Changing Structure of the Economy

Several key trends influence the force field within which policymaking takes place. To begin, the composition of the economy has changed in important ways. Thirty years ago, manufacturing represented the core of the economy, both in terms of economic activity and employment. Since 1980, however, the role of manufacturing has declined significantly. By the late 2000s, it accounted for less than 12 percent of total value added to the GDP. Over the same period, two sectors—finance, insurance, and real estate (FIRE) and professional and business services—experienced meteoric growth, nearly doubling their share of value.

The same pattern has affected trends in employment. In the middle of the twentieth century, one in four workers were employed in manufacturing. By the 2000s, the

---

[12]US Census Bureau, "Subject Reports: Establishment and Firm Size," http://www.census.gov/epcd/www/g97psize.htm.

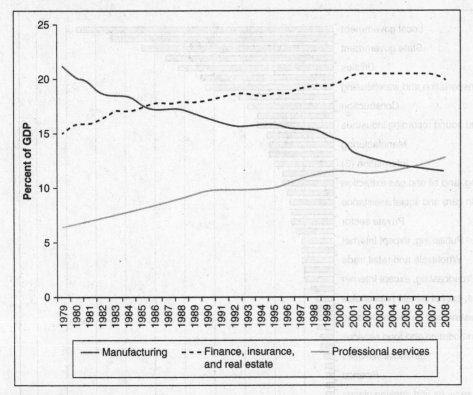

Figure 2.1
Manufacturing, Finance, and Professional Services as a Percent of Value Added to the Gross Domestic Product, United States, 1979–2008
Manufacturing used to dominate the American economy, but it has been replaced by finance and professional services.

Source: Based on *Economic Report of the President, 2009,* Table B12.

proportion had fallen below one in six. Meanwhile, the proportion in FIRE and business and professional services has more than doubled (Figure 2.1).[13]

One impact of industry shifts has been a decline in the role of labor unions in the economy. Manufacturing used to be the most organized industrial sector. As manufacturing has declined, so has the unionized workforce. In the middle of the twentieth century, a third of the civilian nonagricultural workforce was represented by unions; by 2009 that figure declined to 12 percent. The decline appears even more severe if we exclude government workers—a sector that was largely unorganized in the mid-twentieth century but now is the most unionized sector of the economy. In fact, only 7.2 percent of private-sector employees were union members in 2008 (Figure 2.2).[14]

The changing structure of the economy alters the nature of economic need in the United States. One obvious impact has been the increase in economic inequality—a topic we examine in Chapter 4. However, another pattern with an important effect on social welfare has been the increasing volatility of income associated with less steady patterns of employment and earnings.

---

[13]Michael B. Katz and Mark J. Stern, *One Nation Divisible: What America Was and What It Is Becoming* (New York: Russell Sage Foundation, 2006), 69.

[14]Bureau of Labor Statistics, *"Union Members in 2008,"* (Washington, DC: US Department of Labor, 2009), http://www.bls.gov/news.release/archives/union2_01282009.pdf.

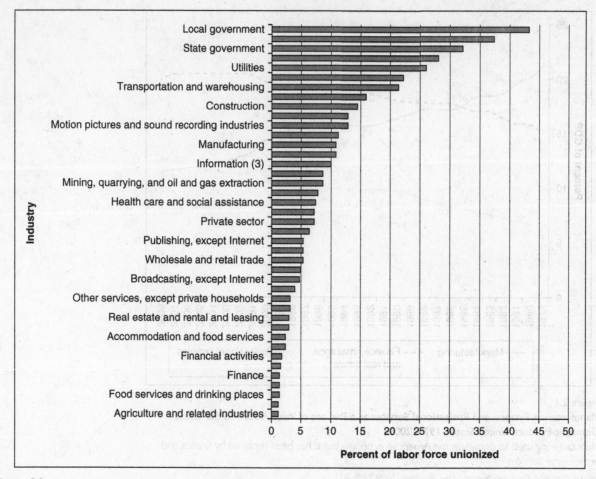

Figure 2.2
Percent of Labor Force Unionized by Industry in 2008
Public employees now make up a large share of labor union members. Service employees have very low rates of unionization.
Source: Author's calculations based on Current Population Survey, 2009.

Read Jacob Hacker's and Elisabeth Jacobs' paper, "The Rising Instability of American Family Income, 1969–2004," to better understand how macroeconomic forces are influencing individual families.

Since the 1970s, families' ability to predict their future income has declined. According to Jacob Hacker and Elisabeth Jacobs, the volatility of household incomes doubled between 1969 and 2004. The proportion of working-age individuals whose income dropped by more than 50 percent in a year increased from 4 to 10 percent of the population.[15]

Another contributor to the declining security of economic life during the past several decades has been a change in how investors and entrepreneurs view business. Before the 1970s, the dominant approach to managing large businesses was to increase predictability and stability. "Vertical integration" (consolidating raw materials, production, and distribution within one firm), reaching accommodations with organized labor and government regulators,

[15]Jacob S. Hacker and Elisabeth Jacobs, *"The Rising Instability of American Family Incomes, 1969–2004: Evidence from the Panel Study of Income Dynamics,"* (Washington, DC: Economic Policy Institute, 2008), http://www.epi.org/publication/bp213/.

and developing organizational structures—all were focused on bringing stability and predictability to the core industries of the economy.[16]

However, the economic shocks of the 1970s—increased global competition, high inflation, and slow economic growth—challenged this existing set of beliefs about how to run a business. Beginning in the 1980s, a new set of ideas—notably "shareholder value"—took hold. Increasingly, both investors and managers began to see firms simply as a set of financial assets whose value should be maximized to please the financial markets. In place of stability, accommodation, and predictability, firms turned to a variety of strategies in pursuit of higher stock prices—mergers and acquisitions, breaking up firms and spinning off less profitable units, laying off workers, investing in technology, and reducing the influence of labor unions. While these strategies had an immense impact on how business was managed and on the labor force, there is little evidence that they increased profitability.[17]

These changes in business ideology and behavior had important implications for social welfare. As a "liberal" welfare state, the United States increasingly relied on employer-based welfare programs to ensure retirement income, health care, and a variety of other services to the population. During the age of stability, corporations accepted these responsibilities to accommodate both labor unions and government and to increase the loyalty and satisfaction of their labor force. However, as "shareholder value" came to dominate business ideology and behavior, welfare programs became one more impediment to maximizing a firm's asset value. The needs of the workforce took a backseat to the demands of investors. This posed a major challenge to the employer-based welfare system—as we shall see when we examine health care (Chapter 7) and retirement security (Chapter 10).

Constraining Business

"Shareholder value" ideology not only changed the nature of employer-based welfare, it also affected regulation of the national economy (*macroeconomics*). "Because public functions in the market system rest in the hands of businessmen," according to Charles Lindblom,

> it follows that jobs, prices, production, growth, the standard of living, and the economic security of everyone all rest in their hands. Consequently, government officials cannot be indifferent to how well business performs its functions.... A major function of government, therefore, is to see to it that businessmen perform their tasks.[18]

Thus, changes in business ideas about the management of a firm had implications for broader economic policy as well. In place of macroeconomic policy focused on maintaining stability, steady economic growth, and high employment, business increasingly demanded—and successfully received—policies that made economic life less predictable and less secure.

---

[16]Alfred D. Chandler, Jr., *The Visible Hand: The Managerial Revolution in American Business* (Cambridge: Belknap Press of Harvard University Press, 1993); Michael Piore and Charles Sabel, *The Second Industrial Divide: Possibilities for Prosperity* (New York: Basic Books, 1986).

[17]Neil Fligstein and Taekjin Shin, "Shareholder Value and the Transformation of the U.S. Economy, 1984–2000," *Sociological Forum* 22, no. 4 (December 2007): 399–424.

[18]Charles E. Lindblom, *Politics and Markets*, 172–173.

For most of the period between World War II and the 1970s, the American economy was guided by the principles of Keynesian economic theory. Named after British economist John Maynard Keynes, this school of thought was based on the observation that the uncertainty of economic decision-making tended to lead market economies to patterns of boom and bust; and as the economic resources became more concentrated, the resilience of the economy tended to decline. Therefore, market economies—left to themselves—were likely to suffer from long-term stagnation.[19]

Keynesianism suggested that the government should play an active role in regulating the business cycle and in protecting workers and families from its impact. While the tactics used by Keynesians varied—manipulation of government spending, public works, social welfare schemes—their overall purpose was to ensure stable economic growth and minimize the risk of stagnation.

From a political standpoint, however, this ideology posed a challenge. If "the chief business of the American people is business," as Calvin Coolidge asserted, how could business be induced into accepting greater regulation and a higher tax burden? One answer to this question was the theory of *countervailing forces*. According to John Kenneth Galbraith, the rise of other institutional forces, especially organized labor and organized consumers, was able to constrain the power of business.[20]

Yet, as business ideology shifted at the firm level, business sought to challenge these countervailing forces as well. Critical scholars have used the term *neoliberalism* to describe big business's efforts to reduce the power of unions, reduce business regulation, and use unemployment to fight inflation. The same ideas that led firms to eliminate or reduce union representation in their firm encouraged business leaders to advocate policies that made it more difficult for unions to organize workers. The need to pursue mergers and acquisitions meant that businesses needed more permissive financial regulations.

This shift in economic policy was most clearly seen in policies toward full employment and inflation. Keynesian policies had a bias toward maximizing employment to benefit individuals and families and reduce the social and economic costs of unemployment. Yet, because full employment allows workers to demand higher wages and businesses then pass these increased costs on to consumers, Keynesians tolerated moderate increases in the cost of goods (*inflation*).

Inflation affects social groups in different ways. If someone has many financial assets (savings accounts, pensions, stocks, or bonds), inflation tends to erode their value. If inflation is running at 5 percent per year, one needs a return of 8 percent to have a "real" return of 3 percent. People who owe money, however, tend to benefit from inflation, because money borrowed in the past can be repaid with money that isn't worth as much. Historically, inflation was seen as good for the poor and bad for the rich. If higher inflation

The Phillips Curve

The relationship between inflation and unemployment is summarized by the Phillips Curve, named after William Phillips, a New Zealand–born economist. It suggests that inflation and unemployment tend to vary together: when one goes up, the other goes down.

Although the relationship is not necessarily constant (the US economy has experienced periods of "stagflation" in which both inflation and unemployment remain high), the relationship of the two remains an important element of economic policy.

---

[19]Robert Skidelsky, *Keynes: The Return of the Master* (New York: Public Affairs, 2009).
[20]John Kenneth Galbraith, *The Affluent Society* (Boston: Houghton Mifflin, 1958).

Organized labor used to operate as a "countervailing force" to the power of business. The decline of unions since the 1950's has increased business's influence over social policy.

is associated with higher employment (which also benefits lower-income groups), this association is even stronger.

The "stagflation" (high inflation and slow economic growth) of the late 1970s, however, caused a major shift in policies toward inflation and employment. Increasingly, economic policy embraced the idea that there was a "natural" rate of unemployment, estimated at 5 to 6 percent. *Monetarist* economists believed that if unemployment were allowed to drop below this level, it would inevitably cause an inflationary spiral, with prices increasing much faster than income. Beginning in the late 1970s, economic policy focused more on inflation than unemployment. Most of the recessions the American economy experienced between the late 1970s and the 2000s were induced as a way to keep inflation in check. In other words, monetarist economic policies that focused on reducing inflation displaced Keynesian policies that focused on keeping employment high.[21]

This shift in macroeconomic policy had implications for institutional control of the economy, with the Federal Reserve System taking a more prominent role after the rise of monetarism. Keynesian economic policies were implemented primarily with the tools of government fiscal policy—that is, how much government spends and how much it taxes individuals and businesses. From the New Deal to the 1970s, elected officials—the president and Congress—made decisions about how much government would spend and how much it would tax the population, with at least one eye on their economic implications. When the economy slowed down and unemployment rose, politicians would cut taxes and increase spending; as the economy recovered, they would cut spending and increase taxes.

When inflation replaced unemployment as the policy priority, however, institutional control passed from elected officials to the governors of the Federal Reserve System—a semiautonomous body that oversees the size of the money supply. Using a set of mechanisms, "the Fed" can boost interest rates, which will slow economic growth and reduce inflation, or they can reduce rates when the economy needs to be stimulated.

As a result, rather than the classic Phillips curve, we find that when inflation increases, the Fed raises interest rates; this increase eventually slows the economy and boosts unemployment. Rather than remaining constant, higher unemployment tends to lag a few years behind inflation.

In contrast to Congress and the president, however, the Fed doesn't have to run for office. Indeed, institutionally it is tied more to the private financial services industry than to government. Thus, the Fed has been willing to undertake policies—like provoking recessions to keep inflation low—that are politically unpopular.

An Economy out of Balance

The United States has always been a *liberal* welfare state that has developed social welfare programs to enhance the functioning of the market economy, not to increase an individual's freedom from it. Having said that, the connection of the market to social welfare policy has undergone important changes in the past several decades. The countervailing forces that encouraged business to accommodate other interests have weakened, and the ideas that drive business involvement in politics have hardened. As a result, the concerns of social welfare—reducing poverty, improving human functioning, increasing opportunity—have become less important for those who control the levers of the economy.

---

[21]Robert M. Solow, "Modigliani and Monetarism," paper presented at "Franco Modigliani and the Keynesian Legacy," New School University, April 14–15, 2005, http://www.newschool.edu/scepa/conferences/papers/050414_solow_modigliani-and-monetarism.pdf.

THE INSTITUTIONAL STRUCTURE OF POLITICS

Economic institutions and ideas have a profound impact on the politics of social welfare. As these institutions and ideas have shifted, they have influenced the types of policy that are even considered. Ideas about health care insurance that were proposed by Republicans and rejected by Democrats as too conservative in the 1970s are now proposed by Democrats and rejected by Republicans as too liberal.

Assess your comprehension of "The Institutional Structure of Politics" by completing this quiz.

Yet, the world of politics and policy does not reflect simply economic interests. Government and politics are composed of a complex set of institutions. The federal government is composed of the three branches established by the US Constitution but has evolved even more institutions that influence what it does and does not do. The federal system within which the federal government, states, and localities argue and horse-trade can determine how policies are implemented. Finally, the organization of politics and the "two-party" system influences the types of issues and policy choices that can succeed.

Making Sense of Politics

Because politics can get confusing, people use *metaphors* as a way to make sense of it. For example, the media often use sports to explain politics. Who's ahead? Who will make a comeback? Who's on the defensive? What's the game-changer?

Although there are times when the sports metaphor seems appropriate, it tends to make us focus only on how personalities are interacting in the present. Here we suggest a set of *models* for making sense of politics and policy. No one model is perfect, so having several to draw upon is useful.[22]

We discuss six models for conceptualizing politics and policy: rational, institutional, process, incremental, pluralist, and elite.

Rational

A rational policy model is based on the assumption that government addresses issues by assessing the effectiveness and costs of all options and then deciding on a policy based on this *cost-benefit* analysis. This model assumes that it is possible to reach consensus about how to measure those costs and benefits and how to evaluate them. In its purest form, therefore, the rational model assumes—if everyone were honest and set aside their narrow interests—that a consensus is possible on the best response to a policy challenge.

Given the current state of politics and policy in the United States, the rational approach to politics seems to be a fantasy. The question is, what kind of fantasy is it? Although no one believes that contemporary politics *are* rational, many policy analysts hope that policy *can become* more rational through the application of science. In recent years, these scholars have advocated *evidence-based* policymaking. Using experimental methods, many scholars have come to believe that we can resolve questions about the efficacy and cost-effectiveness of different policies.[23] Other scholars are skeptical about the potential to resolve these questions. They believe that ideology is such a strong lens

[22]Two examples of these models are W. Joseph Heffernan, *Social Welfare Policy: A Research and Action Strategy* (New York: Longman 1992) and Thomas R. Dye, *Understanding Public Policy* (Englewood Cliffs, NJ: Prentice-Hall, 1972).

[23]For a discussion of experimental designs in social policy, see Robert Sampson, *Great American City: Chicago and the Enduring Neighborhood Effect* (Chicago: University of Chicago Press, 2012), 261–286.

that it is impossible for policy analysts or policy makers to overcome their view of the world in order to reach consensus about policy choices.

In their book *Usable Knowledge*, Charles Lindblom and David Cohen try to carve out a middle ground on this dispute. They argue that professional social inquiry can never achieve *authoritativeness*, that is, it can never fully resolve important social policy disputes. Some policy issues cannot be resolved because they involve deeply held beliefs about what is right and wrong—what we can call *normative beliefs*. While some issues—for example, whether public assistance encourages laziness—might be resolved through empirical research; many others—for example, the desirability of teenagers remaining sexually inactive—cannot be resolved empirically.[24]

An even greater barrier to authoritative, rational policymaking is the divergence of social science findings. For example, a detailed analysis of the Bush administration's abstinence-only sex education programs concluded that they made no difference in when kids become sexually active or in kids' attitudes about sex.[25] Recently, another group of Penn researchers conducted a study that found that certain types of "abstinence-only interventions may have an important role in preventing adolescent sexual involvement."[26] A careful reader would find that the studies were looking at different types of programs, but the overall impact of these disputes is policy *divergence* rather than convergence.

Lindblom and Cohen conclude that the goal of professional social inquiry should not be to provide authoritativeness but rather to make a limited set of contributions to the social interactions through which policy is developed. In other words, policy analysis cannot rationally resolve policy dilemmas, but it can contribute to better processes by which to pursue answers.[27]

Institutional

Institutional approaches to policy and politics focus on the structure of government and how it influences the types of policy that are adopted or sidetracked. This simple approach involves a number of complex issues. It might begin with the formal characteristics of government institutions. For example, as we shall see in Chapter 5, the composition of the US Senate (two senators for each state regardless of size) has made the concerns of farmers and the food industry much more prominent than they would have been if Senate seats were allocated based on population size.

However, less formal elements of the institutional process also play a role. A number of scholars have pointed to the influence of Congressional systems of *seniority* in making committee assignments on important social welfare policies.[28] Opportunities for lobbyists and other special interest groups to influence policy also make a difference. For

---

[24]Charles E. Lindblom and David K. Cohen, *Usable Knowledge: Social Science and Social Problem Solving* (New Haven: Yale University Press, 1979).

[25]Christopher Trenholm, Barbara Devaney, Kenneth Fortson, Melissa Clark, Lisa Bridgespan, and Justin Wheeler, "Impacts of Abstinence Education on Teen Sexual Activity, Risk of Pregnancy, and Risk of Sexually Transmitted Diseases," *Journal of Policy Analysis and Management* 27, no. 2 (2008): 255–276.

[26]John B. Jemmott III, Loretta S. Jemmott, and Geoffrey T. Fong, "Efficacy of a Theory-Based Abstinence-Only Intervention over 24 Months: A Randomized Controlled Trial with Young Adolescents," *Archives of Pediatric Adolescent Medicine* 164, no. 2(February 2010): 152–159.

[27]Lindblom and Cohen, *Usable Knowledge*.

[28]Margaret Weir, Ann Shola Orloff, and Theda Skocpol, "Introduction: Understanding American Social Politics," in *The Politics of Social Policy in the United States*, ed. Margaret Weir, Ann Shola Orloff, and Theda Skocpol (Princeton: Princeton University Press, 1988), 3–36.

example, much was made of a secret group of oil-company representatives who were central to the formulation of the George W. Bush administration's energy policy.[29]

Advocates of the institutional approach often point to the ability of the minority party of the Senate to block legislation through the use of a *filibuster*. During the Bush administration, Democrats (who were then in the minority) used the threat of a filibuster to block many of the administration's judicial nominations. During the first years of the Obama administration, Republicans—who controlled only 41 of the 100 seats—were able to successfully block a number of Democratic initiatives through filibuster.[30]

Occasionally, advocates of the institutional approach have overestimated the influence of these narrow institutional factors and concluded that changes in institutions *by themselves* can change policy outcomes. During 2010, though Republicans did benefit from the filibuster, the perception that the public was disillusioned with many Democratic policies also played an important role in slowing the adoption of some legislation. It is often difficult to separate the influence of institutions from other factors in evaluating which policies eventually are adopted.

Process

Process approaches to policymaking focus on the various steps through which a policy proposal moves from its emergence to its implementation. A common view of the policy model divides it into five stages:

- identification of problem
- formulation of alternative approaches
- choosing a policy
- implementing a policy
- evaluating the policy

The process approach shares elements with both the institutional and rational approaches. By identifying a specific process, it assumes the existence of institutions that undertake each stage of the process. Like the rational approach, it assumes that policy development, implementation, and evaluation follow a relatively orderly and logical set of steps.

The primary appeal of process models is that they provide a descriptive framework through which one can track a policy field over time. The primary disadvantage of process models is that they tend to impose orderliness on what is typically a fairly messy process. Like the rational approach, the process model works best for policy issues for which there is wide agreement about the nature of the social problem to be addressed, the costs and benefits of different approaches, and the approach and findings of any evaluation.

One way to remedy the overly rational and simplistic elements of the process approach is to provide a more complex and detailed view of the process. A United Kingdom government guide to public participation in policymaking, for example, focuses on where the public can influence policymaking. To do so, it breaks down the basic elements of the policy cycle and illustrates its complexity. Rather than portraying problem identification as a simple

---

[29]"How the Energy Dice Were Loaded," *New York Times*, July 23, 2007, http://www.nytimes.com/2007/07/23/opinion/23mon2.html?_r=1&ref=dickcheney.

[30]Jill Quadagno, "From Old-Age Assistance to Supplemental Security Income: The Political Economy of Relief in the South, 1935–1972," in *The Politics of Social Policy*, ed. Margaret Weir, Ann Shola Orloff, and Theda Skocpol, (Princeton: Princeton University Press, 1988), 235–264; Jean Edward Smith, "Filibusters: The Senate's Self-Inflicted Wound," *New York Times*, March 1, 2009, http://100days.blogs.nytimes.com/2009/03/01/filibusters-the-senates-self-inflicted-wound/?scp=20&sp=filibuster+obama&st=nyt.

process, the guide highlights the possibility that different visions and perspectives may clash and that the success of one vision or another influences future policy development.

Incremental

Incremental models of policymaking assume that *inertia* is the primary feature of social policy. Once a policy field is initiated, policies tend to build on what went before without taking a fresh look at program costs, benefits, or effectiveness. Efforts to end a program typically fail because of this inertia.

One can see incremental policymaking—or "muddling through," as it has been called—as the opposite of a rational approach to policy.[31] It is based on the belief that what exists must be working and should be continued. In one way, it's a depressing view of how policy works. Yet, the incremental approach recognizes several important features of social policy. First, once a policy is put into place, it may lead to the development of new institutions tied to the policy. To abandon the policy might require the scrapping of a major investment. Second, as policy is implemented, it tends to generate its own constituencies—beneficiaries, government workers, independent contractors, and politicians who take credit for it—that support the continuation and hopefully the growth of a particular approach. Furthermore, the costs of evaluating every policy continuously may be less rational than a "squeaky wheel" approach that selectively examines issues that generate controversy or protest. Because of these tendencies, as we shall see in Chapter 3, policy *trajectories* develop; once an approach is chosen, future policies tend to build on the past.

One place where incremental approaches are most evident is in the process of budgeting. Although some policy is about laws and principles, much policy is about how government spends money. Instead of opening up every possible policy for inspection, whether a policy is expanded, held stable, or cut may come down to how much government is willing to spend. Thus, a seemingly benign approach to policy—continued funding of a block grant at its current level—may over time lead to a major decline in a program as inflation eats away at the buying power of the dollar.

Conflict models: Pluralist and elitist

Rational, institutional, process, and incremental models generally do not focus on possible disputes in policy formulation. They assume that consensus is possible and that policy decisions will command general agreement or at least acquiescence.

Pluralist and elite models assume that political conflict generally influences policy development. *Pluralist* models focus on processes through which different social groups come together to support common issues. *Elitist* models focus on the ability of powerful minorities—social, economic, and political elites—to impose their preferred solutions on a policy field.

Pluralist models developed during the middle of the twentieth century as a way of highlighting democratic processes of policymaking. They focus on processes of mutual accommodation between different social groups in support of a particular position. As we saw when we discussed Esping-Andersen's theories earlier in this chapter, many of the nation's welfare programs are the result of long-term durable coalitions between different social groups in support of social welfare expansion.

The United States is typically viewed as having a political culture in which durable coalitions are difficult to maintain. Because of its ethnic and regional diversity, the US

---

[31]Charles E. Lindblom, "The Science of 'Muddling Through,'" *Public Administration Review* 19, no. 2 (Spring 1959): 79–88.

political system must accommodate more than the social class or occupational differences characteristic of more homogeneous countries. Coalitions, even when they do form, often have internal conflicts that allow them to win elections but not implement policies.

The classic case was the New Deal coalition of the mid-twentieth century (discussed in more detail in Chapter 3). The coalition—by incorporating African Americans who advocated expanded civil rights and social welfare programs, industrial workers who advocated expanded social welfare but were suspicious of civil rights, and white Southerners who opposed both civil rights and expanded welfare—was successful at controlling Congress for most of the 1930s through the 1970s. Yet, except for a few short periods, these internal conflicts limited its policy successes.[32]

Elite theories focus on the ability of a relatively small group of powerful players to control policy outcomes. Historically, elite theories were identified with conservatives who argued that democracy was impossible because the *masses* did not have the intelligence or self-discipline necessary for self-government.[33] However, during the twentieth century, elite theories became more nuanced and less antagonistic to democracy.

Contemporary elite theory synthesizes two complementary ideas. First, to be successful, elites must hold a broad view of self-interest that moves beyond their narrow social and economic interests. Alexis de Tocqueville coined the term "self-interest rightly understood" to characterize individuals who integrate ideas of self-interest and the public interest.[34] For elites to maintain their position in a democracy, they must pursue an idea of stewardship that includes concern for the well-being of the majority of citizens. The idea of stewardship is complemented by *deference* on the part of the majority. For an elite to continue to rule, the majority must acknowledge the ability of elites and accept their judgments about policy.[35]

Neither the idealized pluralist model (with its image of a number of equally balanced groups competing on a level playing field) nor a pure elite theory (with a small group of the powerful controlling all aspects of the policy process) seem to correspond to the realities of American politics and policy. We need to take into account both the conflict of competing ideas and the power of the powerful.

One approach that overcomes this split argues that an important aspect of elite power is its ability to define which policy decisions are possible and which are "unthinkable." This process—which has been called *nondecision-making*—suggests that elites don't control every decision, but that they are able to limit democratic decision-making to particular choices and are able to steer policy discussions in ways that are acceptable to them.[36] There are a variety of ways that elites can exercise this type of control:

- *Control of the media*—The rise of the mass media and its apparent capacity for persuasion has greatly enhanced the ability of well-funded politicians and interest groups to shape public opinion.
- *Money in politics*—Because of the large amounts of funding needed to run a political campaign, only those politicians who are supported by elites can make

[32]Margaret Weir, "The Federal Government and Unemployment: The Frustration of Policy Innovation from the New Deal to the Great Society," in *Politics of Social Policy*, ed. Margaret Weir, Ann Shola Orloff, and Theda Skocpol, (Princeton: Princeton University Press, 1988), 149–198.

[33]Ettore Albertoni, *Mosca and the Theory of Elitism* (Oxford: Basil Blackwell, 1987).

[34]Alexis de Tocqueville, *Democracy in America*, vol. II, section 2, chap. 7.

[35]Jack P. Greene, "Changing Interpretations of Early American Politics," in *The Reinterpretation of Early American History: Essays in Honor of John Edwin Pomfret*, ed. Ray Allen Billington, (San Marino, CA: Huntington Library, 1966), 173.

[36]Peter Bachrach and Morton S. Baratz, "Decisions and Nondecisions: An Analytical Framework," *American Political* 57, no. 3 (September 1963): 632–642.

a serious effort to get elected. Once elected, politicians must continue to curry favor from elites with an eye toward the next election.

Policy Practice

Practice Behavior Example: Know the history and current structures of social policies and services, the role of policy in service delivery, and the role of practice in policy development.

Critical Thinking Question: Many critics complain that social welfare programs hurt business. What are some examples of social welfare policy allowing the private economy to operate more efficiently?

- *Capital flight*—If government pursues policies that an economic elite sees as contrary to its interest, it can simply move its resources elsewhere. This could influence local, state, or national policy, especially now that the global economy makes it easy to transfer resources electronically. The flip side is the extent to which "creating a good business climate"—with low taxes, friendly regulation, and unorganized and low-cost labor—is seen as in the public interest.[37]

- *Agenda-setting*—Policy begins with the identification of a social problem (see the subheading "Process" above). Because elites have the resources to define what is and what is not a social problem, they are able to control the types of issues that can enter the policy process.[38]

If we are willing to incorporate the idea of a *nondecision* into a pluralist model, we can see how both elite theory and pluralism play a role in policymaking.

FEDERALISM AND PUBLIC POLICY

The federal government plays a unique and central role in social welfare policy. There are four important elements we must consider in examining any field of policy: Congress and the legislative branch; the White House and the executive branch; the courts and the judicial branch; and federal-state relations.

How Laws Are Made: Congress

Congress and its two houses—the Senate and the House of Representatives—are the only body in the federal government that can create new laws, although the *balance of powers* means that the executive and judicial branches can constrain Congress's capacities. Much of the operation of Congress is specified in the Constitution, but other elements of the legislative process are a result of Congressional rules and traditions.

Generally speaking, important legislation leads a "double life" in Congress, with each house carrying on a separate legislative process until it passes a bill. The basic steps of this process involve the introduction of a bill by one or more legislators or *cosponsors*. A large number of bills never get any farther than this. However, bills that have a chance of becoming law are assigned to one or more committees that typically hold hearings on the proposed law and then meet to "mark up" or make changes in the bill. On important pieces of legislation, the committee prepares a report that explains the need and purpose of the bill. If the committees recommend passage, the bill is then slated for debate (See Figure 2.3). In the House of Representatives, the Rules Committee will typically designate the rules governing debate, including how long each congressperson may speak and rules for introducing amendments. In the Senate, debate can be limited only through the support of a *cloture* motion by 60 senators. If supporters are unable to gather the

---

[37]Charles Lindblom, *The Market System: What It Is, How It Works, and What to Make of It* (New Haven: Yale University Press, 2002), 212–226.

[38]John Kingdon, *Agendas, Alternatives, and Public Policies, 2nd* ed. (New York: Harper Collins, 1997).

Calendar No. 54

111TH CONGRESS 1st Session	SENATE	REPORT 111–16

AMENDING THE CONSUMER CREDIT PROTECTION ACT, TO BAN ABUSIVE CREDIT PRACTICES, ENHANCE CONSUMER DISCLOSURES, PROTECT UNDERAGE CONSUMERS, AND FOR OTHER PURPOSES

MAY 4, 2009.—Ordered to be printed

Mr. DODD, from the Committee on Banking, Housing, and Urban Affairs, submitted the following

REPORT

[To accompany S. 414]

The Committee on Banking, Housing, and Urban Affairs, to which was referred the bill (S. 414) to amend the Consumer Credit Protection Act, to ban abusive credit practices, enhance consumer disclosures, protect underage consumers, and for other purposes, having considered the same, reports favorably thereon with an amendment and recommends that the bill as amended do pass.

INTRODUCTION

The Committee on Banking, Housing, and Urban Affairs met in open session on March 31, 2009, and ordered S. 414, the "Credit Card Accountability Responsibility and Disclosure Act of 2009," as amended, favorably reported to the Senate for consideration.

HEARING RECORD AND WITNESSES

On Thursday, January 25, 2007, the Committee held a hearing entitled "Examining the Billing, Marketing and Disclosure Practices of the Credit Card Industry, and Their Impact on Consumers." At that hearing, the Committee heard testimony from Elizabeth Warren, Leo Gottleib Professor of Law, Harvard Law School; Michael Donovan, Esq., Donovan & Searles; Carter Franke, Executive Vice President of Marketing, JP Morgan Chase & Co.; Robert Manning, Professor of Finance, Rochester Institute of Technology; John Finneran, President of Corporate Reputation and Governance, CapitalOne Financial; Tamara Draut, Director, Economic Opportunity Programs, Demos; Richard Vague, CEO, Barclaycard USA; and Travis Plunkett, Legislative Director, Consumer Federation of America.

79–010

Figure 2.3
Example of a Congressional Committee Report
Committees play a central role in developing laws. For particularly important bills, their reports provide explanations of their decisions.
Source: Senate Report 111-15. 111th Congress, 1st session.

60 votes, the opposition can filibuster the bill until it dies. An exception to this rule is a *budget reconciliation* bill, which cannot be filibustered.

Very rarely, once one house passes a bill, the other could vote on it. For example, the Patient Protection and Affordable Care Act originally passed the Senate in December 2009, and the House then passed the same bill in March 2010.[39] However, typically

[39]This legislative history was not the result of sudden consensus between the House and Senate. Rather, because the Republicans gained a Senate seat in January 2010, Democratic leaders believed they could not avoid a filibuster of a conference report. Instead, the House chose to pass the Senate bill and then both houses passed a budget reconciliation bill—that couldn't be filibustered—to reconcile differences between the two houses.

each house considers its own version of a bill. If both houses pass versions, the leadership of the two houses appoint a *conference committee* that attempts to reconcile the two. Both houses then consider the resulting conference committee bill, which, if passed by both houses, is sent to the president.

The president may either sign the bill—at which point it becomes a law—or *veto* it. If Congress is in session when a bill is vetoed, the legislators can override the veto with a vote of two-thirds in each house. If Congress can't override it or if Congress is in recess (what is called a pocket veto), the law dies.

This description provides a *process* perspective of policymaking but also gives a full sense of the *institutional* factors that influence the success or failure of a given piece of legislation. For the past two hundred years, seniority has been an important value among members of Congress. For most of the twentieth century, seniority was paramount in assigning members to committees and appointing committee chairs. During the 1970s, Congress attempted to lessen the influence of seniority, but it still remains the most consistent basis on which these decisions are made.[40]

The importance of seniority takes on added significance because of the *gatekeeping* role of committees in the legislative process. Committees don't simply function as a means of efficiently reviewing the many issues facing Congress. Committees can prevent legislation from moving forward even if a majority of members favor it. As a result, members seek seats on committees that matter to their constituents. For example, agriculture committees are typically dominated by members from farm areas. Committee membership also allows members to steer funding and projects to their states or districts, a process often called *earmarking*.[41]

The issue of earmarking brings us to another important institutional factor: the cost of getting elected or reelected. Through much of nineteenth and first half of the twentieth century, the key asset a person needed to get elected was support of the party. The electronic media didn't exist, and rates of voter participation were generally high. The major political parties were organized in each ward or precinct in the entire country, so if one could win the support of a political party, election was much easier.

Money certainly mattered in this system, but the money that mattered had to do with enlisting the support of party leaders. This system still persists. For example, in older cities like Philadelphia, candidates are much more likely to pursue office successfully if they can contribute "walking-around money" (WAMs) to the local party; party workers then use the WAM to encourage voter participation.

However, since the middle of the twentieth century, the old system has been shaken by three important trends. The old political parties no longer have the capacity to deliver votes as they did in the past. The influence on politics of local voluntary organizations (e.g., the Rotary, the Elks, and labor unions) has been eclipsed by the power of national advocacy groups (e.g., the National Right to Life Association, the American Hospital Association, and the National Federation of Independent Businesses). Finally, the rise

[40]Sara Randes Crook and John R. Hibbing, "Congressional Reform and Party Discipline: The Effects of Changes in the Seniority System on Party Loyalty in the US House of Representatives," *British Journal of Political Science* 15, no. 2 (April 1985): 207–226.

[41]Robert Pear, "House Republicans Urge Earmark Moratorium," *New York Times*, January 26, 2008; Carl Hulse, "How Budget Battles Go without the Earmarks," *New York Times*, February 28, 2011.

of the mass media—first radio, then television, and then the Internet—has changed the ways and means of waging a campaign.[42]

The last trend is particularly important for the economics of getting elected. Today, in order to be effective, candidates running for national or statewide office must be able to pay for media. Since the early 1980s, the total amount spent on Congressional elections increased from less than $400 million to more than $1.4 billion. Congress has sporadically tried to limit campaign finances, but it has been largely unsuccessful for a number of reasons. First, current members of Congress have gained their offices because they are adept at fund-raising, so they often lack motivation to limit their own talent in this area.

Second, political advocates appear to be more successful at finding loopholes in legislation than Congress and the Federal Elections Commission are at filling them. Finally, the Supreme Court has often struck down laws because they violate—in the Court majority's view—either equal protection or free speech aspects of the Constitution. In 2010, for example, the Supreme Court reversed its previous support of campaign finance restrictions in the Citizens United decision. Speaking for the majority, Justice Anthony Kennedy equated restrictions on corporate contributions to campaigns with government seeking "to use its full power, including the criminal law, to command where a person may get his or her information.... This is unlawful. The First Amendment confirms the freedom to think for ourselves."[43]

Implementation and Regulation: Executive Agencies

The president of the United States is now often described as the most powerful person in the world. Certainly, this is a far cry from the office described in the Constitution or actual practice through much of our history. With a few notable exceptions—Washington, Jefferson, Jackson, and Lincoln—until the twentieth century, party leaders selected the president because he was someone who would not interfere with Congress's preeminent role in government. As late as the beginning of the twentieth century, the president's staff consisted of "a secretary, two assistant secretaries, two executive clerks, four lesser clerks, ... and a few doorkeepers and messengers."[44]

By the beginning of the twenty-first century, the president and the departments and agencies that report to him employed 2.7 million civilians compared to only 65,000 employed by Congress or the judiciary. About half of all federal workers are employed by the Defense Department and the Postal Service. Among departments devoted to social welfare, 62,000 are employed by the Department of Health and Human Services, 62,000 by the Social Security Administration, 9,600 by the Department of Housing and Urban Development, and only 4,200 by the Department of Education.

In the Constitution, the executive branch's chief domestic purpose was to carry out and enforce laws passed by Congress, essentially a passive task. Presidents had greater leeway in foreign and military affairs, although the right to declare war rested with Congress. Today, the major roles of the executive branch are control of the federal budget and the development of regulations for enforcing laws.

---

[42]Theda Skocpol and Morris P. Fiorina, *Civic Engagement in American Democracy* (Washington, DC: Brookings Institution Press, 1999), 1–26.

[43]*Citizens United v. Federal Election Commission*, No. 08-205.

[44]Morton Keller, *Affairs of State: Public Life in Late Nineteenth Century America* (Cambridge: Harvard University Press, 1977), 297–98.

The budget

The federal budget represents the most important link between Congress and the executive branch. Typically, in the language of the budget, we distinguish three elements of spending: authorization, appropriation, and outlays. First, Congress must *authorize* spending, that is, pass a law that specifies the amount of funding that should be spent on a particular program.[45] Ideally, it will then pass a separate bill that *appropriates* the funding, that is, gives the executive branch permission to actually spend the funds. The executive branch, however, must put into place any administrative structures necessary to spend the money and make the actual *outlay* of funds. Because authority and appropriations can cover more than one fiscal year, while outlays are tied to the year the spending takes place, the three figures are often different. Generally speaking, the president and Congress reach some agreement on most budget items. However, disputes often arise over particular spending. For example, Congress will often place several appropriations in a single bill as a way of avoiding a presidential veto. Presidents have requested the *line-item veto* that would give them the power to veto some elements of a bill but not others. A line-item veto was enacted in 1996, but two years later the federal courts found that it violated the Constitution.[46] Another tactic used by some presidents is *impounding*—or refusal to spend—appropriations. Richard Nixon used this tactic extensively during the 1970s until Congress took action to prevent it. Finally, in recent years, presidents have issued *signing statements* which explain how they disagree with a law they just signed and how they plan to implement the law, which may vary from Congressional intent.[47]

Currently the basic elements of the federal government's budget process are

- presidential preparation and presentation of budget;
- congressional budget resolution;
- separate appropriation bills or omnibus reconciliation spending bill; and
- President's Office of Management and Budget directives to departments about how to spend the money.

Federal spending is important both for the specific tasks it accomplishes—building roads, providing social services, building tanks—and for its overall impact on the economy. As we've noted, since the 1930s policymakers have recognized that government spending can be an important tool for reducing the impact of economic recessions—an idea associated with Keynesian economic theories.

In the folklore of American government, government budgets should never be out of balance. If this were true, we should truly worry about the state of our economy. For most years since the 1930s, the federal budget has run a deficit. However, there are many economists who argue that—within limits—a budget deficit itself is not harmful. If government spending, for example, reduces unemployment, it can have a positive impact on future economic growth and the gap between potential and actual gross domestic product (GDP).

---

[45]Most budget authority is tied to an appropriation, but less commonly, authorizing legislation can give an agency authority to either borrow funds for a purpose or enter into a contract in advance of appropriation. US Senate Budget Committee, "Glossary of Budget Terms," accessed February 22, 2010, http://budget.senate.gov/democratic/glossary.html#budget_auth.

[46]Thomas J. Nicola, "U.S. Supreme Court 1998 Line-Item Veto Act is Unconstitutional—Order Code 98-690A (August 18, 1998)." http://www.law.umaryland.edu/marshall/crsreports/crsdocuments/98-690a.pdf.

[47]Charlie Savage, "Obama's Embrace of a Bush Tactic Riles Congress," *New York Times* (August 8, 2009). http://www.nytimes.com/2009/08/09/us/politics/09signing.html?_r=1.

Although budget deficits have been typical since the 1930s, the overall budget situation has changed significantly since 1970. First, the character of federal spending changed dramatically. As the Vietnam War wound down in the early 1970s, Congress was able to use the decline in defense spending as a means of expanding social welfare, especially Social Security and social services. At the same time, the emergence of "stagflation" during the late 1970s and the recessions in 1974–75, 1979, and 1980–82 put downward pressure on revenues and upward pressure on spending (Figure 2.4).[48]

The most decisive change during the 1970s, however, was a profound shift in the position of the Republican Party on deficit spending. Previously, Republicans had been the party of budget discipline, opposing deficit spending and calling for a balanced budget. In the late 1970s, however, economic conservatives came to believe that they should advocate for tax cuts, even if they threw the budget into deficit.[49]

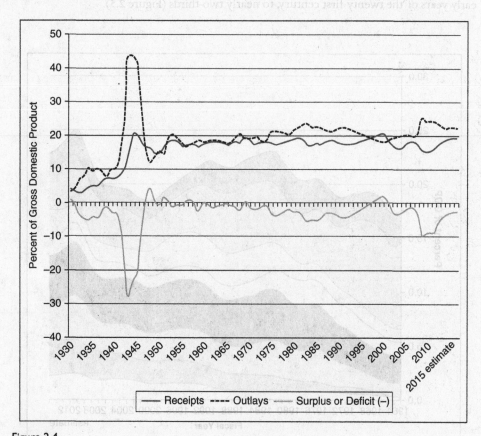

Figure 2.4

Receipts, Outlays, and Surplus as Percent of Gross Domestic Product

The federal government often runs a deficit during economic recessions as social programs like unemployment compensation expand and taxes decline.

Source: Based on Office of Management and Budget, "Historical Tables: Budget of the US Government," http://www.whitehouse.gov/sites/default/files/omb/budget/fy2013/assets/hist.pdf.

---

[48]Morris Janowitz, *Social Control of the Welfare State* (Chicago: University of Chicago Press, 1976), 41–71.

[49]The advocates of tax cuts argued that these cuts would eventually pay for themselves by increasing economic growth. However, they continued to champion tax cuts even after it became clear that this argument—while politically useful—did not square with reality.

The Republican triumph in the 1980 elections allowed them to implement this policy, which—along with the recession of the early 1980s—accelerated the growth of the deficit. Only in the 1990s, with government divided between a Democratic president and a Republican Congress, did policies to reduce the deficit gain support. But this period was short-lived. Large tax cuts implemented by a Republican Congress in 2001 and 2003 pushed the budget back into deficit, a trend that accelerated with the recession that began in 2007.

Although conservatives have been successful in using tax cuts as a means of placing pressure on government spending, they have been much less successful at changing the character of federal spending. Since the expansion of social welfare programs in the 1970s, these programs—especially Social Security and health care—have occupied a much larger share of the budget. In the 1960s, social welfare spending accounted for about a third of federal spending. During the 1980s, it had risen to about half, and in the early years of the twenty-first century, to nearly two-thirds (Figure 2.5).

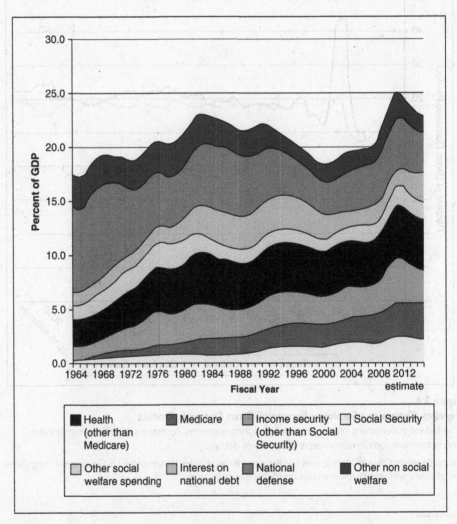

Figure 2.5
Federal Expenditures by Type as Percent of Gross Domestic Product, 1962–2014
Social Security and health now constitute the largest share of all federal spending.

Source: Based on Office of Management and Budget, "Historical Tables: Budget of the US Government," http://www. whitehouse.gov/sites/default/files/omb/budget/fy2013/assets/hist.pdf.

Regulations

The second dimension of executive branch influence on social welfare policymaking is the development of rules for implementing legislation. When Congress passes a law, it specifies the basic requirements for it to be implemented. However, even if a law is very long and detailed, Congress typically won't specify every detail about how it will be interpreted or implemented. This is where executive branch regulation comes in.

Generally speaking, the president's staff assigns the job of writing regulations to the appropriate department, which takes its time drafting regulations and then issues them in draft form for comment. During the comment period, organizations and individuals with an interest in the issue submit recommendations for how to improve the regulations. The department then publishes a set of final rules that are the official guidance for how the law will be interpreted.

Take the example of the welfare reform law of 1996. After being signed by the president in August 1996, the final regulations for the new program, Temporary Assistance for Needy Families (TANF), were not issued until April 1999. One hotly contested issue was "maintenance of effort" (MOE). Because the law provided a block grant to the states for public assistance, members of Congress wanted to make sure that the money was actually used for that purpose. Thus, states were required to maintain their efforts in this area. The actual legislation is shown in the following figure (Figure 2.6):

PUBLIC LAW 104–193—AUG. 22, 1996

"(A) IN GENERAL.—The Secretary shall reduce the grant payable to the State under section 403(a)(1) for fiscal year 1998, 1999, 2000, 2001, 2002, or 2003 by the amount (if any) by which qualified State expenditures for the then immediately preceding fiscal year are less than the applicable percentage of historic State expenditures with respect to such preceding fiscal year.

"(B) DEFINITIONS.—As used in this paragraph:
"(i) QUALIFIED STATE EXPENDITURES.—
"(I) IN GENERAL.—The term 'qualified State expenditures' means, with respect to a State and a fiscal year, the total expenditures by the State during the fiscal year, under all State programs, for any of the following with respect to eligible families:

"(aa) Cash assistance.
"(bb) Child care assistance.
"(cc) Educational activities designed to increase self-sufficiency, job training, and work, excluding any expenditure for public education in the State except expenditures which involve the provision of services or assistance to a member of an eligible family which is not generally available to persons who are not members of an eligible family.
"(dd) Administrative costs in connection with the matters described in items (aa), (bb), (cc), and (ee), but only to the extent that such costs do not exceed 15 percent of the total amount of qualified State expenditures for the fiscal year.
"(ee) Any other use of funds allowable under section 404(a)(1).

Figure 2.6
Excerpt from Public Law 104–193, The Personal Responsibility and Work Opportunity Reconciliation Act (1996)
Federal laws lay out the broad outlines of policies and programs.
Source: Public Law 104–93, August 22, 1996.

The law spends some time explaining what counts as "qualified State expenditures" but does not go into how a state or the federal government will know if the state is meeting this standard. To do so, the Department of Health and Human Services issued an explanation of how it would judge whether the MOE statute was being followed (Figure 2.7):

Federal Register / Vol. 64, No. 69 / Monday, April 12, 1999 / Rules and Regulations   17817

section 403. Therefore, they only affect the use of Federal TANF funds, unless the State commingles its money with Federal TANF funds. If a State commingles its funds, the Federal and State funds become subject to the same rules. Thus, commingling of State and Federal TANF funds can reduce the total amount of flexibility available to the State in its use of Federal and State funds.

Requirements pertaining solely to the use of Federal TANF funds do not apply to families assisted under TANF with State-only funds. Consequently, if a State segregates its TANF State funds from its Federal TANF funds, State expenditures on assistance must comply only with all of the rules that generally pertain to the TANF program, e.g., work and child support requirements. They are not subject to requirements that pertain only to the use of Federal TANF funds.

A State might choose to operate a "segregated" TANF program because certain limitations, e.g., time limitations and certain alien restrictions, apply to the program funded with Federal TANF funds that would not apply to a TANF program funded wholly with State funds.

Whether the expenditure of State funds is within the TANF program or separate from the TANF program, to count toward meeting the State's basic MOE, all expenditures must: (1) be made to or on behalf of an eligible family; (2) provide "assistance" to eligible families in one or more of the forms listed in the statute under section 409(a)(7)(B)(i)(I); and (3) comply with all other requirements and limitations set forth in this part of the regulations, including those set forth in §§ 263.5 and 263.6.

(b) Eligible Families

Section 409(a)(7)(B)(i)(I) provides that State funds under all State programs must be spent with respect to eligible families to count toward the State's basic MOE. Section 409(a)(7)(B)(i)(IV) further clarifies that an eligible family means a family eligible for assistance "under the State program funded under this part." The "State program funded under this part" is the State's TANF program.

Thus, we proposed that, in order to be considered an "eligible family" for MOE purposes, a family must have a child living with a custodial parent or other adult caretaker relative (or consist of a pregnant individual) and be financially needy under the TANF income and resource standards established by the State under its TANF plan. This definition includes two categories of

families. It includes all families funded with MOE funds under TANF, including certain alien families or time-limited families who cannot be served with Federal TANF funds, but who are being served in a segregated State TANF program. (We discuss this alien limitation in detail further on in this section.) It also includes a family that meets these criteria, but is not receiving TANF, and instead is receiving benefits and services from a separate State program. The expenditures to provide these benefits and services under all State programs may count toward the MOE requirement, provided the expenditures also meet all other requirements and limitations set forth in part 263.

A State is free to define who is a member of the family for Federal TANF purposes and may use this same definition for MOE purposes. For example, it could choose to assist other family members, such as noncustodial parents, who might significantly enhance the family's ability to achieve economic self-support and self-sufficiency. By including such individuals within its definition of family, a State could provide them with services through TANF or a separate State program. Noncustodial parents could then engage in State-funded activities such as work or educational activities, counseling, or parenting and money management classes.

The NPRM stated that we expect States to define "child" consistent either with the "minor child" definition given in section 419 or some other definition applicable under State law. The State must be able to articulate a rational basis for the age they choose.

The definition of "eligible family" expressly includes families that "would be eligible for such assistance but for the application of section 408(a)(7) of this Act."

Under section 408(a)(7), States may not use Federal TANF funds to provide TANF assistance to a family that includes an adult who has received federally funded assistance for a total of 60 months. Therefore, if a family becomes ineligible for Federal assistance under the TANF program due to this time limit, but still meets the definition of eligible family, then this family may be considered an eligible family for MOE purposes. (Note: In the NPRM, in § 273.2(c), we did not accurately cite the applicable criteria. The final rule at § 263.2(c) corrects this error; in referencing paragraph (b) of this section, it captures all three criteria for "eligible families.")

Section 5506(d) of Pub. L. 105–33 (the Balanced Budget Act of 1997) clarified

that the definition of an eligible family also includes lawfully present aliens who would be eligible for TANF assistance, but for the application of title IV of PRWORA.

Thus, the definition of eligible family allows States to claim MOE expenditures with respect to three types of family members: (1) those who are eligible for TANF assistance; (2) those who would be eligible for TANF assistance, but for the time-limit on the receipt of federally funded assistance; and (3) those lawfully present who would be eligible, but for the application of title IV of PRWORA. An alien family who meets any one of these three criteria may be considered an eligible family provided they also meet the family composition requirement (i.e., have a child living with a custodial parent or other caretaker relative or be a pregnant individual) and financial eligibility criteria established by the State. These last two requirements are based on the statutory language stating that eligible families "means families eligible for assistance under the State program funded under this part (TANF) * * * and that would be eligible for such assistance."

While this three part definition of eligible families may appear to allow States to claim qualified expenditures with respect to all lawfully present alien eligible family members, i.e., both qualified and nonqualified aliens, as discussed further below, this is not necessarily the case. Nor is it the case that the amendment to the definition under the Balanced Budget Act precludes States from claiming MOE for illegal aliens under certain circumstances.

While we mentioned the 1997 amendment in the NPRM, at that time, we had not fully analyzed the significance of the statutory language defining "eligible families" for MOE claiming purposes, relative to the extant eligibility provisions in title IV of PRWORA. Title IV of PRWORA sets forth the aliens who are eligible for Federal public benefits and for State and local public benefits; whereas, the definition of eligible families limits the expenditures that may be claimed for MOE. While there is obvious overlap between these two concepts, they are distinct and must be analyzed separately.

To understand eligibility for Federal TANF benefits, readers must be familiar with the definition of qualified alien, Federal public benefit, and Federal means-tested public benefits. Section 401 in title IV of PRWORA provides that, in general, only qualified aliens, as defined in section 431 of PRWORA, are

Figure 2.7

Excerpt from the Federal Register, Regulations Pertaining to Public Law 104–193

After a law is passed, the executive branch issues regulations that govern its implementation.

Source: Federal Register, Volume 64, No. 69, April 12, 1999, p. 17817.

Regulatory authority is an important element of the power of the president and the executive branch. It provides a relatively high degree of discretion in assessing Congress's intent and allows the president to place his own distinctive stamp on how a law is actually carried out.

LITIGATING PUBLIC POLICY: THE COURTS

After Congress passes a law and the president issues regulations for implementing it, the third branch of the federal government—the judiciary—may step in to play its role in policymaking. Because the courts are the only branch of the federal government whose members are not elected, their role has been ambiguous since the ratification of the Constitution. Moreover, their interpretation of the application of the Constitution to social welfare has changed over time. Indeed, we are currently in the midst of another major shift in how the courts intervene in social welfare policymaking.

The federal courts are organized in three levels. Ninety-four *district courts* are the entry level where most cases are tried. The district courts are organized into 12 *circuits*, each of which is headed by a *court of appeals* that hears appeals of district court cases. If a party is unhappy with the decision of the appeals court, it can request review by the Supreme Court, although the Court accepts only a small percentage of cases that request review.

All federal judges are nominated by the president and confirmed by the Senate. Once confirmed, they enjoy lifetime appointments. The fact that they are neither elected nor face reelection nor reappointment gives them a unique position in the federal system. Their lack of a popular mandate suggests to some commentators that they should take a secondary role in substantive policymaking. Others see federal judges as the bulwark against what Tocqueville called "the tyranny of the majority" by resisting popular passions.

The principal of *judicial review* (the ability of the courts to nullify actions of the other branches of government) was established in 1803 in the case of *Marbury v. Madison*.[50] For much of American history, the courts—with their emphasis on established precedent, the limits of federal authority, and the protection of individual rights against the power of government—were seen as the most conservative branch of government. The courts of the past generally outlawed a variety of welfare schemes including protective legislation, the recognition of labor unions, and civil rights. As a result, the courts were viewed as the enemy of activist social policy.

During the twentieth century, however, the traditional formalism of legal thinking was challenged on a number of fronts. First, Progressives argued that the courts should defer to the popular branches of government, nullifying laws only when they egregiously violated the Constitution. Second, beginning with *Muller v. Oregon* (1908), the courts began to recognize social scientific evidence as a means of breaking the formalistic reliance on the texts of laws.[51] Finally, at midcentury, the courts began to consider more expansive interpretations of parts of the Constitution, including *equal protections* (14th Amendment), the commerce clause, and protections against self-incrimination and search and seizure.[52]

---

[50]"*Marbury v. Madison* (1803)." National Archives and Record Administration, http://www.ourdocuments.gov/doc.php?flash=true&doc=19.

[51]Melvin I Urofsky, *Louis Brandeis: A Life* (New York: Pantheon, 2009).

[52]Morton J. Horowitz, *The Warren Court and the Pursuit of Justice* (New York: Hill and Wang, 1999).

These trends came together in the early postwar years that, for a time, made the courts the most progressive branch of the federal government. The landmark case *Brown v. Topeka Board of Education* (1954) was critical to the expansion of civil rights. During the 1960s and 1970s, the courts broadened the rights of welfare recipients by outlawing residency requirements, "midnight raids" of recipients' homes, and other state regulations that restricted welfare eligibility. *Roe v. Wade* (1973), which established a constitutional right for abortions, represented the apogee of the expansion of welfare rights by the courts.

Since the 1990s, the courts have returned to their traditional role, exercising a conservative pull on social policy. For example, in *US v. Morrison* (2000), the Supreme Court invalidated a section of the Violence Against Women Act that allowed victims to file a civil suit against attackers for damages by using a narrow interpretation of the commerce clause. Similar retreats into a more formal interpretation of the law have influenced a variety of recent court decisions, including their 2012 decision on the Affordable Care Act.

During the 1970s and 1980s, Progressives and social welfare advocates came to see the courts as the defenders of civil rights and unpopular causes. This era has clearly come to an end. In fact, in a number of cases, Congress has stepped in to reassert its intentions after the courts have invalidated laws on narrow technical grounds. In 2007, for example, the Supreme Court threw out an award to a woman who had unknowingly suffered long-term pay discrimination on the grounds that she had not filed her suit in a timely fashion. The Lily Ledbetter Fair Pay Act of 2009 (PL 111–2) clarified Congressional intent that the time limit should begin only when the victim discovered the discrimination, not when the discrimination itself had covertly begun.[53]

Although the overall trend in judicial review is conservative, there have been some notable counter-trends, the most interesting of which is the increased use of international legal opinions in Supreme Court decisions. In *Lawrence v. Texas* (2003), for example, the Supreme Court reversed its earlier support of antisodomy laws. The majority opinion, written by Justice Kennedy, used decisions by the European Court of Human Rights as one of the bases for this reversal. The use of international court decisions remains controversial but may provide a new direction for expanding the recognition of rights not explicitly protected by the Constitution.[54]

FEDERAL GOVERNMENT AND THE STATES: CHANGING RELATIONSHIPS

For most of American history, state governments were the prime movers of social welfare policy. The poor laws; almshouses; and institutions for the mentally ill, criminals, and other dependent populations were the outcome of state laws. During the twentieth century, however, the federal government supplanted the states as the driver

---

[53]Sheryl Gay Stolberg, "Obama Signs Equal-Pay Legislation," *New York Times*, January 29, 2009, http://www.nytimes.com/2009/01/30/us/politics/30ledbetter-web.html.

[54]Dale Carpenter, *Flagrant Conduct: The Story of Lawrence v. Texas* (New York: W.W. Norton and Company, 2012).

of social welfare legislation. The Social Security Act and the Civil Rights Act of 1964, in particular, stand as monuments to the ability of the federal government to take over the leading role.

In the past several decades, however, the states have staged a comeback. The welfare reform act of 1996, for example, left the states as the primary institution in the fight against welfare dependency, and left the federal government with a much-diminished regulatory and fiscal role.

The reasons for this reversal are complex. To some extent, the federal government has invited the states to assume a greater role in policymaking. At its high point in the late 1970s, the federal government found itself managing an unwieldy set of programs, typically tied to grants-in-aid to the states. One can argue that the decision of the Reagan administration to combine these individual programs into a set of larger block grants was simply an effort to improve administrative oversight.

But that isn't the whole story. Certainly the shift of responsibility back to the states was also a result of the increasing strength of political conservatism. In principle, conservatives have tended to support states' rights as more consistent with the "original intent" of the Constitution. More to the point, conservatives see the growth of the federal government as associated with more activist policies in social welfare and human rights, and they oppose the "imposition" of federal policies on the states. Indeed, the language of "imposition" is associated with the battles over civil rights and states' rights during the 1960s, which explains the appeal of this political language in the South.[55]

One argument often cited in support of this devolution of powers to the states is their role as the "laboratory for democracy." The phrase, attributed to Justice Louis Brandies' dissent in a 1932 Supreme Court decision, suggests that the states have the ability to test policy innovations before they are adopted as national policy. Politically, this means that conservative states can try out conservative innovations while more liberal states can test very different policies. The case of marriage equality (Chapter 9) provides a particularly clear example of this divergence.

The increasing importance of state government in social welfare has left the United States with a patchwork of different approaches to fundamental issues of social policy. We now have some states where welfare systems continue to serve millions of low-income recipients and other states where the welfare system has virtually disappeared. Although the federal courts have defined a right to abortion for all American women; in practice, in many states women who wish to terminate a pregnancy have very few options.

CONCLUSION

The organization of America's political and economic institutions can be a forbidding topic, far removed from the real-life experience of social workers. Yet, understanding these structures and the impact they have on the ability of social workers to help individuals, families, groups, and communities is essential to becoming an effective professional.

---

[55]Donald G. Mathews and Jane S. DeHart, *Sex, Gender, and the Politics of ERA: A State and the Nation* (New York: Oxford University Press, 1992).

Some social workers see part of their practice as working to change the fundamental structure of America's political economy. A number of social workers were involved in Occupy Wall Street and other Occupy movements that swept the country during the fall of 2011. Others are active in political campaigns and advocacy for changes in policies affecting particular social groups. Still others see their primary policy practice as working with individual clients to ensure their rights to services and fair treatment.

Test your understanding and analysis of this chapter by completing the Chapter Review.

However you conceptualize your stance toward policy practice, understanding the broader forces in the American economy and political system will make you a more effective professional. The chapters that follow provide examples of how social workers can combine their knowledge and skills to influence policy and improve the lives of the clients they serve.

3

LIBRARY OF CONGRESS PRINTS AND PHOTOGRAPHS DIVISION [LC-DIG-HIGHSM-12294].

Historical Influences

Ideology and Institutions

INTRODUCTION

This chapter explains how history influences contemporary social policy. It focuses on the role of ideas, institutions, and social movements in charting the course of social welfare policy. First, social thought about the nature of social justice, the capacity of government, and the malleability of human nature influence decisions about the desirability of certain policy outcomes and the possibility of achieving them. Second, social institutions, including government programs, the structure of politics, and the organizations of professions limit the trajectory of social policy. Only at certain critical junctures are there possibilities for significant changes in direction. Finally, the chapter explains how social work's professional values and ethics and its institutional roles provide opportunities for involvement in policymaking.

The first lesson to learn about the history of social welfare is that you can never start from scratch. The nature of past decisions structures both the opportunities and constraints on social policy. If you need an example, look at the French Revolution.

THE YEAR I: WHY HISTORY ALWAYS MATTERS

Seventeen ninety-two (1792) was an exciting year in France. Three years after the storming of the Bastille, the political and social forces of the Revolution had increased in strength. In 1792, Louis XVI and Marie Antoinette were guillotined, and the National Convention abolished the monarchy and declared France a republic. In place of the

Assess your comprehension
of "The Year I: Why History
Always Matters" by
completing this quiz.

old order, the *ancien regime*, the revolutionaries sought to construct a new society governed by reason and freed of the mythologies of the past. In place of religion, a cult of the Supreme Being was instituted. The revolutionaries believed that once the superstitions of the past had been deposed, a new society devoted to reason would emerge.

One expression of the devotion to a clean slate was the "Revolutionary Calendar" instituted in November of 1793. If society were to free itself from the past, then that essential element of life—time—could not continue to be governed by the claptrap of the Gregorian calendar. Instead, a new, more rational way of measuring the passage of time was needed. "The Revolutionary Calendar was introduced in an age which advocated the total obliteration of the old order in the name of progress and modernity: the beginning of the new Republican Era marked the total discontinuity between past and present."[1]

The new calendar divided the year into twelve 30-day months with a five-day hiatus at the end of the year. The year would begin with the fall equinox, and the months would be named after natural events, not ancient gods. The day, too, would be governed by a rational decimal system with 10 hours, each hour having 100 decimal minutes, and each minute, 100 decimal seconds.

The most profound expression of this rejection of the past was the calendar's numbering of the years. Clearly, linking the year to a religious event—such as "the Year of our Lord"—was incompatible with the new secular age. For that matter, history itself was suspect, governed as it had been by kings and emperors. So, the counting of years would begin with the most important date in history—the founding of the Republic. September 22, 1792, became the first day of Vendémiaire (the month of the grape harvest—this was France!) in the Year I.

Things didn't work out well for the Revolutionary Calendar or its creators. By the end of the Year III, Robespierre and many of his supporters had followed the king and queen to the guillotine. After Napoleon came to power in 1799, he signed a *concordat* with the Vatican that reinstituted the traditional days of the week. In 1806, Napoleon—perhaps realizing that a "Revolutionary Calendar" did not really suit an empire—abolished it altogether. Although revived briefly by the Paris Communards of 1871, the Revolutionary Calendar has stood as an example of hubris, of a people trying to impose its will on the unruly body of history.

We start this chapter with the story of the Year I because it poses, in the starkest form, the importance of history. We never start totally new. The past is present in our institutions, in our memories, and in our routines. While societies and people can change, efforts to eradicate the past inevitably fail.

For social welfare, the weight of history manifests itself in a number of ways. Decisions made in the past limit some options and open up others. Policy decisions lead to the creation of institutions. Institutions attract individuals and groups whose interests are served by those institutions. Those groups are unlikely to be swayed by arguments in favor of abolishing institutions in which they are invested.

History manifests itself as well in ideologies—ways of viewing the world. Is the government an embodiment of the public interest or a despotic power interested in stealing our money and our freedom? How a person answers that question will influence her views on a variety of policy issues.

---

[1]Eviater Zerubavel, "The French Republican Calendar: A Case Study in the Sociology of Time," *American Sociological Review* 42, no. 6 (December 1977): 868–877. Quotation on p. 871.

Finally, history influences one's identity. During the years after World War II, for example, many white working-class men identified themselves as union members and supported a variety of social welfare innovations that supported unions. By the 1970s, however, many of these same men—after the first years of the civil rights movement—came to see themselves as white men and, as a result, opposed the expansion of civil rights and programs directed at low-income populations.[2]

Exactly where one's identity comes from is a ticklish question. For social welfare, it points to the important influence of social movements on policy. In addition to informing one's identity, movements mobilize people and resources behind certain institutions and ideas.

The health care reform debate of 2009–10 illustrated this process. The most successful health policy innovation of the past half century is Medicare, the program that insures care for the elderly and disabled (see Chapter 7). Yet, to pay for health care reform, Congress needed to constrain the cost of a privatized element of Medicare, Medicare Advantage.

But recipients of Medicare are now an interest group. They are generally happy with the care they receive and worry that changing the health care system too much will hurt *their* benefits. Medicare Advantage enrollees, in particular, have benefited from the subsidies provided to private insurers—subsidies that cost more than a thousand dollars a year per enrollee—and are unwilling to give them up.[3] So we are faced with a situation in which the success of a publicly run health care program is now a major barrier to expanding coverage in the present.

Jacob Hacker's book *The Divided Welfare State* highlights two ideas that help us understand the history of social welfare and the prospects for change. *Path dependency* refers to the fact that once government makes a particular policy choice, it tends to embellish and expand on that choice rather than reversing course. This tendency to continue to build on past decisions—what Hacker calls a *trajectory*—means that for much of social welfare history, fundamental policy change is not a real option. Any change that occurs is likely to be incremental: refining a past decision, expanding or contracting one or another aspect of a program.[4]

Sometimes, however, the stars align in a set of circumstances that provide an opportunity to change direction, to try something new or stop doing something we've done for years. These moments—what Hacker refers to as *critical junctures*—are times of crisis when more basic change can gain a hearing.

Critical junctures don't happen very often. Two related features make them more likely. First, a system has to be in some degree of crisis. In other words, it's not good enough just to have a better idea. Old ideas have to lose their credibility as well. Second, the political balance of institutional forces—particularly in the

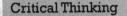

Critical Thinking

Practice Behavior Example: Use critical thinking augmented by creativity and curiosity.

Critical Thinking Question: According to Jacob Hacker, "critical junctures" are relatively rare in national politics. Are we currently in a critical juncture or rather a period when we can only make incremental changes in existing programs?

---

[2]David R. Roediger, *The Wages of Whiteness: Race and the Making of the American Working Class,* revised ed. (London and New York: Verso, 1999); Jonathan Rieder, *Canarsie: The Jews and Italians of Brooklyn Against Liberalism* (Cambridge: Harvard University Press, 1985).

[3]Brian Bliss, Jonah Pozen, and Stuart Guterman, "The Continuing Cost of Privatization: Extra Payments to Medicare Advantage Plans Jump to $11.4 Billion in 2009," (New York: The Commonwealth Fund, 2009), http://www.commonwealthfund.org/~/media/Files/Publications/Issue%20Brief/2009/May/1265_Biles_Extra_Payments_54_v2.pdf.

[4]Jacob S. Hacker, *The Divided Welfare State: The Battle Over Public and Private Social Benefits in the United States* (New York: Cambridge University Press, 2002).

legislative branch (Congress), the executive branch (the president and his appointees), and nongovernmental interests—must have the capability to push through a new approach without compromising with defenders of the old policy path.

Practice Context

Practice Behavior Example: Continuously discover, appraise, and attend to changing locales, populations, scientific and technological developments, and emerging societal trends to provide relevant services.

Critical Thinking Question: Welfare reform was, in part, a response to changes in women's work and family roles during the late twentieth century. How can changing social trends around gender roles affect other social welfare policies and professional practice?

The past 15 years provide two examples of critical junctures in social welfare: the debates over welfare reform and health care reform. We will discuss these issues in more detail later in the book. Here we want to focus on how the concepts of path dependency and critical juncture applied to the debates.

The opportunity for welfare reform came about because of two interdependent crises in welfare policy. First, the core rationale for public assistance for children and their caretakers—the program called Aid to Families with Dependent Children (AFDC)—had been undermined over a number of years. As more women entered the labor force, the idea that poor women should stay home and take care of their children seemed obsolete to more and more Americans. In addition, a large body of research had come to the conclusion that welfare did serve as a kind of *trap*; because welfare recipients were not engaged in the labor force, welfare seemed to increase rather than reduce *social exclusion*.[5]

This change in social conditions was complemented by changes in political ideology. First, Bill Clinton—hoping to reverse 12 years of Republican victories—decided to define himself as a *New Democrat* not tied to old policy decisions. During the 1992 campaign, he vowed to "end welfare as we know it" as proof of this commitment. Second, in 1994 the Republicans captured both the House of Representatives and the Senate for the first time in 40 years. Part of their platform, the "Contract with America," called for radical welfare reform. As a result, during 1995 and 1996—although Clinton and the Republicans had very different ideas about the nature of welfare reform—both Republicans and many Democrats were committed to making welfare a program for temporary aid and requiring welfare recipients to work.

Health care reform is a more complicated story for a number of reasons: the debate has been going on since the 1940s, the health care system is much larger than welfare and affects all citizens, and the bulk of health care is delivered outside of government.

Certainly there is much about the US health care system that appears to be in crisis. A large part of the population lacks health insurance; American health care is extraordinarily expensive by international standards; and, notwithstanding all those expenditures, Americans are less healthy than citizens of most comparable nations. But in spite of these facts, most Americans like their own health care, and many fear that changing the system will hurt them. In addition, because employers pay a large share of the cost of health care, American households do not directly experience the full weight of increasing costs.[6] So, whatever the deficiencies of the health care system, many Americans opposed comprehensive reform.

Although conditions were by and large the same during the two big pushes for health care reform—1993–94 and 2009–10—the politics of the two eras were quite different.

---

[5]Alice O'Connor, *Poverty Knowledge: Social Science, Social Policy, and the Poor in Twentieth-Century US History* (Princeton: Princeton University Press, 2001), 242–283.

[6]Although most workers don't pay the full cost of their health care, the general stagnation of wages over the past generation is at least partially the result of a share of compensation going to health care costs rather than wage increases.

In 1993–94 the Democrats enjoyed a majority in both houses of Congress, but their majority in the Senate was smaller than in 2009–10. Just as importantly, other institutions relevant to the health care debate—particularly the pharmaceutical industry and physicians—were much stronger opponents of health care reform in 1994 than they were 15 years later.[7] As a result, in 2009, although the health care crisis was only marginally worse, the prospects for a critical juncture were much more favorable to reform.

FOUR ERAS OF AMERICAN SOCIAL WELFARE

The ideas of path dependency and critical juncture are a starting point for understanding the history of social welfare. Much of this history is characterized by stable situations in which dominant ideas and institutions define the parameters of social welfare. However, over time, two forces of change encourage reform. First, general social conditions can change. Urbanization, the expansion of women's role in the labor force, and deindustrialization—these big social changes can undermine old conditions and create new ones that push the system to change. Second, social movements can arise that challenge the dominant ideas about social welfare and dominant institutions. As a result, at critical junctures these three forces—ideas, institutions, and movements—come together to cause a shift from one era to another in social welfare history.

Assess your comprehension of "Four Eras of American Social Welfare" by completing this quiz.

We can think of social welfare in the United States as being divided into four eras. A *corporatist era* dominated Colonial America and slowly gave way in the years after the American Revolution. It was followed by the *age of the poorhouse* dominated by voluntary efforts to restrict public welfare. This era, in turn, gave way to the *era of Progressive America* in which government's role in social welfare expanded greatly. Finally, we are in the midst of the *era of conservative America* in which many of the Progressive era's institutions have been under attack.

The Corporatist Era

The history of Colonial social welfare is as close as the United States ever came to what Esping-Andersen would call a truly conservative or corporatist era of social welfare. The organization of Colonial society was dominated by tradition, with a heavy emphasis on paternalism and the involvement of religion. In contrast to later periods of American history, Colonial government often took a very active role in the private lives of citizens. This combination of traditionalism, religion, and strong government gave the corporatist era its distinctive character.

The major social welfare institution of the Colonial era was the *poor laws*. Although they varied from colony to colony, the poor laws generally outlined an active role for

---

[7]Social movements, too, played a critical role in both the welfare reform and health care debates of the 1990s. The late 1970s saw the rapid growth of a conservative movement that went beyond any specific issue. A set of powerful ideas about the causes of economic stagnation, the intrusion of government into many aspects of American life, and the fear of moral decline coalesced a variety of social groups—many of which were not natural allies—into a unified movement. This conservative movement was largely responsible for the nomination of Ronald Reagan by the Republican Party in 1980 but saw its power decline somewhat during the Bush administration (1989–1993). In 1992, much of the movement broke with George H. W. Bush and opposed his reelection; hence, he received less than 38 percent of the vote in the general election.

local government in providing for poor and dependent people. However, the *right* to public assistance was not tied to an idea of citizenship, as it would be later in American history. Rather, two important ideas guided Colonial society and social welfare: hierarchy and localism.

The idea that "all men are created equal" would have been virtually meaningless in Colonial society before the Revolution.[8] Instead, individuals typically saw themselves as located within a set of hierarchical relationships in which they were subordinate to some people and dominant to others. Hierarchical relationships were not restricted to one sphere. Rather, economic, social, political, and religious relationships all fit together into an integrated social order.[9]

The model for Colonial society was the patriarchal family in which a strong father figure held sole authority over other family members. The economy was dominated by these hierarchical relations, in which weaker people—those without land or property— took orders from their superiors. In politics, men of property and standing were seen as natural rulers to whom other elements of society were expected to defer. The religious order too was dominated by hierarchies, beginning with the idea of the Great Chain of Being, in which every angel, human, and animal fit into a neat order.[10]

The place where these social relations were realized was in the local community. While the Colonial governments established the legal framework, local communities generally were charged with implementing the guidelines. In the seventeenth century, when the colonies imported the poor laws from England, they were forced to modify the British idea of *settlement* in which one's right to assistance was based on one's place of birth. In place of settlement, the colonies typically established residency tests that required a person to live in a community for a number of years before becoming eligible for aid.

The paternalism of Colonial society demanded that the "lower classes" show respect and deference toward their social superiors, but it also imposed responsibilities on the social elites. Paternalism carried reciprocal responsibilities for masters and servants. Master workmen who owned their own shops and employed apprentices were expected to consider and contribute to the apprentices' well-being. Even in slave societies, masters were expected to assume responsibility for the basic needs of their workforce.[11]

Thus, the poor laws of the Colonial era reflected the dominant paternalism of the society. The poor members of a community were the responsibility of the community, which had to provide resources to respond to the needs of all residents. Typically, aid to the poor was provided in the home, called *outdoor relief.* If an older or disabled member of the community could not live independently, they were often boarded out at community expense. Dependent children were often let out as apprentices with the expectation that they would learn a trade and become productive members of society.[12]

The idea of the "undeserving" poor had its origins in the Colonial period, but it carried a different meaning than it would acquire later in American history. In Colonial society, one was undeserving of aid because of being an outsider, not because of moral

---

[8]Of course, it wouldn't have occurred to most Colonials to consider women and men as equal.

[9]David Rothman, *The Discovery of the Asylum: Social Order and Disorder in the New Republic,* (Boston: Little Brown, 1971), Chapters 1–2.

[10]William F Bynum, "The Great Chain of Being after Forty Years: An Appraisal," *History of Science* 13 (1975): 1–28. Quote from p. 6

[11]Eugene Genovese, *Roll, Jordan, Roll: The World the Slaves Made* (New York: Random House, 1971), 3–6.

[12]Rothman, *Discovery of the Asylum,* 206–236.

inferiority. For those who did not meet the residency requirements, the poor laws were harsh. Migrant paupers were "warned out" of the community and forced to take to the road. In other places, the workhouse—where extremely spartan conditions were combined with grueling work—was the only option offered outsiders.[13]

The point is that the poor members of Colonial society were seen as a part of their local community who, like all other members, had responsibilities and rights. As part of an integrated society based on tradition, paternalism, and hierarchy, the poor had their place, although certainly not an enviable one.

Yet, the ideas and institutions brought by white men to Colonial America were an uneasy fit with the radically different social conditions they faced. Although colonists saw themselves living in a stable society governed by tradition, they in fact were living in a dynamic social order that would soon transform their lives.

The foundation for the transformation of Colonial society was demography—the balance of births, deaths, and marriages that determines the composition of the population. In Europe of the seventeenth century, death and birth were in a close race with one another. People married relatively late, often because they had to wait to inherit land; and while women might have eight or nine pregnancies, just over half of those might yield children who survived until adulthood. High birth rates and high death rates resulted in slow population growth or, during famine years, actual declines.[14]

In America, the colonists imported the same ideas about family formation, but they yielded radically different results. First, because land was more plentiful, young people did not have to wait as long to acquire land and marry, so women began having children earlier. Second, because food was more plentiful and diseases not so virulent, more of their children survived to become adults. In place of a stable society based on static population, the colonies experienced population explosions.[15] Although for a time, communities tried to hold onto the idea of stable, traditional community, soon the excess population of the new generation was forced to set off into the wilderness to establish new communities.[16] Others took to the road, often leading to the cities along the Eastern Seaboard: Boston, New York, Philadelphia, Baltimore, or Charleston.[17]

The dynamic demography of the colonies set loose another force: individualism. From a fixed social order in which one was born to and lived in one's place, Americans relatively quickly came to "look out for number one." Though the reasons are complex, some are clear enough. During the seventeenth century, the colonies were pulled into extensive commercial networks that linked tobacco cultivation in the South to sugar and rum production in the West Indies and the slave trade. Luck, talent, and moxie could combine to create great fortunes or send men falling into poverty. The hierarchal and traditional religion of the early years gave way to more individualistic evangelical forms of belief like the Great Awakening of the 1740s that overturned the religious hierarchy of

[13]Michael B. Katz, *The Undeserving Poor: From the War on Poverty to the War on Welfare* (New York: Pantheon, 1990), 9–36.

[14]Phillip J. Greven, *Four Generations: Population, Land, and Family in Colonial Andover, Massachusetts* (Ithaca: Cornell University Press, 1970).

[15]The same was true of the slave societies of the South. British North America was the only place in the Western Hemisphere where slave populations grew through natural increase during these years.

[16]Kenneth A. Lockridge, *A New England Town: The First Hundred Years: Dedham, Massachusetts, 1636–1736,* Expanded ed. (New York: Norton, 1985).

[17]Gary B. Nash, *The Urban Crucible: Social Change, Political Consciousness, and the Origins of the American Revolution* (Cambridge: Harvard University Press, 1979).

New England and the Middle Atlantic states. Frontier life with its threats and privations encouraged a rough-hewn sense of democracy in place of the deference and obligation of a hierarchical society.

All of these forces combined to knock the poor laws on their ear. The population explosion increased the number of outsiders who left their homes in search of fortune, many of whom found failure instead. Local communities, in response, increased their residency requirements, which ultimately made the problem worse by disqualifying more and more people from aid.

As the poor more frequently became outsiders, the sense of moral obligation between the poor and the rich broke down. Increasingly, the poor were seen not as members of the community, but as "surplus population" that was artificially supported through the taxation of the well-off and hard-working. Benjamin Franklin, one of the Founding Fathers of the United States, argued for a more punitive system of poor relief to encourage the poor to fend for themselves.[18]

The political controversies of the early Republic had little direct impact on the delivery of social welfare. However, the abandonment of a weak national government based on the Articles of Confederation and the adoption of a stronger federal system based on the Constitution established a set of institutions that continue to define how laws are made and carried out. The three branches of the federal government and the division of responsibilities between the federal and state governments were the most important of these new institutional arrangements.

The battle of religion and republicanism that broke out in the wake of the Revolution had an important influence on social welfare in the late eighteenth and early nineteenth centuries. Many revolutionary leaders—like their counterparts in France—were adherents of deism, the belief that a Supreme Being existed but did not intervene in the affairs of human beings. After the Revolution, the link between republican democratic thought and secularism continued, often reinforced by skepticism about the undemocratic qualities of social elites.

In this context, organized religion found itself in a sorry state in the 1780s. The Revolution had destroyed many churches, and republicanism and the enthusiasm associated with war and revolution sapped much of the population's spiritual fervor. This was soon to change. Within a decade, several religious sects—particularly the Methodists and Baptists—had initiated organizing drives to build churches and expand membership. These organizing efforts sparked the second "Great Awakening," a major expansion of religion in American life that would influence the development of social welfare and social reform for the first six decades of the nineteenth century.[19]

While secular republicanism and religious enthusiasm battled for the hearts of women and men in the early years of the nineteenth century, beneath the struggle the two movements shared a newfound optimism about social improvement. The intellectual traditions of the Colonial period were overwhelmingly gloomy. Sin ("In Adam's Fall, We sinned all," as the *New England Primer* noted) and the need to protect humans from their own darker impulses had informed American religious and political thought.

By the early years of the nineteenth century, fueled by these two social movements—republicanism and the Second Great Awakening—more and more Americans embraced

---

[18]Mark J. Stern and June Axinn, *Social Welfare: A History of the American Response to Need*, 8th ed. (Boston: Pearson Educational, 2011), 28–29.

[19]Donald G. Mathews, "The Second Great Awakening as an Organizing Process, 1780–1830: An Hypothesis," *American Quarterly* 21, no. 1 (Spring 1969): 23–43.

the idea of *perfectionism*, the notion that people, especially Americans, could fundamentally improve the morals of individuals and the collective organization of society. While they split on how to undertake this mission, especially regarding the role of government in the pursuit of perfection, these two movements were central to the breakdown of the corporatist era and the coming of the age of the poorhouse.

The Age of the Poorhouse

Poorhouses had existed in Colonial America, but they were not central to the operation of the poor laws. Typically, they were established when preferred solutions—like having the dependent elderly or people with disabilities board with a family—were in too short a supply to meet the demand.

However, as ideas of perfectionism gained momentum in the early nineteenth century, the poorhouse became central to the two dominant policy initiatives of the century: the move toward institutionalism and the attack on public welfare. The poorhouse was only one of many institutions that increased in popularity during these years. States established penitentiaries to attack criminality. Insane asylums were started to treat and hopefully cure the mentally ill. Orphans, truants, and young delinquents were confined in "houses of refuge" and "reformatories."

All of these institutions went through a similar cycle. They were born in the enthusiasm that this new approach could solve the problem, whether it was crime, insanity, or pauperism. Whether of religious conviction of the perfectibility of the human soul or secular optimism, advocates believed these social problems were caused by defects in the social environment. Change the environment by cutting off individuals from these bad influences, they claimed, and the problem would quickly be solved.[20]

Believing inmates would need only a short stay, these new state institutions recruited inmates widely. For a while, funding and the quality of service kept pace with the demand, but slowly it became apparent that their advocates had overestimated the effectiveness of the new institutions. As their populations shifted from short-term to longer-term inmates, the amount of funding and quality of service declined. The institutions shifted from places of reform and cure to warehouses in which populations that bothered or frightened the general population could be kept out of sight.

Some institutions, especially those serving children and the mentally ill, began as private systems; however, as their custodial role increased, they typically became public. In a way, they represented a major shift in government responsibility. During the Colonial era, criminals, delinquents, and the dependent had been primarily a *local* responsibility; the new institutions, however, were *state* institutions that often shifted responsibility from counties or townships to the state government.

The expansion of state and federal government involvement in social welfare accelerated during and immediately after the Civil War. The war itself transformed the power of the federal government. The abolition of slavery and the Fourteenth Amendment's expansion of the rights of citizens redefined the relationship of individuals to the national government. Before the war, the federal government existed as a compact between itself and the individual states. With the exception of the postal service, individuals rarely interacted with federal government institutions. After the Civil War, American citizenship rights expanded in many ways, including social welfare rights.

---

[20]Gerald N. Grob, *Mental Institutions in America: Social Policy to 1875* (New York: Free Press, 1973).

The Fourteenth Amendment to the US Constitution (ratified 1868)

Section 1. All persons born or naturalized in the United States, and subject to the jurisdiction thereof, are citizens of the United States and of the State wherein they reside. No State shall make or enforce any law, which shall abridge the privileges or immunities of citizens of the United States; nor shall any State deprive any person of life, liberty, or property, without due process of law; nor deny to any person within its jurisdiction the equal protection of the laws.

Section 2. Representatives shall be apportioned among the several States according to their respective numbers, counting the whole number of persons in each State, excluding Indians not taxed. But when the right to vote at any election for the choice of electors for President and Vice President of the United States, Representatives in Congress, the Executive and Judicial officers of a State, or the members of the Legislature thereof, is denied to any of the male inhabitants of such State, being twenty-one years of age, and citizens of the United States, or in any way abridged, except for participation in rebellion, or other crime, the basis of representation therein shall be reduced in the proportion which the number of such male citizens shall bear to the whole number of male citizens twenty-one years of age in such State.

Section 3. No person shall be a Senator or Representative in Congress, or elector of President and Vice President, or hold any office, civil or military, under the United States, or under any State, who, having previously taken an oath, as a member of Congress, or as an officer of the United States, or as a member of any State legislature, or as an executive or judicial officer of any State, to support the Constitution of the United States, shall have engaged in insurrection or rebellion against the same, or given aid or comfort to the enemies thereof. But Congress may, by a vote of two-thirds of each House, remove such disability.

Section 4. The validity of the public debt of the United States, authorized by law, including debts incurred for payment of pensions and bounties for services in suppressing insurrection or rebellion, shall not be questioned. But neither the United States nor any State shall assume or pay any debt or obligation incurred in aid of insurrection or rebellion against the United States, or any claim for the loss or emancipation of any slave; but all such debts, obligations and claims shall be held illegal and void.

Section 5. The Congress shall have power to enforce, by appropriate legislation, the provisions of this article.

Diversity in Practice

Practice Behavior Example: Recognize the extent to which a culture's structures and values may oppress, marginalize, alienate, or create or enhance privilege and power.

Critical Thinking Question: Northern politicians believed that passing a few laws would quickly lead to African Americans achieving equality in the South after the Civil War. What role did the culture's structures and values play in preventing freed slaves from achieving equality?

African Americans were those most immediately influenced by the expansion of public welfare. Although the Civil War transformed their legal and political status, it didn't change their poverty and economic vulnerability. The provision of direct aid to former slaves began during the war and eventually led to the establishment of the Freedman's Bureau, which served as a provider of food, shelter, and other necessities; an employment agency; and legal advocates for the former slaves.[21]

The War also led to the increased federal responsibility for the Northern population. The carnage left behind an increased population of disabled veterans, widows, and orphans who turned to the federal government for aid. As time passed, aging veterans and their dependents also sought aid from the government. Eventually, some historians estimate, one-half of the elderly male population of the North qualified for pensions as hundreds of thousands of Americans turned to the federal government.[22]

[21]Leon F. Litwack, *Been in the Storm So Long: The Aftermath of Slavery* (New York: Random House, 1979), 238–246.

[22]Theda Skocpol, *Protecting Soldiers and Mothers: The Political Origins of Social Policy in the United States* (Cambridge: The Belknap Press of Harvard University Press, 1992), 102–152.

The administration of the Civil War pensions was hardly a model of bureaucratic rationality and efficiency. Pensions soon became an element of political party competition, with both Democrats and Republicans viewing the expansion of eligibility and the easing of qualification requirements as a means of garnering votes. In states where party competition was particularly keen, signing up veterans—many of whom had suspiciously lost their proof of service—became a major election-year activity.

The abuses of the Civil War pension system, in fact, contributed to the other major policy innovation of the period—the expansion of voluntary charity organizations that sought to limit the power of government to care for the poor. Beginning with organizations like the New York Society for the Prevention of Pauperism in 1818 and reaching the zenith of its influence with the Charity Organization Societies of the 1880s, the voluntary charity movement advocated the abolition or at least the curtailment of outdoor relief—providing public assistance to individuals and families outside of the poorhouse. Ideally, all charity would be distributed by voluntary agencies that would carefully investigate recipients to make sure the aid was not used for alcoholic beverages or other illicit purposes. For those unwilling or unable to receive voluntary assistance, the poorhouse became the sole alternative.[23]

Behind the voluntary charity movement was a new image of the nature of poverty and its role in society. The *undeserving poor* of the Colonial period were undeserving because of their residence; they hadn't lived in the community long enough to qualify for local aid. By the early nineteenth century, *undeserving* had taken on a whole new meaning. The poor became undeserving because they lacked the necessary moral constitution. Reformers condemned the two great stereotypes of the poor—the pauper and the tramp—because they used their individualism to choose drink over temperance, charity over work, and deceit over honesty.

The "wickedness" of the poor, reformers believed, was encouraged by the behavior of the well-off. By giving the poor charity without assuring that it was used for moral purposes, the "indiscriminant almsgiver" contributed to poverty. This core argument—that aiding the poor increased rather than ameliorated suffering—was a new idea in the early nineteenth century, but it is one that continues to justify and legitimate public policies even today.

Thus, from an afterthought, the poorhouse moved to the center of public policy. Two reports on poverty—the Yates Report (1824) in New York and the Quincy Report (1821) in Massachusetts—accepted the idea that almsgiving and outdoor relief increased pauperism, but rejected their total abolition. Instead, the reports recommended that each county or town maintain its own poorhouse as the preferred response to poverty. The reports and their advocates claimed that through the labor required of their inmates, the poorhouse would pay for itself.[24]

The same social motivation that spurred institutionalization and voluntary charity animated many of the era's social reform movements. Efforts to attack vices like alcoholism and prostitution, to spread religion to the poor, to expand public education, and, eventually, to abolish slavery all drew their inspiration from religious and secular notions of perfectionism and optimism.

Within a few years of their beginning, these two policy innovations—institutionalization and the expansion of voluntary charity—were failures. By the 1850s, the

[23]Michael B. Katz, *In the Shadow of the Poorhouse: A Social History of Welfare in America*, 10h anniversary ed. (New York: Basic Books, 1996), 3–36.
[24]Katz, *Shadow of the Poorhouse*, 21–24.

optimism that greeted the new institutions had been replaced by exposés of corruption and inhumane conditions. Although it took only a few years for reformatories and insane asylums to sweep across the country, it would take more than a century to begin the process of closing them down.

Voluntary charity—while often dominating intellectual discussions of poverty—had a difficult time imposing its vision on actual charity practices. Local politics in major American cities during the nineteenth century were often dominated by a coalition of small proprietors and working-class voters who were often hostile to the social concerns of social elites. While some municipalities experimented with the abolition of outdoor relief, democratic pressure typically encouraged politicians to maintain aid to poor families. Indeed, the political "machines" (like Tammany Hall in New York) used outdoor relief and public employment as means of maintaining poor people's political loyalties.

Increasing class antagonism played an important role in voluntary charity's last stand during the 1870s and 1880s. Although by then, the formula—restricting aid, increasing investigation, forcing poor people into the poorhouse—was threadbare, the Charity Organization movement attempted to revive it by adding a new twist: "friendly visiting." These visitors, often middle-class women, were supposed to bridge the expanding gap that had opened between the well-off and the poor as a result of the depression of the 1870s. But their actual function was to ensure that aid was restricted and that the intemperate and immoral were refused aid. A similar formula for engaging the poor was taken up by the settlement house movement that saw young women and men take up residence in poor districts in order to better engage working families.[25]

Charity Organization and settlement work weren't any more successful than earlier efforts at imposing voluntary charity's view of the world, but they did spark a change with far-reaching consequences. Friendly visiting was intended to allow the poor to adopt middle-class standards of propriety and industry, but its actual impact was just the opposite. Although originally friendly visitors expected to find immoral paupers that needed to be reformed, what they found instead were families struggling with unemployment, illness, and bad luck. Over time, it was the friendly visitors who changed. The young middle-class women who visited the poor or worked in a settlement house came to understand—in a way that other movements had resisted—that poverty was, at its core, a problem of inadequate *consumption*. After the economic crisis of the 1890s, this new generation of poverty workers, the first generation of social workers, was able to formulate a new way of thinking about the problems of the poor.[26]

It seems remarkable that it would take most of a century for reformers to understand how central unemployment and material deprivation were to the problems of the poor, but it is testimony to the power of ideas. Nineteenth-century economic thought argued that "supply created its own demand," which suggested that long-term economic stagnation and high unemployment were impossible. Because mass unemployment was a new feature of the social landscape, it took literally decades of experience before public policy was ready to address it.[27]

---

[25]Katz, *Shadow of the Poorhouse*, 37–60.

[26]Viviana Zelizer, *The Social Meaning of Money: Pin Money, Paychecks, Poor Relief, and other Currencies* (New York: Basic Books, 1994), 143–199.

[27]Alexander Keyssar, *Out of Work: The First Century of Unemployment in Massachusetts* (Cambridge and New York: Cambridge University Press, 1986).

Progressive America

The poorhouse era did not end until the waning years of the nineteenth century. In the meantime, American society experienced a set of profound changes. Industrialization, which in the early 1800s had hardly begun, was the dominant force in economic life by the end of the century. With economic change, Americans left the countryside, swelling the population of the cities. Some cities that barely existed at the beginning of the century—Chicago is the outstanding example—were vast metropolises by its end.

Increasing wealth and urbanization transformed America's social class structure as well. A new social class made up of professionals and employers that hadn't previously existed became a major presence in cities. Flows of immigrants—first from Germany, Ireland, and Britain and later from southern and eastern Europe—joined a US-born working class. Workers found employment in the emerging mass-production industries—steel, automobiles, and chemicals—that came to dominate the economy.[28] The working class began to experience a new level of material well-being. In the early twentieth century, although the poverty rate probably remained at around 30 percent, mass-production workers could hope to acquire property, drive a Model-T, and send their children to high school.

This new material advantage changed the *family strategies* of low-income families. During the nineteenth century, most working families had to rely on multiple wage earners to survive. Children were still seen as a source of income because the typical child would leave school by her early teens and enter the labor force. Defensive family strategies based on high fertility, little education, taking in boarders, and children's labor dominated the working class. Later in the century, parents could afford to focus

The Changing Nature of the Family Economy

During the early twentieth century, many working families experienced an important watershed that fundamentally altered their economic outlook and family strategy. Through much of the nineteenth century, male workers did not earn enough to support their families. In addition, their wages would often fall as they aged because of illness and the decline in their physical abilities. As a result, families had to supplement husbands' earnings with other sources. Married women rarely entered the labor force, but they were able to supplement their families' income by taking in boarders or contract work (for example, making artificial flowers at home). Children, too, were under pressure to contribute wages, which led to most working-class children leaving school and entering the labor force by the time they were 14 years old.

This work pattern led to a distinctive life-course pattern in which families struggled through their early years of marriage and child-rearing, and then enjoyed relatively "good times" when their children were old enough to go to work. By the time the parents were in their 50s, children's work often made up more than half of the family's income.

By the middle of the twentieth century, this pattern had been replaced by the "breadwinner" family, in which the husband's earnings composed the majority of family income throughout the life course. As opportunities opened up for women, their wages and those of children became important supplements, especially if the husband's wages were lower than average.

While this describes the most common patterns of working-class family life, many families had more diverse experiences. Married African American and Hispanic women, for example, were more likely to work outside the home than white women. In a family headed by a woman, its members were likely to face extreme deprivation, even if they found employment or qualified for public aid.

---

[28]Michael B. Katz and Mark J. Stern, *One Nation Divisible: What America Was and What It Is Becoming* (New York: Russell Sage Foundation Press, 2006), 7–62.

on their children's future. They began to have fewer children and allow them to stay in school longer. Older people—whatever their earlier economic standing—often ended up in poverty, but poverty had ceased to be a typical part of working-class existence.[29]

Yet, the new family strategy had its own vulnerability because it was based on a single, male wage earner—what has been called the "breadwinner" family strategy. The older family strategy, with its several earners, provided the family with a hedge against economic emergencies. If the head of a "breadwinner" family became unemployed, the family could almost immediately enter a crisis. Thus, improving the well-being of working class families increased the pressure for policy solutions to the problem of unemployment.

The middle and upper class were also experiencing changes in their composition. The professions—medicine, law, education, and eventually social work—became important sources of employment and encouraged growth of the college-educated population. Educated women, in particular, created pressure for new occupational opportunities for women. By the early twentieth century, education, nursing, and social work were major employers of women who often brought extraordinary talent and motivation to the field of social reform.

These major social changes, beginning with the depression of the 1890s, sparked a new era of social ferment and mobilization. The growth of big business, the clash of capital and labor, and the flood of new immigrants inspired a set of disparate and often contradictory social movements.

Progressivism—the usual label given to these early twentieth-century social reform efforts—is hard to pigeonhole, but there were some common themes that had particular importance for social welfare. First, Progressives believed that government could be a positive force for social improvement, a belief at odds with many nineteenth-century reformers. Second, Progressives abandoned the moralistic view of poverty in favor of a focus on the material well-being of families. Finally, the new generation of reformers believed that disinterested professionals (like themselves) could establish bureaucracies to represent the public good against the narrow interests of big business and corrupt politicians.

Human Behavior

Practice Behavior Example: Know about human behavior across the life course, the range of social systems in which people live, and the ways social systems promote or deter people in maintaining or achieving health and well-being.

Critical Thinking Question: Only during the twentieth century did policies affecting children take into consideration their developmental needs. For example, how might confining children in a poorhouse along with adult inmates influence their well-being and later development?

The Progressive movement encompassed a variety of causes—from fighting monopolies to conservation to political reform. Its major social welfare goals, however, were associated with protecting dependent women and children, addressing the risks of industrial workers, and improving the environment of the industrial city.

The change in family strategies put a new focus on children. No longer seen as potential workers, children moved from being useful to being "priceless." Much of the reform agitation of the era focused on improving the prospects of poor children, particularly those living in families headed by women. The Progressive education movement focused on "child-centered" education, while institutional reformers sought to remove children from poorhouses and improve the conditions in children's institutions. The establishment of the Children's Bureau in the Labor Department, staffed often by trained social workers, was representative of this approach.[30]

---

[29]Katz and Stern, *One Nation Divisible*, 126–170.

[30]Viviana Zelizer, *Pricing the Priceless Child: The Changing Social Value of Children* (Princeton: Princeton University Press, 1994); Linda Gordon, *Pitied But Not Entitled: Single Mothers and the History of Welfare* (New York: Free Press, 1994).

The most significant lasting innovations of child-saving in the early twentieth century were the state "mothers' pensions" laws. Enacted after active mobilization by women's groups—including the Congress of Mothers (the forerunner of today's Parent-Teacher Associations) and the General Federation of Women's Clubs—mothers' pensions reversed the nineteenth-century attack on outdoor relief, establishing a legal entitlement to public aid for dependent women and children. Eventually, these programs formed the basis for the federal Aid to Dependent Children program in the 1930s.[31]

The creation of the Children's Bureau gave maternalism a role in federal policymaking. At the same time, World War I focused public attention on the health and wellbeing of the nation's children.

Industrial workers faced many problems in the early part of the century. Old age, industrial accidents, and unemployment were a few of the risks to workers supporting themselves and their families. One solution to these problems was factory legislation that regulated working and safety conditions. In the wake of the Triangle Shirtwaist Fire of 1911, in which 146 workers lost their lives in a sweatshop fire (many of them jumping to their deaths from ninth-story windows), the State of New York formed an industrial commission. The introduction of its report embodied the Progressives' belief in government action for the public good:

> The State not only possesses the power and the right, but it is charged with the sacred duty of seeing that the worker is properly safeguarded in case of fire; that he is protected from accidents caused by neglect or indifference; that proper precautions are taken to prevent poisoning by the materials and processes of his industry; and that he works under conditions conducive to good health, and not such as breed disease.
>
> Indifference to these matters reflects grossly upon the present-day civilization, and it is regrettable that our State and national legislation on the subject of industrial hygiene compares so unfavorably with that of other countries.[32]

---

[31]Skocpol, *Protecting Soldiers and Mothers*, 321–524.

[32]David von Drehle, *Triangle: The Fire That Changed America* (New York: Atlantic Monthly Press, 2003), 212–218; New York State Factory Investigating Commission, *Preliminary Report to the Legislature of the State of New York*, 3 vols. (Albany: Argus Company, 1912), vol. 1: 18, http://www.ilr.cornell.edu/ trianglefire/primary/reports/LegislatureOfNYS.html?sto_sec=investigation.

Social insurance, state-sponsored programs based on contributions by employers and employees, were slower to gain acceptance. Although many states adopted workers' compensation laws during the early years of the twentieth century, efforts to enact unemployment and old-age laws would have to await federal action during the 1930s.[33]

Finally, social reformers took aim at the unregulated development of American cities, especially the health and environmental threats of working families' districts. Park and playground building was at the cutting edge of a broader effort to bring rational planning to cities through the adoption of housing and zoning codes. Tenements, large apartment blocks with inadequate ventilation or light, attracted the most attention and led to pioneering efforts to establish minimum standards of decency for rental housing.

While the Progressive movement was brimming with ideas and motivation, it faced a political problem. Middle- and upper-class reformers had great sympathy for working-class families but little or no connection to the major institutions of working-class life, including local politicians, labor leaders, and Catholic and Jewish religious institutions. Without these connections, the movement often lacked the political muscle to translate its ideas into legislation. Over time, however, a new generation of leaders—often the children of immigrants themselves—discovered ideas and relationships that could link workers and reformers politically. The New Deal of the 1930s provided a political moment when these ideas finally took center stage. The nationalization of mothers' pensions and maternal and child health programs, the enactment of unemployment and old age insurance, and comprehensive worker safety and housing legislation were all enacted during these years and continue to form the foundation for key elements of the social welfare system. (See Chapters 7, 8, 10, and 11.)

Read "Franklin Roosevelt's Radio Address Unveiling the Second Half of the New Deal (1936)" to better understand the substance and rhetoric of the New Deal.

One problem that Progressivism avoided was *racial discrimination*. At the beginning of the twentieth century, most African Americans continued to live in Southern states. White reformers rarely saw a reason to upset the caste system that replaced slavery after the Civil War. In fact, in the South, Progressives often took the lead in disenfranchising African Americans under the guise of bringing "honest" government to the region.[34]

During World War I, however, African Americans began a great migration that would ultimately transform black Americans from a Southern rural to a Northern urban population. Once in the North, blacks discovered that even without Jim Crow laws, schools, employment, and housing remained tightly segregated. The founding of a set of civil rights organizations, like the National Association for the Advancement of Colored People, set the stage for efforts to expand the Progressive agenda to include the rights of black Americans.

These efforts faced a major institutional barrier. The national Democratic Party, which had become the party of social reform by the 1930s, included "lily-white" Southern state parties that were uncompromising in their opposition to civil rights. If Democrats were to embrace civil rights, they would have to choose between black and Southern white votes.[35]

The struggle over civil rights within the Democratic Party began during the 1930s but was not resolved until the 1960s when the strength of the civil rights movement and its success in defining the black struggle as part of an international struggle for human

---

[33]Roy Lubove, *The Struggle for Social Security, 1900–1935* (Pittsburgh: University of Pittsburgh Press, 1968).

[34]C. Vann Woodward, *The Strange Career of Jim Crow* (New York: Oxford University Press, 1955).

[35]Ira Katznelson, *When Affirmative Action Was White: An Untold History of Racial Inequality in Twentieth-Century America* (New York: W.W. Norton, 2005).

rights pushed Democrats to embrace a comprehensive definition of civil rights in housing, education, and the justice system. The cost of this choice was to split the New Deal coalition and usher in the era of Conservative America.

Conservative America

Often, reform creates the condition for its own undoing. Certainly, many of the successes of the New Deal set the stage for the reassertion of conservatism after the 1960s. As we noted earlier, one function of social movements is to define or redefine the identities of their participants. During the 1930s and 1940s, millions of Italian, Polish, and Jewish workers stopped defining themselves as distinct based on their ethnicity and began to define themselves as united because of their economic status.[36]

The success of New Deal legislation during and after World War II, including the GI Bill of Rights passed in 1944, set the stage for new processes of identity and social movement formation. Federal housing legislation encouraged the expansion of segregated suburban development over integrated urban redevelopment. Working families came to think of themselves as homeowners, suburbanites, and—most importantly—taxpayers. At work, white union members who had supported labor reform questioned whether affirmative action efforts to integrate unions were in their interest.

Perhaps the biggest revolution in identity was the emergence of "whiteness" as an identity. Until the 1930s, many Americans equated race and ethnicity. Government and scholarly literature regularly referred to the Italian or Hebrew "race." The same efforts that led to overcoming these ethnic divisions led to the contrast between *whites* and *blacks*.[37]

The conflicts over the civil rights movement itself created a new vocabulary that spread to other movements. In the South, segregationists interpreted the efforts of federal courts to enforce civil rights as a form of "imposition" by the government. In later years, this image of an overreaching federal government would be used to oppose the Equal Rights Amendment (intended to ensure gender equality) and "forced busing" to enforce integration. During the 1950s, "states' rights" was the demand of segregationists who opposed federal civil rights efforts. By the 1980s, conservatives argued that the federal government was too big and too distant to respond to local conditions. Taxpayer revolts were fueled by the idea that government waste and abuse were responsible for high taxes.

Conservative ideology took on a split personality when it came to social welfare. Again tied to opposition to civil rights, conservatives identified *welfare* as a key element of the waste and abuse of government. Where *welfare* originally applied to all social welfare programs, beginning in the late 1950s, conservatives restricted the term to programs that were income tested (restricted to low-income families) and whose beneficiaries were disproportionately black or Hispanic. Critics demonized public housing and public assistance, in particular—including Aid to Families with Dependent Children. To do so, however, critics needed to ignore the bulk of public spending on social welfare. Old age insurance, Medicare, disability insurance and assistance (SSI), and nutritional assistance all remained popular.[38]

[36]Lisabeth Cohen, *Making a New Deal: Industrial Workers in Chicago, 1919–1939*, 2nd ed. (New York: Cambridge University Press, 2008).

[37]Roediger, *The Wages of Whiteness*.

[38]Michael B. Katz and Lorrin Thomas, "The Invention of 'Welfare' in America," *Journal of Policy History* 10 (November 1998): 399–418.

At the same time, conservatism tried, often unsuccessfully, to spread a set of ideas about the economy that were a hard sell. What came to be called neoliberalism argued that government intervention harmed the economy, and that the best economic policy intervened the least. Rather than attempt to reduce unemployment, neoliberals argued that there is a "natural" rate of unemployment; if policy tries to shift unemployment below this rate, it could damage the economy by sparking high rates of inflation. Rather than protecting Americans from risk, government should encourage Americans to protect themselves by assuming more risk.[39]

These ideas, on the face of it, were never that popular. Despite increasing skepticism about the effectiveness of government, Americans continued to look to public programs to help them deal with the predictable problems of life. For example, when conservatives advocated privatizing Social Security—Barry Goldwater in 1964, Ronald Reagan in 1981, and George W. Bush in 2005—they were soundly defeated.

However, the combination of unpopular ideas and popular politics did foster a new set of institutions in Conservative America. Between the expansion of public programs they opposed and leaving Americans to fend for themselves, conservatives increasingly turned to the tax system as a means of reducing taxes while providing for common concerns. The entire health care system was based on a set of tax expenditures that allowed employers to use spending on health insurance to offset federal taxes. A similar set of tax breaks fueled the expansion of pension programs. After the 1970s, individual tax breaks encouraged workers to invest in 401(K)s and IRAs as the way to support themselves during retirement.[40]

This institutional innovation led to some remarkable results. After 30 years of conservative political success, the US government was spending as much as more established European welfare states on health care and pensions, but a large share of the funding was associated with these tax breaks. At the same time, the lion's share of these benefits went to the richest Americans, leaving low-income families worse off in spite of the expansion of government spending.

The Achilles' heel of conservatism became apparent during the financial crisis of 2008. Beliefs that "government was the problem, not the solution" and that "the era of big government has ended" encouraged a generation of economic deregulation. Combined with the new institutions of globalization, deregulation of the financial industries fed an increase in risk taking—typically with other people's money—that eventually threatened the entire world financial structure. After decades of calling for shrinking government, major financial players called on the federal government to come to their rescue. The price for abandoning sound financial regulation was trillions spent on bailouts and an economy so injured that unemployment continued to rise for two years after the onset of the crisis.

Spanning the crisis, conservatives suffered a series of political defeats that brought centrist and liberal Democrats back into control of the federal government. The Obama administration began with an ambitious agenda in which the comprehensive health care reform was the most important element. Yet, the passage of the reform bill in 2010 contributed to a Republican gain in that year's midterm elections.

It is still an open question whether events between 2006 and 2012 represented the transition to a new era of social welfare history or a continuation of Conservative America. In other words, we don't yet know if this represents a critical juncture or not. Much will depend on what choices and decisions political leaders make over the next several years and the reaction of the American political system to those changes.

[39]David Harvey, *A Brief History of Neoliberalism* (New York: Oxford University Press, 2005).
[40]Hacker, *Divided Welfare State*.

PATHS TAKEN AND NOT TAKEN

As we noted at the beginning of this chapter, the history of social welfare has opened particular paths for the development of social programs and closed others. As a way of summarizing the points in this chapter, this section examines how each era contributed to the current structure of social welfare and its possible future impact.

Assess your comprehension of "Paths Taken and Not Taken" by completing this quiz.

Colonial social welfare laid a foundation of enduring ideas and institutions for our current social welfare system. The most important of these has been a belief in *local* solutions to the problems of poverty and the establishment of a set of local institutions to carry out those programs. Although states and then the federal government became important players in social welfare, localities continued to play an important role. Even today, when the vast majority of social welfare spending comes from the federal government, a complex system of block grants and grants-in-aid channel the money through state and local government. Sometimes the federal government has defined special jurisdictions for funding—for example, the Area Agencies on Aging (AAA) established by the Older Americans Act—but more often it has used counties or townships as a means of sending national dollars to localities.

The age of the poorhouse laid out a set of ways of thinking and acting that continue to inform social welfare. Many major social institutions—those large forbidding structures that dot the landscape even today—had their origins during this era. At different times during our subsequent history, we've tried to reduce our dependency on institutional solutions—for example, by closing state mental hospitals during the 1970s and 1980s—but these efforts have often been frustrated by a combination of public indifference and fear. The explosion in America's prison population, which we discuss in Chapter 9, shows that the appeal of institutions as a way to get bothersome populations off the streets and out of sight continues to animate social policy.

The other major legacy of the poorhouse era is the stigmatization of the poor and a set of robust stereotypes used to explain their condition. The poorhouse era was the first time that the poor were seen as an actual *threat* to the social order. However, as we explore in Chapter 4, the tendency to see low-income people as deviants has continued to influence social welfare policy to the present day.

The death of Progressivism has been exaggerated. While the conservative resurgence certainly placed many Progressive ideas and programs on the defensive, conservatives have been more successful in *limiting the growth* of Progressive institutions than in killing them. The large public role in social welfare, while it can be traced back to the Colonial era, was firmly established during the Progressive era. The other pillars of Progressivism—a material view of poverty and need and a belief in the importance of bureaucracies and experts—continue to influence social policy, even as they have competed with other ideas. Certainly, many of the institutions that determine social welfare policy—the expanded structure of the federal government, the role of professions, patterns of federal-state cooperation, and the role of the courts in defining rights—are still firmly in place, even if they are not always used for Progressive purposes.

The long-term impact of conservative resurgence on social welfare is the hardest to assess, partly because much of contemporary conservatism is a return to older traditions. For example, the popularity of local solutions is really a return to eighteenth- and nineteenth-century ideas, not a wholly new idea. Similarly, the sweeping use of market models in social welfare to assess the effectiveness of programs would have been familiar to nineteenth-century reformers who argued that poorhouses would pay for themselves. Likewise, the antitax sentiment and stigmatization of dependency that has motivated much conservative thought echo earlier traditions in social welfare.

Ironically, one of the legacies of Conservative America may be a new willingness to consider radical restructuring of social programs. For much of the last three decades, it has been conservatives who have proposed abandoning historical commitments—for example, an entitlement to aid for mothers and children or a guaranteed payment from Social Security—and considering entirely new arrangements. Thrown on the defensive, liberals have often functioned as the true conservatives, defending established programs and questioning the wisdom of radical breaks from the past.

It may be a time for Progressives to learn from this legacy, to propose more fundamental changes in how America addresses its problems of need and its redefinition of social rights. The Obama campaign of 2008 raised many supporters' hopes that they would experience change they could believe in. Whether hope will translate into action is still an open question.

CONCLUSION: A NEW GENERATION OF "YOUNG TURKS"

The contemporary debates over social welfare pose a major challenge not only to social workers and our clients but to all Americans. History influences our institutions, our ways of viewing the world, and our identity. In many ways, this leads to an inherent conservatism in social welfare. Institutions, once established, generate patterns of action that tend to reproduce themselves. The groups associated with those institutions defend their interests, often by disseminating ideas that justify and legitimate their role. Finally, while social movements can act as agents of social change, their institutional weakness is often no match for the status quo.

One additional lesson we can draw from history is that the tendency toward conservatism—toward protecting what exists and resisting change—becomes a bigger problem as a nation evolves. The Ottoman Empire that ruled Turkey, much of the Mideast, and a good part of Europe from the fourteenth through the twentieth centuries is a good example. During the late nineteenth century, the problems of the empire were overwhelming. Restive minorities attempted to break the power of the central authority. The cost of the established order—layers and layers of bureaucracies, courts, and religious leaders—had bankrupted the central government. A society based on military prowess, albeit five centuries earlier, had trouble accommodating industrial capitalism and the new strength of competitors.

In the face of social disintegration, a new movement, the Young Ottomans, organized to break with the past and bring modernity to the empire. Its leader eventually succeeded in wresting power from older elites and in setting up a new path for the empire, what we might call a critical juncture. Yet, the Young Turks ultimately failed. The layers of ossification that had developed over centuries were too great to overcome, and the choices the Young Turks did make—especially their alliance with the German Empire—proved disastrous during World War I. Although they failed in remaking the empire, one of their number, Ataturk, was able to remake Turkish society after its dissolution.

We began this chapter with a warning: don't ignore history. We end it with another: don't become captive to it. If social change is to occur, we need to neither ignore what has gone before nor take on a cynicism that things will never change. This is the real lesson that history has to teach us.

Test your understanding and analysis of this chapter by completing the Chapter Review.

4

Poverty and Inequality

PAUL FUSCO / MAGNUM PHOTOS

INTRODUCTION: THE TWO USES OF POVERTY

Poverty is the elemental problem of social welfare. Once government takes on the task of ensuring its citizens' welfare, providing for their basic needs—food, shelter, and clothing—is the starting point for any broader notion of well-being.

In its simplest form, we should think of poverty as an *indicator* of public policy success in meeting these basic needs. Most welfare states have adopted a poverty measure as a means of judging their success in addressing the basic consumption requirements of their populations and whether their success (or failure) in doing so changes over time.

With the coming of recession to the United States in 2007, a variety of indicators were used to judge the overall performance of the economy: stock market indexes (like the Dow Jones' Industrial Average or the Standard and Poor's index), change in gross domestic product (GDP), and the unemployment rate. These indicators tell us if the economy is growing, if the profits of corporations are strong, and how many people are unable to find work, but they don't tell us about the ability of people to meet their basic needs.

This is the role of the poverty rate. When the government announced that poverty increased from 12.5 to 15.1 percent between 2007 and 2010, it was the starkest demonstration that the economy was not working effectively and that government policy was failing to ameliorate the problems of the economic system. If we look at the poverty rate over time, we should be able to judge how well the political economy is functioning.

If life were only that simple! First, developing a poverty index is complicated. The definition of poverty must enjoy widespread acceptance, and government needs a method for systematically

CHAPTER OUTLINE

collecting and analyzing data connected to that definition. We'll talk about these challenges later in this chapter.

But there is a more fundamental problem. Ideally, poverty should function as simply an indicator, but the word *poverty* carries a lot of baggage. Not only does it refer to lack of material resources, but common usages include ideas of deficiencies and inferiority. The reality is that while poverty *is* simply a neutral indicator of economic well-being, in common speech it carries heavy connotations expressing the inherent qualities of the people who are in that condition. People are poor—it seems—not just because they lack income, but rather because they possess certain *deficiencies* that make them *inferior*.

These deficiencies have come in a variety of forms. During the early years of the nineteenth century, commentators focused on the *moral inferiority* of poor people. The image of the pauper was that of a morally degraded person who turned to mendacity and trickery to receive charity. At the turn of the century, this moral lens gave way to a genetic interpretation of the poor's inferiority. In 1912 Henry Goddard, the director of the Vineland (NJ) Training School, published the history of the *Kallikak* family. According to Goddard, there were two branches of the family, one a product of Martin Kallikak's illicit liaison with a feeble-minded "tavern girl" and the other the result of his marriage to a well-off Quaker woman of good standing. The first branch, Goddard claimed, produced a generation of "'mental defectives' who were plagued by illegitimacy, prostitution, alcoholism, epilepsy, and lechery" while the other branch "yielded generations of society's finest citizens."[1] Goddard's work was just one example of a "feeble-minded" mania that swept through American intellectual circles during the early twentieth century; it eventually led to more than half of the states passing compulsory sterilization laws.

Later in the twentieth century, these individual approaches to the "inferiority" of the poor gave way to cultural interpretations. Originally proposed by progressive academics during the 1930s as a means of making sense of the persistence of poverty and dependency, the cultural interpretation of poverty eventually migrated to the conservative side of the political spectrum.[2]

The key point here is that whatever its specific form—moral, genetic, or cultural—the association of poverty with inherent deficiency has made it difficult to treat poverty simply as an indicator of economic need. The vast majority of people who enter poverty leave after a few months. While this should not cause us to ignore the problem of long-term or persistent poverty, it does point to how we tend to confuse poverty as a transitory material state for many families and the persistent idea that the poor are somehow different.

The symbolic meaning of poverty has implications for the politics of social welfare as well. Through much of our history, Americans have viewed society through imagery that divides the social order into three classes. The "middle class," which accounted for the vast majority of the population, was the carrier of core American values like self-reliance and respectability. However, two parasitic groups beset this class—an upper

[1] J. A. Plucker, ed., "Human Intelligence: Historical Influences, Current Controversies, Teaching Resources," http://www.intelltheory.com.

[2] Alice O'Connor, *Poverty Knowledge: Social Science, Social Policy, and the Poor in Twentieth-Century U.S. History* (Princeton: Princeton University Press, 2001), 74–99.

class that lived off the hard work of the middle and a lower class populated by the lazy, criminal, and feeble-minded.[3]

This three-class imagery has often been in a struggle with a two-class model that contrasts the well-off to the "working people." For example, during the Progressive era, reformers often contrasted the special "interests" against the "people" as a way of galvanizing support.

This conflict between two- and three-class models has had great implications for the success of social welfare reform. When the three-class model is dominant, the interests of middle-income people are contrasted to those of the poor. During the debate over changes in public assistance during the 1990s, welfare recipients were characterized as predatory "wolves" that gained from taxes paid by hard-working Americans.[4]

In contrast, the two-class model encourages us to see the interests of middle- and low-income Americans as aligned. In a 2009 article in the *New England Journal of Medicine*, for example, researchers emphasized the common interests of working and middle-class Americans in heath care reform. "Growth in health care spending is disproportionately felt by middle-income working families."[5]

One way to shift the debate on economic need in a progressive direction, therefore, is to refocus the discussion of economic need from poverty to economic inequality. Where extreme economic need focuses policy on the bad decisions made by individuals and families, the issue of economic inequality focuses on the functioning of the economic system as a whole. It provides an opportunity to show the similarities in the condition of poor people and the "uncomfortable" class that lives between poverty and affluence.

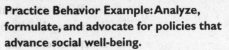

Policy Practice

Practice Behavior Example: Analyze, formulate, and advocate for policies that advance social well-being.

Critical Thinking Question: Coalition building is an essential element of successful policy advocacy. How can a focus on broader trends in economic inequality help build support for programs that benefit our clients?

TYPES OF INEQUALITY AND DEMOCRATIC VALUES

The discussion of inequality goes back to our discussion of the economy. Markets are useful. They promote choice and allow for the production, distribution, and consumption of goods that produce the greatest utility for the entire population while reducing the need for large government bureaucracies to do so.

Markets are often too much of a good thing. The same emphasis on innovation and efficiency that we love can undermine the stability of people's lives in a way that is ultimately destructive to society. The process of "creative destruction" tends to slant the odds that past winners will continue to win and past losers will ultimately lose.[6] This purely economic tendency is reinforced by politics. The well-off and well-connected are more likely to influence laws that govern economic relationships in a way that benefits them. The tax system and the regulation of the financial industries provide two examples of how this process works.[7]

---

[3]Stanislaw Ossowski, *Class Structure in the Social Consciousness* (London: Routledge and Kegan Paul, 1963).

[4]O'Connor, *Poverty Knowledge*, 284–296.

[5]Daniel Polsky and David Grande, "The Burden of Health Care Costs for Working Families: Implications for Reform," *The New England Journal of Medicine* (July 30, 2009): 438.

[6]Joseph Schumpeter, *Can Capitalism Survive?* (New York: Harper and Row, 1950), 38–47.

[7]Charles Lindblom, *Politics and Markets: The World's Political Economic System* (New York: Basic Books, 1977).

THEORIES OF DISTRIBUTIVE JUSTICE

Assess your comprehension of "Theories of Distributive Justice" by completing this quiz.

Just as the market can undermine social relationships, this drive toward inequality can undermine democratic values in the political system. Take a moment to consider three distinct visions of economic justice: utility, equality of condition, and opportunity.[8]

Utility

Utility theories of justice focus on maximizing economic growth with little consideration for how economic benefits are distributed. The theory behind this approach is that everyone benefits when the pie gets larger faster, even if not everyone gets an equal share of the new benefits. This approach is often identified with "trickle down" economics because it asserts that aiding the well-off will be more productive and ultimately benefit poor people.

While this central tenet is highly debatable, there are situations where trickle down may be the best approach. Housing is an example. Building affordable housing is expensive, so the number of units that can be built is limited. Despite some success in innovative approaches to affordable housing, the gap between the housing needs of low-income families and the supply has not closed much. However, if well-off people decide they want new, bigger houses—like the McMansions that proliferated during the 1990s and 2000s—they provide the opportunity for "sifting" within the housing stock. That is, less affluent families move into houses given up by the very rich, and low-income people move into housing that has been turned over by the middle-class.

Let's not get carried away. Even in this example, the gap between the rich and poor increases, and a general rise in housing prices—like that of the early 2000s—may keep poor families from taking advantage of residential opportunities as they open up.

Equality of Condition

The most comprehensive approach to equality is to demand that everyone in society has exactly the same living standard—the same amount of housing, food, and disposable income. Because this "ideal" is often hard to accomplish and may have negative consequences for the creation of wealth, the most common equality of condition position is less rigid. The philosopher John Rawls, for example, argues that the only defendable amount of inequality is the amount that creates enough wealth to leave the least well-off in a better position than they would have been if there were less inequality. In short, it's all right for the rich to become richer, if it means that the poor are better off.

While this approach has been popular among many political philosophers, it has never been hugely popular among Americans, who prefer a fair amount of "rugged individualism" in their society.

Opportunity

Equal opportunity is the grand consensus of equality thought, but here again the key is in the fine print. Life should be a fair race. We should all start from the same line so that whoever "wins" (or loses) won't question the fairness of their position.

---

[8]The following discussion draws on Julian Lamont and Christi Favor, "Distributive Justice," in *The Stanford Encyclopedia of Philosophy,* Fall 2008 edition, ed. Edward N. Zalta, http://plato.stanford.edu/archives/fall2008/entries/justice-distributive/.

Yet, what does it mean to start the race from the same line? We know that all sorts of things influence a person's capacity, starting before birth and continuing throughout life. Biological, psychological, and cultural factors influence how prepared people are for the "race." So, while everyone accepts the desirability of equal opportunity, it tends to be an unreliable guide for influencing policy decisions.

Take the example of early childhood development (see Chapter 11). An individual's emotional and cognitive development is heavily influenced by a host of factors early in his life. If he has poor nutrition, lacks a stimulating environment, or is at risk of violence, he will not make it to the start line with an equal chance to win the race.

This type of argument is often persuasive and probably accounts for the considerable support for early childhood development in the past several decades. It is difficult to help children without helping their parents, however, and interest in early childhood development has expanded at the same time as policy that stigmatizes poor adults. As a result, the focus of early childhood efforts has been on education rather than ensuring that children's home environments provide adequate food, shelter, and safety.

The flip side of the equal opportunity argument is the affirmative action debate and the issue of "color blindness." For most of American history, the opportunity "race" was not equal for African Americans. During the civil rights movement, government leaders decided that black Americans were so disadvantaged by that history that all sectors of society—government, education, business, and the labor market—needed to take "affirmative action" to compensate for historical discrimination.

Yet, since the 1970s, many people have objected to affirmative action as a form of "reverse discrimination" that violates "equal opportunity."[9] Beginning with the Bakke decision in 1978 and continuing through its 2003 expectation that affirmative action would have run its course by 2028, the Supreme Court has been increasingly concerned about affirmative action's harm to white Americans. Conservative opponents of affirmative action took Martin Luther King's hope that people be judged "by the content of their character not the color of their skin" as support for their position.[10]

The point is that while equal opportunity is the consensus position on economic equality, it does not provide a reliable basis for social welfare policy, because widely divergent approaches are all premised on equal opportunity.

One way of articulating with more precision the concept of opportunity has been suggested by the *capability approach* to social welfare. As Amartya Sen has noted, the issue of poverty should be framed as one of freedom or more precisely *lack of freedom*. What defines well-being is one's ability to make decision about how one is and what one does: *beings* and *doings*.[11] Martha Nussbaum has taken up Sen's approach and attempted to specify the nature of those capabilities. She outlines a set of capabilities by which to judge the well-being of a society:

Human Rights and Justice

Practice Behavior Example: Understand that each person, regardless of position in society, has basic human rights, such as freedom, safety, privacy, an adequate standard of living, health care, and education.

Critical Thinking Question: Concern about clients' material standard of living often obscures other forms of deprivation. How might Martha Nussbaum's idea of capabilities inform a social worker's engagement with a client?

[9]See, for example, Nathan Glazer, *Affirmative Discrimination: Ethnic Inequality and Public Policy* (New York: Basic Books, 1975).

[10]"Affirmative Action," *New York Times*, http://topics.nytimes.com/topics/reference/timestopics/subjects/a/affirmative_action/index.html.

[11]Amartya Kumar Sen, *On Economic Inequality* (Oxford: Clarendon Press, 1997).

1. Life
2. Bodily Health
3. Bodily Integrity
4. Senses, Imagination, and Thought
5. Emotions
6. Practical Reason
7. Affiliation
8. Other Species
9. Play
10. Control Over One's Environment[12]

As Nussbaum's list makes clear, the capability approach incorporates traditional notions of economic well-being as well as the ability of individuals and particularly vulnerable populations to thrive in a society.

INEQUALITY'S CHALLENGE TO SOCIAL WORK VALUES AND ETHICS

Assess your comprehension of "Inequality's Challenge to Social Work Values and Ethics" by completing this quiz.

The core ethical dilemma faced by social workers is the gap between their responsibility for addressing social injustice and ameliorating human suffering and the resources they have available to do so. Poverty and inequality are at the center of this dilemma. On the one hand, poverty and inequality are critical to creating the "supply" of needs in society. Among the conditions that have been correlated with poverty are higher rates of crime, mental illness, obesity, and social alienation.

One of the implications of the capability approach is that the study of inequality should not be confined to the narrow measure of income and wealth. For a start, we need to expand the economic indexes that enter into well-being. For example, in a 2009 report, Stiglitz and Sen have suggested that "gross domestic product" (GDP) is an inadequate measure of social progress. Moving beyond economic indexes, they suggest that the issue of sustainability must also inform our measure of social development.

Social workers must become part of this debate. While economists have developed sophisticated means of measuring income and poverty, their focus is too narrow. Most importantly, to the extent that their measures become the standards we use to measure how well our society is doing, they skew our perspective to a one-dimensional view of human well-being.

If Sen is right that inequality is about human freedom, then the issue of poverty is the central ethical issue of our civilization. If we are a society that truly prizes freedom as a value, we can hardly allow the ultimate "unfreedom"—poverty—to remain so common a condition. Social workers can work with others to make the case for a broader idea of human well-being and freedom.

Engage, Assess, Intervene, Evaluate

Practice Behavior Example: Develop, analyze, advocate, and provide leadership for policies and services.

Critical Thinking Question: What strategies can social workers use to provide leadership in advocating for policies that benefit our clients?

---

[12]Martha C. Nussbaum, "Capabilities as Fundamental Entitlements: Sen and Social Justice," *Feminist Economics* 9: vols. 2–3 (2003): 33–59.

On a more practical level, the capability approach provides a way for social workers to reengage the policy debates over poverty. Since the 1960s, economists have taken "ownership" of poverty as a social issue. When government or the media want to find an "expert" on poverty, they turn to economists. Yet, as social workers and other professionals know, well-being is multifaceted and cannot be restricted to a certain basket of consumer items. Furthermore, these other aspects of well-being— like emotions, affiliation, and play—are dimensions where social workers have considerable expertise. The capability approach provides a means for social workers to use *their* expertise in the debate over economic inequality and its alleviation.

TRENDS IN POVERTY AND INCOME INEQUALITY

The issue of poverty raises many philosophical and conceptual issues, but at some point, we need to translate those ideas into data we can measure. In this section, we address choices in how we define and measure inequality and poverty. We also examine data on inequality from an international perspective, and we will examine poverty trends in the United States.

Defining Economic Inequality

What do we mean by economic inequality? In essence, the term refers to the distribution of economic resources across an entire society. This sounds like a simple concept, but in reality, measuring the level of inequality is complicated. Let's look at just three of the challenges.

First, we have to define our *unit of measurement*. The idea of economic inequality means that we are comparing the resources of different entities. Typically, we could think of income as measured at one of three levels—individuals, families, or households—each of which has its own challenges.

Individuals

The definition here is simple. If we are interested in individual inequality, we would compare the income of every single person in society. But this could get a bit confusing. If we simply measure the income that each person earns, there would be many people with no income— children, for example. Usually, this is not what we mean by individual income. Instead we take the income of a total family or household (see below) and divide it by the number of people in the family or household. For example, if a family's total income is $65,000 and the family has five members, then each member's *per capita income* would be $13,000.

You might ask, If we're going to use the total family income anyway, why bother to do the calculation of individual per capita income? It's simply because an important recent trend in American domestic life is the explosion in people living alone. Suppose you have two households, one with one person (say a recent college graduate living by himself) and one with five members. The new college grad is earning $35,000, and the family has a total income of $50,000. If we ignore the size of family, we're liable to see the large family as better off than the college grad, but if we calculate per capita income, we find that the college grad's economic standing ($35,000 per capita) is much higher than the large family ($10,000 per capita).

Because household size has dropped so much during the past four decades, per capita income gives a much different picture of trends in income than family or household income, a fact often missed.

Households and families

The question of exactly what constitutes a *family* has become a hot political issue in the past generation. The debate over same-sex marriage has made it a particularly touchy subject (Chapter 9). The box entitled "Official Census Bureau Definitions of Family and Household" explains how the Census Bureau defines these terms.

In essence, a household is defined by a place of residence. Everyone living in the same housing unit—whether that is a house, an apartment, or a room—lives in the same household. In contrast, families are defined by the relationship between people, but only certain types of relationships qualify as family relationships: those based on birth (a child), marriage (a spouse), or adoption. Because the Census Bureau definition of a family has to have two or more people, single-person households are not families, nor are groups of people who are either unrelated (say, roommates) nor those related in a way not recognized by this definition (e.g., an unmarried gay or straight couple). Given the increase in these "nonfamily" households, about 19 percent of the US population in 2008 are not included in the calculation of median family income.

Measuring resources

The second issue in measuring economic inequality is the question of what resources to consider. The most common measure is *cash income*, that is, the amount of money received by an individual (or a family or household) during the previous year. But even this straightforward concept can get complicated. For example, *disposable income* refers to the economic resources that a family has available for meeting its consumption needs. This differs from cash income in two ways. First, it includes noncash government bene-fits that individuals or families receive—for example, the value of SNAP (what used to be called Food Stamps). Second, it deducts the amount of taxes paid by the family because this income is not available to spend.

A second approach to resources focuses on an individual or family's total assets, what we commonly call *wealth*. Wealth is notoriously difficult to measure, primarily because so much of it isn't cash (e.g., securities and real estate) and because noncash assets change in

Official Census Bureau Definitions of Family and Household

A household consists of all the people who occupy a housing unit. A house, an apartment or other group of rooms, or a single room is regarded as a hous-ing unit when it is occupied or intended for occupancy as separate living quarters; that is, when the occupants do not live and eat with any other persons in the structure and there is direct access from the outside or through a common hall.

A household includes the related family members and all the unrelated people, if any, such as lodgers, foster children, wards, or employees who share the housing unit. A person living alone in a housing unit, or a group of unrelated people sharing a housing unit such as part-ners or roomers, also count as a household. The count of households excludes group quarters. There are two major categories of households: "family" and "nonfamily."

A family is a group of two people or more (one of whom is the householder) related by birth, marriage, or adoption and residing together; all such people (including related subfamily members) are considered as members of one family. Beginning with the 1980 Current Population Survey, unrelated subfamilies (referred to in the past as secondary families) are no longer included in the count of families, nor are the members of unrelated subfamilies included in the count of family members. The number of families is equal to the number of family households; however, the count of family members differs from the count of family household members because family household members include any nonrelatives living in the household.

http://quickfacts.census.gov/qfd/meta/long_58579.htm.

value frequently. During the stock market crash of 2008 and 2009, for example, the total value of stock owned by Americans dropped by more than 40 percent. For other assets, it's difficult to assign a dollar value. Real estate, the most common asset among American families, may have a current market value; however, because most people keep their houses for a long time, its immediate value is likely of less concern than its longer-term value—or at least its value when sold. Because so much of Americans' wealth is tied up in their homes, many researchers have excluded the value of homes (or more precisely home equity—the difference between the value of a house and how much the family owes on its mortgage) and focus on net financial assets.[13]

View "Income Inequality: Evidence and Policy Implications" for more in-depth information on current tends in inequality.

A third complicating issue is the noneconomic dimensions of inequality. In a recent report, Stiglitz and Sen argued that current measures of social progress—based primarily on standard economic indexes—understate the level of inequality within society. Take the case of personal insecurity.[14] Clearly, the risk of crime and accidents can have a profound effect on people's standard of living. If certain groups are particularly likely to be victimized by personal violence (e.g., women or ethnic minorities) this dimension may reinforce economic differences.

The World Health Organization has identified marital violence as a major health concern (WHO, 2000, 2002). Although still largely underreported, estimates indicate that worldwide between 10 percent and 50 percent of women ever married report having experienced physical violence from spouses (Population Reports, 1999), with this phenomenon cutting across countries and economic groups. Psychological abuse is even more common. Marital violence is found to cause serious physical and mental injury to women (Dannenberg et al., 1995; Harper and Parsons, 1997; Maman et al., 2000)....Physical or mental injury can adversely affect her job market prospects, productivity, regularity of work life, and chances of upward mobility (Brown et al., 1999; Lloyd et al., 1999). Marital violence can also erode a woman's social opportunities by undermining her relationships and social capital. Neighbors and friends tend to shun families where violence is common, and a woman's self-confidence can get so eroded that she withdraws from social contact. The "battered woman syndrome" implies that a woman's sense of self is so damaged that she begins to believe she deserves the abuse. It also makes her fearful to seek help when she needs it. Marital violence can similarly undermine a woman's political freedom—her ability to be an active citizen or seek her entitlements.[15]

Personal insecurity is only one of many noneconomic issues that contribute to overall inequality. Economic insecurity—as distinct from economic deprivation—can have a profound impact on individual and family quality of life. At any point in time a relatively small proportion of the workforce may actually be unemployed. Yet, elevated unemployment, like the 10 percent rate in the United States during 2009, means that a much larger number of workers fear that they may lose their jobs. This forces them into a range of decisions—such as seeking less expensive educational opportunities for children—that

[13]Edward N. Wolff, *Top Heavy: The Increasing Inequality of Wealth in America and What Can Be Done About It* (New York: New Press, 2002).
[14]Joseph E. Stiglitz, Amartya Sen, and Jean-Paul Fitoussi, "Report by the Commission on the Measurement of Economic Performance and Social Progress," September 2009, http://www.stiglitz-sen-fitoussi.fr/documents/rapport_anglais.pdf.
[15]Sen, Stiglitz, and Fitoussi, "Measurement of Economic Performance and Social Progress," 194.

may carry long-term consequences. In addition, there is a strong association between economic insecurity and negative health and mental health outcomes.

Job insecurity can also be measured through self-reports of individual workers. Fears of job loss can have negative consequences for the quality of life of each worker (e.g., physical and mental illness, tension in family life), for firms (e.g., adverse impacts on workers' motivation and productivity, lower identification with corporate objectives) and for society as a whole (De Witte and Näswall, 2003). Various surveys provide information about *perceived* job insecurity, by asking workers either to evaluate their satisfaction with the security of their present job or to rate their expectation of job loss with either probabilistic questions ("What do you think is the percent chance that you will lose your job during the next 12 months?") or qualitative questions ("Thinking about the next 12 months, how likely do you think it is that you will lose your job or be laid-off?"). Data on satisfaction with job security among European countries in the early 2000s show large cross-national differences, with greater fear of job losses in southern European countries compared to northern ones.[16]

Our ability to measure these noneconomic factors is still quite rudimentary. Yet, it is clear that the purely economic approach to measuring inequality is limited. More importantly, for social workers and other members of the helping professions, the amplification of economic inequality in noneconomic factors like personal security or social connectedness are central to the problems they address in their professional practice.

Measuring Inequality

The final issue is how should we measure economic inequality. The most common single measure used is the Gini coefficient. The Gini coefficient measures how far the actual distribution of resources in a society differs from a perfectly equal distribution. If income were distributed equally (Line A), 10 percent of the population holds 10 percent of its income, 20 percent holds 20 percent, etc. Line B represents the distribution of personal income among Americans in 2009; the top 10 percent of the population holds about 35 percent of the income, while the bottom 50 percent holds only 16 percent (Figure 4.1).[17]

The Gini coefficient, in a perfectly equal society, is equal to zero, and it can range as high as one (in the unlikely case where one individual or family had *all* of a nation's income). The Gini coefficient can be interpreted as the proportion of all of a nation's income that would have to be redistributed to create a totally equal society.

International patterns

The world is characterized by significant differences in the level of inequality. Among these 30 member countries of the Organisation for Economic Co-operation and Development, the United States has the fourth highest Gini coefficient. The American Gini coefficient of .37 means that 37 percent of all income would have to be shifted from richer to poorer families to produce a totally equal society. More tellingly, the number of countries with a very high standard of living but a very low Gini coefficient—Denmark, Sweden, and Austria, to take just three examples—shows that a country needn't promote inequality to prosper.[18]

---

[16]Sen, Stiglitz, and Fitoussi, "Measurement of Economic Performance and Social Progress," 198.

[17]Author's calculation from 2010 American Community Survey.

[18]Organisation for Economic Co-operation and Development, *Growing Unequal: Income Distribution and Poverty in OECD Countries* (Paris: OECD, 2008), http://www.oecd.org/social/socialpoliciesanddata/growingunequalincomedistributionandpovertyinoecdcountries.htm.

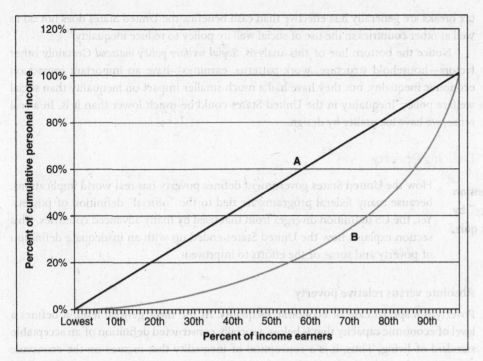

Figure 4.1
Example of the Lorenz Curve
The Lorenz Curve and Gini coefficient measure income inequality. Line A represents the perfectly equal distribution of income. The larger the curve in Line B, the greater the level of income inequality.

Over the past 20 years, generally speaking, economic inequality has increased within these societies. Some nations with historically low inequality—like Denmark and Sweden—have experienced upticks in inequality. The United States stands out in that it both has a history of high inequality and has experienced an above-average increase in income inequality during the past two decades.

Perhaps the most telling international data, however, compare very poor (bottom 10 percent) and very rich (top 10 percent) Americans with their counterparts in other countries. On average, Americans are quite well off. The average American's disposable income ranks fourth out of the 30 OECD countries. Rich Americans, as we might expect, are richer than the rich in any other country; their annual disposable income in the mid-2000s was $90,000. Poor Americans, however, are much worse off than the poor of most advanced economies. Their average income puts them behind all of the countries of northern and western Europe and only slightly ahead of southern and eastern European countries like the Czech Republic, Italy, and Spain.

There are a variety of reasons why economic inequality has increased over the past several decades. The household changes noted, especially the rise of more one- and two-person households, tend to increase economic inequality. In addition, earnings have been distributed less equally, which has pushed up inequality internationally.

Government social welfare policy has counterbalanced these changes to some extent. Here, the United States has a distinctive profile. On the one hand, thanks to special tax breaks for low-wage families and families with children, the United States has used the tax system more effectively to reduce inequality than most countries. On the other hand, American families get less help to reduce inequality through cash benefits. Overall, because tax breaks are generally less effective than cash benefits, the United States does not do as well as other countries in the use of social welfare policy to reduce inequality.[19]

Notice the bottom line of this analysis. *Social welfare policy matters!* Certainly other factors—household structure, work patterns, earnings—have an important impact on economic inequality, but they have had a much smaller impact on inequality than social welfare policy. Inequality in the United States could be much lower than it is. In a real sense, we have inequality by design.

Defining Poverty

Assess your comprehension of "Defining Poverty" by completing this quiz.

How the United States government defines poverty has real-world implications, because many federal programs are tied to the "official" definition of poverty. Yet, the US definition diverges from that used by many advanced countries. This section explains how the United States ended up with an inadequate definition of poverty and some of the efforts to improve it.

Absolute versus relative poverty

Poverty is a special case of economic inequality. At the most general level, it defines a level of economic capacity that is below a socially constructed definition of an acceptable standard of living. Thus, it is a conception of inequality that focuses on the economic situation at the bottom of the income ladder. Two concepts of poverty have dominated social welfare thinking: relative poverty and absolute poverty.

Relative poverty defines an acceptable standard of living as a percentage of the income of average households. As an example, the "Fuchs line" (named after economist Victor Fuchs) defines poverty as one-half of the income of the average American. In 2008, the median family income was $50,303, so the Fuchs line would be one-half of that or $25,152. The European Union has begun to use a relative measure—60 percent of average income (controlled for family size)—as its poverty measure.[20]

Absolute poverty defines an acceptable standard of living by calculating the cost of a minimum acceptable standard of living and estimating what proportion of the population has an income below that level.

The two approaches to poverty have very different intellectual foundations. Relative poverty is closely connected to concerns about inequality. By starting with the income of the average family, it proposes a conception of poverty that focuses on how low-income families are faring *relative* to average families. In contrast, the absolute concept of poverty is concerned only with a minimally acceptable standard of living. If the average family income increases, it doesn't directly influence the measurement of absolute poverty.

As we have seen in the previous section, America's level of inequality is much higher than that of other countries with comparable standards of living. In contrast to other affluent nations, the United States has done relatively little, in terms of social welfare policy, to compensate for inequalities in the market.

Many European nations have incorporated a relative definition of poverty into their social policy processes. Using a poverty line based on 60 percent of median income,

[19]OECD, *Growing Unequal*, 97–115.

[20]John Cassidy, "Relatively Deprived: How Poor Is Poor?" *The New Yorker* (April 3, 2006); OECD, *Growing Unequal*.

the EU estimates that about 16 percent of EU member states' population was at risk of poverty in 2007. Using this relative measure, poverty ranged from 10 percent in the Czech Republic to 25 percent in Bulgaria.[21]

The European data, however, bring out another problem with relative definitions of poverty. Because poverty is measured relative to the median, the poverty line is much lower in some European countries than in others. For example, while the Czech Republic can boast of having the lowest poverty rate, part of the reason is that its median income is so low. In fact, the poverty line for a family of four in the Czech Republic was only about half the line used in Denmark. So while fewer Czechs fall below the poverty line, it's because the line is so low.

The same issue can arise with measurement of poverty over time. For example, if the economy slows down and average incomes drop, the poverty rate of a country could actually fall even though more and more people have suffered a decline in income. This counter-intuitive result—poverty lower in low-wage countries, poverty declining as the economy declines—is one argument in favor of an absolute measure of poverty.

Unfortunately, while there are good reasons for the United States to use an absolute measure of poverty, there is no reason why it should use our current "official" poverty line.

The official poverty line

Since 1969, the US government has recognized an official definition of poverty that is based on work done by the Social Security Administration in the early 1960s. It uses a set of poverty thresholds or lines based on family size, number of children, and age of householder. The thresholds are adjusted every year for changes in the cost of living using the Bureau of Labor Statistics' Consumer Price Index Research Series (CPI-U-RS). The thresholds for 2011 are listed below (Figure 4.2).[22]

To determine if a family is living in poverty, one compares the family's income to the appropriate poverty threshold. Specifically, the income figure used is *pretax cash income* from all sources during the previous year. This includes all government cash benefits (like unemployment compensation, Social Security, and public assistance) but excludes the value of nutritional assistance and any housing subsidies a family might receive. The official poverty rate is computed using an annual government survey, the Current Population Survey conducted every March.

We have long recognized that there are a number of serious problems with the official method for calculating poverty.[23] Among the most prominent are

- *The poverty thresholds are simply too low.* As an example, the Department of Housing and Urban Development (HUD) issues annual figures for "fair market rent." In 2008, the average FMR for the nation was $10,338 for the year. In other words, a family of three living in a two-bedroom apartment would need to spend

---

[21]OECD, *Growing Unequal*, 125–149.

[22]US Census Bureau, *Income, Poverty, and Health Insurance Coverage 2010*, Current Population Report P60-239 (Washington, DC: Government Printing Office, 2011), http://www.census.gov/prod/2011pubs/p60-239.pdf.

[23]For critical analysis of the official poverty measures, see Center for Economic Opportunity, "The CEO Poverty Measure," (August 2008), New York City Center for Economic Opportunity, http://www.nyc.gov/html/ceo/downloads/pdf/final_poverty_report.pdf; and Kathleen Short, "The Research Supplemental Poverty Measure: 2010," Current Population Reports P-60-241, http://www.census.gov/prod/2011pubs/p60-241.pdf.

(Dollars)								
Size of family unit	**Related children under 18 years**							
	None	**One**	**Two**	**Three**	**Four**	**Five**	**Six**	**Seven**	**Eight or more**
One person (unrelated individual):									
Under 65 years	11,702								
65 years and older	10,788								
Two people:									
Householder under 65 years	15,063	15,504							
Householder 65 years and older	13,596	15,446							
Three people	17,595	18,106	18,123						
Four people	23,201	23,581	22,811	22,891					
Five people	27,979	28,386	27,517	26,844	26,434				
Six people	32,181	32,309	31,643	31,005	30,056	29,494			
Seven people	37,029	37,260	36,463	35,907	34,872	33,665	32,340		
Eight people	41,414	41,779	41,027	40,368	39,433	38,247	37,011	36,697	
Nine people or more	49,818	50,059	49,393	48,835	47,917	46,654	45,512	45,229	43,487

Figure 4.2
Poverty Thresholds for 2011 by Size of Family and Number of Related Children
The poverty "line" is made up of a number of thresholds that range from under $10,000 for a one-person household to over $50,000 for a family of nine or more people.

Source: US Census Bureau, "Income, Poverty, and Health Insurance Coverage in the United States: 2011," 60–243.

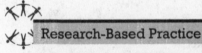

Research-Based Practice

Practice Behavior Example: Use practice experience to inform scientific inquiry.

Critical Thinking Question: How can social workers use their practice experience to dramatize the shortcomings of the "official" poverty measure?

60 percent of its poverty threshold just on rent and would have only about $7,000 left to spend on all other cash expenses.[24]

- *The thresholds ignore the value of cash-like benefits.* When the poverty line was first constructed, these benefits were a small part of government benefits for the poor, but over the past half century they have grown faster than means-tested cash benefits.
- *The thresholds do not take geographic differences in the cost of living into account.* For example, the HUD fair market rent mentioned above in 2008 varied from $5,688 in Acadia Parish, Louisiana, to $19,704 in Fairfield County, Connecticut. Obviously, a uniform national poverty line undercounts the poor in Connecticut and overcounts them in Louisiana.
- *The thresholds ignore taxes.* One of the major sources of aid to the working poor is the Earned Income Tax Credit, yet this doesn't figure at all in calculating poverty rates. Other families that don't qualify for the EITC may actually fall into poverty because of taxes.[25]

[24]"Fair Market Rents: HUD USER," US Department of Housing and Urban Development, http://www.huduser.org/portal/datasets/fmr.html.
[25]Mark J. Stern, "Crossing City Line: Alternative Measures of Poverty for Metropolitan Philadelphia 2005–2007," a paper delivered at the Association for Public Policy Analysis and Management, Washington, DC, November 2009.

The Orshansky line

The story of the current official poverty line has all of the twists and turns of a great mystery. It began with the work of a generation of dedicated women in the Social Security Administration and other federal agencies who worried about the well-being of women and children before it seemed important enough to be "men's work." These women pioneered the study of poverty as part of "home economics" before the economics profession paid much attention to the field.[26]

One such woman was Mollie Orshansky. As the War on Poverty began to gain steam in the early 1960s, Ms. Orshansky worried that the men at the Council of Economic Advisors (CEA) had begun to study poverty without paying enough attention to the economic needs of families of different sizes and composition. Where the CEA had proposed a flat poverty threshold of $3,000 for all families, Orshansky believed that the number of adults, the number of children, and other circumstances of the family made a difference in the amount of cash a family needed to survive. She set about developing a set of detailed thresholds that eventually numbered 124, depending on the size of the family, its composition, the gender and age of the family head, and whether the family lived on a farm or not.

In developing her poverty line, Orshansky was limited by time pressures and a lack of data. As a result, she made several decisions that were more or less "on the fly" or provisional, but they eventually became permanent elements of the official poverty line.[27]

First, Orshansky wanted to calculate the amount of money a family needed to feed itself. Unfortunately, the most recent US Department of Agriculture data on food budgets at the time dated from 1955. She decided to use two sets of food budgets: a "low-cost" plan that represented the typical diet of low-income families and an "economy" plan that was about 20 percent lower and represented the type of food a family might eat if it was experiencing an economic emergency. Only the "economy" estimates became part of the official poverty line. *So the poverty line we use today is based on the diet that a poor family would have eaten in 1955 during an extreme emergency.*

Second, Orshansky ran into a data problem. Her food budgets were based on income *after taxes* (i.e., disposable income), but the only available data on income related to *before-tax* income. If she had adjusted her food budget to pretax, the poverty line would have been 20 percent higher.

Third, Orshansky needed to multiply the food budget by some figure to take into account other family expenses. Orshansky chose a *multiplier* of three, based again on the 1955 Agriculture Department data. By the 1960s, this figure did not reflect the actual behavior of low-income families. This depressed the poverty line further.

This may all seem like ancient history to a student interested in poverty in the twenty-first century, and it would be except for one fact: *these issues are still integral to how we define poverty.* As a result of a variety of institutional and political reasons, Orshansky's work—which she saw as preliminary—eventually became the foundation of the official poverty measure in 1969. Two factors account for this inability to revise the poverty line to reflect current reality:

- In 1968, when the Social Security Administration was ready to revise the poverty line using more current data, the Johnson administration's budget office stopped it because new thresholds would lead to bureaucratic headaches for other

---

[26]O'Connor, *Poverty Knowledge*, 183–184.

[27]Gordon Fisher, "The Development and History of the Poverty Thresholds," *Social Security Bulletin* 44, no. 4 (Winter 1992): 3–14.

agencies that used the poverty line. The issue of *bureaucratic inertia* continues to block changing the poverty line.

- The polarization of American politics has impeded a sensible revision of the poverty line. During the 1970s, many social scientists and social welfare experts advocated increasing the threshold, which would tend to push up the poverty rate. During the 1980s, many conservatives argued that the value of food and housing subsidies should be counted as income, which would push the poverty rate down.[28]

Supplemental Poverty Measure

In November 2011, the Census Bureau released guidelines to address some of the well-known shortcomings in the official poverty measure.[29] Although the new Supplemental Poverty Measure (SPM) does not influence the allocation of social programs, the Bureau hopes that its dissemination will provide a more accurate standard for judging the extent and distribution of economic need in the United States. The SPM closely follows a set of recommendations made by a panel of the National Academy of Sciences in the 1990s for increasing the accuracy of the poverty measure. In place of the Orshansky line, the SPM uses government data on consumer expenditures to determine poverty. It incorporates data on the geographic variation of housing costs, includes the costs of out-of-pocket medical expenses, and makes some adjustments for estimating the number of members of each domestic unit. The most important changes, however, relate to the estimates of income. In place of a narrow measure of pretax cash income, the SPM includes data on in-kind benefits like food stamps and housing subsidies and the impact of taxation on a family's income. As a result, the role of the Earned Income Tax Credit, which had been ignored by the official measure, is now clearly evident in the data.

When all of these changes were incorporated, the estimated poverty rate in 2010 rose from 15.2 to 16.0 percent. In other words, it defined 2.5 million more poor people than the old measure. In the next section we compare the impact of the official poverty line and the SPM on different population groups.

Trends in Official Poverty

In 2011, 15.0 percent of Americans lived in poverty, a significant increase from the 2007 figure of 12.5 percent. In both 2010 and 2011, 46.2 million Americans had incomes below the official poverty measure, an increase of 8.9 million people since 2007. This is the highest number of poor people ever recorded by the government.

Since the 1960s, the American poverty rate has been marked by a number of continuities as well as several important changes. We need to distinguish two different ways of thinking about changes in poverty: the *risk* of being poor and the *composition* of the poverty population.

By *risk* of poverty we are estimating the likelihood that someone will be poor based on his group membership. Risk is measured using the *poverty rate*, that is, the percent of a particular group with incomes below the poverty line. The *composition* of the poverty population tells us about the representation of a particular group within the population living below the poverty line.

---

[28]A possible third reason for inaction is that no president wants to see poverty increase during his administration, even if it's simply a statistical correction. The direct evidence on this is harder to come by, although the television show, *West Wing*, had an episode devoted to this theme in its third season.
[29]Short, "Research Supplemental Poverty Measure: 2010."

Let's take an example. In 2008, 17.7 million men and 22.1 million women lived in poverty. The *risk of poverty* was slightly higher for women (14.4 percent) than for men (12.0). With respect to composition of the poverty population, however, women made up 56 percent of all poor people.

Keeping the risk and composition of poverty straight is important because it influences how we understand change. For example, a group's poverty risk could remain the same, but if its share of the population increases, so will its share of the poverty population.

The risk of poverty has been strongly related to ethnicity and family structure since the United States began calculating official poverty in the 1960s. Americans who live in married-couple families have consistently had lower poverty rates than those living in single-parent families. While the poverty rate of female-headed families has declined over time, the rapid increase in the number of female-headed families has increased their share of the poverty population dramatically.

In 1960, 42 percent of female-headed families lived in poverty, approximately 2 million of the 4.6 million people comprising families headed by unmarried women. But female-headed families only made up 23.7 percent of all poor people. By 2008, the risk of poverty for these families had dropped significantly, from 42.4 to 28.7 percent. However, because so many more Americans now live in female-headed families and because the poverty risk for other family types had fallen more quickly, their share of the poverty population had increased from 23.7 to 51.1 percent.

The racial and ethnic ordering of poverty has remained relatively stable since the 1970s. White Americans have generally had the lowest risk of poverty. Since the mid-1970s, their poverty rate has remained largely unchanged. Black Americans continue to have the highest poverty rates, although their risk of poverty has dropped more sharply than that of any group since the mid-1970s. Two groups that were quite small when poverty data were first collected—Hispanics and Asians—now occupy very different places in the poverty hierarchy. The Asian poverty rate, while higher than whites, is much lower than that of African Americans. Hispanics, who in the mid-1970s had a rate much lower than African Americans, now have a poverty rate that is only slightly below that of black Americans.

Although the risks of poverty for the different ethnic groups have remained generally stable, the ethnic composition of the poverty population has undergone significant changes. In the mid-1970s, whites accounted for three-quarters of the poverty population. By 2008, their share had declined to 56 percent. African Americans' share of the poverty population has remained stable, while that of Hispanics has mushroomed. In 1976, only 8 percent of poor people were Hispanics. In 2008, their share had increased to 22 percent.

While the family and ethnic risk of poverty has remained largely stable since the 1960s, the age structure of poverty has undergone dramatic transformation. When the government first began keeping poverty statistics, more than one-in-three older Americans lived in poverty, roughly twice the rate of working-age Americans. Children under the age of 18 had a higher-than-average poverty rate as well, but at 27 percent, it was significantly below the rate for older Americans. During the 1960s, all three age groups—children, working-age adults, and older Americans—saw their poverty rates decline. During the 1970s, however, things began to change. While the rate for older Americans continued to decline, the rates for children and working-age adults first stabilized and then increased during the recessions of the early 1980s. By the early 1990s, older Americans' poverty rate was lower than those for the working-age and child populations.

LEONARD FREED / MAGNUM PHOTOS

Female-headed households with children account for an increasing share of the population living in poverty.

In contrast, children—whose poverty rate had fallen as low as 14 percent in the early 1970s—have suffered an increase in poverty that pushed their rate as high as 23 percent during the 1990s. In 2011, the child poverty rate stood at 22 percent (Figure 4.3).

The reasons for the shift in the age structure of poverty are not hard to understand. As we explore in later chapters, older Americans have benefited from two associated changes in social welfare policy. First, during the late 1960s and early 1970s, the Social Security system was expanded and its benefits made more generous. Second, since the 1970s, the government has provided a set of generous tax breaks to encourage saving for retirement.

Social welfare policy toward children's poverty has been more complex. Some changes in policy, including the expansion of Social Security and the enactment of the Earned Income Tax Credit, have benefited some groups of children. However, the ambivalence of policymakers toward female-headed households—particularly those headed by unmarried women—has blocked many initiatives that would have reduced the poverty of these children. Instead, the neglect of public assistance benefit levels during the 1970s and 1980s and the passage of welfare reform legislation during the 1990s left the children of single mothers more vulnerable than many other groups. The fact that these children were more likely to be black or Hispanic made this neglect easier to sustain.

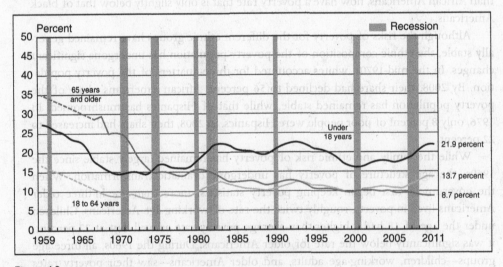

Figure 4.3
Poverty Rates by Age, 1959–2011
Since the 1970s, older Americans have enjoyed a declining poverty rate while other age groups have seen their poverty rates increase.
Source: US Census Bureau, "Income, Poverty, and Health Insurance Coverage in the United States: 2011," 60–243.

The release of the Supplemental Poverty Measure in 2011 changed our perception of the poverty gap between children and older Americans.[30] The incorporation of in-kind benefits and the Earned Income Tax Credit into the calculation of poverty resulted in a decline of the child poverty rate from 22.5 to 18.2 percent. The poverty of older Americans, however, rose from 9.0 to 15.9 percent. Using the official rate, child poverty was 150 percent higher than that of older Americans. Using the SPM, the child poverty rate was only 14 percent higher.

EXPLAINING PERSISTENT POVERTY

Imagine a waiting room in an airport. It's morning and a flight is about to leave when the airport personnel announce that because of mechanical difficulties, the flight will be delayed. Several hundred disappointed travelers shift in their seats.

As the day progresses, other flights come and go, hundreds and eventually thousands of travelers enter the waiting area, take a seat for a few minutes, and then leave as their flights board. Finally, late in the day, the delayed flight is ready to leave.

Think about the population flow in the waiting room during the day. At any point in time, the delayed passengers would make up a majority of the people in the waiting room. However, if we look at everyone who had spent any time in the waiting room, the delayed passengers would represent only a small proportion of the total.

This story mirrors a paradox in the story of American poverty. Most people who are poor remain poor for only a short time, like the majority of travelers in our waiting room. But a small minority of this total is poor for a very long time. As a result, at any one point in time, they make up a large share of the poor.

Looking only at people who were poor for at least two months between 2001 and 2003, Sharon Stern discovered that half of the individuals were poor for between two and four months and 14 percent were poor for more than two years.[31] However, if we ask what proportion of all of the months spent in poverty each group represented, we find that the group that was poor four months or less accounts for only 16 percent of all months spent in poverty, but the long-term poor (over 24 months) account for 42 percent of all months spent in poverty.

The implications of this split in the poverty population for social welfare policy are gigantic. One could say that the United States in fact has two distinct poverty problems, each of which calls for its own policies. On the one hand, the short-term poor are typically individuals and families who are always living close to the poverty line but are pushed below the line by some emergency or dislocation. Illness, the loss of a job, the end of a marriage or relationship, or an unexpected change in housing arrangements—any one of these situations can take a family that was just making ends meet and push it over the edge. On the other hand, a much smaller group of individuals simply can't cope. For whatever reason, they can't find the resources to cover their expenses. They live in poverty month after month.

How do we explain these two patterns? Generally speaking, explanations of poverty have fallen into one of two camps, which we can call structural or cultural/psychological.[32]

---

[30]Short, "Research Supplemental Poverty Measure:2010."

[31]Sharon M. Stern, "Poverty Dynamics: 2001–2003," May 15, 2008, http://www.census.gov/hhes/www/poverty/publications/dynamics01/PovertyDynamics.pdf.

[32]O'Connor, Poverty Knowledge, 284–296.

Structural explanations point to problems with the organization of America's social structure or political economy as the cause of poverty. Structural theories typically point to the inadequacy of wages, discrimination, and the unequal distribution of resources.

Cultural and psychological explanations date back to the early twentieth century. In essence, these theories see the problem of poverty as a product of the choices that poor people make. The classic example of a cultural explanation is Oscar Lewis's "culture of poverty" theory. Lewis argued that many poor people share a set of characteristics or traits. In 1966, Lewis listed some of those traits as

> a high incidence of maternal deprivation, of orality, of weak ego structure, confusion of sexual identification, a lack of impulse control, a strong present-time orientation with relatively little ability to defer gratification and to plan for the future, a sense of resignation and fatalism, male superiority, and a high tolerance for psychological pathology of all sorts.[33]

While some writers take either a pure structural or cultural approach to explaining poverty, many attempt to carve out a middle ground between the two extremes. The sociologist William J. Wilson, for example, argued that some of the features identified with the culture of poverty were in reality a product of structural features, specifically the social isolation of the poor in urban neighborhoods with high concentrations of poverty.[34]

CONCLUSION: RECONNECTING THE CONVERSATIONS OF INEQUALITY AND POVERTY

One final consequence of the artificially low poverty thresholds used by the United States is its impact on our understanding of the relationship between poverty and inequality. As we have seen, the distance between middle-income Americans and the officially poor has widened in recent decades. While the poverty line in the 1960s was equal to about half of the median family income, in 2007 it represented only 40 percent of the median. The conversation about poverty has been disconnected from the conversation about middle-income working families.

This is too bad, because over the past several decades the number of American families who live between poverty and affluence—what we might call the "uncomfortable" class—has increased. During most of the twentieth century, it grew because of declines in poverty. Over the past 20 years, however, it's increased as the proportion of American families with above-average income has fallen. By 2000, 51 percent all families with children were part of this uncomfortable class. Virtually all of these families have members in the labor force, working in occupations as varied as truck driver, child-care worker, or retail sales. Most of them own their home.

At first glance, their family incomes—between $27,000 and $70,000 per year in 2007—don't warrant concern. Members of the uncomfortable class don't go to bed hungry, fall into homelessness, or rely on welfare. Parents suffer from a quieter desperation: sitting at the kitchen table wondering which bills NOT to pay this month, watching their adjustable-rate

---

[33]Oscar Lewis, *La Vida: A Puerto Rican Family in the Culture of Poverty—San Juan and New York* (New York: Random House, 1966), xlviii.

[34]William J. Wilson, *The Truly Disadvantaged: The Inner City, the Underclass, and Public Policy* (Chicago: University of Chicago Press, 1987).

mortgage eat up a larger share of their income, wondering if they will be able to help their kids get a college education, and wondering what to do if they or their kids get sick.

The Supplemental Poverty Measure released by the Census Bureau in 2011 is an important contribution to bringing our statistical portrait of poverty into line with the realities faced by Americans of modest means. By using a more realistic estimate of what one needs to survive in America, the new measure will allow us to more accurately pinpoint those groups that need the most help and those places where our current policies fall short. Predictably, conservatives have claimed that the SPM does more harm than good and represents a hidden agenda to promote the redistribution of wealth. It seems likely that Congressional opposition will prevent the SPM from influencing poverty policy, at least in the short term.

Whatever the outcome, it will not change the reality faced by millions of American families—those above and below the official poverty line—trying to cope with the challenge of providing for their economic necessities. Poverty will continue to cast a long shadow over those families and, to the extent that widespread poverty in an affluent country is an indictment of an entire civilization, over the rest of us as well.

POLICY PRACTICE: THE FINANCIAL VICTIMIZATION OF THE POOR[35]

In a market economy, *caveat emptor—let the buyer beware*—has always been the operating principle. A half century ago, in his study of *The Other America*, Michael Harrington pointed to the role of exploitive business practices in the victimization of the poor. Over the past several decades, the character of this victimization has changed. In the past, it was marginal shopkeepers and businessmen who were the dominant players in this market. Now, the exploitation of the poor has become big business and, in 2008, shook the foundations of our economic system.

The financial services industry is one of the major exploiters of the poor. During the past several decades, regulated financial institutions like banks and savings and loan associations have become less interested in serving low-income neighborhoods. In place of these regulated institutions, a set of "fringe banking" institutions has moved into poor neighborhoods.[36] In addition to pawnshops—that provide high-interest loans to customers that provide jewelry, appliances, and other valuables as collateral—check-cashing outlets and "payday" lenders make money off the financial vulnerability of the poor. Cashing a $500 check at one of these outlets can cost between $5 and $50. Payday loan outlets that provide short-term loans to the poor typically charge fees of about $15 for each $100 advanced. When the short duration of the loan is taken into consideration, the annual interest rates on these loans can be as high as 400 percent.

As we've noted, the US tax system is fairly generous to low-income families with children. Yet, because the poor often have to wait to receive their refund check, tax services can make big profits off of *refund anticipation loans*. Marketed as "quick refunds," these loans get filers their refund two or three weeks in advance, but at the cost of annual interest rates of between 70 and 1,000 percent.

---

[35]This section is based on Matt Fellowes, *From Poverty, Opportunity: Putting the Market to Work for Lower-Income Families* (Washington, DC: Brookings Institution, 2006), http://www.brookings.edu/research/reports/2006/07/poverty-fellowes.

[36]John P. Caskey, *Fringe Banking: Check-Cashing Outlets, Pawnshops and the Poor* (New York: Russell Sage Foundation, 1994).

The limited consumer choices available to the poor also open up opportunities for business to profit. Supermarkets have often completely abandoned neighborhoods with concentrated poverty. As a result, many poor people must rely on smaller stores with lower-quality goods and higher prices. A recent study, for example, found that two-thirds of the goods in a typical market basket cost more at smaller grocery stores.

Perhaps the most significant exploitation of the poor was the explosion of predatory mortgage lending during the early years of the twenty-first century. Using aggressive and misleading marketing techniques, predatory lenders were able to lure millions of unwary homeowners into financing or refinancing their homes with mortgages with high front-end fees and ballooning interest rates. Operating largely outside the purview of government regulators, these lenders often undermined the financial security that low-income homeowners had taken years to build.

Can We Do Better?

Thanks to the financial meltdown of 2008, the federal government has shown increased interest in expanding the number and types of financial services that it regulates. While not motivated by the victimization of the poor, the issue may provide an opportunity for more effective regulation of fringe banking.

A national movement among community development advocates, meanwhile, is pushing to expand the consumer choices open to poor neighborhoods. Pennsylvania, for example, funded a loan pool to encourage the construction of supermarkets in urban areas. The fund led to the construction of 60 supermarkets in the Philadelphia metropolitan area.

Finally, consumer counseling—for new homeowners, for example—provides an important means of blocking predatory lending from resurfacing.

Social workers can make contributions to all of these efforts. By viewing their clients from a holistic perspective, social workers take into account the issues that clients present as well as their entire social environment. The financial exploitation of poor families means that their meager paychecks don't go as far. Being knowledgeable about consumer finance and housing counseling can make social workers more effective in addressing these concerns. Finally, given their firsthand knowledge of the impact of financial exploitation on everyday lives, social workers can be effective advocates not only for individual clients but also for changes in how laws and public agencies monitor these activities and affect broader policy.

Test your understanding and analysis of this chapter by completing the Chapter Review.

5

Food and Nutrition

INTRODUCTION

This chapter uses food and nutrition to show the connections between the needs of all Americans and the special challenges of low-income Americans. It begins with an overview of the American food system's accomplishments and challenges and then focuses on targeted public nutritional programs.

Food is the most fundamental of human needs. Humans have been able to live without shelter and other "necessities," but nourishment is a requirement. It represents the most basic connection between people and nature.

Yet, at the same time, food represents a highly developed dimension of our society and culture. "Culinary arts" are an important form of human creativity. The notion that "we are what we eat" suggests that our identity, our view of the world, and our culture are tied to what we put in our mouths.

Thus, the discussion of social welfare and nutrition is multidimensional. At its most basic level, it is about the availability of adequate nutrition for the entire population. But it encompasses as well how we make decisions as a society about our use of natural resources, how we organize our labor force, and how we connect to our families and the rest of society.

This chapter examines the role of food and nutrition in contemporary America. Within the narrow world of policy development, the social welfare perspective on nutrition is concerned primarily with "food insecurity," the extent to which a share of the population is unable to obtain adequate nutrition on a daily basis. We have developed a range of targeted programs—such as Supplemental Nutrition Assistance Program (SNAP, formerly Food Stamps); Women, Infants, and Children (WIC); and school lunch programs—to address the nutritional needs of low-income people.

Yet, in recent years, the wider world of policy—changing ideas about the organization of food production and consumption, the changing institutional world of food production and distribution—has begun to expand the framework within which we view the issue of social welfare and nutrition.

Take the issue of obesity. We know that as a society we have become more overweight. Today, approximately 34 percent of American adults are judged to be obese. The Centers for Disease Control estimate that 17 percent of children are obese. The child obesity rate ranges from a low of 21 percent in Colorado to a high of 32.2 percent in Alabama.[1]

America stands out in international comparisons. The only other country with an obesity rate over 30 percent is Mexico. Among rich European countries, the American rate compares unfavorably with that of Denmark (11 percent), France (11 percent), and Germany (14 percent).[2]

The issue becomes more complex when we ask who is obese. Nearly half of African Americans females (48 percent) are obese, as are 38 percent of those with less than a high school diploma. One out of seven low-income, preschool-aged children are obese. Is there a contradiction here? Can we claim that a large proportion of low-income Americans are "food insecure" and at the same time say that many of them are overweight?

We can't address this seeming contradiction if we focus just on the food consumption of poor people. We need to understand the broader organization of food production in the United States, and indeed in the world. In addition, systems of food distribution play an important role in determining what we eat and how it affects us.

This broader frame of reference has implications for how we think about social welfare policy and nutrition. Some of the more innovative approaches to nutrition policy now target food production and distribution, not just the availability of food. In addition, ideas about food quality that have had an impact on how all Americans eat are filtering their way into social welfare policy discussions.

Much of this new thinking about food challenges us to consider "food environments"—an ecological perspective—rather than merely individuals making decisions about what they eat. When a middle-school student passes five convenience stores on her way home from school—all selling nothing but junk food—does it make sense to talk about her individual decision to eat junk, or should we rather see it as an environmental issue? When a working single mother pops a couple of frozen dinners in the microwave for her family, should we see this as her bad decision or frame it within a wider time/space challenge of working families? Adopting an environmental framework allows us to make sense of some of the nutritional contradictions and reframe some of the policy questions we face.

Study "Percentage of the Adult Population Considered to be Obese" to understand how the United States compares with other countries.

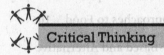

Critical Thinking

Practice Behavior Example: Distinguish, appraise, and integrate multiple sources of knowledge, including research-based knowledge and practice wisdom.

Critical Thinking Question: How do we reconcile the contradiction of widespread obesity and food insecurity? What additional information allows us to make sense of this?

---

[1] "Childhood Obesity Facts," Centers for Disease Control and Prevention, http://www.cdc.gov/healthyyouth/obesity/facts.htm.

[2] "Percentage of the Adult Population Considered to be Obese," Organization for Economic Cooperation and Development (OECD), 2010, "OECD Health Data," OECD Health Statistics database, www.census.gov/compendia/statab/2012/tables/12s1342.xls.

HOW AMERICANS OBTAIN THEIR FOOD

The policy-in-environment approach suggests that we make sense of food by looking at the ideas and institutions that frame policy and behavior. In this respect, food stands out as an extreme example of *cultural lag*—the gap between our ideas and our institutions.[3] On the one hand, most Americans think about food and food policy in the context of an idealized image of the American farm and countryside. On the other hand, the production of food is now a sphere dominated by a few giant corporate players who apply technology, mass production techniques, and sheer economic power to shape the food industry to maximize its profitability. Our ability to evaluate policy choices is limited by our poor understanding of the social context of food production, distribution, and consumption.

The Agrarian Ideal

> The instant I enter on my own land, the bright idea of property, of exclusive right, of independence exalt my mind. Precious soil, I say to myself, by what singular custom of law is it that thou wast made to constitute the riches of the freeholder? What should we American farmers be without the distinct possession of that soil? It feeds, it clothes us, from it we draw even a great exuberancy, our best meat, our richest drink, the very honey of our bees comes from this privileged spot. No wonder we should thus cherish its possession, no wonder that so many Europeans who have never been able to say that such portion of land was theirs, cross the Atlantic to realize that happiness. This formerly rude soil has been converted by my father into a pleasant farm, and in return it has established all our rights; on it is founded our rank, our freedom, our power as citizens, our importance as inhabitants of such a district. These images I must confess I always behold with pleasure, and extend them as far as my imagination can reach for this is what may be called the true and the only philosophy of an American farmer.[4]
>
> —*J. Hector St. John de Crevecoeur, 1782*

No occupational group in America is fraught with more meaning than farmers. Since Crevecoeur penned these lines in 1782, the image of the American farmer has been tied to a complex set of values: the importance of property ownership, the conquering of the wilderness, and independence as the cornerstone of democracy. The agrarian ideal was fixed by Thomas Jefferson, whose *Notes on the State of Virginia* argued for the superiority of rural over urban, small over big, landed over unlanded.

Yet, after the Civil War, as America became an industrial nation, farmers found themselves on the economic defensive. The vagaries of crop prices, the weather, and the power of the railroads turned the agrarian ideal into a nightmare of debt and dispossession. Wave after wave of rural protest built up during the last decades of the nineteenth century, culminating in the populist revolt of the 1890s.[5]

---

[3]William F. Ogburn, "Cultural Lag as Theory," *Sociology and Social Research* 41, no. 3 (January 1957): 167–174.

[4]J. Hector St. John de Crevecoeur, *Letters From an American Farmer*, reprinted from the original ed. with a prefatory note by W. P. Trent and an introduction by Ludwig Lewisohn (New York, Fox: Duffield, 1904), 27–28.

[5]Lawrence Goodwyn, *Democratic Promise: The Populist Moment in America* (New York: Oxford University Press, 1976).

Imperceptibly, the centrality of the farmer to the American political economy faded. Keeping food cheap for the urban masses, not keeping American farmers prosperous, became the dominant force influencing farm policy. Increasingly, as the twentieth century progressed, the consolidation of the food industry increased its political power, again at the expense of farmers.

The image of the independent farmer continues to dominate much of the political and social rhetoric of food policy. But in recent years, the image of the farmer has changed subtly. While still held up as a paragon of distinctly American virtues, Crevecoeur's focus on democracy has given way to the farmer as a global economic force. As President George W. Bush told a group of Future Farmers of America in 2001[6]

> America's farmers and ranchers are feeding those who are hungry, those who need foodstuffs. We're the best in the world at growing products. Our farmers and ranchers are not only some of the hardest working people in the world, but we're better at it than everybody else is, too. And therefore, we ought to work hard to open up all avenues, all markets, so we can feed people.

The rise of agribusiness and the rapid decline in the farm population has not challenged this old agrarian ideal. Ironically, even as farmers have disappeared, the agrarian ideal was recharged by what would appear to be its opposite, the rise of organic and natural foods.

Organic farming had its origins in early twentieth-century concerns about environmental degradation associated with the Industrial Revolution. However, only in the 1960s and 1970s did an alternative approach to agriculture and increasing consumer concerns about food quality and safety combine to fuel the popularization of organic food. Ideas about small-scale agriculture, family farms, and conforming food production to environmental concerns and consumer preferences are now more readily associated with organic farming than conventional industrial agriculture, even as the realities of organic and conventional agricultural production have continued to converge.[7]

PUBLIC POLICY AND THE FOOD CHAIN: AGRICULTURAL SUBSIDIES AND PUBLIC REGULATION

A century ago, farmers were the largest occupation in the United States. Their numbers steadily declined over the twentieth century, first because the city attracted more and more workers and then, after the 1930s, because the mechanization of agriculture reduced the viability of smaller farms.

In the past three decades, however, the institutional context in which food is produced underwent another profound change. First, a wave of consolidation hit all aspects of the American food system. A few companies—Archer Daniels Midland (ADM), Monsanto, and Cargill—became central to all aspects of the food chain: selling seeds and

[6]John T. Woolley and Gerhard Peters, "The American Presidency Project," Santa Barbara, CA, http://www.presidency.ucsb.edu/ws/?pid=63838.

[7]Patricia Allen, "Reweaving the Food Security Safety Net: Mediating Entitlement and Entrepreneurship," *Agriculture and Human Values* 16 (1999): 1117–129.

fertilizer to farmers, controlling the massive feedlots and grain elevators, developing new uses for products and marketing them worldwide.[8]

The increasing importance of large vertically integrated companies was facilitated by changes in government policies in the 1980s. Historically, farmers faced a core problem. Because of the dependence of their production on the natural environment, the weather and seasons defined the size of a farmer's crop and when it was ready for market. As a result, farmers always faced bad timing. They were ready to sell when everyone else was, so prices were low. If weather was bad, prices went up, but they had little to sell. If the weather had been good, they had a lot to sell, but so did everyone else, so prices were low.

Since the 1880s, farmers had developed an idea about how to deal with this dilemma. Government should provide storage facilities and a means for farmers to borrow against their stored crop until prices were more advantageous. The "subtreasury" system, as it was called, was one of the more radical demands of the Famers' Alliances and Populists of the late nineteenth century. But it was only with the New Deal that the federal government adopted a similar system. The New Deal's focus on preventing an oversupply of farm commodities—including paying farmers to leave land unplanted—was the dominant trend in agriculture policy for four decades.[9]

One of the consequences of policies focused on overproduction, however, was to keep food prices high. Recall from Chapter 4 that in the early 1960s, food still represented nearly 30 percent of the monthly budget of modest-income Americans. During the 1970s, a combination of high world demand, lower supplies, and a general inflationary environment drove food prices even higher. In the early 1970s, food's share of family budgets remained at 19 percent, well above the 14 percent share of the 1990s.

During the 1970s, as a result, the Nixon administration and Congress transformed the farm subsidy program from one that would control production to one that would, in effect, encourage overproduction. The contemporary food subsidy system pays farmers the difference between market prices and price floor. As a result, the system provides farmers an incentive to produce more crops even when the prices for those crops is below the cost of producing them.[10]

According to Michael Pollan, the chief beneficiary of this system has been large agribusinesses like ADM and Cargill. At the front end, they profit from selling farmers the seeds, fertilizers, and other products to push up crop yields. At the same time, they profit from the distribution system and abundance of cheap grain that has fueled the proliferation of new products derived from subsidized agriculture.[11]

Corn provides the outstanding example of this use of food technology to absorb the excess production of subsidized crops. High-fructose corn syrup (HFCS) has taken over a large share of the sweetener market for soft drinks and many other foods because its low, subsidized cost has squeezed out cane sugar. Corn is now broken down into a dizzying array of compounds that show up as additives in virtually all of our food. At the same time, cheap corn has displaced other crops as feed for cattle, chicken, and other animals. Even farm-grown salmon are now being "taught" to live on corn-based feed.[12]

[8]Michael Pollan, *The Omnivore's Dilemma: A Natural History of Four Meals* (New York: Penguin Press, 2006), 15–122.

[9]Goodwyn, *Democratic Promise.*

[10]Pollan, *Omnivore's Dilemma*, 52–54.

[11]Pollan, *Omnivore's* Dilemma, 63.

[12]Pollan, *Omnivore's Dilemma*, 67.

FOOD INSECURITY

Assess your comprehension
of "Food Insecurity" by
completing this quiz.

Through most of human history, hunger was a constant threat. Because of the low productivity of farming, most of the population were cultivators. The vicissitudes of the agricultural economy—bad weather, crop disease, and soil exhaustion—meant that famine was always a possibility. With the entire population laboring to produce food to feed itself, there was no margin of error. Small disturbances in production could lead to famine.

Famine led to hunger. For months, sometimes for years, entire populations would find themselves living on insufficient calories, often exacerbated by the lack of vitamins and minerals. As the entire population became weaker, women became less likely to have children, those who were born would be more likely to die, and people would become more susceptible to disease. Years of famine would often be followed by years of plague, often leading to a third or half of the population perishing. After the famine and plague had run their course, those remaining would start again to rebuild their lives, their families, and their communities.[13]

In the global North, famine became less common as the twentieth century progressed. Still, during the 1930s and 1940s, Europeans experienced a series of famines that led to millions of deaths. In the twentieth century, however, the causes of famine became more complex. In the Soviet Union in the 1930s and in China in the 1950s, millions perished because efforts to collectivize agriculture led to sharp declines in output at the same time that the government sought to channel a large share of food to urban populations. Modern medicine's successes at curing common deadly illnesses have led to population explosions that put great pressure on local agricultural economies. Political disputes in places like Zimbabwe or the Sudan have led to famine and hunger for large populations.

Within the history of hunger and famine, the nature of food insecurity in the United States may seem trivial. Robert Rector of the Heritage Foundation writes

> [T]he government's own data show that, even though they may have brief episodes of reduced food intake, most adults in food insecure households actually consume too much, not too little, food. To improve health, policies must be devised to encourage these individuals to avoid chronic overconsumption of calories and to spread their food intake more evenly over the course of each month to avoid episodic shortfalls.[14]

In one way, Rector is right. Certainly, the food insecurity experienced by low-income people in the United States today is different from the prolonged periods of hunger experienced by populations in the past and present. He is also correct that the food challenges experienced by low-income Americans can't be addressed simply by the expansion of food programs.

Ultimately, the food problems of poor people are an exaggerated form of the problems we all face with our current food

Diversity of Practice

Practice Behavior Example: Appreciate that, as a consequence of difference, a person's life experiences may include oppression, poverty, marginalization, and alienation as well as privilege, power, and acclaim.

Critical Thinking Question: Those who are never hungry can easily trivialize food insecurity. How can social workers appreciate the impact of marginalization on the life experience of the poor without having experienced it?

---

[13]E. A. Wrigley, *Population and History* (New York: McGraw Hill, 1976).

[14]Robert Rector, "Hunger Hysteria: Examining Food Security and Obesity in America," Web memo #1701 (November 13, 2007), accessed February 4, 2010, http://www.heritage.org/research/welfare/wm1701.cfm.

systems. Contemporary agriculture's lack of sustainability, its dependence on huge inputs of fossil fuels, its vulnerability to disease, and its ultimate product—highly processed food with too much sugar, too much fat, and too little nutrition—are problems for us all, but problems that the poor experience most keenly.

What Is Food Insecurity?

The US Department of Agriculture (USDA) defines *food security* as access by all members at all times to enough food for an active, healthy life. Food security includes, at a minimum

- ready availability of nutritionally adequate and safe foods, and
- assured ability to acquire acceptable foods in socially acceptable ways (i.e., without resorting to emergency food supplies, scavenging, stealing, or other coping strategies).

Food insecurity, therefore, is the opposite:

Food insecurity is limited or uncertain availability of nutritionally adequate and safe foods or limited or uncertain ability to acquire acceptable foods in socially acceptable ways.[15]

The USDA differentiates four levels of food security:

1. *High food security*—Households had no problems, or anxiety about, consistently accessing adequate food.
2. *Marginal food security*—Households had problems at times, or anxiety about, accessing adequate food, but the quality, variety, and quantity of their food intake were not substantially reduced.
3. *Low food security*—Households reduced the quality, variety, and desirability of their diets, but the quantity of food intake and normal eating patterns were not substantially disrupted.
4. *Very low food security*—At times during the year, eating patterns of one or more household members were disrupted and food intake reduced because the household lacked money and other resources for food.

In order to determine the level of American food security, the USDA, in cooperation with the Census Bureau, adds a set of questions to the Current Population Survey once a year. In 2008, the survey covered 44,000 households, which constituted a representative sample of the US civilian population.[16] In order to determine the level of security or insecurity of a particular family, the survey asked a set of questions about the experience of obtaining food by members of the household over the previous year:

- *Least severe*—Was this statement often, sometimes, or never true for you in the last 12 months? "We worried whether our food would run out before we got money to buy more."

[15]"Food Security in the United States: Measuring Household Food Security," accessed February 4, 2010, http://www.ers.usda.gov/Briefing/FoodSecurity/measurement.htm.

[16]Mark Nord, Margaret Andrews, and Steven Carlson, "Household Food Security in the United States, 2008," USDA Economic Research Report No. ERR-83, accessed February 4, 2010, http://www.ers.usda.gov/Publications/Err83/. See also, Alisha Coleman-Jensen, Mark Nord, Margaret Andrews, and Steven Carlson, "Household Food Security in the United States in 2010," USDA Economic Research Report No. 125, accessed September 2011, http://www.ers.usda.gov/media/121076/err125_2_.pdf.

- *Somewhat more severe*—Was this statement often, sometimes, or never true for you in the last 12 months? "We couldn't afford to eat balanced meals."
- *Midrange severity*—In the last 12 months, did you ever cut the size of your meals or skip meals because there wasn't enough money for food?
- *Most severe*—In the last 12 months, did you ever not eat for a whole day because there wasn't enough money for food? In the last 12 months, did any of the children ever not eat for a whole day because there wasn't enough money for food?

Trends in Food Insecurity

Over the past 15 years, the USDA has found that between 10 and 12 percent of Americans were food insecure, with between 4 and 5 percent experiencing very low food security.

The recession that began in late 2007 had a particularly large impact on food security. According to the USDA report, the proportion of the population experiencing food insecurity jumped from 11 to 15 percent of households between 2007 and 2008. The number of households who experienced very low food security went from 4.7 to 6.7 million households, representing an increase from 4 to 6 percent of households (Figure 5.1).

Some groups face much higher risks of food insecurity than the general population. Those groups more likely to be poor—female-headed households, households with children, households headed by an African American or Hispanic—had food insecurity rates more than 50 percent higher than the national average.

Although food insecurity is associated with poverty, it extends much higher in the income distribution. Among households with incomes 85 percent above the poverty line in 2008, 33 percent were food insecure, more than twice the national average (Figure 5.2). Indeed, the prevalence of food insecurity among the near poor can be seen as one indicator of the inadequacy of our current poverty line (see Chapter 4).

Not everyone agrees with the official government definition and measurement of food insecurity. The Food Research and Action Center (FRAC) commissioned its own survey of food hardship, which collected information from over one-half million adults through monthly surveys between January 2008 and December 2009. FRAC concluded that 19 percent of the population experienced "food hardship" (the lack of money to buy food that families need) during this period. Because the FRAC survey collected monthly

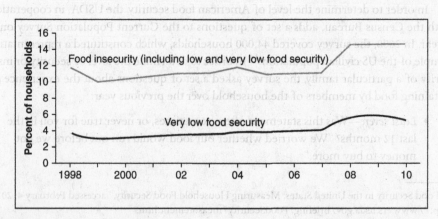

Figure 5.1
Food Insecurity in the United States, 1998–2010
Food insecurity increased during the recession of 2008–09.

Source: Alisha Coleman-Jensen, Mark Nord, Margaret Andrews, and Steven Carlson, "Household Food Security in the United States in 2010," http://www.ers.usda.gov/media/121076/err125_2_.pdf.

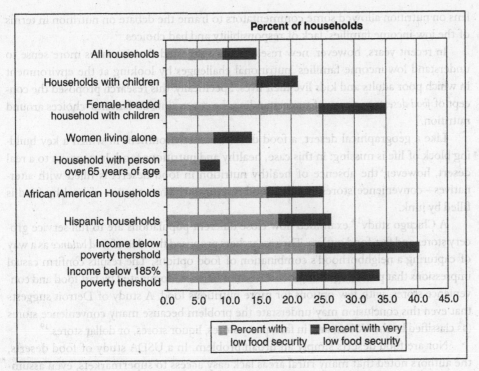

Figure 5.2
Percent of Households Experiencing Low or Very Low Food Security, by Selected Characteristics, 2010
Food insecurity mirrors the poverty rate, with female-headed households with children having the greatest risk of food insecurity.

Source: Based on Alisha Coleman-Jensen, Mark Nord, Margaret Andrews, and Steven Carlson, *"Household Food Security in the United States in 2010,"* http://www.ers.usda.gov/media/121076/err125_2_.pdf.

data, it was able to track the trend in food hardship as the recession took hold in 2008. In early 2008, FRAC concluded that 16 percent of American households did not have enough money to buy the food they needed, but by the last three months of the year, this percentage had grown to 19.5. A variety of policy changes in late 2008 and early 2009 that broadened eligibility for SNAP and increased benefit levels appear to have had an immediate impact, driving the food hardship rate down to 17.9 percent by the fall of 2009.[17] Yet, in the face of high unemployment, the rate remained high by historical standards.

ECOLOGICAL APPROACHES TO FOOD INSECURITY: FOOD DESERTS

Much of the research on inequality and nutrition has focused on individual-level behavior. The food insecurity literature, like that on obesity and diabetes, examined the options available to individuals when they purchase, prepare, and consume food. This individual

---

[17]Food Research and Action Center, "Food Hardship: A Closer Look at Hunger: Data for the Nation, States, 100 MSAs, and Every Congressional District," January 2010, http://frac.org/reports-and-resources/food-hardship-data/new-data-reveal-extent-of-hunger-in-every-corner-of-the-us/. See also, Food Research and Action Center, "Food Hardship in America: Data for the Nation, States, 100 MSAs, and Every Congressional District," March 2011, http://frac.org/wp-content/uploads/2011/03/food_hardship_report_mar2011.pdf.

lens on nutrition allowed some commentators to frame the debate on nutrition in terms of the low-income families' lack of responsibility and bad choices.

In recent years, however, new research has suggested that it makes more sense to understand low-income families' nutritional challenges by looking at the environment in which poor adults and kids live their lives. Specifically, this research proposed the concept of *food deserts* as a way of understanding the constraints on families' choices around nutrition.

Like a geographical desert, a food desert is an environment in which a key building block of life is missing: in this case, healthy and nutritious food. In contrast to a real desert, however, the absence of healthy nutrition in food deserts is filled with alternatives—convenience stores and fast-food restaurants. The vacuum of healthy food is filled by junk.

A Chicago study[18] examined how close different populations are to full-service grocery stores and fast-food outlets. The researchers proposed the idea of *food balance* as a way of capturing a neighborhood's combination of food options. The results confirm casual impressions that poor neighborhoods are out of balance, dominated by fast food and convenience stores, with few options for more nutritious food. A study of Detroit suggests that even this conclusion may understate the problem because many convenience stores (as classified by the USDA) are, in fact, party stores, liquor stores, or dollar stores.[19]

Nor are food deserts simply an urban problem. In a USDA study of food deserts, the authors noted that many rural areas lack easy access to supermarkets, even assuming automobile access (Figure 5.3). In the midst of the wheat belt of South Dakota, for example, residents of much of the state are farther than 20 miles from the nearest supermarket. For the 5 percent of rural residents who don't own a car, the situation is even more difficult.[20]

Using a different approach, Amy Hillier tracked the actual routes that Philadelphia school kids took to and from school and the *food opportunities* they experienced. The results were eye opening. The average student in her study encountered more than 20 food opportunities, most of which were corner stores where they could convert one dollar into a bag of chips and a soda that gave them 200 calories, filled with saturated fats and sugar (Figure 5.4).[21]

The food desert approach to the nutritional problems faced by low-income Americans provides a means of addressing issues of food insecurity while acknowledging that the issue is no longer just insufficient food, but the types of food available. It also opens up a number of policy alternatives that could supplement the traditional approach of reducing the cost of food for poor people. Supermarket initiatives, community gardens, and other fresh food initiatives will be discussed later in this chapter.

---

[18]Mari Gallagher Research and Consulting Group, "Examining the Impact of Food Deserts on Public Health in Chicago" (Chicago: Mari Gallagher, 2006), http://www.marigallagher.com/site_media/dynamic/project_files/1_ChicagoFoodDesertReport-Full_.pdf.

[19]Mari Gallagher Research and Consulting Group "Examining the Impact of Food Deserts on Public Health in Detroit" (Chicago: Mari Gallagher, 2007), http://www.marigallagher.com/site_media/dynamic/project_files/1_DetroitFoodDesertReport_Full.pdf.

[20]Economic Research Service, "Access to Affordable and Nutritious Food—Measuring and Understanding Food Deserts and Their Consequences: Report to Congress," June 2009, http://www.ers.usda.gov/publications/ap-administrative-publication/ap-036.aspx.

[21]Amy Hillier and Stella Volope, "Fed-up with Childhood Obesity: The Things Kids Eat on Their Way to and from School," in *The Shape of Philadelphia,*. ed. Cartographic Modeling Lab (Philadelphia: CML, 2009), http://works.bepress.com/amy_hillier/28.

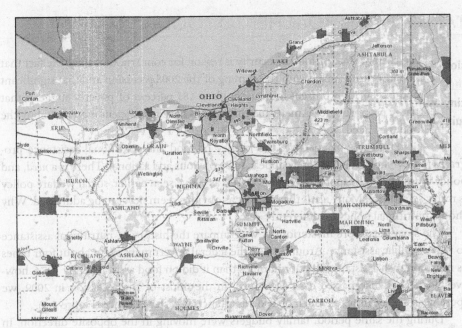

Figure 5.3
Census Tracts with Low Income and Low Access to Food in North Ohio, 2010
Rural areas often suffer from both low food security and low access to food.

Source: United States Department of Agriculture, Food Desert Locator, http://www.ers.usda.gov/data-products/food-desert-locator/go-to-the-locator.aspx.

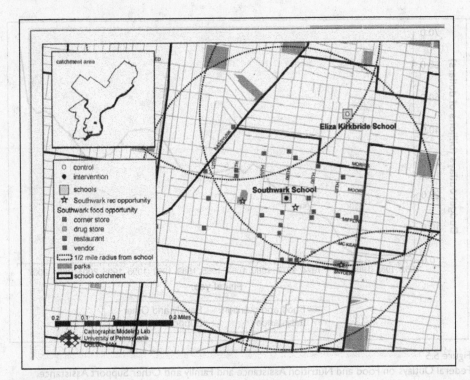

Figure 5.4
Food Access Near Several Public Schools in South Philadelphia
Food access in many urban neighborhoods is restricted to corner stores that are more likely to stock junk food than fresh fruits and vegetables.

Unpublished map created by Amy Hillier, University of Pennsylvania.

TARGETED APPROACHES TO FOOD

The current state of food insecurity is reason for concern. Certainly, the fact that food insecurity spiked with the coming of the 2008 recession and that significant food insecurity is present in households at 185 percent of poverty suggests that a large proportion of Americans continue to have insufficient income to buy the food they need.

From this perspective, the history of food and nutritional assistance programs for low-income people may appear to be obvious and rational. There is a *need*, and policy is designed to respond to that need. Yet, as we've seen earlier, social welfare policy is rarely so rational. Many *needs* that are just as obvious seem never to be addressed. Why should nutritional policy be different?

The story gets more mysterious if we compare the history of nutritional assistance to that of public assistance. Around 1970, the federal government spent about four times as much on cash assistance to poor families than it did on food assistance. By 1974, however, food assistance passed cash assistance. In the midst of the recession in 2009, we spent nearly three times as much on food assistance as cash assistance (Figure 5.5).

During the same period, family budgets were moving in the opposite direction. In 1960, 24 percent of average expenditures were spent on food and 30 percent on housing. By 2008, the figures were 13 and 34 percent respectively. As food has become cheaper

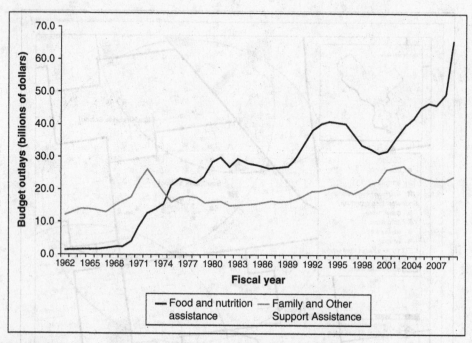

Figure 5.5

Federal Outlays on Food and Nutrition Assistance and Family and Other Support Assistance, 1962–2009

Thanks to the support of farm-state legislators, food assistance has grown while cash assistance stagnated since the 1960s.

Based on Office of Management and Budget, "Historical Tables: Budget of the US Government," http://www.whitehouse.gov/sites/default/files/omb/budget/fy2013/assets/hist.pdf.

relative to other goods, we have been willing to spend more to ensure low-income families' access to it.[22]

The answer to this puzzle lies in the combination of politics and institutional structures. The same institutional players that structured farm policy to benefit the industrialization of agriculture also supported the expansion of cheap food, including the slow but steady expansion of nutritional assistance. While this has increased low-income people's access to food—clearly a good thing—it has created a large split between food assistance and other ways that we support low-income people. In 2009, we spent more on food assistance than we did on the two largest cash programs for families with children—TANF and EITC—combined.

Supplemental Nutritional Assistance Program (SNAP)

When food stamps were first implemented, they really were stamps or coupons. During the last years of the Great Depression and World War II, the federal government implemented the first food stamps program. Eligible families could buy orange stamps at their face value (a dollar for a dollar), and they would receive a 50 percent bonus in blue stamps (50 cents for each dollar of orange stamps). At its peak, the first food stamps program served four million Americans, but with the coming of full employment—and Republican successes in the 1942 midterm elections—the program, along with many other New Deal programs, came to an end in 1943.[23]

The idea of targeted food assistance then languished for almost two decades. Although Congress authorized the USDA to operate a new food stamps program in 1959, the Eisenhower administration never used this authority. It was only during the Kennedy administration that a new pilot program was put in place in 1961 and then made permanent by Congress in 1964.

From their beginning, food stamps have led a charmed life compared to other anti-poverty programs. Administered by the USDA, food stamps legislation has often been embedded in the horse-trading over farm bills. This type of horse-trading provided food stamps with political support—and at times political cover—not enjoyed by other programs serving the same population.[24] For example, the expansion of food stamps in the 1970 authorization bill was the result of a collaboration of George McGovern (the Democrats' 1972 nominee for president) and Bob Dole (who would be nominated by the Republicans for vice president in 1976 and for president in 1996).[25]

This political resilience explains why welfare reform, which eliminated the entitlement of poor families to public assistance in 1995 and 1996, left food stamps relatively unchanged. Although efforts to balance the budget in the late 1990s did limit food stamp expansion for a time, during the 2000s the program has steadily expanded. The horse-trading that protected food stamps, however, may be less effective than it once was. During 2012, Congressional Republicans proposed a $33 billion cut in the program over the coming decade. A coalition of Democrats and more moderate Republicans defeated the proposal but approved a $16.5 billion cut.[26]

---

[22]"Consumer Expenditure Survey," Bureau of Labor Statistics, http://www.bls.gov/cex/tables.htm.

[23]"A History of Food Stamps Use and Policy," *New York Times*, http://www.nytimes.com/interactive/2010/02/11/us/FOODSTAMPS.html.

[24]David G. Abler, "Vote Trading on Farm Legislation in the U.S. House," *American Journal of Agricultural Economics* 71, vol. 2 (August 1989): 583–591.

[25]Dole Institute, "Food Stamps," http://www.doleinstitute.org/archives/wordsFoodStamp.html.

[26]Ron Nixon, "Split Among House Republicans Over How Deeply to Cut May Delay Farm Bill," *New York Times*, July 12, 2012, http://www.nytimes.com/2012/07/13/us/politics/house-agriculture-committee-agrees-on-farm-bill.html/.

Who is eligible for SNAP?

SNAP is a selective program with both income and resource eligibility requirements. If all members of a household receive TANF, SSI, or (usually) General Assistance, the household will qualify for SNAP. Otherwise, if a household's gross income is below 130 percent of its poverty threshold, it is eligible for SNAP. In 2010, this translated into an annual income of $28,668. A household is defined as a group of people who live together and purchase and prepare meals together. In some instances, a group of people who might be considered a single household by the Census Bureau—because they share one dwelling unit—might be considered more than one household for SNAP because they don't purchase or prepare meals together.

In addition to the gross-income test, applicants must pass a net-income test that makes a number of deductions and adjustments to income, like child support, high medical costs, and higher-than-average shelter costs.

Since 1996, "able-bodied adults without dependents" who do not work or participate in an employment or training program can receive SNAP only for three months during a three-year period. However, the American Recovery and Reinvestment Act of 2009 eliminated this limit from April 2009 through September 2010.

Historically, most food stamp recipients were eligible for cash public assistance as well. When Congress reformed public assistance in 1996, however, the number of people eligible for food stamps but NOT eligible for cash assistance grew. This, in turn, led to a decline in the proportion of eligible households that actually received food stamps. The high unemployment of 2009 led to an explosion in the number of households with no income other than food stamps. At the recession's low point, six million Americans received food stamps but no other government benefit. As the *New York Times* reported on January 2, 2010, this represented a 50 percent increase in the number of households in this situation.[27]

Unfortunately, this tells only half the story. Because millions of Americans are eligible for SNAP but for no other assistance program, a large number of families that would benefit from the program are not enrolled. Although local governments and nonprofits have sought to redress the problem, many eligible families still receive no food stamps.

Finally, immigrants were largely excluded from SNAP by the 1996 welfare reform law. However, rules around immigrant eligibility for food stamps have changed several times since then. The 2002 authorization allows legal immigrants to receive SNAP if they have lived in the United States for five years or are receiving disability assistance. In addition, there is no longer a waiting period for children.

SNAP benefits

SNAP benefits consist of an allotment that can be used for the purchase of American-produced food products. Originally, food stamps were distributed as coupons that could be used like cash. Now, the allotment is usually distributed as an electronic benefit transfer (EBT) in the form of a debit card.

Benefits are tied to size of household. As discussed earlier, the SNAP definition of a household differs from that used by the Census Bureau because it includes information on the number of people who purchase and prepare food together. The impact of this definition is to increase the number of households and decrease the size of households.

[27]Jason DeParle and Robert M. Gebeloff, "Living on Nothing but Food Stamps," *New York Times*, January 2, 2010, http://www.nytimes.com/2010/01/03/us/03foodstamp.html.

About the Benefit Bank

The Benefit Bank is owned and operated by Solutions for Progress, Inc.

Billions of dollars in public funds go untouched each year because applying for state and federal benefits such as food stamps or Medicaid is confusing, intimidating, time consuming, or embarrassing. Additional billions in tax credits are also left unclaimed due to lack of knowledge. The Benefit Bank removes these obstacles—bringing people closer to stability and closer to self-sufficiency.

The Benefit Bank (TBB) is a web-based service that simplifies and centralizes the process of applying for many state and federal benefits for low- and moderate-income individuals and families. Through its eligibility screening tool, TBB can ensure that people are fully aware of the benefits to which they are entitled and, as an expert system, it helps maximize the benefits and tax refunds they can secure. The "one-stop shop" concept of TBB reduces the amount of time needed to apply for benefits. Further, the information a person enters is stored securely, so an individual who wishes to reapply for benefits, apply for new benefits, or file future tax returns simply needs to enter his or her user-name and password to initiate this new action.

The Benefit Bank is a free service. No consumer can be charged for using TBB. TBB is free for use by host organizations. If a TBB site provides counselor candidates, a computer, a printer, Internet access, and a phone in a setting that is respectful and private, then they can use The Benefit Bank. From the start TBB has been structured to ensure the privacy and confidentiality of all client data.

Developed for use by a wide range of community-based, faith-based, governmental, job-training, health care or social service agencies, The Benefit Bank can be part of a community-wide response to poverty. TBB not only provides the opportunity to help neigh-bors but also provides information for organizations to more effectively advocate for policies that better serve their communities. An innovative public-private partnership of state-local governments and a broad, statewide coalition committed to helping neighbors move towards self-sufficiency by utilizing The Benefit Bank have resulted in tens of millions of dollars being returned each year to low- and moderate-income individuals and families.

http://www.thebenefitbank.com/About, accessed January 6, 2012.

For example, a single mother and child living with her parents would be considered one household by the Census Bureau but might be defined as two households if the mother reported that she purchases and prepares food separately from her parents.

In addition to the eligibility standards, SNAP benefits are reduced by 30 percent for each dollar of net monthly income. For example, if a four-person household has a net monthly income of $1,154, its allotment would be reduced by $346, from the maximum of $668 to $321.[28]

SNAP administration and financing
SNAP is administered by the Food and Nutritional Service (FNS) agency of the USDA. State agencies carry out most administrative tasks associated with the program, including determining eligibility, with the FNS covering a majority of the states' administrative costs.

SNAP is an entitlement funded by the federal government. During the efforts to reduce the deficit in the 1990s, the USDA was required to report to Congress if the total cost of food stamps exceeded the amount appropriated for it. However, this requirement was never exercised and subsequently dropped.

[28]American Recovery and Reinvestment Act of 2009, US Department of Agriculture, http://www.fns.usda.gov/fns/recovery/recovery-snap.htm.

The FNS carries out an extensive program of outreach and nutritional education associated with its programs. In the past, Congress has sometimes restricted the USDA's funding for these efforts. Currently, the FNS pays 50 percent of the administrative costs of outreach efforts by state agencies.

Women, Infants, and Children (WIC)

WIC is a supplemental food program for pregnant women, new mothers, and their children. Its goal is to ensure adequate nutrition for these particularly vulnerable populations.[29]

WIC eligibility

In order to receive WIC, one must meet four types of requirements: categorical, residential, income, and nutritional risk.

- *Categorical*—Recipients must be pregnant, postpartum (up to six months after giving birth), breastfeeding (up to the infant's first birthday), and have an infant under the age of one or a child under the age of five.
- *Residential*—Applicants must be a resident of the state in which one applies. In some states, applicants are required to live in a particular service area and apply at a WIC clinic serving that area. There is no length-of-residency requirement.
- *Income*—States set their own income standard for WIC. However, it can be no lower than the federal poverty threshold and no higher than 185 percent of the poverty threshold. Generally, women and children who are already receiving SNAP, TANF, or Medicaid are automatically eligible for WIC.
- *Nutritional risk*—Applicants must be examined by a health professional (physician, nurse, or nutritionist) to determine if they are at nutritional risk. Nutritional risk means that "an individual has medical-based or dietary-based conditions. Examples of medical-based conditions include anemia (low blood levels), underweight, or history of poor pregnancy outcome. A dietary-based condition includes, for example, a poor diet."

During most the 1990s and early 2000s, seven to eight million individuals were enrolled in WIC, including around two million infants, three to four million children, and one to two million women. During the recession of 2007–10, this number spiked. In April 2008, 9.5 million women and children were enrolled in the program. Average monthly participation remained above nine million through 2009. During this period, approximately three-quarters of eligible infants but only 40 to 50 percent of one- to five-year-olds were enrolled in the program.

WIC benefits

Those women and children found eligible for WIC can receive the WIC food package consisting of "a wider variety of foods including fruits and vegetables and whole grains." Eligible foods include breakfast and infant cereals, "baby food" (fruits, vegetables, and meat), infant formula, milk and cheese, tofu and soy-based beverages,

---

[29]Information on WIC can be found at "WIC Eligibility Requirements," USDA Food and Nutrition Service, http://www.fns.usda.gov/wic/howtoapply/eligibilityrequirements.htm.

fruits, vegetables, legumes, canned fish, whole grains and whole-grain bread, juice, and eggs.[30]

Benefits are distributed in a variety of ways. Historically, recipients would literally receive a monthly food package including a standard set of items. Later, in many states, the program was shifted to vouchers that recipients could redeem at eligible food outlets. Increasingly, WIC is now included in EBT, although the restrictions on types and amounts of food pose a challenge for EBT implementation.

WIC administration and financing

Unlike SNAP, WIC is not an entitlement. The FNS administers a grant program for states, sets minimum requirements, and monitors compliance, but the bulk of WIC administration is done by state agencies and local clinics.

School-Based Nutritional Programs

The USDA administers three school-based nutritional programs:

- National School Lunch Program (NSLP)—provides free and subsidized lunches to eligible students
- School Breakfast Program—provides breakfast
- Free Milk Program

The NSLP, the largest of the three, was created by the National School Lunch Act of 1946. Within a year, more than seven million children were receiving subsidized lunches through the program. By 2007, more than 30 million children were receiving free or reduced-rate lunches, at a cost of $9.3 billion.

Eligibility for NSLP is broader than for SNAP. Children with family income below 130 percent of poverty qualify for free lunches, while those between 130 and 185 percent of poverty qualify for reduced-rate lunches.

In recent years, questions have been raised about the cost-effectiveness of the program's administration. During the Bush administration, concerns were raised that many children received free or reduced-rate lunches even though their families did not qualify. The USDA initiated efforts to ensure that children who did not meet the income limits were excluded from the program. In addition, states were required to undertake direct certification of children who were TANF or SNAP recipients. Although direct certification increased the number of children enrolled in NSLP, it picks up only about half of children who qualify for subsidized lunches.

At the same time, others have pointed to the School District of Philadelphia's Universal Feeding program. Under Universal Feeding, schools with very high proportions of eligible students receive free lunches for the entire student body, without the need for individual applications and review. Given the high concentration of children who qualify for free or subsidized lunches in urban districts, Universal Feeding advocates argue blanket eligibility for entire schools could save money and feed more children by reducing the considerable time and paperwork required to establish eligibility.

Policy Practice

Practice Behavior Example: Know the history and current structures of social policies and services, the role of policy in service delivery, and the role of practice in policy development.

Critical Thinking Question: Historically, governments have limited access to social benefits by increasing the paperwork required. What lessons can social workers draw from the Universal Feeding program about how they can make a program more efficient and more effective?

[30]"Benefits & Services: WIC Food Packages," USDA Food and Nutrition Service, http://www.fns.usda. gov/wic/benefitsandservices/foodpkg.HTM.

COMMUNITY-BASED AND ALTERNATIVE APPROACHES TO FOOD AND NUTRITION

Assess your comprehension of "Community-Based and Alternative Approaches to Food and Nutrition" by completing this quiz.

Food and nutritional policy in the United States, from one perspective, has led a charmed life. While virtually every other field covered in this text has faced mounting pressure to cut benefits and reduce eligibility, the amount that the federal government spends on food and nutritional assistance continues to grow.

Food and nutrition are different largely due to the political coalitions that have supported program expansion. In addition to the—typically liberal—interest groups that support most welfare expansion, food and nutritional programs have won support from important interests in the food industry. Moreover, rural political actors, including influential US senators, have consistently supported program expansion, even as their usual political allies on the Right have voiced skepticism about the extent of food insecurity in the United States.

Still, though food and nutrition seem to be the model of policy success, all is not well. The nature of the political coalitions that have supported program expansion mean that current policy has not addressed a number of important issues. On the supply side, the nature of industrial agriculture, the safety of current practices, and the threats of the system to the environment and the nation's health have largely been sidestepped. From the consumption side, the spread of obesity and other health conditions, including diabetes and cardiac disease, associated with the American diet have likely been made worse by food policy. The fact that low-income Americans are the most common victims of food-associated illness underlines the significant policy issues posed by the current system.

Yet, as the successes of food and nutritional policy have prevented a reexamination of some of its assumptions, the past several decades have witnessed ferment at the local level. Grassroots social movements and ordinary citizens seek to challenge existing practices and develop alternative ways of promoting sustainable food systems and more healthy approaches to food.

Emergency Feeding Programs

Despite the expansion of food and nutritional programs, a significant proportion of the population continues to experience high food insecurity. More broadly, cuts in other program areas have stimulated philanthropic and religious concern for the well-being of poor people. This concern for the poor is often expressed in the proliferation of a variety of voluntary feeding programs.

The largest national network of emergency feeding programs, Feeding America (FA), had 205 certified members in 2010. These programs include several types of services:

- *Food banks*—charitable organizations that solicit, receive, and distribute food to agencies that directly aid clients
- *Partner distribution organizations*—charitable organizations that serve as intermediaries between larger food banks and agencies that directly aid clients
- *Food rescue organizations*—organizations that gather prepared and perishable foods from supermarkets, distributors, restaurants, and other food service organizations
- *Agencies and food programs*—charitable organizations that distribute food directly to clients[31]

---

[31]"Feeding America," http://feedingamerica.org.

Among food programs, we distinguish between nonemergency programs directed at special populations, like children or seniors, and emergency programs. The three common emergency program types are: emergency food pantries that distribute non-prepared foods, emergency soup kitchens that provide prepared meals, and emergency shelters that provide shelter and meals to temporary residents.[32]

According to a 2009 survey of the FA network, affiliated organizations served 37 million people, an increase of nearly 50 percent since 2005. Seventy percent of people served were below the federal poverty line and 75 percent had been food insecure at some point during the previous year.

Most emergency food programs are operated by faith-based organizations and staffed by volunteers. The 2009 survey found that 93 percent of pantries, 87 percent of kitchens, and 72 percent of shelters surveyed were dependent on volunteers. A significant number—including 68 percent of pantries and 42 percent of kitchens—were entirely dependent upon volunteers.[33]

By and large, emergency food programs are viewed as providing an important service to a very needy stratum of society, reducing waste (through food rescue operations), and fostering a spirit of service to individuals and communities. However, some commentators have suggested that their service is essentially symbolic rather than being of real practical use to poor people, while others have raised questions about whether they seek to manage rather than alleviate food insecurity.[34] Sociologist Janet Poppendieck went a step further, arguing that food banks serve many community needs, but not necessarily those of the hungry.

What I have found in seven years of studying the growth and institutionalization of the emergency food system is that emergency food has become very useful indeed.... The United States Department of Agriculture uses it to reduce the accumulation of...agricultural surpluses. Business uses it to dispose of...unwanted product, to...avoid dump fees,...and to accrue tax savings.... Churches use it to express their concern for the least of their brethren.... Environmentalists use it to reduce the solid waste stream.... A wide array of groups, organizations, and institutions benefits from the halo effect of "feeding the hungry."...If we didn't have hunger, we'd have to invent it.[35]

Although emergency food programs mobilize important resources directed at low-income Americans, the intellectual underpinnings are often a traditional view of charity in which issues of the character of the American food system and social justice are largely ignored.

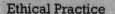

Ethical Practice

Practice Behavior Example: Tolerate ambiguity in resolving ethical conflicts.

Critical Thinking Question: Who benefits from emergency food programs? How should social workers respond to the ambiguity in the distribution of these benefits?

---

[32]James Mabli, Rhoda Cohen, Frank Potter, and Zhanyun Zhao, *Hunger in America 2010: National Report Prepared for Feeding America* (Washington, DC: Mathematica Policy Research, 2010), 9–12, http://feedingamerica.issuelab.org/research/listing/hunger_in_america_2010_national_report.

[33]Mabli, Cohen, Poter, and Zhao, *Hunger in America 2010*, 4–5.

[34]Valerie Tarasuka, Joan M. Eakin. "Charitable Food Assistance as Symbolic Gesture: An Ethnographic Study of Food Banks in Ontario," *Social Science & Medicine* 56 (2003): 1505–1515; Mark Winne, "Outlook: The Futility of Food Banks: Generosity of Donors and Volunteers Hasn't Addressed Underlying Problem—Poverty," *Washington Post*, November 19, 2007, http://www.washingtonpost.com/wp-dyn/content/discussion/2007/11/16/DI2007111601442.html; Mark Winne, *Closing the Food Gap* (Boston: Beacon Press, 2008).

[35]Quoted in Mark Winne, Closing the Food Gap (Boston: Beacon Press, 2008), 77; Janet Poppendieck, *Sweet Charity?: Emergency Food and the End of Entitlement* (New York: Penguin Books, 1999).

Community Food Security

An alternative approach to feeding programs focuses on the concept of community food security. Where much government and voluntary action has been focused on individuals and households, the advocates of community food security believe a comprehensive approach must examine how production, distribution, and consumption systems work to ensure adequate nutrition for the entire community.

A variety of efforts have spun off from this emphasis on local and metropolitan food systems. A new emphasis on urban agriculture, for example, has taken a variety of forms, from futuristic ideas of turning green roofs into farms to tiny community gardening plots on vacant land in low-income communities.[36] *Community supported agriculture* (CSA)—in which urban dwellers "subscribe" for part of the product of a local farm—is one way to link urban dwellers with fresh food and provide needed cash for farmers. Advocates also argue that community gardening affords a more effective way of pursuing nutritional education than typical classroom approaches.

For example, Weavers Way, a Philadelphia food cooperative, started a set of community programs that include farm education based at the co-op's urban farm at a local arboretum and a vegetable garden at a local homeless shelter. They also run a variety of marketplace programs in partnership with area schools that use urban agriculture as a way to teach students about collaboration, democratic decision-making, and running a small business.[37]

If emergency feeding can be criticized for lack of social justice rhetoric, community food security advocates can be challenged on the grounds that their democratic efforts don't necessarily include low-income residents. CSA arrangements, in which urban families make a lump-sum payment at the beginning of the growing season and receive produce during the summer and fall, are unlikely to be of interest to cash-strapped families. Indeed, a study of California CSA members found that they were overwhelmingly white, educated, and middle- or upper-income.[38]

POLICY PRACTICE: USING UNIVERSAL FEEDING TO REDUCE RED TAPE AND INCREASE ACCESS

As we noted in Chapter 1, income-test "selective" programs require program administrators to devote significant resources to verifying eligibility. Typically, this is justified to ensure that benefits are targeted to the truly needy and that only eligible individuals receive aid.

But eligibility procedures can have a number of negative effects. Most obviously, they reduce the amount of funding available to provide benefits. In essence, the program can become a way of funding administrative staff rather than providing benefits to needy families. Furthermore, involved administrative procedures can discourage eligible families from applying because it is too time-consuming, too intrusive, and too stigmatizing.

The downside of eligibility procedures raised questions about the USDA's School Lunch program, especially in poor American cities. In many cities, like Philadelphia, virtually all public school students may be eligible for subsidized or free breakfast and lunch.

---

[36]Michael Nairn and Domenic Vitiello, "Lush Lots: Everyday Urban Agriculture: From Community Gardening to Community Food Security," *Harvard Design Magazine* 31 (Fall/Winter 2009/10).

[37]Weavers Way Community Programs, nd., "The Next Crop Starts with You," pamphlet.

[38]Allen, "Reweaving the Food Security Safety Net."

Does it make sense to devote huge amounts of time and staff to determining individual eligibility when the ultimate cost of those requirements is to leave many eligible children without benefits?

The School District of Philadelphia didn't think so. As a result, during the 1990s it worked with the USDA to develop a Universal Feeding program that treated all students as eligible if they attend a school with a high proportion of low-income students. The following brief from The Reinvestment Fund reports on the effort.

Test your understanding and analysis of this chapter by completing the Chapter Review.

Capital at the point of impact.

National School Meals Program:
Increasing Efficiency and Access

The Reinvestment Fund (TRF) recently completed a study for the School District of Philadelphia that estimates the percentage of students that are income-eligible for free or reduced-price lunches in each of its schools. With the results of the report, the School District will be able to reevaluate and improve its school lunch program.

The traditional method for determining income-eligibility for the free or reduced-price lunch program is to collect applications from students. These applications must then be evaluated for income-eligibility and a portion must be validated by District officials, including principals, teachers, and support. In Philadelphia, this added unnecessarily to over-burdened School District staff, as well as to the paperwork required from parents and the stigma of being identified as the "poor student."

Through a unique partnership with the U.S. Department of Agriculture (USDA), the School District of Philadelphia will designate many of its schools as free for all students, without requiring the collection or processing of applications. While the School District provides free meals to all students in these schools, the USDA reimburses the School District according to the number of income-eligible students.

This pioneering approach, started in Philadelphia in the early 1990s, ensures that the maximum number of students benefit from free or reduced-price meals and removes the stigma children often experience because they receive free lunches. It has also proved to be much more cost-effective than the application process common across the nation.

This method of feeding students under the National School Lunch Program has made the School District of Philadelphia's lunch program more efficient, more equitable, and more cost-effective. While Philadelphia is the first city with this program, the USDA may consider allowing other school districts to implement similar programs. The initiative's success in Philadelphia has led other cities to explore with TRF the possibility of implementing similar studies in their school districts.

Study Design
In 1991, the School District of Philadelphia commissioned a study for its pilot universal feeding program. The study was updated in 1994 and again this year. To deliver a high-quality product, TRF brought together a team of professionals that offered expertise in: study design and statistical consultation, public outreach and marketing, survey design and interviewing, and research and information. TRF's Director of Policy and Information Services, Ira Goldstein, Ph. D., was a principal on the pilot study in 1991. This year, Dr. Goldstein led the analysis, applying his knowledge of the program and his widely-recognized expertise in statistical analysis to the project. The team worked directly with the School District of Philadelphia, the Pennsylvania Department of Education, and the U.S. Department of Agriculture.

The School District of Philadelphia identified students who were automatically qualified for free lunches by matching student records to state public assistance and food stamp records. Previous studies suggest that schools with a high percentage of students that are automatically qualified for free meals (directly certified) have higher percentages of students income-eligible for free or reduced-price lunches. This observation, coupled with the desire to obtain the most precise and statistically reliable estimates of income-eligibility, led to the use of a stratified sample design.

This map shows the residential location of sampled households, distinguished by their participation in the telephone survey only or in both the telephone survey and validation survey.

Figure 5.6
National School Meals Program: Increasing Efficiency and Access
Universal feeding programs, like that implemented in Philadelphia, promise to increase food security and reduce administrative costs.
Source: The Reinvestment Fund, www.trfund.com/resource/downloads/.../SchoolLunch_Summary.pdf

A stratified random sampling process led to the selection of nearly 2,000 students, representative of the approximately 102,000 active on-roll but non-directly certified students in the District. Random samples of the non-directly certified households were drawn from each stratum. Those households were surveyed by telephone and categorized in terms of their income and household size. Based on this, students were categorized as income-eligible for free lunch, income-eligible for reduced price lunch, or not income-eligible for either.

What distinguishes our effort from the previous studies of 1991 and 1994 is an income validation component. In this study, households with reported incomes below 250% of poverty were encouraged to provide interviewers documentation to support their reported income. They were offered an incentive to participate and told that interviewers would meet with them at any convenient location. The purpose of this effort was to understand the extent to which the telephone survey gives answers that are representative of those that would be derived through this alternative method of data collection. The results obtained from both samples were remarkably similar.

Outreach

Because the integrity of our analysis depended on the participation of as many students in our sample as possible, we made a great effort to reach out to the community to encourage participation. A letter from the CEO of the School District of Philadelphia preceded any contact with households; so too did a variety of public education and outreach efforts designed to raise the level of comfort and voluntary cooperation. Taken together, we believe these efforts maximized both overall participation and uniform participation across racial, ethnic and demographic groups.

Efficiency and Access

The universal feeding program in Philadelphia is receiving national attention. The approach is saving the city's school district time and money, while maximizing the number of students benefiting from the National School Lunch Program. All students in schools with universal feeding are benefiting, including students whose family incomes may have been just above the qualification level. TRF's analysis in Philadelphia provides the foundation to realize these benefits.

Our Team

Shirley Robinson Watkins, M.ED, FCSI, will work with district, local, state, and federal officials to help them understand and implement universal feeding. Ms. Watkins is a food service consultant and the principal founder of SR Watkins & Associates, where she leads her firm's efforts in School Nutrition Strategic Business Issues. Ms. Watkins was formerly the USDA Under Secretary for Food, Nutrition and Consumer Services, prior to which, she was Deputy Assistant Secretary for Marketing and Regulatory Programs. In 1993 she joined USDA as the Deputy Assistant Secretary for Food, Nutrition and Consumer Services. Prior to that, she Directed the award-winning Nutrition Services program in Memphis, Tennessee. In 1988-1989, Ms. Watkins served as President of the 60,000 members American School Food Service Association (now School Nutrition Association).

MYRO Associates, LLC will play an active role, primarily in coordination with the school district and publicizing the study to maximize representative participation. MYRO Associates is a management consulting partnership focusing on school business operations and specializing in school food service. Tom McGlinchy, Partner, was Director of Food Services for the School District of Philadelphia f from 1986 to 1996, Executive Director of Facilities Management and Services from 1996 to 1999 and Managing Director/Chief Operating Officer at the time of his retirement from the District. Eric Shapiro, Partner, spent eleven years with the District's Procurement Office and later was the Assistant Director of Food Services for Administration, Executive Director of Facilities Management of Services and Director of Operations for Charter Schools/EMOs during his tenure with the District. Eric Shapiro and Tom McGlinchy coauthored and designed the original Paperwork Reduction and Alternatives for Meal Counting Pilot Program in 1989. Tom and Eric are intimately familiar with the requirements of the National School Lunch Program and the operations of school foodservice programs.

About TRF

Established in 1985, The Reinvestment Fund's mission is to build wealth and opportunity for low-wealth people and places through the promotion of socially and environmentally responsible development. TRF achieves its mission by making loans and equity investments; by applying high quality market analysis to distressed areas, and by providing development services to nonprofit, government, and for-profit partners. TRF manages $484 million in assets from over 850 investors and is recognized as a national leader and innovator in neighborhood and economic development. We have invested over $790 million in the mid-Atlantic region.

To learn more about TRF's analysis, contact:
Cathy Califano
The Reinvestment Fund
718 Arch Street, Suite 300N
Philadelphia, PA 19106
Tel: 215.574.5831
Email: cathy.califano@trfund.com

Figure 5.6
Continued

6

Housing and Community Development

CHAPTER OUTLINE

INTRODUCTION

We know that people are influenced by their environment. When social workers make this observation, they usually are speaking about a person's social and emotional environment. But the statement is just as true with respect to one's physical environment.

In this chapter, we examine two dimensions of the physical environment and how they influence social welfare. First, we discuss housing policy. Shelter is one of the basic needs of people, but of course housing is more than shelter alone. Housing is an important policy field that is strangely invisible. Few people think of their housing choices as being determined by government policy, but they are. Public policy has a variety of programs that influence most of the population and a smaller set of policies directed at low-income families. We then examine the problem of homelessness and the way public policy has responded to it.

Next, we discuss community place-based policies. Community development is directed at improving the quality of life in neighborhoods, especially low-income urban neighborhoods. Many of these policies have their origins in the War on Poverty, when community-based interventions were believed to be the key to ending poverty in the United States. Since the 1960s, although aspirations have been tempered, community development corporations (CDCs) and other community-based programs continue to make a difference in urban neighborhoods.

HOUSING

Two generations ago, Americans spent a third of their income on food and a sixth on housing. Today, the proportions have been reversed. Even as the quality of shelter has improved, the search for affordable housing has become a challenge to a larger proportion of the population.[1]

Assess your comprehension of "Housing" by completing this quiz.

Public policy has made a huge contribution to improving the housing options open to most Americans. However, a large and growing proportion of households face a yawning affordability gap between their ability to pay for housing and its cost. In contrast to food, where SNAP has provided a federal entitlement to nutritional aid for low-income Americans, the United States has no entitlement to shelter. Those programs that provide rental assistance are limited by funding caps that allow them to serve only a fraction of eligible families.

The Social and Economic Meaning of Housing

Housing serves many roles in Americans' social welfare. At a most basic level, it provides shelter against the elements and provides a place for humans to rest, socialize, and work. In this respect, housing in the United States shares much with the issue of shelter for people around the world.

Housing, however, has additional meaning in the United States that complicates its social welfare function. Housing—and home ownership in particular—have emerged as a major element of Americans' strategy for *wealth creation*. Through much of American history, families have viewed property ownership as a hedge against an impoverished old age. Indeed, through much of the twentieth century, home ownership was more common among households headed by the elderly than those headed by younger adults. Only after World War II did this pattern change as new mortgage instruments and public policy encouraged home ownership among younger families (Figure 6.1).[2]

Since World War II, the expansion of home ownership has continued to serve as the cornerstone of most families' wealth-creation strategies. Seventy-two percent of American families in 2010 had no significant assets other than their home. As these assets became more liquid with the introduction of home equity loans and reverse mortgages, property became a means of financing a college education or a more comfortable retirement.

Just as importantly, property ownership became a badge of honor for many Americans, a sign that they had achieved a level of independence and decency. When Eli Chinoy interviewed automobile workers during the 1950s, he found that the drive for autonomy—represented by small business and home ownership—was the key aspiration of his informants.[3] Owning one's own home freed one from the control and intrusions of a landlord and marked a family as stable and trustworthy.

This layering of meanings—shelter, asset, and honor—has driven much of housing policy in the United States. Yet, it has been a combustible mixture. Efforts to expand home ownership have run up against countercurrents, including discrimination on the

---

[1]Bureau of Labor Statistics, "Consumer Expenditure Survey," http://www.bls.gov/cex/.

[2]Mark J. Stern, "The Un(credit)worthy Poor: Historical Perspectives on Policies to Expand Assets and Credit," in *Assets for the Poor: The Benefits of Spreading Asset Ownership,* eds. Thomas M. Shapiro and Edward N. Wolff (New York: Russell Sage Foundation, 2001), 269–301.

[3]Eli Chinoy, *Automobile Workers and the American Dream* (Boston: Beacon Press, 1955).

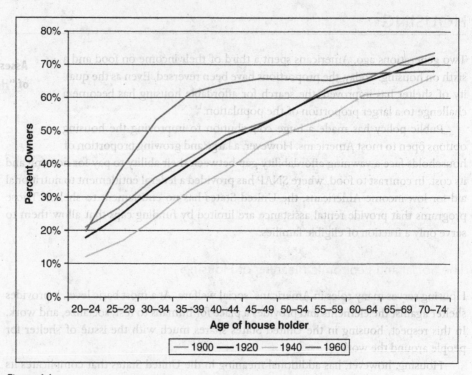

Figure 6.1
Property-Ownership Status of Householder, by Age, 1900–1960
Until the 1960s, young adults rarely owned their home. Increased access to mortgage financing led to increasing homeownership during the years after World War II.

Source: Author's calculations from Steven Ruggles, J. Trent Alexander, Katie Genadek, Ronald Goeken, Matthew B. Schroeder, and Matthew Sobek, Integrated Public Use Microdata Series: Version 5.0 [Machine-readable database] (Minneapolis: University of Minnesota, 2010).

part of lenders (at times, the federal government) and the lag of average wages over the past generation. In addition, while the importance of home ownership has inspired a variety of public policies to make it accessible, by limiting aid to renters, housing policy has also played a role in reinforcing a dimension of *duality* in the social welfare system.

This section focuses on public policies that influence the access and affordability of housing in the United States. Most Americans are only vaguely aware of how these affect them because the most important one—the mortgage interest tax expenditure—tends to be viewed more as a right than a policy. Yet, the economic crisis of 2008 played a certain *consciousness-raising* role in this regard, because policies toward mortgage access and how the private sector used those policies were largely responsible for the crisis.

In contrast, public policy toward renters, particularly the availability of subsidized rental housing, has highlighted the role of public policy in the most unflattering light. The widespread view of public housing as a catastrophe has undermined progressive social policies in this sector and contributed to the stigmatization of low-income people and their advocates.

American's negative view of public housing and the resulting limits on low-income rent subsidies have also played a role in the third element of housing policy: homelessness. One of the more remarkable elements of contemporary social welfare policy has been its accommodation to a widespread homeless population. Two generations ago, homelessness was identified as a social problem that needed to be eliminated. Today, for the most part, it is viewed as inevitable and "natural"—a problem to be managed, not eliminated. Fortunately, in recent years, we have seen renewed efforts to divert more families and individuals who are at risk of becoming homeless into permanent housing, although the reach of these efforts remains limited.

Two economic principles play an important role in explaining the challenges of housing policy. First, land—the stuff on which housing is inevitably located—is a rather unique economic entity. Although in the United States we treat land as a *commodity* that can be bought and sold, several features differentiate land from other commodities with which we are concerned. Second, in many cases, property ownership is a *positional good*; that is, expansion of its supply has a tendency to degrade its quality. We need to take a moment to explain these issues before we can make sense of current housing policy.

Land: A False Commodity

For home ownership to be possible, land must be turned into a commodity. Why do I say "turned into"? Because land is not created as a commodity. Many years ago, the economist Karl Polanyi explained that a commodity is something produced for sale. Notice it must be both produced and sold. However, Polanyi goes on to note

> The crucial point is this: labor, land, and money are essential elements of industry; they also must be organized in markets.... But labor, land, and money are obviously not commodities; the postulate that anything that is bought and sold must have been produced for sale is emphatically not true in regard to them.... [L]and is only another name for nature, which is not produced by man.[4]

Polanyi's point is that these three "false commodities" have qualities that differentiate them from other elements of the market basket of goods that people need. In the case of land, the two most obvious aspects that differentiate it are its *immovability* and the source of its value in *externalities*.

Land is immovable. This seems obvious enough, but notice the implications of this feature. Many objects are difficult to move. Large appliances like washers or refrigerators are difficult and expensive to move, but for a price they can be relocated. Even houses, the structures themselves, can be moved from one location to another. But the actual location—the land upon which a shelter is built—is just that, a location. The immovability of land means that the relationship of people to the land is the reverse of people's relationship to other objects. If a person needs to move to another job or to take care of a family member, he usually packs up belongings and moves. Not so with land. As a result, land often constrains its owner's mobility. Because land is difficult to buy or sell, decisions about property ownership often dictate other life decisions rather than the other way around.

A property's value is a function of its externalities. An externality is the impact of an economic transaction on a third, uninvolved party. Externalities come in two flavors: positive and negative. A *positive* externality is a positive gain that a third party receives without having to pay for it. If my neighbor gets Wi-Fi Internet service (and neglects to add security to it), I may gain access to the Internet without having to pay for it. Likewise, if someone in my office makes coffee every morning, I may benefit without having to pay for it (or clean out the pot!). A *negative* externality is a cost that a third party must bear without being compensated for it. If my roommate plays loud music (that doesn't

---

[4]Karl Polanyi, *The Great Transformation: The Political and Economic Origins of Our Time* (Boston: Beacon Press, 2001) (Originally published in 1944), 75.

jibe with my taste), he might make it impossible for me to study in my room. If a polluter dumps poison into a stream that my town uses for its water supply, we've been asked to bear a huge cost without compensation.

Land, for the most part, is nothing but externalities. Certainly, agricultural land and land that covers deposits of oil, coal, or minerals may have value tied to its inherent qualities. But urban land particularly derives its value from what is around or not around it. A suburban lot may derive its value from its fresh air, proximity to a park, and the socioeconomic status of the people next door. Likewise, an urban lot may have a low value because of the local crime rate, the quality of schools, and the poverty of others in the neighborhood.

Homeowners, when they buy a property, make a decision about the current value of the externalities associated with it. How good are the schools? Are the neighbors friendly? Are the neighbors of the "right" social class or ethnicity? Yet, although an individual might make accurate judgments about these factors at the time of purchase, he has little control over them as time passes. As a result, property owners want to reduce uncertainty, which pushes their decision-making in a conservative direction.

Positional Goods

A positional good is a special type of externality. It refers to something that is subject to absolute or socially imposed scarcity (that is, the supply cannot be expanded) or subject to congestion (that is, increasing the supply has a tendency to decrease the quality of the good).[5] A few examples will fill out the concept:

- *A vacation home*—There is a limit to how many homes can be built on a highly preferred site. So, a vacation home can be positional both because of its absolute scarcity and because over-building homes in a desirable site can make the existing homes less desirable.

- *A slot in the entering class of an elite university*—The proportion of Americans with a college degree has expanded. Although this has been associated to some extent with increases in incomes and social status, the positional nature of academic credentials can have a contradictory effect. As the number of college graduates increases—mostly as a result of the expansion of public universities and colleges— the value of a public university degree will tend to fall in relative terms and that of an elite private degree will tend to rise because of the socially imposed scarcity of an elite college degree.

Economists have shown that positional goods introduce a number of irrationalities into the market that have implications for social welfare. First, one means of dealing with the over-competition for positional goods is to make the screening procedures more complicated in a way that doesn't actually improve the final outcome. The individual has no choice but to submit to these elaborated procedures if he wants to compete for the good, even though, from a collective standpoint, no one benefits from the extra effort.

The recent history of the college admissions process provides a particularly striking example. The SAT was introduced in the early post-World War II years as a means of imposing a standardized screening process on potential college applicants.[6] Over time,

---

[5]Fred Hirsch, *Social Limits to Growth* (Cambridge: Harvard University Press, 1976).
[6]Nicholas Lemann, *The Big Test: The Secret History of the American Meritocracy* (New York: Farrar, Straus and Giroux, 2000).

however, businesses began to sell test preparation materials to help individuals improve their scores. Later, other wrinkles were added to the process. Admissions consultants, summer internships, campus visits, and advanced placement courses have all become standard parts of the college applicant gauntlet. From the standpoint of an individual student with aspirations to attend a high-quality college, these steps have become nearly mandatory, even though from the view of the entire society, applicants have no better chance of succeeding than they did when no one engaged in these activities. In short, American high school seniors (and their parents) invest huge amounts of time and resources in activities that leave no one better off.

Housing has many of the characteristics of a positional good. There are only so many houses that can be built in desirable neighborhoods. If those neighborhoods allow too many houses, the quality of the existing houses declines. All sorts of processes—zoning, neighborhood associations, and redlining, for example—have been used as screening mechanisms to assure that only the "right" kinds of people can enter particular neighborhoods.

In this respect, the social politics and policy of housing differ from those for food and nutrition. Nutrition is not a positional good. In an affluent society, addressing one person's food insecurity does not undermine that of others. Given that we can and have *overproduced* certain types of food, finding ways that more people can access those goods can benefit both producers and consumers. To some extent this explains the willingness of food producers to support the expansion of nutritional assistance.

Housing is different. Because housing is not a commodity in the normal sense, because its value is tied to the uncertain state of its externalities, and because it is a positional good, the social politics of housing have been quite different. In the end, they have worked to limit rather than expand the housing choices available to low- and moderate-income families and individuals.

Neighborhood Effects

Positional goods and externalities are economic concepts, but there is a sociological dimension to them as well. *Neighborhood effects* refer to the impact that one's immediate environment has on behavior. For example, if two people with the same characteristics—same income, ethnic background, educational attainment, family composition—act differently depending on the type of neighborhood they live in, we refer to this as a neighborhood effect.

One challenge to understanding neighborhood effects is the issue of scale. Historically, sociologists have used the notion of neighborhood as "a natural area"—"a collection of both people and institutions occupying a spatially defined area influenced by ecological, cultural, and sometimes political forces." Yet, the more researchers looked for this "natural" community, the less clear it became. People often see themselves as residing simultaneously in areas of different sizes and boundaries. For example, when discussing local issues, neighbors might differentiate persons living on one block from another but use a larger unit when the issue relates to citywide or regional issues. Eventually, a consensus emerged that "local community is best thought of not as a single entity, but rather as a hierarchy of progressively more inclusive residential groups."[7]

---

[7] Robert J. Sampson, Jeffrey D. Morenoff, and Tomas Gannon-Rowley, "Assessing 'Neighborhood Effects': Social Processes and New Directions in Research," *Annual Review of Sociology* 28 (2002): 443–478. Quotation on p. 445.

A variety of social mechanisms create neighborhood effects. At the most basic level, we can think about the environment as providing *constraints* and *opportunities*. The types of services or transportation available in a neighborhood influence what a person can do. In Philadelphia, residents who don't live near Center City have relatively long commutes to work because they don't own cars and bus service is relatively poor.

One step removed from the actual opportunities available is one's *perception* of opportunities and constraints. Take the example of crime. As we'll see in Chapter 9, although actual crime has declined quite dramatically in American cities over the past generation, Americans still see crime as a major problem. Whatever the actual crime rate in your neighborhood, if you decide to stay home as a result of your perception of crime, it is a neighborhood effect.

A third type of neighborhood effect is a result of the types of *social networks* that people create as part of their everyday life. These networks can be formal (like those associated with one's workplace) or informal (like a group of neighbors who get together regularly for dinner). These social networks can function as a source of opportunities or constraints. As we note in Chapter 8, most people find jobs as a result of social networks.

Many people now use the term *social capital* to describe people's ability to use their social networks as a resource. Some people use the term to refer to the ability to use one's relationships to accomplish specific outcomes—get a job, organize a protest, or get a street light fixed on your block. For others, the outcomes are less specific and more psychological. For example, some authors suggest that generalized social trust, whether for the entire society or one's specific neighborhood, is the best example of social capital. However one defines it, social capital can have an impact on one's behavior in a particular context.[8]

Finally, Robert Sampson has suggested that one source of neighborhood effects is *selective mobility*. People make subjective assessments of the desirability or lack of desirability of a particular neighborhood. People who share those subjective assessments are likely to make the same decisions about where to live. If some people like ethnically diverse neighborhoods with high density and others like ethnically homogeneous neighborhoods with low density, over time they will tend to sort themselves that way. The residents of the dense, diverse neighborhood will be reinforced in the view that their neighborhood is the right place to live, as will the homogenous, low-density residents. Indeed, the Move To Opportunity (MTO) initiative that we discuss later in this chapter tried to push low-income residents to move to different types of neighborhoods but found that, within a few years, its participants tended to relocate to places that were quite similar to the places they had left.[9]

The idea of neighborhood effects is a bit of a double-edged sword when it comes to policy interventions. On the one hand, it suggests that policies directed *only* at individuals will fail to take into account how the environment influences their opportunities and aspirations. On the other hand, it shows that individual decisions and actions are always influenced by a complex of environmental conditions. Rather than count on a one-to-one relationship between policy incentives and outcomes, we should see that *unanticipated outcomes* are the rule, not the exception. Indeed, as the MTO example suggests, what appear to be obvious and desirable changes in the social environment won't necessarily produce the outcomes you expect.

---

[8]Alejandro Portes, "Social Capital: Its Origins and Applications in Modern Sociology," *Annual Review of Sociology* 24 (1998): 1–24.

[9]Robert J. Sampson, *Great American City: Chicago and the Enduring Neighborhood Effect* (Chicago: University of Chicago Press, 2012), 287–308.

Neighborhood effects are important because of the behaviors they reinforce and those they discourage. In his study of Chicago, Sampson found that neighborhoods show remarkable continuity in some features—poverty, crime, level of civic engagement—because these outcomes aren't simply individual problems but are influenced by neighborhood effects. Sampson suggests that "collective efficacy"—residents' belief that they can influence their social environment and their willingness to act on that belief—works against the persistence of these features. For example, Sampson found that various measures of physical and social disorder are influenced both by the poverty and social disadvantage of a neighborhood and by its level of collective efficacy.[10]

How Americans Obtain Housing

Before World War II, most American families rented their accommodations. After the war, however, a combination of factors—pent-up demand, a rise in family formation, and government policies including the GI Bill of Rights—accelerated the rate of home ownership. By 1960, the rate jumped to 62 percent. Between 1960 and 2004, it rose more slowly to 69 percent. By 2013, as a result of the recession, home ownership fell to 65 percent.

Most Americans obtain housing without any direct or conscious involvement with public policy. Typically, if they wish to purchase a home, they engage one or more realtors in their search. When they find a suitable property, the realtor typically handles the legal elements of the sale while the buyer seeks out a mortgage broker or lender and applies for a mortgage. Various services—housing inspectors, assessors, underwriters, and others—will deal briefly with the physical structure or the mortgage. The deal is closed, and the property changes hands.

For a renter, the process is typically less involved. They seek out a suitable dwelling either through word of mouth or published sources. In tight rental markets, they might have to engage an agent in helping them find a unit. The landlord may require a set of credit checks or references. The landlord and tenant sign a contract—either a lease or rental agreement—and the tenant submits a set of deposits and initial rent payment.

Yet, this ground-level view of the process provides only a hint of housing's policy ecosystem. Some of the actors that our prospective buyer or tenant encounter play an important role in the political economy of housing. Realtors and their national organization, the National Association of Realtors, have had a significant impact on housing policy through the years, because they can be mobilized as grassroots advocates in virtually every Congressional district. The financial services industry, because of its relationship to the mortgage market, too, has had a large political footprint. Furthermore, the vast restructuring of the sector since the savings-and-loan crisis of the late 1980s has changed what happens to mortgages and the many derivative financial instruments they have spawned.

Other private economic players who are crucial to housing were left out of our examples altogether. Ordinary buyers or tenants will rarely encounter the developers who decide to build or renovate housing. Real estate development engages a huge number of occupations and industries related to residential construction—from planners, architects, and hydrologists to painters, carpenters, and day laborers. It is no accident that housing constitutes about one-fifth of the entire GDP of the United States.[11]

---

[10]Sampson, *Great American City*, 152–160.

[11]Alex F. Schwartz, *Housing Policy in the United States: An Introduction* (New York and London: Routledge, 2006) 3–4.

Almost totally invisible to the ordinary buyer or tenant is the role of federal and state social policy in obtaining housing. They may notice that they must sign an "Equal Opportunity Lender" form. Some will seek out an FHA or other government-guaranteed mortgage. But for the most part, obtaining property appears to be a private market affair.

To a great extent, this is deliberate. The real estate and financial-services industries have played a dominant role in policymaking around housing for many years. As a result, although the government is central to all aspects of the housing market, its actions happen behind the scenes, especially through the tax system. Furthermore, the strength of the housing lobby has often prevented public policy from addressing a number of the inequities of the housing market that disadvantage low-income, African American, and Latino households.

Residential Segregation and Discrimination

No features have been more important in defining the contemporary American city than segregation and concentrated poverty. In recent years, we have come to understand the deadly interaction of the two. Racial segregation has created the context within which poor African Americans and Latin Americans find themselves crammed into particular neighborhoods. The concentrated poverty that results reinforces the "otherness" of poor people of color, which in turn motivates other social groups to keep their distance.

Douglas Massey and Nancy Denton use the Detroit Area Survey to provide a particularly striking example of the dynamic. They discovered that the majority of African Americans see the ideal racial balance in a neighborhood as a 50/50 division between African Americans and other social groups. However, whites' ideal balance is closer 90/10, white majority. As a result, as African Americans move into a neighborhood, they see its composition approach an ideal state; however, once the African American population exceeds 10 percent, whites are more likely to see the neighborhood as becoming "too black" and often will decide to leave. Within a few years, the neighborhood will become *hyper-segregated*.[12]

Segregation, however, is not simply a product of the individual choices of residents. Although the idea of segregation goes back centuries in the United States, the critical chapters of its story occur during the years after the Civil War when whites looked for ways of reconstructing a system of social exclusion.[13] Ultimately in the South, whites were able to use a variety of laws to enforce the separation of the races at work, school, and in neighborhoods—what we call "Jim Crow" laws[14] This *de jure* (of the law) segregation often drifted north, as in 1910 when the city of Baltimore identified each block in the city as either "black" or "white."[15] In some issues, like voting, Jim Crow ran up against the Civil War amendments to the US Constitution that ostensibly assured the citizenship rights of African Americans. In these cases, a variety of subterfuges—like poll taxes, literacy tests, or "grandfather clauses" (the voting status of one's grandfather determined yours)—were used to assure the exclusion of African Americans.[16] The attack on Jim

---

[12]Doug Massey and Nancy Denton, *American Apartheid: Segregation and the Making of the Underclass* (Cambridge: Harvard University Press, 1993), 92–93.

[13]Carl H. Nightingale, *Segregation: A Global History of Divided Cities* (Chicago: University of Chicago Press, 2012).

[14]The classic study of this process is C. Vann Woodward, *The Strange Career of Jim Crow* (New York: Oxford University Press, 1966).

[15]Antero Pietila, *Not in My Neighborhood: How Bigotry Shaped a Great American City* (Chicago: Ivan R. Dee, 2010), 5–21.

[16]Alexander Keyssar, *The Right to Vote: The Contested History of Democracy in the United States* (New York: Basic Books, 2009).

Crow began to show results in the 1940s, but the system was still in place when the 1964 Civil Rights Act and 1965 Voting Rights Act were passed.

In the North, with a few exceptions, legal segregation took less direct forms. During the early years of the twentieth century, the *restrictive covenant* became the preferred way to ensure the racial purity of a neighborhood. These covenants were attached to deeds as part of a real estate transaction and bound the purchaser to sell a property only to a member of the white race (prohibitions against selling to Jews were often included as well). For several decades they provided a durable method of maintaining residential segregation, but enforcing them usually required the cooperation of virtually all land-owners in a particular district. Eventually, in the *Kramer v. Shelley* decision in 1947, the Supreme Court ruled that they were unenforceable.[17] Although these covenants contin-ued to be observed in many parts of the country, by the late 1940s, other methods for reinforcing segregation were necessary.

The real estate industry remained the key to enforcing segregation. Since the 1950s, two methods have been the most reliable ways to exclude African Americans and other racial and ethnic minorities from particular neighborhoods—redlining and steering.

Redlining consists of financial institutions agreeing not to invest in particular neigh-borhoods. The method evolved in the early twentieth century and was institutional-ized by the federal government in the 1930s. During the Great Depression, the Home Owners' Loan Corporation (HOLC) focused on helping property owners refinance their properties in order to avoid foreclosure. To make their work easier, they adopted the real estate industry's method of identifying desirable and undesirable sections of the city.[18]

Community-based discrimination has a long history. Both the real estate industry and the federal government endorsed using neighborhood characteristics to assess loan decisions through much of the twentieth century. The most common form of community-based discrimination was "redlining," literally drawing a red line around a section of the city and deciding not to offer mortgages within that area. The Home Owners' Loan Corporation, a federal agency, produced a set of redlined maps in the 1930s that accurately identified those communities in which neither the federal government nor private lenders offered mortgages from the 1930s through the 1960s. Typically, "hazardous" areas were character-ized by an aging housing stock and the presence of "undesirable" groups including newer European immigrants, African Americans, and Latinos (Figure 6.2).

Redlining was outlawed in a set of housing acts during the late 1960s and early 1970s. Although redlining was outlawed, African Americans still faced discrimination. To the extent that these difficulties were a result of their income, work stability, or credit his-tory, it was legal. Thus, there is always ambiguity when a low-income African American applicant is denied a mortgage; is he rejected because of his financial status or because he is African American?

Because of the continuing problems that African Americans faced in the mortgage market, Congress passed the Home Mortgage Disclosure Act (HMDA) in 1975, which required lenders to collect and make public data about their mortgage decisions. Generally these data have shown a considerable gap between the treatment of whites, blacks, and Latinos, with black and Latino applicants' denial rate generally two to three times that of white applicants. A more detailed analysis of the role of discretion and creditworthiness

---

[17]Colin Gordon, *Mapping Decline: St. Louis and the Fate of the American City* (Philadelphia: University of Pennsylvania Press, 2008), 71–82.

[18]Kenneth T. Jackson, *Crabgrass Frontier: The Suburbanization of the United States* (New York: Oxford University Press, 1987), 190–218.

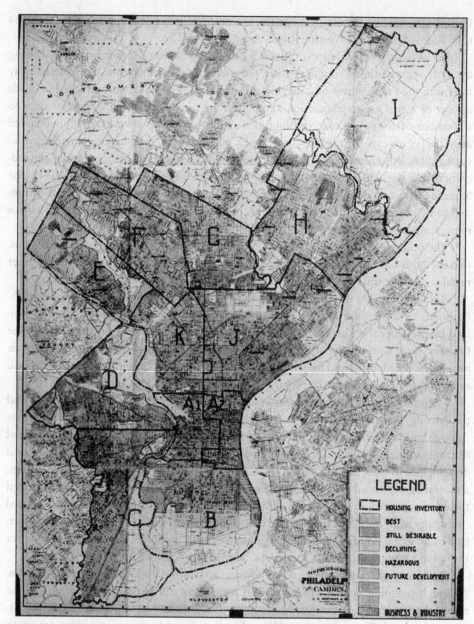

Figure 6.2
Redlining Map of Philadelphia, Home Owners' Loan Corporation
Redlining—identifying neighborhoods that were ineligible for conventional mortgages—was critical to urban decline. The federal government in the 1930s endorsed this real estate industry practice.

Source: Cartographic Modeling Lab, "HOLC's 1936 Security Map of Philadelphia," University of Pennsylvania, http://cml.upenn.edu/redlining/HOLC_1936.html.

conducted by the Federal Reserve Bank of Boston found, among applicants with flawed credit, "that for the same imperfections, whites seem to enjoy a general presumption of creditworthiness that black and Hispanic applicants do not, and that lenders seem to be more willing to overlook flaws for white applicants than for minority applicants."[19]

---

[19]Alicia Munnell, Lynn E. Browne, James McEneaney, and Geoffrey M. B. Tootell, *Mortgage Lending in Boston: Interpreting HMDA Data* (Boston: Federal Reserve Bank of Boston, 1992), 3.

In contrast to redlining, which can be detected through an analysis of HMDA, *steering* results from real estate agents showing clients only particular properties based on their race. A significant body of research—typically conducted by sending black and white "testers" to the same real estate offices and comparing the homes they are shown—has demonstrated that steering is widespread in the industry.[20]

During the Clinton and Bush administrations, the US Department of Housing and Urban Development (HUD) undertook a variety of initiatives to increase home ownership, especially among blacks and Latinos. In response, the private mortgage industry shifted its practices to make *subprime* mortgages available to individuals and families with less-than-perfect credit. This expansion of the subprime mortgage market, however, accompanied an explosion in *predatory lending*. Predatory lending is defined by a number of characteristics:

> Generally speaking, three features—alone or in combination—define predatory
> lending practices. Those features include targeted marketing to households on the
> basis of their race, ethnicity, age or gender or other personal characteristics unre-
> lated to creditworthiness; unreasonable and unjustifiable loan terms; and outright
> fraudulent behavior that maximizes the destructive financial impact on consum-
> ers of inappropriate marketing strategies and loan provisions. Although a loan
> involving any one of these tactics might legally be considered predatory, most
> predatory lenders use some combination of all three to extract the greatest profit
> and, as a consequence, cause the greatest financial harm to the borrower.[21]

In a sense, the story of discrimination in housing had come full circle. After decades in which creditworthy minority applicants were denied credit because of their race or ethnicity, the expansion of the subprime loan market and the predatory lending syndrome led to members of these racial and ethnic groups being sought after by the purveyors of overpriced mortgages that are economically ruinous.

Public Policy and the Housing Market: Universal Approaches

Universal (that is, non-income-tested) housing policies are focused on home ownership. The tax benefits provided to homeowners are among the largest expenditures made by the federal government. They are widely popular but rarely viewed by ordinary Americans as part of the social welfare system.

Yet, the existing system of homeowner subsidies has some serious flaws. First, from the standpoint of distributive justice, they go disproportionately to well-off families and individuals. Second, innovations in the mortgage markets have had a number of serious side effects. The explosion in subprime lending in the mid-2000s and the global financial crisis of 2008–09 are both associated with the American mortgage market.

Human Rights and Justice

Practice Behavior Example: Recognize the global interconnections of oppression and be knowledgeable about theories of justice and strategies to promote human and civil rights.

Critical Thinking Question: During the housing boom of the early 2000s, financial firms made billions by selling ruinous mortgages to low-income homeowners and reselling them on global markets. What actions can social workers take to explain these connections and ensure that they aren't repeated?

---

[20]Gordon, *Mapping Decline*, 87.

[21]James H. Carr and Lopa Kolluri, *Predatory Lending: An Overview* (Washington, DC: Fannie Mae Foundation, 2001), 2.

The mortgage tax expenditure

Homeowners benefit from two tax expenditures. First, interest paid on home mortgages, including second or third homes, is deductible from one's income. Second, all property taxes paid during the previous year are also deductible.

The origins of the home mortgage tax deduction are hazy. When the first income tax was instituted during the Civil War, it included a deduction for interest, and this deduction was maintained when a permanent income tax was instituted in 1913. After World War II, the expansion of the income tax to cover most families along with the housing boom made the mortgage tax deduction an important part of a family's economic standing. When most interest deductions were eliminated by the Tax Reform Act of 1986, the mortgage interest deduction remained, for many families, the only way to use debt to reduce their tax burden.[22] As a result, it continues to be a popular policy.

However, as with many tax expenditures, lack of transparency hides its distributional impact. First, if a family's income is low, it is unlikely to itemize deductions and benefit from interest and tax deductions. The higher one's income, the more one benefits from the deduction. Low-income households who pay no income tax receive no benefit from the deduction, while the lowest-income taxpayers (if they itemize deductions) will save only one in ten dollars they spend on a mortgage. High-income households, in contrast, are in the 35 percent bracket. In absolute terms, the differences are even larger; because low-income taxpayers are more likely to live in more modest homes, the size of their tax break will be much smaller.

As a result of these cumulative distributional effects, affluent individuals enjoy the lion's share of all the benefits of the mortgage and property tax deductions. As of 2004, households earning less than $30,000 per year (roughly 44 percent of all tax returns in that year) gained less than 2 percent of the mortgage interest deduction and 2.5 percent of the property tax deduction. In contrast, households earning over $200,000 —only 2 percent of all tax filers—received 23 percent of the mortgage interest deduction and 17 percent of the property tax deduction.[23]

In aggregate, these two tax expenditures represented more than $94 billion in tax breaks in 2010. More than half of this amount went to the top 11 percent of all tax filers. If the government announced that it was sending more than $40 billion to people earning over $100,000 a year, there would be widespread consternation. That is exactly what the government is doing, but because it is in the form of tax breaks rather than checks, the redistribution of income is less clear.

The home ownership tax breaks have been criticized on other than fairness grounds. Some economists worry that the deductions cause imbalances in capital markets, "drawing more resources into housing," according to W. F. Hellmuth, "than would occur in the absence of such preferences."[24]

This point is reinforced by international comparisons that suggest that the tax incentives are inefficient. Many other advanced economies have similar rates of property ownership, including Canada, Australia, and several European countries, without granting such generous tax incentives.

---

[22]C. Howard, *The Hidden Welfare State: Tax Expenditures and Social Policy in the United States* (Princeton: Princeton University Press, 1997).

[23]Schwartz, *Housing Policy*, 74–75.

[24]W. F. Hellmuth, "Homeowner Preferences," in *Comprehensive Income Taxation*, ed. J. A. Richman, (Washington, DC: The Brookings Institution, 1977), quoted in C. Dolbeare, "How the Income Tax System Subsidizes Housing for the Affluent," in *Critical Perspectives on Housing*, eds. B. G. Bratt, C. Hartman, and A. Myerson (Philadelphia: Temple University Press, 1986), 265.

A number of alternatives to the current system have been proposed over the years. The most straightforward would be limitations on the scope of the deduction, for example, by placing a stricter limit on the total amount of interest that qualifies or restricting the benefit to only one residence. In his 2010 and 2011 budgets, President Obama proposed a milder approach by limiting the benefit for those with incomes over $250,000. Even this small effort provoked a successful lobbying effort by the National Association of Realtors, National Association of Home Builders, and the Mortgage Bankers Association.[25]

Predatory lending and global financial networks

Despite the success of the housing lobby in blocking reform of the mortgage interest deduction, there is abundant evidence that money flowing into home mortgages has the ability to imbalance credit markets and, indeed, to bring the global financial system to its knees.

The expansion of home ownership after World War II was the result of a two-tier system of financing. Most mortgages were offered by savings-and-loans and mutual savings banks (often called "thrifts") that used depositors' savings to fund them. The dominant home finance system remained close to the ground because of this link between depositors and mortgagees (reinforced by bank regulations that required most institutions to serve individual communities). The Federal Housing Administration (FHA) insured a smaller number of mortgages, usually offered by mortgage brokers and independent mortgage companies that then sell them to investors, most often insurance companies.[26]

This system was transformed after the savings-and-loan crisis of the late 1980s, because new capital requirements reduced the role of savings and loans and increased the need for mortgage originators to sell their mortgages to investors. This *secondary mortgage market* provided fertile ground for the financial service industry, which developed ways to bundle a set of mortgages into a single security and then sell shares or *tranches* of these *mortgage-backed securities*. During the late 1990s and early 2000s, these securities themselves were combined into *collateralized debt obligations* (CDOs), placing even more distance between the original mortgage and the investors who owned them.

The process of turning home mortgages into investment securities—*securitization*—allowed investors from anywhere in the world to buy a share of a mortgage. We had come a long way from the time when local banks used local deposits to fund local mortgages. What is more, the acceleration of securitization occurred at a time when the demand for fixed-rate investments was exploding. Taken together, these conditions created unprecedented demand for mortgage-backed securities and their derivative.

The market's response to these conditions was the explosion in subprime lending.[27] The expansion of these mortgages began in the late 1990s but accelerated greatly after 2000. The demand for mortgages by the investment industry led as well to a weakening of standards for mortgages. Applicants were no longer required to produce a down payment or documentation of their income or assets, what one participant called a "liar's loan."[28]

[25]"Plan to Cut Mortgage Interest Deduction Stirs Opposition," *Los Angeles Times*, March 14, 2009.

[26]Schwartz, *Housing Policy*, 52–53.

[27]Souphala Chomsisengphet and Anthony Pennington-Cross, "The Evolution of the Subprime Mortgage Market," Federal Reserve Bank of St. Louis *Review* (January/February 2006): 31–56.

[28]NPR and This American Life, "The Giant Pool of Money," first broadcast May 9, 2008, http://thislife.org/radio-archives/episode/355/The-Giant-Pool-of-Money.

Review Harvard University's Joint Center for Housing Studies **for up-to-date information on the American housing market.**

The explosion of subprime lending was sustainable only as long as housing prices continued to rise. When the bubble burst in 2006–07, a tidal wave of foreclosures shook the market, first crushing the subprime market and then hitting the "alt-A" market, heavily funded by quasi-governmental corporations like the Federal National Mortgage Association (Fannie Mae) and the Federal Home Loan Mortgage Corporation (Freddy Mac). By 2010, it was estimated that one in four mortgages in the United States was "underwater," that is, that the mortgage amount exceeded the value of the property.[29]

Ultimately, the crash of subprime lending had repercussions that went far beyond the low-income families that were its target. The world financial structure had become so heavily invested in low-quality mortgages that, when they went bad, world credit markets seized, the world economy went into recession, and unemployment in the United States reached 10 percent for the first time in a generation.

The story of subprime lending is tragic, not only because of its impact on the economy. Lack of access to credit has always dogged low-income families. Without access to credit, it is virtually impossible for poor people to acquire assets—either a home, small business, or substantial savings. If regulated in a thoughtful way, the expansion of credit for those with flawed credit history could have contributed to a significant reduction of economic inequality.

Unfortunately, those who managed world financial markets and who enabled the predatory lenders were left to their own devices. In the early years of the twenty-first century, the financial system generated a new generation of bankruptcies, which effectively assured that the expansion of credit for low-income people would become a political and economic impossibility for the foreseeable future.

Targeted Approaches to Housing

The vast majority of funding devoted to housing, especially the tax expenditures for mortgage interest and property taxes, is focused on home ownership. By comparison, the amount of funding devoted to rental housing for the poor is paltry. In 2008, for example, the federal government spend $144 billion on tax breaks for homeowners, of which less than 2.4 percent went to families earning less than $40,000 a year. In the same year, the government spent a total of $46 billion on low-income rental housing assistance.

Since the 1930s, the federal government has tried a variety of methods of funding housing for low-income people. The first effort—public housing—provided funding for local housing authorities to build units devoted to low-income families. During the 1970s, the focus shifted to programs to encourage private developers to provide units for low-income renters and subsidies for low-income families: a set of initiatives usually labeled "Section 8." Finally, beginning in the 1980s, housing policy moved from a focus on extreme poverty to families with slightly higher income who faced affordability problems. The low-income housing tax credit was the most notable of the third generation of federal housing policy.

The problem of affordability

As we noted previously, food and shelter—the two key elements of the family budget—have switched places during the past half-century. While food now occupies a much smaller proportion of the budget of average and low-income families, housing occupies a much larger share. Part of this increase is the result of the improvement in the average

---

[29]Casey B. Mulligan, "The Housing Crisis and the 'Resentment' Zone," *New York Times*, March 24, 2010, http://economix.blogs.nytimes.com/2010/03/24/the-housing-crisis-and-the-resentment-zone/.

housing stock over those years, but most of it is the result of housing costs increasing more quickly than the incomes of moderate- and low-income families.

Until the 1980s, a family spending more than 25 percent of its income on housing was considered to be facing an affordability problem and qualified for some type of housing assistance. By the early twenty-first century, the affordability cutoff has risen to 30 percent. Yet, even this increase did not fully compensate for the increasing housing cost burden. Between 1989 and 2008, the average amount spent on housing by all households increased from 30 to 34 percent. Among households in the bottom 20 percent by family income, the increase was from 35 to 40 percent. Even households in the second family-income quintile (20–39 percentiles) faced a new level of desperation; their average housing costs increased from 33 to 37 percent during these years. Only a small fraction of Americans used to face an affordability challenge, but it has now become more common.

This shift upward in the affordability problem provides one explanation of the change in rental housing policy. During the first two generations of housing policy, the focus of intervention was primarily on extremely low-income families. However, since the 1990s, much housing policy—including the refocus on public housing and the expansion of low-income housing tax credits—has targeted the needs of low-income, but not poor, households.

Approximately five million units of housing qualify for rental assistance. Public housing—projects owned by local housing authorities that receive operating subsidies from the federal government—accounts for 1.2 million units. Section 8—subsidized units that are privately owned—accounts for 3.2 million units. More than two million of these units are tied to housing vouchers that allow families to find housing in the private market. The remaining Section 8 units are *project-based*, meaning that landlords receive subsidies to make units available to qualified families. The low-income housing tax credit—a program that funds privately developed units—accounts for an additional 1.9 million low-income units (Chart 6.1).

Public housing

Public housing, for most Americans, epitomizes the failure of low-income housing policy. The "projects" that came to dominate many poor neighborhoods since the

Chart 6.1   A Picture of Subsidized Housing, 2012 (HUD)

Program	Total units	Percent occupied	Total residents
All programs	5,019,563	94	10,042,471
Public housing	1,156,839	94	2,323,646
Housing choice (Section 8) vouchers	2,339,198	93	5,341,128
Section 8 moderate rehabilitation	24,487	88	37,667
Section 8 new construction, substantial rehabilitation	816,959	96	1,241,643
Section 236 multifamily	98,153	93	166,281
Other multifamily	511,985	95	932,104
Low-income housing tax credit	1,974,163	—	—

Note: — missing data.

Source: http://www.huduser.org/portal/datasets/pictures/files/US_2012_2010geography.xlsx.

1950s—typically high towers surrounded by derelict green space—are seen as one of the abject failures of social policy in the late twentieth century. The implosion of the Pruitt-Igoe project in St. Louis in 1972 represented the concession by local officials that the concentration of poor families in a few high-rise towers created unlivable social conditions.

Yet, the story of public housing in the United States is more complex. It is a product of the dreams of generations of housing reformers running up against the realities of American politics and the interests of powerful elements of the housing and construction industry. The realities of public policy represented unanticipated outcomes of these compromises.

American reformers imported the idea of "social housing" from Europe, where model developments in Vienna and elsewhere raised the vision of decent housing for working people. Philanthropies and labor unions sponsored a number of small projects during the early years of the twentieth century, but it took the Great Depression of the 1930s to turn social housing into a public program. By the time the first federal program became law in 1937, a number of states and cities—particularly New York City—had already begun ambitious programs to replace their tenement districts with modern housing.[30]

From its start, public housing was pulled in two directions by ideology and by special interests. The philosophical debate centered on whether public housing should focus on the needs of average working people or on the most destitute. This division was reinforced by the interest of the emerging housing lobby—mortgage bankers, real estate brokers, and developers—who sought a guarantee that public housing would not compete with the private housing market.

As a result, from its inception, two features characterized public housing. First, it would be controlled by local authorities, not by the federal government. This meant that communities that wished to exclude low-income people could do so simply by not building public housing. Second, federal legislation placed strict limits on construction costs, which assured that units would be built in undesirable locations, using low-cost designs and materials, and—most consequentially—that local housing authorities would lower land costs by building high-rises.

The public housing program made little headway before the passage of the Housing Act of 1949. The postwar housing shortage increased localities' interest in a construction program. During the 1950s, the number of public housing units increased from 170,000 to 422,000.[31] The growth of public housing, however, quickly ran into another public policy conundrum: racial discrimination.

When the 1949 housing act was passed, Southern legislators insisted that the act exclude antidiscrimination language. As a result, virtually all public housing built during the 1950s was racially segregated. When civil rights advocates sought to change these laws during the 1950s, they encountered stiff resistance. In Chicago, for example, when the executive director of the Chicago Housing Authority implemented a desegregation plan, she quickly found herself out of a job, and black residents who moved into previously all-white projects experienced harassment and intimidation.[32]

[30]Gail Radford, *Modern Housing for America: Policy Struggles in the New Deal Era* (Chicago: University of Chicago Press, 1997) 29–84.

[31]M. Stegman, "The Role of Public Housing in a Revitalized National Housing Policy," in *Building Foundations: Housing and Federal Policy*, eds. D. DiPasquale and L. C. Keyes (Philadelphia: University of Pennsylvania Press, 1990), Table 13.3.

[32]Arnold Hirsch, *Making the Second Ghetto: Race and Housing in Chicago, 1940–1960* (Cambridge and New York: Cambridge University Press, 1983).

The public housing boom continued into the 1960s, when another 370,000 units were added, but the policy ecosystem had shifted in a number of ways. First, the passage of federal civil rights legislation in 1968 made the maintenance of segregated housing projects illegal. The policy tilt toward home ownership and the declining housing shortage meant that public housing became the home of the most destitute members of society. Increasingly, public housing slots were reserved for welfare families, meaning that the economic diversity that characterized public housing in the 1950s gave way to projects dominated by single-parent families dependent on public assistance.

At the same time, the decision to entrust the maintenance of public housing to local housing authorities accelerated a decline in the quality of life for residents. Although some critics contend that the decision to build high-rises condemned public housing to failure, other analysts have pointed to New York City, where public housing was able to maintain its quality and livability.[33] However, the level of managerial oversight that contributed to New York's relative success was absent in many housing authorities, where corruption and poor management allowed vandalism, crime, and physical deterioration to undermine the physical and social environment. By the 1970s, although a majority of projects continued to function satisfactorily, the image of public housing as a policy failure was deeply fixed in the public mind.

Hope VI

Public housing policy began a decisive turnaround in 1989 with the establishment of the National Commission on Severely Distressed Public Housing. The Commission's recommendation led to the passage of the Hope VI program in 1993. The Hope VI goal was to demolish and redevelop public housing projects. Housing authorities were encouraged to combine Hope VI funding with other sources (including the low-income housing tax credit, see below) to construct mixed-income projects characterized by better design, public amenities, management innovation, resident involvement, and social services.

After 1993, because Hope VI projects typically began with the destruction of an existing project, the program contributed to a loss of 173,000 public housing units. Although the Hope VI legislation included a guarantee that public-housing residents would either return to the redeveloped site or another form of subsidized housing, analysts concluded that many never returned. A 2004 study, for example, found that only 19 percent of former residents of eight Hope VI sites returned to the revitalized site, while 62 percent were living in other public or subsidized housing and 18 percent were living in unsubsidized units.[34]

In spite of the public perception of public housing as a failure, the projects have remained popular among residents because they are affordable. Originally, public housing rents were intended to cover all operating costs, after the federal government paid construction costs. However, during the late 1960s and early 1970s, amendments to the Public Housing Act limited rents, currently to 30 percent of household income. As a result, operating subsidies by the 2000s came to comprise about half the budget of local housing authorities.[35]

[33]Nicholas Dagen Bloom, *Public Housing that Worked: New York in the Twentieth Century* (Philadelphia: University of Pennsylvania Press, 2009).

[34]S. J. Popkin et al., *A Decade of Hope VI: Research Findings and Policy Challenges* (Washington, DC: The Urban Institute, 2004), 28.

[35]Schwartz *Housing Policy*, 113.

Since the 1990s, federal housing policy has encouraged mixed-income developments rather than traditional public housing projects.

Since the 1990s, policymakers have focused on tightening resident selection and eviction policies to reduce behavioral problems in public housing projects. The Clinton administration implemented a "one-strike" policy that made an offense committed by any household member grounds for evicting the entire household. The law provided for eviction in cases where a tenant "engaged in a pattern of disruptive alcohol consumption or illegal drug use" or "any drug-related criminal activity, any violent activity, or any other criminal activity" if the housing authority considered it a safety risk.[36]

Public housing, since it began, has swung back and forth between a focus on lower-middle income and desperately poor families. Since the 1990s, public housing—like other housing programs—has swung back toward a vision of mixed-income projects. One cost of this policy direction has been a net loss of subsidized units and displacement of some of the most desperately poor tenants. At the same time, Hope VI and current initiatives have raised hope that public housing can shed its reputation for failure and again become a means of improving the housing options of low- and middle-income families.

Section 8 and other rental housing subsidies

The second generation of federal rental assistance began with the Housing and Community Development Act of 1974. As part of the consolidation and devolution of poverty policy at the end of the War on Poverty, Congress created a new program of rental subsidies, known as Section 8.

Section 8 originally included three sets of subsidies: new construction, substantial rehabilitation, and existing housing. During the Reagan administration, a voucher program was added to the program, and in 1998 the existing housing and voucher programs were merged to form the Housing Choice Voucher program.

The first two subsidies—for new construction and substantial rehabilitation—are provided to developers who receive funding to create subsidized housing. The federal government pays the landlord the difference between the HUD-defined "fair market rent" (FMR) and 30 percent of the tenant's income. In addition, developers are able to take advantage of a number of tax breaks and access below-market rate financing available through state housing finance agencies.

The chief challenge posed by these subsidies is their time limit. In accepting the subsidy, owners agree to make units available to qualifying families for a fixed number of years, originally between 20 and 40 years. In the 1990s, as these contracts expired, HUD began spending a larger share of its budget on renewing contracts rather than bringing new units on line. Because these units had relatively high rents, the maintenance of older Section 8 project-based units has become a chronic fiscal challenge,

---

[36]Schwartz *Housing Policy*, 125.

often absorbing up to half of HUD's budget authority.[37] In spite of efforts to preserve the stock of project-based Section 8 units, about 360,000 units have been lost since the mid-1990s, primarily as a result of owners deciding to shift their properties to market-rate rents.[38]

The existing housing and voucher programs award certificates to qualifying families, who then seek housing on the open market. The original program covered households with incomes up to 80 percent of the area's median income, and units could not rent for more than the area's FMR. Families were required to pay 25 percent of their income (later raised to 30 percent) with the government obligated to make up the difference. When the voucher program began in 1983, it retained the same subsidies but allowed families to pay additional rent (up to 40 percent of income) if they chose to. Families displaced by Hope VI or the conversion of project-based Section 8 developments swelled the number of vouchers. But because the voucher program is not an entitlement, the number of families who actually receive vouchers is far fewer than those with eligible incomes.

Some analysts see vouchers as the most cost-effective means of increasing low-income families' access to rental housing. However, in addition to the obvious gap between the number of vouchers and number of eligible families, critics have noted a number of problems with the program. First, in very tight housing markets, voucher holders often fail to gain access to eligible units. This problem was particularly acute in cities with large numbers of Hope VI redevelopments. In these situations, existing voucher holders must compete with a flood of former public housing residents who receive vouchers. Even when units are identified, they are often disqualified because they do not meet HUD's standards.

Vouchers have also been criticized for reinforcing patterns of racial and economic segregation because voucher holders are most likely to find places to rent in higher-poverty and racially segregated neighborhoods. During the 1990s, HUD operated a social experiment—Move to Opportunity (MTO)—that made some vouchers contingent on the household finding housing in neighborhoods with lower poverty rates. The evaluation of MTO discovered that many families, although they found qualified units, remained in racially segregated neighborhoods. Overall, the hope that MTO would generate side effects that would improve the social and economic standing of MTO families has, for the most part, not been realized.[39]

Using markets: Low-income housing tax credits

The low-income housing tax credit (LIHTC) is the most recent innovation in funding subsidized rental housing. Created by the Tax Reform Act of 1986, the LIHTC provides a transferable tax credit that developers can sell to investors to raise capital for construction. During the heady days of the economic booms of the late 1990s and the 2000s,

---

[37]Schwartz, *Housing Policy*, 42.

[38]Douglas Rice and Barbara Sard, *Decade of Neglect Has Weakened Federal Low-Income Housing Programs: New Resources Required to Meet Growing Needs* (Washington, DC: Center for Budget and Policy Priorities, 2009), 17.

[39]Xavier de Souza Briggs, Susan J. Popkin, and John Goering, *Moving to Opportunity: The Story of an American Experiment to Fight Ghetto Poverty* (New York: Oxford University Press, 2010). For a more critical view of MTO, see Sampson, *Great American City*, 261–287.

Wall Street investors could use these credits to offset a share of their profits from other investments. However, the collapse of the real estate market in 2007 spelled trouble for the LIHTC. As the market for the tax credit dried up, the federal government—as part of the 2009 economic stimulus package—allowed states to convert a share of their credits to a direct subsidy as a means of continuing to support the subsidized rental market.

The most popular LIHTC is a limited tax credit.[40] Each state's housing finance agency receives an annual allotment of credits that it can allocate to qualified housing development projects based on a state plan. The size of the credit for a development is determined based on the total development cost of the project, the proportion of units that are designated for low-income occupants, and the characteristics of the project's neighborhood (projects in "difficult development areas" receive a 30 percent bonus). Credits can be used for 10 years, as long as the low-income units are made available for 15 years.

As with the securitization of mortgages, the value of the tax credit is realized only when it is sold, usually to banks, government-sponsored enterprises (like Fannie Mae or Freddie Mac), or insurance companies. Until the collapse of the housing market, developers could typically get 80 percent of the value of a tax credit in capital to fund the development. However, after 2008 when the demand for the credits declined, their price fell below 60 percent in 2009 before recovering.

The LIHTC represents a new approach to building low-income rental housing that has led to the construction of nearly two million housing units since its inception. By enlisting the support of the financial services industry, LIHTC represents a much broader political coalition in support of expanding subsidized rental housing.[41]

Yet, LIHTC raises two questions. First, the economics of LIHTC allow it to successfully construct quality housing for struggling working families but not for the poorest families. Thus, it can be part of a successful housing strategy but must be complemented by direct subsidies for those households with lower incomes.

Second, the dependency of LIHTC on the financial services industries raises questions about its possibilities for revival. Government-sponsored institutions like Fannie Mae and Freddie Mac were important parts of LIHTC financing during its heyday.[42]

The emergence of the LIHTC as the key policy for building subsidized rental housing was complemented by changes in the policy environment. According to David Erickson, the current system is the result of a new social network of grassroots interests—ranging from community development corporations to private developers to Wall Street investors—who had a stake in the new system. Whether this new system can eventually close the gap between the supply and demand for subsidized rental housing remains an open question.[43]

---

[40]In addition to the main, more highly subsidized tax credits that are controlled by state housing finance agencies (often called 9 percent credits), there is a lower-subsidized credit that is automatic (often called a 4 percent credit).

[41]David Erickson, *The Housing Policy Revolution: Networks and Neighborhoods* (Washington, DC: Urban Institute Press, 2009).

[42]Buzz Roberts, "Strengthening the Low Income Housing Tax Credit Investment Market," *Cascade* 72 (Fall 2009), http://www.philadelphiafed.org/community-development/publications/cascade/72/03_strengthening-low-income-market.cfm.

[43]Erickson, *Housing Policy Revolution*.

Housing the homeless

The largest challenge facing the United States concerning shelter is the yawning afford-ability gap—the gap between the price of available housing and what low-income fami-lies can afford to pay—which has led to an increase in shelter insecurity. One indicator of that insecurity is the presence of large numbers of homeless individuals and families in many parts of the United States.

Many younger Americans are surprised that homelessness was not a recognized social problem until the 1980s. Although many people before that time faced housing insecurity, they did not resort to living on the street. Typically, "skid row" sections of American cities were home to an amalgam of single-resident occupancies (SROs) and missions—often run by religious orders, like the Salvation Army—that catered to indi-viduals without permanent housing.

A variety of factors contributed to the emergence of homelessness as a public prob-lem during the early 1980s. Some had to do with actual changes in the shelter options of individuals and families. The closing of many state mental institutions increased the number of people with mental illness living in the community. The Vietnam-War vet-eran generation includes many individuals with significant mental health and substance-abuse problems. Cutbacks in state general assistance programs limited the number of single persons who could maintain themselves in permanent housing, while federal public assistance programs for families began a long period of eligibility restriction and benefit decline.

Yet, it is unclear if the new attention that homelessness attracted was simply a response to the demography of the population. The rising conservatism of the 1980s appears to have reduced public interest in the "root causes" of social problems (that often had their origins in the broad contours of poverty and inequality discussed earlier) and increased focus on the concrete, immediate problems faced by people.[44]

The homeless population is quite diverse. According to the 2008 recent Annual Homeless Assessment Report, on a single night in January 2008, there were approxi-mately 664,000 homeless persons in the United States of which 60 percent were living in shelters and 40 percent were "unsheltered."[45] About three-fifths of this population were individuals; the rest were members of families.

Although "only" 600,000 individuals were homeless on a single night, 1.6 million people—one-half of one percent of the US population—were homeless at some point during 2008. The homeless were more likely to be male, older than 31, and alone. About 40 percent of the sheltered homeless have a disability.

As these numbers suggest, there are several distinct types of homeless persons facing different challenges. The *chronically homeless* individuals, who use shelters as long-term housing, comprise only about 11 percent of the shelter population but account for more than 50 percent of all occupied beds on a given day. The *transitional homeless*, who often use a shelter for a day or two in a three-year period, represent 80 percent of all individuals who ever use a shelter but account for only a third of total days. Between the transitional and chronic shelter users is an *episodic* set of residents who represent 9 percent of persons and 17 percent of total days. The same divisions are present among homeless families.

[44]Mark J. Stern, "The Emergence of Homelessness as a Public Problem," *Social Service Review* (June 1983).
[45]US Department of Housing and Urban Development (HUD), *The Third Annual Homeless Assessment Report to Congress*, Executive Summary (2008), 1–2, http://www.huduser.org/portal/publications/povsoc/ahar_4.html.

However, the proportion of families with long stays is nearly twice as large as its share of homeless individuals.[46]

Homelessness became a significant social problem during the 1980s. Whatever uncertainty there is about the reasons for its emergence as a social problem, it is clear what the policy response was. Within a very short period of time, a system of homeless shelters focused on providing minimal shelter and food for the homeless had emerged in virtually every major city in the United States. Funded through a mix of public and philanthropic sources, some shelters sought to integrate themselves with other social welfare systems. But for the most part they stood apart, providing a minimal source of survival for a desperately poor population that included both individuals and families.

This pattern—a separate system providing a variety of services—became the model for federal involvement with the passage of the McKinney-Vento Homeless Assistance Act in 1987. The McKinney Act provided funding for a variety of purposes, including rental assistance for SRO residents, emergency shelter aid, and educational aid for homeless children.

In 1994, HUD instituted its Continuum of Care (CoC) policy, which encouraged a variety of health, mental health, employment, legal and other services for residents of homeless shelters. The impact of CoC was to institutionalize a separate social welfare system for the homeless built around the shelter. By effectively segregating services for the homeless, "mainstream social welfare services...[were] able to largely ignore their clients' housing problems."[47]

During the past decade, advocates have led a major reorientation of homelessness programs. Instead of focusing on improving the shelter system, the new approach has taken as its goal the elimination of homelessness through a focus on linking the homeless and those at risk of homelessness to permanent housing. The 2000 reauthorization of the McKinney-Vento Act required that 30 percent of homeless funding be used for permanent housing rather than shelter maintenance, and in 2003 the Bush administration set the ending of homelessness as a national goal. In 2009, the Obama administration continued this shift in policy with inclusion in the stimulus bill of the Homeless Prevention and Rapid Re-Housing program and the reauthorization of McKinney-Vento.

Yet, the shift in policy—while supported by local advocates and policymakers—faces a number of challenges. The new approach calls for the diversion of funding from shelter programs to new permanent housing solutions. Over the past generation, an entire shelter industry has developed, supported largely by public funding. Although supportive of the long-term goal of ending homelessness, these providers have resisted the cuts in their funding that would be necessary to achieve this goal.

In addition, homelessness prevention and re-housing will not come cheaply. Some data suggest that shifting chronically homeless individuals and families to permanent housing could be achieved without a significant increase in the amount spent. Nationwide, the average cost of maintaining a person in a shelter is over nine thousand dollars a year. The cost of providing permanent housing would be less than a thousand dollars a year more per person, certainly an achievable objective—*if we could effectively shut down the shelters.*

---

[46]Stephen Metraux, "Waiting for the Wrecking Ball: Skid Row in Postindustrial Philadelphia," *Journal of Urban History* 25, no. 5 (July 1999): 690–715.
[47]Dennis Culhane and Stephen Metraux, "Rearranging the Deck Chairs or Reallocating the Lifeboats?" *Journal of the American Planning Association* 74, no. 1 (Winter 2008): 112.

Finally, the goal of ending homelessness faces a vicious paradox, because although shelters are expensive, they act as a deterrent to homelessness. The affordability gap in the general low-income population means that many families are avoiding homelessness through a variety of strategies—doubling up, living in substandard units, squatting. To the extent that homeless shelters constitute a new system of poorhouses, low-income people have taken extraordinary steps to avoid entering this system.

Thus, if homeless programs successfully switch to a model that combines permanent, subsidized housing with supportive services, it is likely that many more individuals and families would want to take advantage of these services. While a targeted program with clear eligibility requirements could mitigate this problem, it could exacerbate a "notch" effect where those working hard to avoid homelessness find themselves worse off than families who have not tried as hard.

The Housing Policy Ecosystem

Homelessness represents only the most acute symptom of the shelter insecurity faced by low- and moderate-income Americans. The crash of the housing market after 2007 sent millions of properties into foreclosure and families into bankruptcy. Efforts to rehabilitate public housing and build new low-income rental housing showed no signs of meeting the needs of low-income families or individuals *before the 2008 crisis hit*, and it is clear that the need has grown considerably as a result of the crisis. Finally, homeless policy, although newly focused on the brave goal of eliminating homelessness, finds itself hamstrung by past policy decisions, especially the existence of an extensive separate system of services tied to the continuum of care.

Generally, the policy ecosystem within which shelter policy is formulated is not susceptible to rapid innovation. The housing lobby that successfully tipped policy toward the funding of home ownership is unlikely to look kindly on a shift toward the needs of low-income Americans, especially after the subprime debacle. Although the LIHTC won a new set of champions of rental housing development on Wall Street, it is unclear if their support will survive. Finally, homeless service providers are likely to resist the shift toward permanent housing if it leads to sharp cuts in the funding of shelters.

In other words, the two great elements of the policy ecosystem—ideas and institutions—find themselves moving in different directions. The 2007–09 economic crisis has given impetus to a number of innovative ideas for improving the shelter prospects of low- and moderate-income Americans, but the institutional structure that has developed around past policy decisions is likely to resist change to accommodate these new ideas.

COMMUNITY DEVELOPMENT

Space matters. The environment in which people live and work influences the decisions they make, the opportunities they enjoy, the challenges they face, and the ideas they have. In addition, a large share of social welfare policies—in the past and currently—are focused on *place-based* changes.

Generally, social workers pay little attention to the role of social ecology and geography in their work. When social workers use the term *community*, they are more likely to think of it as a social network rather than a geographical phenomenon. The *Encyclopedia of Social Work*, for example, defines community as a set

Assess your comprehension of "Community Development" by completing this quiz.

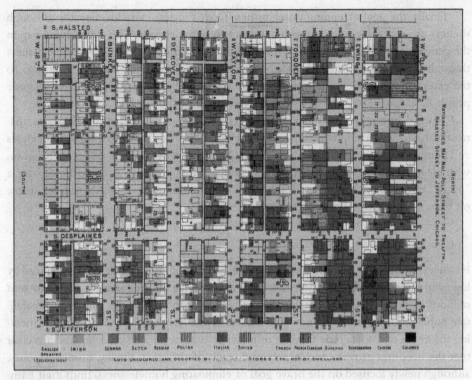

Figure 6.3

Detail of a Hull House Map

Social workers at Hull House pioneered research on urban housing conditions around the turn of the twentieth century.

Source: http://homicide.northwestern.edu/docs_fk/homicide/HullHouse/NATMAP1.pdf.

Professional Identity

Practice Behavior Example: Know the profession's history.

Critical Thinking Question: Compare the role of social workers in Hull House's neighborhood with contemporary social workers' role in housing and community development issues.

of relationships.[48] Certainly, using community to refer to a set of social relations makes sense, but a focus on relationships that transcend location leads us away from the place-specific dimension of community that we address in this section.

This was not always the case. In the early days of the profession, one of the key methods used by social workers was the community investigation. Social workers would prowl a neighborhood, documenting dimensions of community life that were relevant to their work. Chicago's Hull House compiled an extensive collection of maps, like the one below, which showed the distribution of different ethnic groups within its neighborhood (Figure 6.3).

Geographic communities continued to be an important area of social work intervention throughout the Progressive period and into the 1920s. The social unit plan in Cincinnati was one of the most significant efforts of social workers to concentrate their efforts in a particular district of an American city.[49] During the 1930s, 1940s, and 1950s, settlement houses remained active in cities across the United States. However, as social

---

[48]Calvin L. Streeter, Dorothy N. Gamble, Marie Weil, "Community," in *Encyclopedia of Social Work,* e-reference edition, eds. Terry Mizrahi and Larry E. Davis (New York: Oxford University Press, 2008).

[49]Robert Fisher, *Let the People Decide: Neighborhood Organizing in America* (Boston: Twayne Publishers, 1984), 1–28.

workers increasingly viewed psychological theories and casework as their major "commodities," they were less likely to see communities as an ecological construct.[50]

In this section, we examine efforts to intervene in poor communities since the 1960s. During President Johnson's War on Poverty, the federal government tried an experiment: What would happen if the federal government funded grassroots mobilization that bypassed local government? That experiment—community action—lasted a little over two years before it was shut down. The presidents who succeeded Johnson—Nixon and Ford—were hostile to the War on Poverty and proposed a variety of alternatives. Ironically, one of those alternatives, the Community Development Block Grant program, became one of the most durable efforts of the federal government to improve the economic and social environment of low-income neighborhoods.

The War on Poverty and the Rise of Community Development

Community organizing has long been recognized as a method of social work practice. During the 1940s and 1950s, however, it lost prestige within the profession as casework's focus on depth psychology emerged as the most sophisticated social work intervention.

The interest in community-level intervention took an unexpected turn during the 1960s. Based on a variety of youth interventions sponsored by the Justice Department and the Ford Foundation, the idea of *community action* emerged as a major focus of President Johnson's War on Poverty.[51]

The emergence of community action is a complicated story. On the one hand, it was the result of social psychological theories of the period. Ohlin and Cloward—who taught at the Columbia School of Social Work—argued that delinquency was the result of a set of psychological strains associated with the differential opportunities that low-income youths faced in the legitimate and illegitimate economy.[52] This posed the possibility that intervention at the community level that changed the opportunity structure faced by youths could have a significant impact on juvenile delinquency. Along different lines, Oscar Lewis's "culture of poverty" theory argued that poor people's view of the world included a variety of traits, including a tendency toward fatalism and apathy. It was reasoned that efforts to mobilize the poor at the community level would serve to overcome these barriers and encourage their social integration. On a more practical level, the Johnson administration had been frustrated by the unwillingness of local and state political leaders—most of whom were not dependent on the votes of African Americans—to take initiative in addressing poverty or to use antipoverty funding effectively. So, in addition to its theoretical appeal, community action offered a means of circumventing established political leaders in addressing the problems of poor neighborhoods.

In order to accomplish these varied goals, the Economic Opportunity Act of 1964 authorized the establishment and funding of community action agencies. These organizations were typically nonprofits that, in many cities, had already been working on poverty and civil-rights issues. The Act mandated the "maximum feasible participation" of low-income residents, but how this mandate would be translated on the ground became a bone of contention.

[50]Stanley Wenocur and Michael Reisch, *From Charity to Enterprise: The Development of American Social Work in a Market Economy* (Urbana: University of Illinois Press, 1989).

[51]Peter Marris and Martin Rein, *Dilemma of Social Reform: Poverty and Community Action in the United States*, 2nd ed. (New York: Aldine Transaction, 2006).

[52]Richard A. Cloward and Lloyd E. Ohlin, *Delinquency and Opportunity: A Theory of Delinquent Gangs* (Glencoe, IL: Free Press, 1960). See also, Alice O'Connor, *Poverty Knowledge: Social Science, Social Policy, and the Poor in Twentieth-Century US History* (Princeton: Princeton University Press, 2001), 128–30.

You might say that community action was *too* successful. Where its architects had hoped that poor people might eventually be mobilized to engage in planning programs for their neighborhoods; in fact, community action projects in many cities were soon challenging established interests, including city officials, in vocal and attention-getting ways. The energy released in many low-income neighborhoods by the civil rights movement fed these nascent efforts.

Thus, within a year, many community action projects found themselves on the defensive. Right from the start, some organizations found themselves under attack as "subversive" and were forced to fire staff and change tactics.[53] Even when this wasn't the case, confusion about how to incorporate the poor and at the same time satisfy organized constituencies hampered the projects. Ultimately, Congress took action to place the projects more firmly under the control of local politicians.

As government backed away from its volatile elements, community action moved toward more conventional efforts to target funding to poor communities. The Demonstration Cities and Metropolitan Development Act (1966) created the Model Cities program, which provided categorical aid to cities for the purpose of planning and coordinating services for poor neighborhoods more effectively. In contrast to community action, however, the design and implementation of Model Cities programs were left to local government. Although originally designed to target the most severely impacted cities like Detroit, Cleveland, and Newark, Congressional negotiations led to the inclusion of earmarks for lower priority projects in small cities and towns. The Special Impact program provided grants directly to *community development corporations*, community-based organizations that focus on housing development and social services.

In very short order, the community action emphasis of the War on Poverty was subordinated to social service–oriented programs like Head Start. During the 1980s, the Reagan administration shifted the funding into a block grant, which continues to be distributed to agencies providing a variety of services directed at low-income populations.

The Nixon and Ford administrations were generally hostile to the goals of the War on Poverty. They were faced, however, with Democratically controlled Congresses that continued to give priority to programs serving low-income populations. The tension between a conservative administration and a liberal Congress became particularly acute after the Watergate scandal forced Nixon to resign and led to a Democratic landslide in the 1974 elections.

The Housing and Community Development Act of 1974 (PL 93–383) was passed literally days after Nixon's resignation. It represented a melding of Republican efforts to decentralize urban investments with Democratic efforts to target low-income communities for federal aid. The core of the program was the establishment of the Section 8 program discussed earlier, which focused federal rental-housing policy on subsidizing the private market, and the Community Development Block Grant (CDBG), a set of grants to cities and counties that they could use for a wide range of community development efforts. Over the course of the four decades since it was passed, the CDBG has grown and declined, and the amount of federal regulation on how the funding can be used has waxed and waned.

The key to the CDBG program's durability has been its extensive geographic distribution. The program has two parts: an *entitlement* program that makes awards to cities and counties based on size and need and *a state-administered or non-entitlement* program that makes awards to smaller jurisdictions. Over a thousand individual cities, towns, or

[53]George Brager, "Commitment and Conflict in a Normative Organization," *American Sociological Review* 34, no. 4 (August 1969): 482–491.

counties receive CDBG allocations, meaning that every member of Congress has a stake in the program.[54]

More importantly, CDBG represented a shift—one might say a *retreat*—in policy. After 1974, the grandiose rhetoric of the War on Poverty was replaced by an emphasis on funding effective organizations to accomplish tangible goals: build or rehabilitate housing units, deliver services, repair sidewalks. The disconnect between the magnitude of the problems and the size of the government's fiscal commitment has become the defining feature of place-based policies since the 1970s.[55]

Types of community development strategies

Community development strategies fall into one of three categories:

- Organization-based community development
- Community capacity building
- Social movements

Organization-based community development

Organization-based strategies grow most clearly out of the efforts of the 1960s and 1970s. Community development corporations (CDCs) originally began as local efforts to organize antipoverty efforts in inner-city neighborhoods. Eventually, philanthropies and the Special Impact Program discovered CDCs as a means of channeling funding to local communities for housing and other development efforts. Although usually identified with affordable housing and commercial economic development, many operate in a variety of fields, often serving as the intermediary between local communities and regional funders.[56] At the same time, another level of national and regional intermediaries, including community development financial institutions, developed specialized skills in evaluating and funding community development.

CDCs, therefore, perform a wide range of functions and require a variety of capacities to succeed. Not only must they access external funding (often combining resources from philanthropies, government, and banks fulfilling their Community Reinvestment Act obligations), they must develop political and networking capacity to carry out projects effectively. Glickman and Servon suggest that successful CDCs build their capacity in five areas: resources, politics, organization, networks, and program capacity.[57]

Community capacity building

Community capacity building was a product of a variety of philanthropic efforts beginning in the 1990s. They built on organization-based efforts but used a broader idea about points of intervention. Advocates believed that community capacity was a product of

---

[54]Todd Richardson, *CDBG Formula Targeting to Community Development Need* (Washington, DC: Department of Housing and Urban Development, February 2005), http://www.huduser.org/portal/publications/CDBGAssess.pdf.

[55]Alice O'Connor "Swimming against the Tide: A Brief History of Federal Policy in Poor Communities," in *The Community Development Reader,* eds. James DeFilippis and Susan Saegert (New York and London, Routledge, 2008), 3–27.

[56]Robert Halpern, *Rebuilding the Inner City: A History of Neighborhood Initiatives to Address Poverty in the United States* (New York: Columbia University Press, 1995), 131–148.

[57]Norman J. Glickman and Lisa J. Servon, "More than Bricks and Sticks: Five Components of Community Development Corporation Capacity, " in *Community Development Reader,* eds. James DeFilippis and Susan Saegert, 48.

the interaction of individual, organizational, and informal associational resources (social capital). They worked to intervene at all three of these levels using four major strategies:

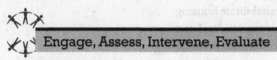

Engage, Assess, Intervene, Evaluate

Practice Behavior Example: Develop a mutually agreed-on focus of work and desired outcomes.

Critical Thinking Question: How might a community-capacity approach facilitate a mutually agreed-on focus for work with a coalition of neighborhood groups?

- *Leadership development*—to build individuals' capacity to engage in change efforts
- *Organizational development*—to allow CDCs and other community-based organizations to successfully pursue projects
- *Community organizing*—to build trust and social capital within the community and increase the community's ability to engage formal institutions
- *Collaborations*—to link community-level efforts to wider regional players[58]

Some critics suggest that although the rhetoric of community building focused on community-level efforts, the outside funders used their influence to tailor initiatives to their priorities.[59]

Social movements

Social movements also focus on the link between individuals and wider communities, but in contrast to capacity-building efforts, social movements are focused on changing individuals' sense of identity and their membership in a collective. Typically, social movements aren't restricted to an individual community, although local grievances are often the context within which they organize.

One debate in the social movement literature surrounds the relationship of mobilization to organizing. Most theories of social movements see a movement's development as moving from spontaneous protest to more strategic, organized efforts. However, Frances Fox Piven and Richard Cloward—formerly professors at the Columbia University School of Social Work—argued that spontaneous protest that disrupts the normal functioning of society is the only means through which "poor people's movements" can bring about lasting change.[60]

Drawing inspiration from the civil rights movement, many "new" social movements have emerged in the past several decades, including the women's movement, the disability rights movement, and the LGBT movement. These movements share a focus on using individuals' rethinking of their identity as the basis for social action. They also share similarities in the types of tactics and organizational forms used.[61]

Community Development and Policy Practice

Social workers continue to work in low-income communities. As a result, they often come into contact with a variety of individuals, organizations, and informal associations that work at the community level. For the most part, however, these professional interactions are in the context of delivering services to individuals. We suggest that if social

[58]Robert J. Chaskin, Prudence Brown, Sudhir Venkatesh, and Avis Vidal, *Building Community Capacity* (New York, Aldine de Gruyter, 2001).

[59]Sudhir Venkatesh, *Off the Books: The Underground Economy of the Urban Poor* (Cambridge, MA: Harvard University Press, 2006) pp. 245–257.

[60]Frances Fox Piven and Richard A. Cloward, *Poor People's Movements: Why They Succeed, How They Fail* (New York: Random House, 1977).

[61]Hank Johnson, Enrique Laraña, and Joseph R. Gusfield, "Identities, Grievances, and New Social Movements," in *New Social Movements: From Ideology to Identity*, eds. Enrique Laraña, Hank Johnston, and Joseph R. Gusfield (Philadelphia: Temple University Press, 1994), 3–35.

workers were to pay more attention to the potential of community-level interventions, they could be more effective both in delivering services and in promoting broader social change around economic and cultural equity.

IMMIGRANTS AND THE ECONOMIC REVITALIZATION OF AMERICAN CITIES

One of the major contemporary developments influencing communities in the United States is mass immigration. Historically, immigration has gone through cycles in American history, influenced by changes in the economy, international relations, and public policy. Between the 1920s—when Congress imposed a set of strict quotas on immigrant entry—and 1965—when the Hart-Celler Act (Immigration and Nationality Act) replaced those quotas—immigration was a minor element of social welfare policy. Since 1965, however, we've seen an explosion in legal immigration and in the flow of undocumented persons into the United States, flows that have changed the profile of neighborhoods, the labor force, and the very nature of race relations (Figure 6.4).

Assess your comprehension of "Immigrants and the Economic Revitalization of American Cities" by completing this quiz.

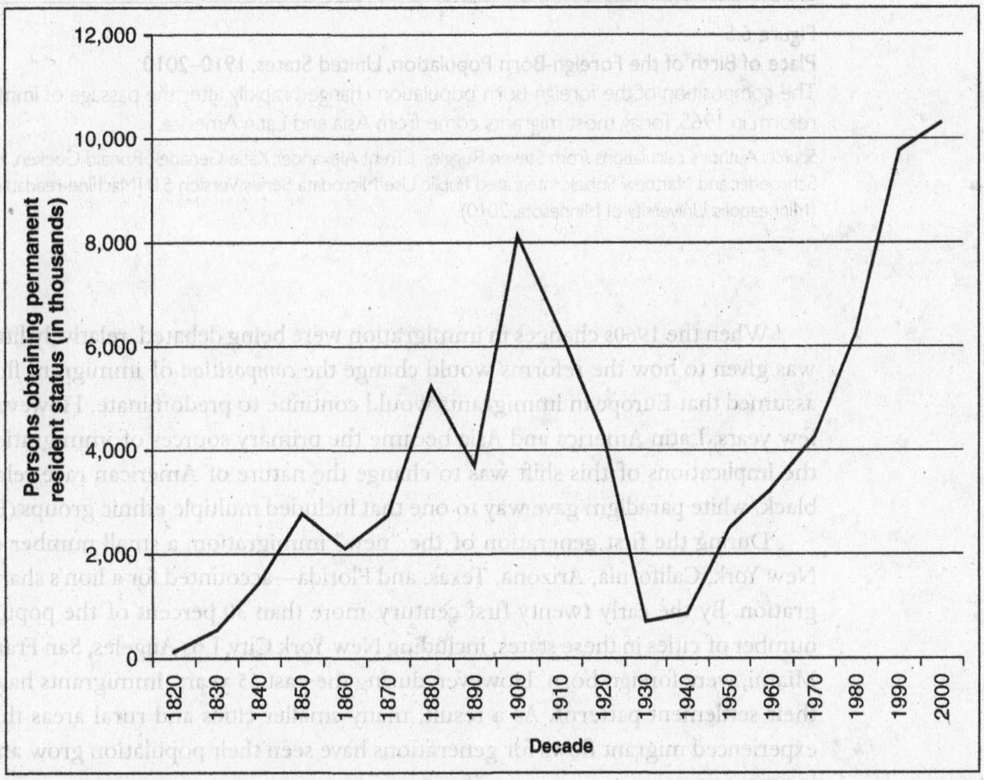

Figure 6.4
Immigrants Entering the United States, by Decade, 1820–2010
More immigrants enter the United States today than at any time in American history.

Source: US Department of Homeland Security, "Yearbook of Immigration Statistics, 2012," http://www.dhs.gov/sites/default/files/publications/immigration-statistics/yearbook/2012/LPR/table1.xls.

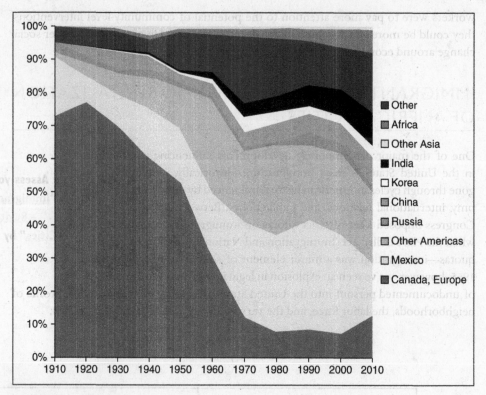

Figure 6.5
Place of Birth of the Foreign-Born Population, United States, 1910–2010
The composition of the foreign-born population changed rapidly after the passage of immigration reform in 1965. Today, most migrants come from Asia and Latin America.

Source: Author's calculations from Steven Ruggles, J. Trent Alexander, Katie Genadek, Ronald Goeken, Matthew B. Schroeder, and Matthew Sobek, Integrated Public Use Microdata Series: Version 5.0 [Machine-readable database] (Minneapolis: University of Minnesota, 2010).

When the 1960s changes in immigration were being debated, relatively little thought was given to how the reforms would change the *composition* of immigrant flows. It was assumed that European immigrants would continue to predominate. However, within a few years, Latin America and Asia became the primary sources of immigration. One of the implications of this shift was to change the nature of American race relations, as a black/white paradigm gave way to one that included multiple ethnic groups (Figure 6.5).

During the first generation of the "new" immigration, a small number of states—New York, California, Arizona, Texas, and Florida—accounted for a lion's share of immigration. By the early twenty-first century, more than 30 percent of the population of a number of cities in these states, including New York City, Los Angeles, San Francisco, and Miami, were foreign-born. However, during the past 15 years, immigrants have widened their settlement patterns. As a result, many smaller cities and rural areas that had not experienced migrant flows for generations have seen their population grow and diversify in recent years.

In addition to normal immigration, refugee policy has had an important role in remaking the population of many communities. As the United States emerged as a world leader after World War II, and especially since it began to emphasize human rights as a foreign-policy priority in the 1970s, the United States has accepted, on average, approximately 50,000 refugees per year. During the first decade of the twenty-first century, Africa, Asia, and Eastern Europe accounted for the largest number of refugees.

Unauthorized persons have emerged as a particularly hot political issue. Although it is difficult to count accurately the number of unauthorized migrants, a 2010 study estimated that between 11 and 12 million residents were unauthorized migrants, with Mexico as the largest source of unauthorized migration. Much of the debate over immigration policy has focused on how to address the status of these people. At one extreme are groups that advocate militarization of the border and mass deportation as the best solutions to the problem. Others have proposed developing channels through which unauthorized residents could have their status legitimated.

One group that has attracted sympathy is unauthorized children, who are seen as less culpable than their parents. The DREAM (Development, Relief, and Education for Alien Minors) Act would have provided permanent residency status to young adults in this group who meet certain requirements. In 2010, the Act was passed by the House but failed to break a filibuster in the Senate. In 2012, President Obama used an executive order to stop the deportation of young adults who would have qualified for permanent status under the DREAM Act.[62]

The increase in immigration has driven policymaking at federal, state, and local levels. Since the 1980s, issues of border security and concerns about terrorism have driven most successful federal legislation. The massive increase in funding for border security has had little impact on the actual inflow of unauthorized migrants, although it has substantially increased the danger and cost of entering. Ironically, one result of militarizing the border has been to discourage authorized residents from seasonal migration back to their countries of origin. As a result, a larger share of unauthorized migrants are now year-round residents.[63]

Historically, the national politics of immigration have been complicated. Issues of whether to allow more immigrants to enter the country legally and whether and how quickly they should acquire full citizenship have tended to split rather than unite political parties. For example, business groups tend to support immigration because it increases the labor supply, while other Republican-oriented groups tend to be hostile to immigration. Among Democratic-leaning groups, liberals tend to favor immigration while organized labor has been more skeptical; recently, however, labor has been more open to immigrants as a potential source of new recruits.

Because of these complications, federal immigration policy tends to change rarely, but dramatically. The restrictions of the 1920s and liberalization of the 1960s represented radical changes in policy, which were followed by long periods of continuity. In spite of widespread mobilization, federal policy has not changed fundamentally in the past half century.

States and localities have become involved in immigration policy for a variety of reasons. Most directly, increased immigration is associated with greater demands for social services, which fall disproportionately on states and cities. In addition, state and local policymaking have provided activists with opportunities to change policy at a time when federal changes aren't likely. For example, Arizona passed a set of immigrant restrictions in 2010 that require all immigrants to have proof of status on their person at all times and

[62]Julia Preston and John H. Cushman Jr., "Obama to Permit Young Migrants to Remain in US," *New York Times*, June 15, 2012, http://www.nytimes.com/2012/06/16/us/us-to-stop-deporting-some-illegal-immigrants.html?pagewanted=all.

[63]Douglas S. Massey, Jorge Druand, and Nolan J. Maline, *Beyond Smoke and Mirrors: Mexican Immigration in an Era of Economic Integration* (New York: Russell Sage Foundation Press, 2003).

authorize police to check the documents of persons if they have reasonable suspicion that they are not authorized to be in the United States. In 2012, the Supreme Court invalidated several aspects of the Arizona law because they infringed upon the federal government's constitutional authority but allowed others—including the document requirements—to go into effect, pending proof that they were applied in a discriminatory way.

Not all local and state efforts have been anti-immigration. Many cities have seen attracting immigrants as a key economic development strategy. New York Mayor Michael Bloomberg was instrumental in establishing the *Partnership for a New American Economy*, which advocated making the economic benefits of immigration the driving force in reform. As Latin American and Asian immigrants have become an increasingly significant part of the voting public, local and state politicians have become more sensitive to their needs and less likely to stigmatize immigrants.

At the neighborhood level, new immigration has radically changed the character of racial segregation, particularly in American cities. Taking Philadelphia as an example, in 1990 less than one in five Philadelphians lived in an ethnically diverse neighborhood (defined as a census block group in which less than 80 percent of the population was of a single race or ethnicity). By 2010, more than half of the city's population lived in an ethnically diverse block group. But the story was not entirely positive. The one group for which this was the exception was African Americans. Although more African Americans now live in diverse neighborhoods than in the past, the vast majority of African Americans still live in segregated black neighborhoods (Figure 6.6).

Immigrants pose another challenge to social welfare service providers. Historically, social service organizations have located in neighborhoods with high levels of need, which, more often than not, have been poor African American and Latino neighborhoods. New immigrants, however, are often locating in other neighborhoods. As a result, we are witnessing a geographic mismatch between the location of immigrants and the presence of social services.

Consult the <u>Pew Research Hispanic Center</u> for current information on immigration.

This mismatch is only one element of the broader problem of immigrant integration into American society. In recent years, there has been significant evidence that immigrants are less connected to the political and civic life of their communities. Notably, the proportion of immigrants who choose to become citizens has been declining for several decades.

In a comparative study of the United States and Canada, Irene Bloemraad has argued that the combination of government policy and grassroots mobilization have been critical to the political incorporation of immigrants in Canada. Not only do more Canadian immigrants become citizens, they have become more active in all aspects of civic and political life than those in the United States. The risk of social exclusion among US immigrants—whether documented or not—poses a grave risk for the quality of life of immigrants and the rest of the population.

A hundred years ago, social workers were active in low-income communities and played a critical role in the social, political, and cultural inclusion of a generation of immigrants into American society. Although much has changed in American society over the past century, we again face a moment in history where the need

Policy Practice

Practice Behavior Example: Collaborate with colleagues and clients for effective policy action.

Critical Thinking Question: Local policy may be more important than national policy in speeding the social integration of new Americans. What constituencies could social workers engage in collaborations to influence local government?

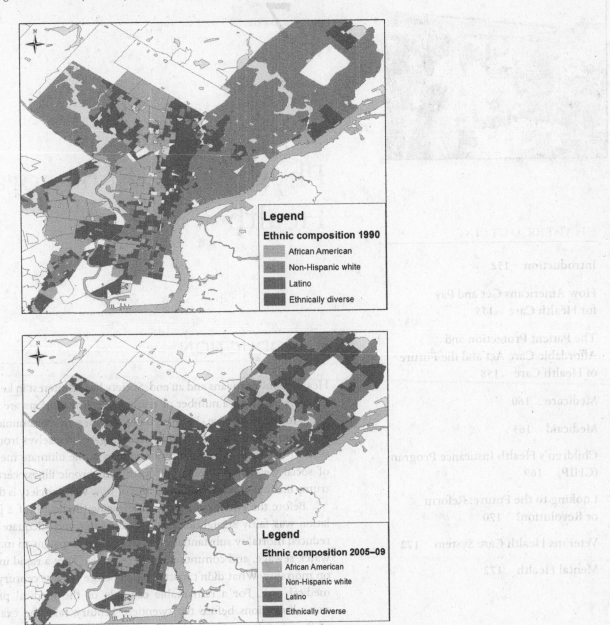

Figure 6.6
Ethnic Composition of Block Groups, Philadelphia, 1990 and 2005–09
After the 1990s, cities like Philadelphia became more ethnically diverse as homogeneous black and white neighborhoods became less common. Still, a majority of African Americans continued to live in segregated sections of the city.

Source: Author's calculations from Steven Ruggles, J. Trent Alexander, Katie Genadek, Ronald Goeken, Matthew B. Schroeder, and Matthew Sobek, Integrated Public Use Microdata Series: Version 5.0 [Machine-readable database] (Minneapolis: University of Minnesota, 2010).

for outreach is necessary. For new professionals entering the field, we encourage the well-being of communities as a field of practice and, particularly, working with new American communities as an important area of endeavor.

Assess your analysis and evaluation of the chapter's content by completing the Chapter Review.

LARRY TOWELL / MAGNUM PHOTOS

7

Physical and Behavioral Health

INTRODUCTION

Health is both a means and an end. Society has an interest in keeping people healthy for a number of reasons. Healthy workers are more likely to be productive. Because many diseases are communicable, it is often difficult for the healthy to segregate themselves from the sick. At the same time, health can be seen as the ultimate measure of social well-being. Premature death and chronic illness certainly trump income or poverty as measures of how well a society is doing.

Before the twentieth century, improving the health of a population was fairly straightforward. Clean water and adequate food reduced mortality substantially. Public health campaigns to manage water, sewage, and communicable disease also have a rapid impact on mortality. What didn't matter much before the last century was medical care. For a remarkable example of the medical profession's limitations before the twentieth century, take the example of President James Garfield, who in 1881 survived an assassination attempt *until* he was turned over to the physicians. American doctors of Garfield's time largely ignored recent strategies for fighting infection and abjured even washing their hands before surgery. The "good old surgical stink" would be Garfield's undoing, as doctors probed his wound with unwashed fingers that ultimately spread infection throughout his body.[1]

Things changed by the twentieth century. The application of germ theory; the development of vaccines to combat many common diseases; and improvement in the training of physicians,

---

[1]Kevin Baker, "The Doctors Who Killed a President," *New York Times Book Review,* September 30, 2011, review of *Destiny of the Republic: A Tale of Madness, Medicine, and the Murder of a President* (NY: Doubleday, 2011).

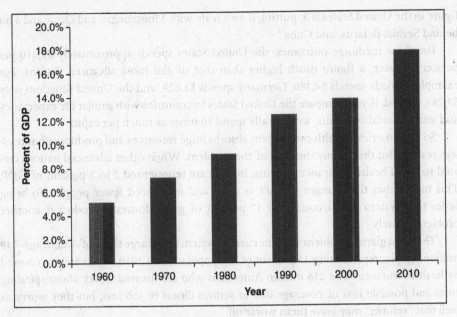

Figure 7.1
National Health Expenditures as Share of Gross Domestic Product, 1960–2010
Health expenditures now account for 17 percent of the US economy, which makes health care
reform more important ... and more difficult.

Source: Based on Centers for Medicare & Medicaid Services, Office of the Actuary, National Health
Statistics Group; US Department of Commerce, Bureau of Economic Analysis; and US Bureau of the
Census, accessed January 8, 2012, https://www.cms.gov/NationalHealthExpendData/02_NationalHealthAccounts
Historical.asp.

nurses, and other professionals led to rapid improvement in the effectiveness of health
care. Still, during the early decades of the century, the medical profession's role in health
care continued to be tenuous.

At the same time, until the end of the twentieth century, health care as an industry
remained a relatively minor part of the American economy. As late as 1960—despite sizable expansion of the health care system and private health insurance after World War
II—the health care sector still accounted for only 5 percent of GDP, less than a third of its
current proportion (Figure 7.1).

In short, although issues of health and medical treatment have very long histories,
the nature of our current challenges around health care are relatively novel both in scope
and nature. So, what is the nature of our current health care
challenge?

First, Americans are relatively healthy compared to the rest
of the world, but indicators of health do not jibe with the nation's
overall wealth. Americans' average life expectancy (79 years)
compares unfavorably to that of many other advanced industrial nations, like Japan (83); Australia, Switzerland, Spain (all
82); France (81); and Germany (80). Indeed, the countries with
which the United States shares average life expectancy—including
Chile, Costa Rica, Portugal, and Slovenia—are not our usual company. The data on infant mortality are even starker. While most
European nations have 2 to 4 child deaths per 1,000 live births, the

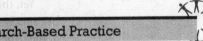

Research-Based Practice

**Practice Behavior Example: Use research
evidence to inform practice.**

Critical Thinking Question: How should the
United States' relatively high infant mortality
rate inform social work practice? Are there
particular practice arenas that should be the focus
on this effort?

figure in the United States is 8, putting it on a scale with Montenegro and Qatar and a bit behind Serbia, Belarus, and Cuba.[2]

For these mediocre outcomes, the United States spends approximately $7,410 per person per year, a figure much higher than that of the most advanced nations. For example, Canada spends $4,380, Germany spends $4,629, and the United Kingdom only $3,285. Indeed, if you compare the United States to countries with similar life expectancy and infant mortality results, we typically spend 10 times as much per capita.

So the American health care system absorbs huge resources and produces unimpressive results. But this is only the start of the problem. When other advanced nations created national health insurance systems, health care represented 2 to 3 percent of GDP. This meant that the changes weren't as great and influenced fewer people. To bring order to a system that accounts for 17 percent of gross domestic product is another problem entirely.

The most glaring problem with the current system is the large share of Americans—49 million people, representing 15 percent of the population in 2010—who are not covered by health insurance. The 256 million Americans who are insured worry about spiraling costs and possible loss of coverage due to serious illness or job loss, but they worry as well that "reform" may leave them worse off.

These health care realities have created a policy dilemma. On the one hand, America's health care system devotes excessive resources and produces inferior results. Ideally, health care reform should lower its cost, expand access, and improve quality. On the other hand, many Americans worry that change will do more harm than good. Older Americans worry that cost cutting will harm Medicare, and working Americans have the same concern about their employer-provided care. People who make a living off health care—hospital workers, doctors, insurance companies, pharmaceutical manufacturers, and a host of others—fear that their working lives and incomes will be threatened by reform.

As a result, everyone acknowledges the need for reform, but many—perhaps most—Americans oppose any specific plan to change the system. Since the 1970s, efforts to reform the health care system through federal policymaking have generally failed. However, the outcome of the 2008 elections presented a unique *window of opportunity* for reform. Recession created support, at least in the short term, for a more activist role of the federal government, and the Democrats controlled both houses of Congress and the presidency for the first time since 1995. Although it was hardly inevitable, Democrats were able to take advantage of that window to pass the Patient Protection and Affordable Care Act of 2010 (PL 111–148). The act required virtually all Americans to be covered by insurance; provided a set of subsidies and program reform to provide insurance for lower-income Americans; and introduced a host of measures to make health care more equitable, effective, and efficient.

Yet, the passage of the Affordable Care Act represented not the end of the process, but simply the end of the beginning. Within weeks of its passage, the Republican Party at the national and state levels attacked the bill through legislation, executive actions, and litigation. With the main provisions of the law not scheduled to begin until 2014, opponents had ample time to block its implementation. Indeed, fears about the law's impact on Medicare were critical to the Republicans' electoral victories in 2010. The rise of the "Tea Party" fueled hopes among opponents and fears among supporters that the main elements of the law would never go into effect.

---

[2]World Health Organization (WHO), *World Health Statistics 2011*, http://www.who.int/whosis/whostat/2011/en/index.html.

This chapter outlines the current state of health care policy before the implementation of the Affordable Care Act, reviews the main provisions of the act, and traces changes in the American mental health system.

HOW AMERICANS GET AND PAY FOR HEALTH CARE

In 2010, some form of health insurance covered 85 percent of Americans. The majority—55 percent of the population—were covered by employers. About a third of the population was covered by government-run health care plans: 15 percent by Medicare (which covers older Americans, people with disabilities, and people with end-stage renal disease), 16 percent by Medicaid or the State Children's Health Insurance Plan (S-CHIP) (which covers low-income populations), and 3 percent by military health care (Chart 7.1).[3]

Assess your comprehension of "How Americans Get and Pay for Health Care" by completing this quiz.

The remaining 15 percent have no health coverage. Several decades ago, it was common for families to pay for health care out of pocket, but as health care costs have outpaced inflation, this alternative has become less viable. As a result, a large proportion of the uninsured receives relatively little care at all and typically relies on emergency room care when necessary. The Emergency Medical Treatment and Active Medical Labor Act of 1986 provides Americans with an explicit right to emergency treatment at hospitals that participate in Medicare.

The Emergency Medical Treatment Act (EMTA) brings us back to the concept of moral hazard discussed in Chapter 1. If you don't receive health insurance through your job or

Chart 7.1   Health Insurance Coverage, United States, 2008–2010

	All persons	Heads of households	Unemployed
Percent with no health insurance	15.3%	13.3%	44.6%
Private health insurance	67.2%	72.9%	37.0%
Employer-based	56.0%	59.6%	28.7%
Purchased directly	13.3%	17.0%	8.9%
TRICARE (military)	2.9%	3.4%	1.7%
Public coverage	28.7%	31.3%	22.0%
Medicaid	16.3%	10.4%	17.7%
Medicare	14.8%	23.9%	4.0%
Veterans Administration	2.1%	4.0%	1.9%
Indian Health Service	0.5%	0.4%	0.7%
N	306,738,434	114,597,490	14,043,057

Source: Author's calculation from Steven Ruggles, J. Trent Alexander, Katie Genadek, Ronald Goeken, Matthew B. Schroeder, and Matthew Sobek, Integrated Public Use Microdata Series: Version 5.0 [Machine-readable database] (Minneapolis: University of Minnesota, 2010).

---

[3] Author's calculation from Steven Ruggles, J. Trent Alexander, Katie Genadek, Ronald Goeken, Matthew B. Schroeder, and Matthew Sobek, Integrated Public Use Microdata Series: Version 5.0 [Machine-readable database] (Minneapolis: University of Minnesota, 2010).

from the government, you have to pay for it out of pocket or join the ranks of the uninsured. If you had no other options, you would be more likely to get insurance. If you know that ERs must treat you when you get sick and that you probably won't ever pay for the care, you might take the chance of going without insurance. Thus EMTA creates an incentive (guaranteed care) to do something that is undesirable (go without insurance). It's a moral hazard.

Whether one has health insurance is strongly related to age. Children under the age of 18 have been a particular focus of policy. Their uninsured rate—10 percent in 2010— was well below the population figure, with both the proportion covered by employment-based programs and those covered by government programs higher than the figures for the entire population. Twenty million individuals between 18 and 35 have no health insurance, 40 percent of the entire uninsured population.

The *individual mandate* was included in the Affordable Care Act to address the moral hazard of "free" care for the uninsured. Because health care isn't *free* and because everyone else pays the cost of care for those who lack insurance, the individual mandate was an effort to balance the guarantee of care with a responsibility. You must either obtain insurance or pay a tax to compensate the rest of us.

Employer-Provided Health Care

About half of all Americans receive health care through their employers or the employer of a family member. Although employer-based health care is the foundation of the American health insurance system, it emerged more by accident than as a result of conscious planning or policymaking.

The growth of employer-provided health care is an example of an important dimension of policymaking: the impact of past decisions (or nondecisions) on current policy choices. Although employer-based health care emerged willy-nilly during the 1940s and 1950s, its existence has limited alternatives for reforming the system.

In 1993–94, for example, when President Clinton proposed his plan for health care reform, the existing system generated an unanticipated set of opponents—labor unions. Clinton's plan hoped to achieve cost containment by introducing market discipline through "managed competition." One strategy was to establish ceilings on the generosity of plans. Because this proposal might have reduced the comprehensiveness and increased the out-of-pocket costs associated with some labor union plans, many unions took an ambivalent stance to the Clinton plan. The absence of strong labor union support, a political necessity for virtually any progressive reform proposal, contributed to the failure of health care reform in 1994.[4]

Employer-provided health care grew out of the *welfare capitalism* experiments of the 1920s. In the years after World War I, employers fought a two-front war against the threats of militant unions and socialists. Repression was one approach. Corporations were able to call upon the cooperation of local government and judges and the mobilization of private police forces like the infamous Pinkertons to suppress labor agitation. In 1919, the perceived threat of organized labor—highlighted by a general strike in Seattle, industry-wide strikes in steel and coal, and the Boston police strike—prompted the use of state and federal troops and the "Red Scare" that led to the arrest and deportation of hundreds of leftist activists.[5]

---

[4]Laurence A. Weil, "Organized Labor and Health Reform: Union Interests and the Clinton Plan," (Faculty Publications, 1997), paper 242, http://digitalcommons.ric.edu/facultypublications/242.

[5]Nick Salvatore, *Eugene V. Debs: Citizen and Socialist* (Urbana: University of Illinois Press, 1982).

Welfare capitalism was the second front in this war. Many employers developed a range of programs to increase the loyalty and satisfaction of their employees. These programs ranged from "hard" services like fledgling unemployment and retirement systems to "softer" services like "welfare secretaries" who would visit employees' families. Health care—typically in the form of company-based clinics—was often incorporated into these schemes. Although welfare capitalism did not survive the Great Depression, the idea of companies taking administrative and financial responsibility for welfare services remained popular as an alternative to government-centered approaches.[6]

Although welfare capitalism failed, the *voluntarist* impulse in welfare provision found another champion in the creation of the Blue Cross and Blue Shield systems. The origins of these plans are usually dated to 1929 when the first prepaid hospital insurance plan began in Texas. Between 1930 and the 1950s, these prepaid plans for hospital and doctors' services organized on a group basis grew in popularity, aided by state charters that exempted the plans from taxation and other restrictions under which insurers usually operated. Although the "Blues" incorporated many elements of nonbusiness practices— like covering family members and "community ratings" (in which rates were not linked to individuals' personal health status)—their core business remained selling insurance. By 1946, 67 percent of large corporations had some form of health and accident plan.[7]

By the time the federal government seriously considered national health insurance (in the Wagner-Murray-Dingell proposals of the 1940s), the link between employers and health insurance was well established. It was given greater impetus during the 1940s by the Taft-Hartley Act and the Supreme Court's *Inland Steel* decision that provided legal sanction for union negotiations over fringe benefits. As unions increasingly saw labor-management negotiation, rather than national legislation, as the way to expand coverage for their members, employer-provided health care became institutionalized.

Employer-provided health care, which remains the foundation of the American health care system, retains a number of shortcomings. Because employers are not required to offer plans, many workers are forced to seek more expensive individual coverage. This is particularly true for employees of smaller firms that are the least likely to provide insurance. In addition, employees typically must hold a job for a number of months before they can be included in a group plan. As a result, workers who switch jobs (and their families) can find themselves without insurance.

Of course, employer-provided insurance means that losing one's job means losing one's health insurance. Although the Consolidated Omnibus Budget Reconciliation Act (COBRA) of 1986 required some employers to allow terminated employees to continue their coverage, the coverage is temporary and the employee must pay the full cost of the plan. As a result, in 2008–2010, only 28 percent of the unemployed were still covered by an employer plan (including some covered through another family member). Indeed, 45 percent of the unemployed had no health insurance, 16 percent received Medicaid, and 8 percent were covered under other plans.

With such a large proportion of the population covered through employers, a number of health care reform efforts (including Bill Clinton's) have focused on requiring all employers to cover their employees—an *employer mandate*. This approach has been hard

[6]David Brody, "The Rise and Decline of Welfare Capitalism," in *Workers in Industrial America: Essay on the 20th-Century Struggle,* ed. David Brody (New York: Oxford University Press, 1980) 48–81.
[7]Jacob Hacker, *The Divided Welfare State: The Battle over Public and Private Social Benefits in the United States* (New York: Cambridge University Press, 2002), 229; Paul Starr, *The Social Transformation of American Medicine* (New York: Basic Books, 1982), 290–334.

to sell politically. First, small business and its political arm—the National Federation of Independent Business—have effectively fought against an employer mandate. Big business showed some interest in an employer mandate early in the 1990s because it was already providing health care. It ultimately rejected the Clinton approach out of fear of increased government regulation and its general alignment with the Republican Party.[8]

Still, reflecting the general desire to implement cost containment policies, employer-provided health care has changed dramatically over the past two decades. Today, employees are likely to pay more out of pocket for health care and to find their choice of providers more limited. *Managed care* plans, like health-maintenance organizations (HMOs) and preferred provider plans, require employees to obtain referrals to specialists from their primary care provider (PCP) and seek preapproval for many procedures. Although this approach might improve the quality of individual health care (because the PCP can coordinate care), it often discourages patients from seeking care, and in certain circumstances it limits the care that they receive.

These concerns may explain why those who receive health care through their employer are somewhat less satisfied with their health insurance than those covered by government-run plans. According to 2009 data from the Kaiser Family Fund, 51 percent of Medicare recipients rated their health care plan as excellent compared to only 33 percent of working-age adults who are covered through an employer. Still, with the 60 percent of employer-covered Americans who rate their plan as "good," the vast majority of people getting insurance through their employers are satisfied enough with their existing coverage to resist plans for fundamental change. Along with Medicare recipients, they stand as a restraining force to reform.[9]

THE PATIENT PROTECTION AND AFFORDABLE CARE ACT AND THE FUTURE OF HEALTH CARE

Assess your comprehension of "The Patient Protection and Affordable Care Act" by completing this quiz.

If there were no history, the reform of the American health care system would probably follow that of other Western countries. It might look like the British National Health Service in which the actual provision of health care services is managed by the government. Or it might look more like Canada in which the government is the "single payer" for all health care but does not actually run the system.[10]

But there *is* history, so health care reform in the United States has had to adapt to the existing system rather than start new. In particular, reform has to accommodate the interests of various groups of providers and consumers of health care:

- *Workers who receive health care through their employers*—As we've noted, this is a majority of the population. Any reform that threatens their health care is likely to generate widespread opposition.
- *Employers who offer health care insurance*—The tax treatment of health care insurance is very favorable, so reform can't fiddle with those benefits.

[8]Paul Starr, *Remedy and Reaction: The Peculiar American Struggle Over Health Care Reform* (New Haven: Yale University Press, 2011) 103–128.

[9]Kaiser Family Foundation, *Health Tracking Poll* (conducted August 4–11, 2009).

[10]Charles Webster, *The National Health Service: A Political History* (New York: Oxford University Press, 2002); Malcolm G. Taylor, *Insuring National Health Care: The Canadian Experience* (Chapel Hill: University of North Carolina Press, 1990).

- *Medicare recipients*—Most older Americans are happy with the existing system and resist change. Enrollees in the Medicare Advantage program, which offers large subsidies to private insurers to provide an enhanced, privatized version of Medicare, tend to be particularly satisfied with the existing system.
- *Insurers*—Providing health insurance is a business and a profitable one. Any change that increases regulation or costs is likely to be resisted, unless the increase in market share will compensate for it.
- *Small business*—Most uninsured workers are employed by small businesses that benefit from not paying for health care. Any effort to compel small businesses to provide health care is likely to be resisted.

Despite these interests, which exert a conservative counterweight to reform, the current system has a number of problems that provide an impetus for reform.

- *Spiraling costs*—The system is tremendously expensive and getting more expensive every year. Ultimately, health care costs are likely to be a drain on the entire economy.
- *Lack of coordination*—The health care system is really no system at all but rather a mishmash of many systems and stand-alone elements. Many people find themselves neglected, which may explain why America's health care outcomes are so mediocre relative to other countries.
- *The uninsured*—Lack of health insurance has personal costs in terms of psychological stress and delayed health care. It also has social costs because of its impact on the overall productivity of the labor force and the increased costs for those who do have insurance. Less concretely, it weakens our sense of social citizenship (the idea that we all share common rights and responsibilities) and fosters social exclusion.

Because of these problems, and in spite of the daunting prospects for success, the Obama administration championed health care reform. The chances for success became even slimmer early in 2009 when the Republican Party united in opposition to the Obama plan. The legislative history of the reform proposal went through many twists and turns. Ultimately, in March 2010, Congress passed two bills that made important changes in the health care system: the Patient Protection and Affordable Care Act (PL 111–148) and the Health Care and Education Reconciliation Act (PL 111–152).[11]

Although the laws were passed in 2010, it would take four years for the acts to take full effect. Because of the extent of Republican opposition to reform, the fate of reform remained in considerable doubt. Some of that doubt was removed in June 2012 when the Supreme Court upheld the constitutionality of the "individual mandate" and in November 2012 when President Obama was reelected.

Major Elements of the Health Care Reform

Expanding coverage. The act includes no guarantee of health insurance for Americans. However, it includes two mandates—an individual mandate and an employer mandate—that are expected to reduce considerably the number of uninsured. All US citizens and

[11]It took two bills to implement health care reform because the original bill (PL 111–148) had passed the Senate in December 2009 with 60 Democratic votes and no Republican votes. While the House and Senate negotiated over the conference report that would reconcile each version, the special election for Edward Kennedy's Senate seat in Massachusetts led to the election of a Republican. As a result, after January 2010, Democrats could not break a Republican filibuster to bring the conference report to a vote. To avoid a filibuster, Democrats transformed their changes into a *budget reconciliation* bill that could not be filibustered. Although the changes were enacted with two laws, we will refer to the Obama reform as the Affordable Care Act.

legal residents who do not otherwise have insurance are required to purchase coverage or pay a penalty that will rise to 2.5 percent of taxable income in 2016. Employers with more than 50 workers are required to offer coverage or pay a penalty.

Medicaid expansion. One of the major elements of reform—as it was originally passed—was the expansion of Medicaid to cover virtually all Americans with an income below 133 percent of the poverty line. However, at the same time that it affirmed the constitutionality of the individual mandate, the Supreme Court ruled that the federal government could not compel states to expand their Medicaid programs. There is a risk, therefore, that some states with very large low-income uninsured populations will resist expanding Medicaid.

Subsidies for individuals and employers. The act includes generous subsidies so that individuals and families that do not qualify for Medicaid, but have an income below 400 percent of the federal poverty line, will be able to obtain affordable health insurance.[12] In addition, small businesses with fewer than 25 employees will receive subsidies of up to 50 percent of the cost of insurance.

Establish state insurance exchanges. For the minority of the population that must purchase its own insurance, each state is required to set up an exchange that allows consumers to compare and purchase insurance in one location. In order to make the purchase of insurance more transparent, the act established a set of standard program tiers (bronze, silver, gold, and platinum) as well as a "catastrophic" option for young adults (under 30 years of age) and those exempt from the mandate. If states choose not to create their own exchanges (as a number of states with Republican-controlled legislatures and governors have done), the federal government will step in to establish the exchange.

Restrict insurance companies. The act requires private insurance companies to use only age, geography, family composition, and tobacco use in setting the price of policies. In other words, the act requires a "community rating" that does not tie the cost of a policy to one's prior medical history. In addition, insurance policies are required to cover adult children up to age 26 under their parents' plans, to impose no lifetime limits on care, and to cover a standard package of routine care.

In addition, the act required a number of changes to existing programs that we cover below.

MEDICARE

No population is more sensitive to the need for health care than the elderly. Older Americans are more likely to suffer from disabilities and chronic conditions and need health care than the rest of the population. During the years after World War II, when working-age Americans increasingly came to rely on prepaid insurance, the lack of insurance for the elderly combined with their higher-than-average poverty rates made them a particularly vulnerable population with respect to health insurance.

---

[12]The affordability of the subsidies may be compromised by an Internal Revenue Service (IRS) interpretation of the law. Instead of calculating an employee's ability to pay based on covering her entire family, the IRS ruled that the calculation should only consider individual insurance for the worker. Thus, the IRS would expect a worker earning $35,000 per year to pay more than 12 percent of her income for health insurance before she qualified for a subsidy. Robert Pear, "Ambiguity in Health Law Could Make Family Coverage Too Costly for Many," *New York Times,* August 11, 2012, http://www.nytimes.com/2012/08/12/us/ambiguity-in-health-law-could-make-family-coverage-too-costly.htm?_r=1.

Although the failure to achieve universal health care during the 1940s was a setback for groups that supported an expansion of social welfare programs, by the late 1940s and early 1950s, they had identified the expansion of care for the elderly as an important goal. During the 1950s and early 1960s, support for what became Medicare gained momentum, particularly after the 1958 election when the Democrats made substantial gains.

Yet, those supporting Medicare faced formidable opposition from conservatives who feared that Medicare would be an opening for a more thorough nationalization of health care. Conservative opposition was spearheaded by physicians' organizations, in particular, the American Medical Association. Still, the electoral landslide of 1964 provided the Democratic Party with the votes it needed in the following year to add both Medicare and Medicaid to the Social Security Act.

Major Elements of Medicare

Title XVIII of the Social Security Act—Health Insurance for the Aged and Disabled, what we usually call Medicare—includes four major elements. The first two, hospital and supplementary medical insurance, were part of the 1965 bill.

- *Part A*—Provides hospital insurance for older Americans, people with disabilities, and people with advanced kidney disease.
- *Part B*—Often called Supplementary Medical Insurance or SMI, it provides a voluntary system that helps Medicare recipients pay for physician, outpatient hospital, home health care, and other health-related services. To be covered by Part B, recipients must pay a monthly premium.
- *Part C*—The Medicare Advantage program was added in 1997 and modified in 2003. It created a system whereby seniors could forgo traditional Medicare and instead purchase private insurance, and it provided a set of generous subsidies for the program.
- *Part D*—Prescription drug coverage was added to the program in the Medicare Improvement and Modernization Act of 2003. Part D followed Medicare Advantage in establishing a program of subsidies through which Medicare recipients could purchase private prescription insurance.

Eligibility

Generally speaking, Medicare is provided to persons 65 years of age or older who are eligible for Social Security (or Railroad Retirement) benefits, whether or not the individual has retired or is collecting those cash benefits. Over the years, a variety of other groups have been added to the program. Persons with disabilities who qualify for Disability Insurance or Railroad Retirement disability insurance and have received benefits for two years are eligible for Medicare. Persons with end-stage renal disease (ESRD) who are eligible for Social Security (and insured workers' spouses and children with ESRD) are also eligible.

Overall, 47 million Americans are covered by Medicare. Of these, eight million are under the age of 65 and covered through disability or ESRD. By 2030, as the baby boom reaches the age of 65, the number of recipients is projected to reach 80 million.

Because Medicare covers older Americans (whose poverty rate is somewhat below the national average) and people with disabilities (whose poverty rate is somewhat above average), the overall poverty rate of Medicare recipients in 2008 was 16 percent, only slightly above the national average in that year. Yet, 47 percent of Medicare's recipients have a family income less than twice the official poverty line. Among the under-65 beneficiaries, most of whom have a disability, the proportion is 67 percent. The very old (those over the age of 85)—one of the fastest growing groups in the American population—who are covered by Medicare have a 58 percent chance of having an income below 200 percent of the poverty line. More than two-thirds of black and Hispanic recipients are also below this income standard.[13]

Benefits

Hospital Insurance (Part A) provides reimbursement for beneficiaries' use of inpatient hospital care, skilled nursing facilities, home health agencies, and hospice care. Hospital care is covered (after an initial deductible) for the first 60 days of a hospital stay with an additional 30 days covered with a co-payment. Skilled nursing facility and home health coverage is limited to 100 days and must occur within 30 days of a hospital stay of 3 days or more. Hospice care is provided to terminally ill patients who decide to forgo standard hospital care and whose life expectancy is less than six months.

Home health and skilled nursing care have been particularly ticklish issues for Medicare. First, because Medicare provides no coverage for nursing home care, policy and implementation are vigilant to prevent these services from substituting for long-term coverage. At the same time, the potentially open-ended needs of older Americans with disabilities and chronic conditions pose a challenge for administrators.

In contrast to young children, for whom parents have a clear and unqualified responsibility, sick older people have an ambiguous relationship to their adult children. In principle, there is a social expectation that children will care for their parents, but the legal and normative support for these expectations are much weaker than in the case of young children. As a result, even relatively marginal changes in policies regarding availability can have a significant impact on the utilization of home health services.

In 1980, Congress liberalized what had been a limited home health care benefit, turning it into what one administrator characterized as "an unlimited benefit—one that serves the chronic needs of patients as well as the needs of those who require more short-term, recuperative care after a hospital visit."[14] During the early years of the Reagan administration, the Health Care Financing Administration (the predecessor to the Centers for Medicare and Medicaid Services, CMS) attempted to contain the program through increased review of claims and reporting requirements. However, these administrative actions provoked lawsuits. The 1988 Supreme Court decision in *Duggan v. Bowen* led to a dramatic increase in home health care utilization. The 1997 Balanced Budget Act attempted to limit its growth by changing the reimbursement system in a way that provided incentives for home health care agencies to limit care.[15]

Supplementary Medical Insurance (Part B) is a voluntary insurance program that carries a monthly premium ($99.90 in 2012). As a means of reducing adverse selection—healthy older Americans waiting until they get sick to join SMI—the program imposes a penalty of 10 percent for each year in which a person was eligible for SMI but failed to join.

Part B covers a range of medical services, including physician, surgeon, and other health practitioners' services, emergency room and outpatient surgery, a share of home

[13]Kaiser Family Foundation, "Poverty Among Medicare Population 2008," accessed March 7, 2012. http://facts.kff.org/chart.aspx?ch=1722.

[14]Bruce Vladeck, Testimony on Reforming the Medicare Home Health Benefit, March 5, 1997, accessed March 9, 2012, http://www.hhs.gov/asl/testify/t970305a.html.

[15]Joan Davitt, "Racial/Ethnic Disparities in Home Health Care: Charting a Course for Future Research," *Home Health Care Services Quarterly* 31, no. 1 (January–March 2012): 1–40.

health care, and laboratory and radiology tests. Under regular Medicare, services are subject to deductibles and co-payments. These have increased over the history of Medicare, producing an interest in Medicare Advantage and "Medigap" programs.

Medicare Parts A and B—what might be called "traditional" Medicare—were developed as a *single-payer* system of health care, similar to the health care system of Canada and other nations, in which government plays the role of insurer, receiving bills and negotiating with providers over payment. However, conservatives and the private insurance industry have been hostile to this approach because it is government centered and reduces the role of for-profit entities in the health care market. With the increased influence of conservatives over social policy after the Republicans' takeover of Congress in 1995, Parts C and D were based on a system of subsidies to private insurance companies to provide services.

In the case of Part C, the size of the subsidies was particularly notable. Medicare Advantage (originally known as Medicare + Choice) was passed in 1997 on the ideological assumption that private insurers could more efficiently administer Medicare. The program provided a set of subsidies to private insurers who enrolled seniors. The program was expanded and its subsidies increased in 2003, at the same time that Part D was added. A Congressional commission concluded in 2008 that the government was paying private insurers to provide benefits that could be provided by the government for $1,000 less per person per year.[16]

Beneficiaries of private Medicare Advantage plans ended up with the best of all worlds. The overly generous subsidies allowed insurers to provide additional services to their enrollees and still turn a handsome profit. At the same time, they were free to target younger and healthier beneficiaries, thereby reducing their costs and increasing profits. From the standpoint of individual older Americans, Medicare Advantage looked like a great deal. They received more benefits and paid lower out-of-pocket fees. The fact that this "private market efficiency" was made possible by generous subsidies was invisible to beneficiaries.

This policy trap sprung closed in 2010 when the Affordable Care Act cut the subsidies under Medicare Advantage. More affluent and healthy seniors viewed this as an attack on Medicare. As a result, they were a key segment of the electorate that shifted allegiance to the Republican Party in the November elections.

The preference of Republicans for private-sector Medicare reform carried over to the prescription drug program (Part D). The program provides subsidized access to prescription drug coverage through private insurers with payment of a premium. Medicare beneficiaries may enroll in either a stand-alone prescription drug plan or one that is integrated into a Medicare Advantage plan. One confusing element of Part D is variation in *formularies*—the drugs covered and their pricing—from insurer to insurer. Because these formularies cover different drugs and charge different prices for the same drug, recipients are forced to evaluate which plans provide them with the best coverage for their particular set of prescriptions. Although beneficiaries are allowed to change plans once a year, these plans leave great potential for recipients to choose a plan that disadvantages them.

Financing

No social welfare program poses a greater fiscal challenge than Medicare. The combination of health care inflation (costs for health care services increasing faster than those for other goods and services) and the aging of the population suggest that the cost of the

---

[16]Medicare Payment Advisory Commission, *Report to Congress: Medicare Payment Policy* (Washington, DC: MEDPAC, 2011), http://medpac.gov/documents/Mar11_EntireReport.pdf.

program will outstrip the willingness of Americans to pay for it. How this plays out in the future will be the critical pivot of American politics. Will we use our intelligence and values to craft a program that continues to serve older Americans or will we sacrifice the program to our commitment to low taxes and limited government?

Current funding for Medicare comes from a number of sources. The largest shares come from payroll taxes and general revenue. These are supplemented by beneficiary payments (primarily for Part B, Supplemental Medical Insurance), interest on the trust fund, and payments from states (for costs that had been shifted from state Medicaid spending to Part D, the prescription drug program).

The challenge for the program lies in the future. First, the proportion of gross domestic product—that is, our entire economy—that will be devoted to Medicare is likely to increase from around 3.2 percent in 2010 to more than 5 percent by the 2030s. In addition, an increasing share is likely to come from general revenue, not from earmarked sources like payroll taxes and premiums. As a result, as we move forward, the program will increasingly find itself in direct competition with other government functions (Figure 7.2).

Why is Medicare so expensive? The most obvious answers are that *all* health care has become increasingly expensive and the population is aging, so the proportion of the population covered by the program is expanding and will continue to do so.

An additional factor bears consideration. Who receives Medicare dollars and when those dollars are spent influence the cost of the program. In particular, a small number of beneficiaries account for a large share of total Medicare spending, and a large share of those beneficiaries are in their last year of life. One study estimates that only 10 percent of Medicare beneficiaries account for more than half (58 percent) of

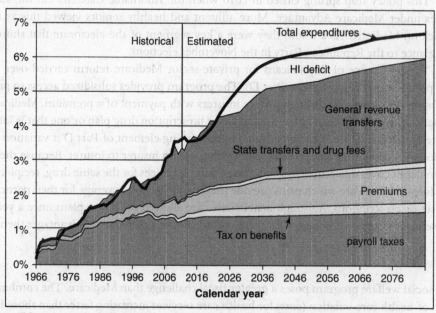

Figure 7.2
Medicare Sources of Income and Expenditures as Percent of GDP, 1966–2086 (Estimates)

Source: 2012 Annual Report of the Boards of Trustees of the Federal Hospital Insurance and Federal Supplementary Medical Insurance Trust Funds, (Washington, DC: 2012), Figure II.D2, p. 24, http://www.cms.gov/Research-Statistics-Data-and-Systems/Statistics-Trends-and-Reports/ReportsTrustFunds/downloads/tr2012.pdf.

all Medicare spending.[17] Another study found that about a quarter of all Medicare outlays occur in the last year of life.[18] Although this share has not increased much over the past 20 years, it is likely to do so in the future as the very old (those over 85 years of age) become a larger share of the population (see Chapter 10 on programs for older Americans).

The issue of end-of-life care is tremendously complicated. Whether an individual (or her family members) choose to take extraordinary measures to keep her alive or to focus more on quality of life is likely to remain an individual decision, not the result of broad policy. Yet, one would hope that these decisions happen in a private and informed way. It appears, however, that such private, informed discussions will be hard to accomplish. A sensible element of the health care reform proposals of 2009—compensating physicians for end-of-life care discussions with their patients, on a voluntary basis—was characterized by opponents of health care reform as advocating "death panels" that seek to euthanize the elderly.

The Kaiser Family Fund website provides up-to-date information on the challenges facing Medicare.

MEDICAID

In contrast to Medicare—which was the focus of a decade-long political battle—Medicaid was added to the Social Security Act in 1965 practically as an afterthought. Originally focused on providing health care for welfare recipients, the program has been retrofitted to the post-welfare reform world of need. Finally, although it is an income-tested program for poor people, a large share of Medicaid spending goes to people who weren't poor for most of their lives but were impoverished by the cost of nursing home care.

Medicaid is distinguished from Medicare by two features. First, Medicaid is an income-tested, selective program, so only people with low incomes can qualify for it. Second, Medicaid is a joint federal-state program. Although the federal government pays the majority of its cost (ranging from about 50 percent to over 80 percent, depending on the state's per capita income), much of the initiative for determining the program's features rests with the states. Furthermore, although the federal government expends most of the money, Medicaid represents a much larger share of states' budgets than of the federal government budget. As a result, when states run into fiscal problems—as virtually all states did after 2008—cutting Medicaid is an attractive alternative (Figure 7.3).

Eligibility

Historically, Medicaid was designed to provide medical assistance to people receiving some form of federal government benefits. Before 1996, this consisted primarily of recipients of Aid to Families with Dependent Children and Supplemental Security Income (SSI), which provides for low-income older Americans and people with disabilities. However, after welfare reform reduced the number of recipients, the link between cash assistance and Medicaid was loosened to some extent. Still, at the time that the Affordable Care Act was enacted, the federal government identified a set of mandatory "categorical needy," which included SSI recipients and families with children. Low-income individuals living alone or in families without children were typically not eligible for Medicaid.

---

[17]Lisa Potetz, Juliette Cubanski, and Tricia Neuman, "Medicare Spending and Financing: A Primer," http://www.kff.org/medicare/upload/7731-03.pdf.

[18]Christopher Hogan, June Lunney, Jon Gabel, and Joanne Lyn, "Medicare Beneficiaries Costs of Care in the Last Year of Life," *Health Affairs* 20, no. 4: 188–195 (doi: 10.1377/hlthaff.20.4.188).

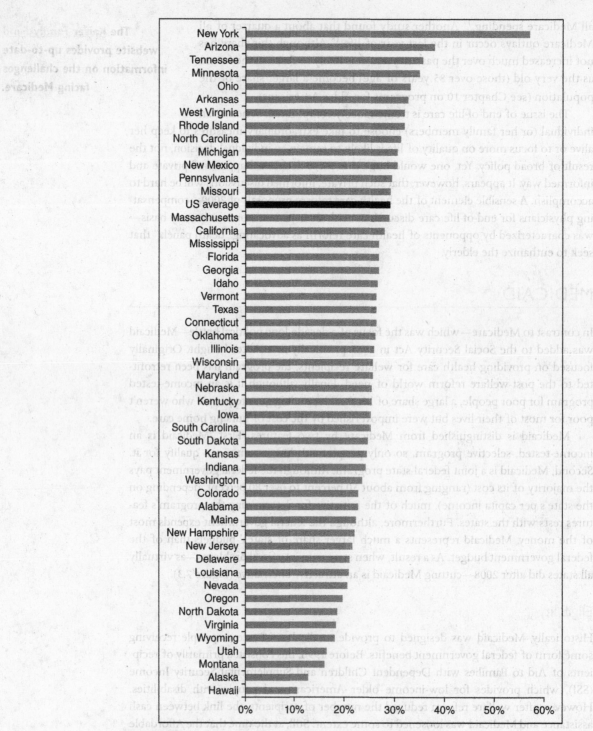

Figure 7.3

Medicaid Payments as Percent of Direct Expenditures, 2008

Because Medicaid is a state-administered program, payments vary widely from state to state.

Source: Based on *Statistical Abstract of the US* 2012, Tables 152, 454.

The Affordable Care Act, as passed, would extend Medicaid eligibility to all citizens and legal residents under 133 percent of the poverty line.[19] The Urban Institute estimates that the extension could potentially cover more than 22 million uninsured Americans or 47 percent of the uninsured. Thus, it would reduce the number of uninsured more than any other feature of the ACA. To assure that states move ahead with this expansion, the law covered 100 percent of the cost of the extension during the first several years and after that continued to pay 90 percent of the cost. The expansion was mandatory unless the state elected to withdraw from the entire Medicaid program.

However, as noted above, the Supreme Court ruled in June 2012 that the all-or-nothing nature of this reform was unconstitutional. Instead, it ruled that states could choose to continue their Medicaid program without the expansion of eligibility. The implications of this ruling are significant. For example, of the 47 million people who potentially would be newly eligible for Medicaid, 5 million lived in Texas, 4 million lived in Florida, and 2 million lived in Georgia—all states dominated by Republicans.[20]

"Making Medicaid Expansion an ACA Option," provides estimates of the impact of the Supreme Court 2012 Medicaid decision on low-income Americans.

Still, although a state's decision in 2012 may be guided by partisan considerations, there is reason to believe the impact of the court's decision may not be so great in the long term. Politicians may want to score points during election season; but the real-world impact of the expansion of Medicaid, especially for hospitals that provide uncompensated care and state governments that absorb much of its cost, are likely to be more persuasive in the long term.

The other major group eligible for Medicaid is nursing home residents. Overall, 34 percent of Medicaid spending is devoted to long-term care.[21] Typically, to qualify for Medicaid, a person needing long-term care must spend down her assets. To prevent individuals from simply giving away their assets in order to qualify for Medicaid, the program includes a "look back" feature that delays Medicaid eligibility for a number of months proportionate to the assets that the person transferred.

Benefits

There is wide variation among the states in the types of services covered by Medicaid. Generally speaking, states must provide inpatient and outpatient hospital care, pregnancy-related services, vaccinations, physicians' care, nursing facility services, and a variety of more specialized services. States vary considerably in their coverage of diagnostic and clinical services, rehabilitation and physical therapy, hospice care, and case management.

In recent years, the high cost of institutional care has led Medicaid to encourage states to invest in care that diverts recipients from institutions. For example, the Balanced Budget Amendments of 1997 established the Programs of All-Inclusive Care for the Elderly (PACE) that provides an alternative to institutional care through a team offering health, medical, and social services. States may also request a waiver to offer a variety of services not otherwise covered if they prevent a recipient from being institutionalized.

---

[19]Because 5 percent of income is disregarded in calculating Medicaid eligibility, the figure is actually 138 percent of the poverty line.

[20]Genevieve M. Kenney, Lisa Dubay, Stephen Zuckerman, and Michael Huntress, "Making the Medicaid Expansion an ACA Option: How Many Low-Income Americans Could Remain Uninsured," (Washington, DC: Urban Institute, June 29, 2012), http://www.urban.org/publications/412606.html.

[21]Kaiser Family Foundation, "Long-Term Care Spending as a Percent of Total Medicaid Spending FY2007," http://facts.kff.org/chart.aspx?cb=56&sctn=153&ch=994.

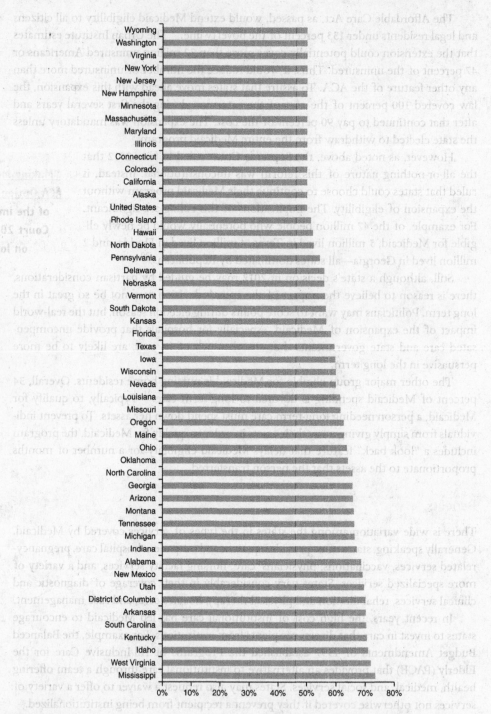

Figure 7.4

Medicaid, Federal Medical Assistance Percentage, 2013

The federal share of Medicaid expenses is tied to a state's poverty rate and other indicators.

Source: Kaiser Family Foundation, StateHealthFacts.org, http://www.statehealthfacts.org/comparetable.jsp?ind=184&cat=4.

In recent years, an increasing number of states have turned to managed care models for Medicaid recipients. These models—which may include health maintenance organizations, prepaid health plans, and similar programs—have been attractive to states as a means of controlling program costs. Managed care is also seen as a way to improve the quality of care by assuring that services are coordinated. This is particularly important for recipients who suffer from a variety of chronic conditions, where treatment for one condition may influence another. As the federal and state governments have sought to contain Medicaid reimbursement levels, the number of health care providers accepting Medicaid patients has decreased, which has made managed care systems still more attractive.

Administration and Financing

Medicaid is jointly funded by the federal government and the states. Richer states pay a higher proportion of the program's cost. The Federal Medical Assistance Percentage (FMAP) ranges from 50 percent in more affluent states to over 75 percent in poorer ones. The stimulus law passed in 2009 increased the FMAP by between 9 and 14 percent for a limited time (Figure 7.4).

The federal government also pays 100 percent of the cost of services provided to American Indians and Alaska Natives through the Indian Health Service.

CHILDREN'S HEALTH INSURANCE PROGRAM (CHIP)

The Children's Health Insurance Program was enacted in 1997, as legislators turned from the Clinton administration's failed efforts at comprehensive reform to piecemeal reform. The Bush administration resisted efforts to expand the program, twice vetoing bills. In 2009, President Obama signed CHIP reauthorization that provided additional funding to expand the program and to conduct outreach efforts.

The program, Title XXI of the Social Security Act, operates similarly to Medicaid. The federal government provides matching funds to the states in support of their efforts to provide health insurance to needy children not enrolled in Medicaid. The federal matching fund rate for CHIP is roughly 15 percentage points higher than the Medicaid rate. This raised the average share of CHIP paid for by the federal government to 93 percent. The program has experienced rapid growth during its existence. In 2000, only 3.4 million children were enrolled. By 2010, this number had increased to 7.7 million.

States have three options in accessing CHIP funding. They may choose to enroll children in their existing Medicaid program, create a separate CHIP program, or create a combined program. As of 2011, 7 states and the District of Columbia had opted for Medicaid expansion, 17 had established separate CHIP programs, and the remaining 26 had some combination.

The Affordable Care Act requires states to maintain their current eligibility levels for children in Medicaid and CHIP through 2019 and extends funding for the program through 2015. Children who are eligible for CHIP but are unable to enroll in the program because of state-imposed limitations (for example, a freeze on new enrollments) will qualify for tax credits through state exchanges.

KATHRYN SCOTT OSLER/DENVER POST/GETTY IMAGES

The Affordable Care Act seeks to expand preventative care like vaccinations (even if they hurt).

LOOKING TO THE FUTURE: REFORM OR REVOLUTION?

In 2013, the United States was at a turning point in health care policy. Although the Affordable Care Act had been upheld as the law of the land, Republicans continued to call for its repeal. In attacking the law, they characterized it as a revolution in which the federal government was undertaking a power-grab.

> Most egregiously, it puts the federal government in command of the health sector, giving bureaucrats immense new power to decide matters ranging from what services must be covered in every American's insurance plan to how doctors and hospitals organize themselves and do business.[22]

Capretta and Moffit argue that for opponents to be successful in repealing the ACA, they need to come together around a single proposal to replace it. They advocate what they characterize as a "market-based" response and outline a proposal based on seven principles.

- *Shift government programs to "defined" contribution*—By forcing Americans to absorb a larger share of the true cost of their health care, they will become more "cost-conscious."
- *Personal responsibility and continuous-coverage protection*—In place of the individual mandate, Capretta and Moffit propose that, if a worker and her family remain continuously covered, insurance companies be required to use "community ratings" in setting their insurance rates. This is a big "if" because it's precisely the disruption of one's work history (and the financial emergencies associated with it)

---

[22]James C. Capretta and Robert E. Moffit, "How to Replace Obamacare," *National Affairs* (Spring 2012): 3–21. Quote on p. 7.

that leads one to forgo insurance coverage. Once a worker misses a month of coverage, they would lose this protection.

- *A genuine partnership with the states*—The authors would abolish the requirement that states set up exchanges and leave it to the states to use their wisdom in setting policies that makes sense for them. Given the reactions of many governors to the Supreme Court's decision to make Medicaid expansion optional, one can assume that this freedom would not necessarily lead to improved care for low- or middle-income families.

- *Abolish the tax treatment of employer-sponsored plans*—The authors propose instead that individual workers receive a tax credit that they would use to purchase individual insurance. In a nod to reality, they suggest that the tax exclusion for small employers be abolished first, because those employers often don't provide insurance anyway.

- *Improve health care for the vulnerable*—This sounds good as a goal, but the authors use it to abolish the entitlement to Medicaid (and the S-CHIP) and turn the funding into a block grant that states could use as they see fit. Again, the reaction of states to Medicaid expansion suggests that the block grant might not lead to better care for low-income families.

- *Replace traditional Medicare with a "premium support" plan*—In other words, rather than guarantee health care for older Americans and people with disabilities, the authors propose that the government pay a share of the cost of private insurance.

- *Fiscal responsibility*—Any additional cost of health care should be offset with cuts to other programs, including raising the retirement age, reducing benefits under Supplemental Medical Insurance (Medicare Part B), or income testing all of Medicare.

The conservatives' alternative to the Affordable Care Act suggests that they, not its supporters, are the true radicals on health care policy. Where the Affordable Care Act includes incremental changes to the existing health care system based on employer-provided benefits, Medicare, and Medicaid, the conservative proposal would essentially abolish all three of these approaches. Instead, most Americans would have to seek private insurance as individuals but without the exchanges that will bring greater transparency to that market.

Should social workers support incremental change that seeks to improve an existing system or support radical change that essentially starts from square one? As we've argued throughout this book, we cannot turn our backs on history. Especially in the case of health care, it seems unlikely that the public would rally around any policy that terminates the programs they currently count on. This suggests, indeed, that the conservative "replacement" is more window dressing than serious policymaking. As the authors note: "the law cannot be reversed without a credible proposal for what should take its place."[23] Rather than lay out a true alternative, the conservative proposal is more a "credible" set of ideas that—they hope—make the repeal of the Affordable Care Act more appealing.

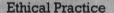
Ethical Practice

Practice Behavior Example: Make ethical decisions by applying standards of the National Association of Social Workers Code of Ethics and, as applicable, of the International Federation of Social Workers/International Association of Schools of Social Work Ethics in Social Work, Statement of Principles.

Critical Thinking Question: It is often said that the "perfect" should not be the enemy of the "good." How might the NASW Code of Ethics standard that social workers should "promote policies that safeguard the rights of and confirm equity and social justice for all people" come into conflict with a political need to defend "good" but not "perfect" legislation?

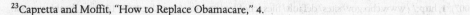

[23]Capretta and Moffit, "How to Replace Obamacare," 4.

If social workers want to consider a radical alternative to the current health care system, they could start by examining what many consider the most successful element of the American system—but not yet discussed—the veterans health care system.

VETERANS HEALTH CARE SYSTEM

The Veterans Administration (VA) currently operates the nation's largest integrated health care system. In contrast to other elements of US health care policy, the VA system is a direct service provider rather than an insurance program. Historically, VA services were directed at persons with service-related injuries, but the current system is open to all vets. About eight million veterans are enrolled in the system.

Eligibility and cost-sharing levels are tied to an eight-point priority system that ranges from vets with a service-connected disability (SCD) rated as 50 percent or more disabling (P1) to those without SCDs and with income or net worth above the VA's means-tested thresholds. Although income restrictions remain, in 2009 eligibility was broadened and enabled an additional 266,000 vets to qualify for services, raising the total population served to eight million.[24]

The system provides to all enrollees a uniform Medical Benefits Package that includes preventive, outpatient, and inpatient services, as well as prescription drugs. In addition, the system offers a wider set of services, including dental care and long-term care, to higher-priority groups.

Beginning in the 1990s, the VA system transformed itself. It broadened its range of services and increased attention to preventative services. Because persons who enter the VA system are likely to remain in it for the rest of their lives, the system invested in electronic medical record systems that allow providers to coordinate care and identify risk factors early. The system also adopted a set of performance measures targeted toward improving care and reorganized services to "share decision-making authority between officials in the central office, regional managers, and key personnel at dispersed medical facilities."[25]

We have no way of knowing if the Affordable Care Act will succeed or even be fully implemented. It's likely to stand as one milestone in the ever-evolving American health care system. However, as we examine alternatives to current policies, it makes sense to consider the success of the VA system's integrated approach.

MENTAL HEALTH

Assess your comprehension of "Mental Health" by completing this quiz.

No field of social welfare policy has undergone a more thorough transformation over the past two generations than mental health. In 1950, the centerpiece of mental health policy was the state mental hospital, where a few psychiatrists and a flood of orderlies were charged with warehousing a mass of mentally disabled wards. Three revolutions have swept through the field since then. Psychotropic drugs and a variety of therapeutic interventions have been found to be an effective treatment for a

---

[24]US Department of Veterans Affairs, "VA Reopening Health Care Enrollment to Thousands of Veterans," June 19, 2009, http://www1.va.gov/opa/pressrel/pressrelease.cfm?id=1703.

[25]US Congressional Budget Office, "The Health Care System for Veterans: An Interim Report," (December 2007), 1, http://www.cbo.gov/sites/default/files/cbofiles/ftpdocs/88xx/doc8892/12-21-va_healthcare.pdf.

variety of conditions. Deinstitutionalization led to the closing of many state hospitals and the shifting of persons with mental disabilities to community settings. Finally, the labor force that treats and cares for this population has diversified, with social workers now occupying a significant role in the field.

The most recent expression of the shift in policy was the New Freedom commission appointed by President George W. Bush, which released its report in 2004. The commission laid out six goals for the future development of the system:

- Americans understand that mental health is essential to overall health.
- Mental health care is consumer and family driven.
- Disparities in mental health services are eliminated.
- Early mental health screening, assessment, and referral to services are common practice.
- Excellent mental health care is delivered and research is accelerated.
- Technology is used to access mental health care and information.[26]

With its emphasis on an inclusive, community-based conception of mental health, focused on consumers, prevention, and improved quality of services (thanks to research and technology), the New Freedom report sought to build on changes in the system over the past generation.

The evolution of mental health policy was the result of changes in *who* the "players" were in policymaking. In the "small world" of policy—around tables where decisions on rules and funding take place—the major shift was from the states to the federal government. Despite the continuing rhetoric about devolution, the national government now is the key decision maker regarding these matters. In the "big world" of policy—where practice meets policy—the critical change was the increasing and active role of people with mental disabilities and their relatives in challenging existing policies. Several professions, including social work and law, have played a critical intermediary role in helping to translate the concerns of consumers and their families into concrete innovations.

Practice Context

Practice Behavior Example: Keep informed, resourceful, and proactive in responding to evolving organizational, community, and societal contexts at all levels of practice.

Critical Thinking Question: What changes in the mental health system provided the context for the New Freedom goals, and how might these goals promote further innovations in the system?

Innovations in Treatment

In the middle of the last century, the treatment of mental illness was rudimentary. Talk therapies that were largely ineffective for serious mental illness were teamed with a variety of electroshock therapy or surgical procedures, of which lobotomy was the most notorious.[27]

The most notable advance has been in the development of antipsychotic drugs. Beginning with the marketing of chlorpromazine in the early 1950s, a variety of drugs were found to be effective in treating schizophrenia, depression, anxiety disorders, and attention deficit hyperactivity disorders. During the next decade, a variety of therapies—including *supportive therapies* for schizophrenia and *cognitive-behavioral therapy* for anxiety disorders—that focused on present behavior (in contrast to psychotherapy's focus on past experience) gained

---

[26]President's New Freedom Commission on Mental Health, *Final Report*.
[27]Edward Shorter, *A History of Psychiatry: From the Era of the Asylum to the Age of Prozac* (New York: John Wiley and Sons, 1997), 190–238.

wider acceptance in the field.[28] Treatment sites for less serious conditions have also shifted. For example, primary care physicians now frequently treat less severe forms of depression.

Deinstitutionalization

The drug revolution opened up the possibility of maintaining persons with serious mental illness in the community. However, the story of deinstitutionalization was hardly an automatic reaction to the changing technology of mental illness. Deinstitutionalization was the result of political and legal processes that brought new funding sources, new players, and new legal doctrines into play in policy development.

The starting point for deinstitutionalization, of course, was the gross failure of institutions for the mentally ill. When "insane asylums" were first constructed before the Civil War, their advocates argued that removing the mentally ill from their environment and confining them in a controlled environment would cure them. Yet, within a few years of their establishment, most asylums had become custodial facilities that varied in the level of care or brutality they provided. Typically, inmates had been involuntarily committed, and state hospitals (as they were renamed during the Progressive Era) functioned more to protect the wider public from the mentally ill than to help the inmates. Yet, the asylum persisted for another century, testimony to the tendency of institutions, once established, to persist.[29]

After the creation of the National Institute for Mental Health in the late 1940s, the interaction of state and federal officials initiated the review of ways to move beyond the asylum. The creation of the Joint Commission on Mental Illness and Health in the 1950s and the release of its report in 1961 outlined a top-down strategy focused on improving conditions and capacity in the state hospitals and developing community-care facilities. The Joint Commission's report provided the outlines for the Community Mental Health Centers Act (CMHCA) of 1963 that provided a number of grant programs for states. Its most important institutional innovation was the establishment of *community mental health centers* that would serve a particular *catchment area*. Originally conceived as the focal point for the assessment and treatment of mental illness, cuts in funding in the 1970s and 1980s circumscribed the role of these centers.

A more significant cause of the decline of the state hospitals, however, was the enactment of Medicare and Medicaid in 1965. Although mental health benefits through Medicare were quite restrictive in the 1960s and 1970s, by the late 1980s they were broadened with respect to the types of services and service providers covered by the program. Medicaid, however, had a much more immediate impact on state policy. Even after the passage of the CMHCA, state hospital systems had been funded almost exclusively by the states. Medicaid posed the possibility that a large share of the financial burden of the mentally ill could be shifted to the federal government. What some have called "transinstitutionalization" was a rapid shift of many older residents of state mental hospitals to nursing facilities. Between 1960 and 1970, nursing homes' share of all institutionalized persons rose from 25 to 44 percent.[30] In effect, after 1965, state mental health policy became much more tied to federal Medicaid policy.

[28]Richard G. Frank and Sherry A. Glied, *Better But Not Well: Mental Health Policy in the United States Since 1950* (Baltimore: Johns Hopkins University Press, 2006), e-book version, Chapter 3.

[29]David Rothman, *The Discovery of the Asylum: Social Order and Disorder in the New Republic* (Boston: Little, Brown, 1971).

[30]William Gronfein, "Incentives and Intentions in Mental Health Policy: A Comparison of the Medicaid and Community Mental Health Programs," *Journal of Health and Social Behavior* 26, no. 3 (September 1985): 192–206.

The enactment of Supplemental Security Income and the expansion of Disability Insurance during the 1970s, although not focused on the mentally disabled, had a decisive effect on mental health policy. For the first time, the issue of community-based policies was constrained by the question of the poverty of mentally disabled people. With access to modest income support from the federal government, states were more open to providing options that allowed people with mental illnesses to remain in their community.

Litigation played a critical role in the shift from institutional care. First, beginning in 1966 (*Baxstrom v. Herald*), the courts recognized and eventually expanded the equal protection rights of persons with mental disabilities under the Fourteenth Amendment. During the 1970s, these decisions changed the nature of state commitment laws. Just as important, beginning with the *Wyatt v. Stickney* decision in 1972, the Supreme Court recognized a "right to treatment." More recently, the Americans with Disabilities Act has been invoked to justify the presumption that people with mental disabilities will be placed in communities rather than institutions.[31]

Finally, people with mental disabilities themselves have become important players in policymaking. As part of the broader community of people with disabilities, they played a role in the expansion of disability rights (see Chapter 9). In addition, the increasing emphasis on consumers, as exemplified by the report of the President's New Freedom Commission on Mental Health, has expanded the role of people with mental illness within the system. Organizations like the National Alliance on Mental Illness play an important role in monitoring policy and practice developments and in mobilizing support for and opposition to changes.

Although deinstitutionalization, compared to an earlier era, represents a net improvement in the lives of people with mental illness, it has generated its own problems. In fact, much of deinstitutionalization has resulted in the transferring of people from one institution to another, not necessarily to their benefit. In addition, efforts to maintain people with mental disabilities in the community have consistently fallen short of the need. Many commentators have attributed the increasing visibility of homeless persons in major American cities to the shift to community-based treatment. In the area of substance abuse, a variety of grassroots efforts have emerged to bridge the gap between the resources available to those in recovery and their needs for subsistence and treatment.[32]

Critical Thinking

Practice Behavior Example: Distinguish, appraise, and integrate multiple sources of knowledge, including research-based knowledge and practice wisdom.

Critical Thinking Question: Commentators often draw a direct line between deinstitutionalization and the expansion of the homeless population. Is this type of argument convincing? What evidence would a social worker introduce to provide a more thorough analysis of the connections between the two?

Social Workers in the Mental Health System

During the state hospital era, the labor force of the mental health system was essentially made up of two groups—psychiatrists, who typically both provided limited services and administered facilities, and a large group of unskilled custodial workers. Although other innovations influenced the system during the 1940s and 1950s, there was little change in the number of professional workers until the mid-1960s. Between 1964 and the mid-1970s, the system experienced explosive growth in its professional labor force. The number of psychiatrists doubled and the number of psychologists tripled between 1972 and the late 1990s. However, social workers more than quadrupled, increasing from under

[31]Frank and Glied, *Better But Not Well*, Chapter 6.

[32]Robert Fairbanks, *How It Works: Recovering Citizens in Post-Welfare Philadelphia* (Chicago: University of Chicago Press, 2009).

20,000 in 1972 to over 70,000 in 1998. In 2009, nearly half of the clinically trained mental health professionals in the United States were social workers.[33]

Social workers' involvement in mental health has expanded since the adoption of managed care after 1980. As insurers sought ways to contain costs, they turned to managed behavioral health care organizations to direct clients to cost-effective settings. These organizations had an interest in directing patients and clients to agencies with lower fees, which typically meant settings that employed more social workers. One outcome of this redistribution of professional services has been a convergence between the incomes of social workers and other mental health professionals. In 1969 psychologists earned nearly 50 percent more than social workers, but by 1999 the gap had been reduced to less than 10 percent.[34]

Impact on Well-Being

By the early twenty-first century, the institutional structures that influence the lives of people with mental illness had improved markedly. Still, moving forward, the system faces many challenges. First, policies adversely affecting low-income populations, which we explore elsewhere in this book, disproportionately affect people with mental disabilities. The proportion of persons who could be diagnosed as suffering from a disability far outnumbers the proportion actually seeking care. Although managed care agencies may have provided benefits for containing costs and matching clients with the most appropriate services, they also have the tendency to discourage people needing services from accessing them.

The Affordable Care Act may provide some improvement to the overall functioning of the system. The expansion of Medicaid promises to connect many persons who need mental health services, but have no insurance, to those services. Reducing the gap in prescription coverage in the original Medicare prescription plan will reduce the number of older Americans who suffer from depression and other conditions who go without their medication.[35] After several attempts to assure that coverage of mental health conditions achieves *parity* with physical health, the reform law mandates universal coverage of mental health services.

Assess your analysis and evaluation of the chapter's content by completing the Chapter Review.

---

[33]SAMHSA, *Mental Health, United States, 2010*, http://www.samhsa.gov/data/2k12/MHUS2010/MHUS-2010.pdf.

[34]Frank and Glied, *Better But Not Well*, Chapter 5.

[35]Richard A. Friedman, "Good News for Mental Illness in Health Law," *New York Times*, July 9, 2012.

8

Employment,
Public Assistance,
and Job Training

INTRODUCTION

Most of us are dependent on work to support our families and ourselves. Before the nineteenth century, working for wages or a salary was a relatively rare experience. The majority of the population was self-employed, working a plot of land or running a small store or workshop. With the coming of a market economy, working for wages became common, and finding work became the central dilemma for individuals and families.

Welfare states, too, need an employed population. First, income support programs are based on the assumption that most of the population is able to work to support themselves and their families. Otherwise, the programs would be overwhelmed. Second, the welfare state needs people to work and generate the taxes needed to support social programs. This double edge—that a rise in unemployment leads to both increases in assistance and decreases in taxes—motivates welfare states to adopt policies that maximize employment and economic growth.

In the twentieth century, social welfare systems tried to differentiate between people who should work and those who should not. Groups that weren't expected to work—older people, people with disabilities, children and their caretakers—were treated differently by the social welfare system, because there was no threat that benefits would reduce their incentive to work. The "able-bodied" population, men and unmarried women, typically received less generous benefits with more conditions attached to them.

By the end of the twentieth century, however, the neat division between nonworkers and workers had broken down. Older people and people with disabilities rebelled against the *assumption* that they would not work. Instead, they argued that they had a civil right to work that should be protected.

Human Behavior

Practice Behavior Example: Know about human behavior across the life course, the range of social systems in which people live, and the ways social systems promote or deter people in maintaining or achieving health and well-being.

Critical Thinking Question: Many twentieth century policy innovations were based on the "breadwinner" family, yet now less than a quarter of households conform to this model. How has the emergence of alternative household structures challenged the existing social welfare system?

The case of women with children was more complex. Women likewise demanded more choice in terms of entering the labor force and more protection of their civil and economic rights. But where the expansion of rights was *added* to the social protection of the disabled and the aging, the entry of women into the labor force reduced the willingness of the welfare state to support them and their children.

The changing status of women both in the labor force and in domestic life had wide-ranging implications for social welfare. It not only affected equal pay and gender discrimination policy but also struck at the center of the old model of welfare programs. An array of social programs had been based on the idea that families would be supported by the wages of a single male head—what some have called the *breadwinner family*. Implicitly, old age and survivors' insurance, unemployment compensation, and many public assistance programs were tied to this model. As the actual lives of Americans changed, the model too came into question.

At the same time, these changes challenged the institutional structure of existing programs. All social welfare programs exist within a particular force field in which political and economic forces are channeled by ideologies, institutions, and social movements. The contemporary United States is in the midst of an experiment to integrate distinct policy fields, each with its own unique history and force field. Thus, while we often speak of *welfare reform*, in reality the restructuring of social welfare since the 1990s aims to integrate public assistance (a means-tested system of cash and in-kind aid) with employment and job training (programs to increase the efficiency of linking individuals with employment). Changes in these systems, although left out of the debate over welfare reform, also have implications for unemployment insurance.

Furthermore, policymakers are attempting to integrate these systems in a decidedly unfavorable political and economic environment. The antigovernment ideology that has driven conservative social welfare policy since the 1990s has wavered between radical restructuring and simple cost cutting. Because cost cutting has usually won this struggle, there has been relatively little funding to push ahead with systems integration. When Democrats gained control of Congress in 2007 and the presidency in 2009, the nation quickly entered a nasty recession that gave the unemployment compensation system new prominence.

This chapter examines a set of programs associated with employment—unemployment compensation, public assistance, and job training. It begins with an examination of changes in the work and family status of Americans and the impact of these changes on these systems.

THE NEW LANDSCAPE OF WORK AND FAMILY

Assess your comprehension of "The New Landscape of Work and Family" by completing this quiz.

One way that social workers can contribute to social welfare policy is through exploring the links between people's family and work lives. Here we examine the shifting patterns of men's and women's work life and its implications for how families make ends meet.

Who Works? Who Stays Home?

These two questions form the critical link between the private sphere of home and family and the public sphere of work and the economy. Because this linkage is so central to social welfare, the answers to these questions are the starting point for understanding social welfare policy around work.

Americans' answers to these questions over the past two generations have changed in three important ways. First, the number of married women who stay home has declined, while the proportion that participate in the labor force has expanded quickly. Second, but less noticed, the proportion of men involved in the labor force has declined sharply. Finally, the most common family form of the 1950s—a breadwinner family with dad working and mom taking care of the kids—has lost its predominance.

Women's Work

At the turn of the twentieth century, few women were members of the labor force. Only 21 percent of all women worked. Among women with children, only 4 percent of those in two-parent households and 45 percent of those in female-headed households worked.

All of these figures increased by 1960. Overall, the proportion of women in the labor force had increased to 41 percent. Twenty-nine percent of women in two-parent households with children were working, and 57 percent of women who headed households with children did so.

By 2007 a new normal had emerged. Seventy-one percent of all adult women were in the labor force. Women in two-parent households with children were just as likely to work as those with husbands but no children. Women who headed households with children remained those most likely to work.

Men's Work

In 1900 virtually all adult men (95 percent) were in the labor force. This number had changed only slightly by 1960 (93 percent); however, as women entered the labor force after 1960, the departure of men accelerated, falling to 88 percent in 1980 and to 83 percent in 2000. The decline in male labor force participation cut across all groups, although those with working wives were most likely not to work (79 percent). Looked at another way, in 1900 the labor force was 83 percent male; this figure declined to 68 percent in 1960 and to 53 percent in 2000 (Chart 8.1).

Household Structure

The changing labor force interacted with personal decisions. Increasingly, men and women delayed marriage. In 1900, half of all men were married by age 26 and half of all women by age 23. By 2000, both of these figures had increased: age 27 for men and age 26 for women. At the same time, marital status was changing; marriage became less likely as the proportion of adult men and women who identified themselves as divorced or separated increased from less than 1 percent to 9 percent during the twentieth century. Finally, the number and timing of children affected family structure. Where in 1900 fertility remained significant across women's childbearing years, by the end of the century, it had become concentrated in a smaller number of years.

The US Census Bureau provides the most recent data on changes in Americans' living arrangements.

Chart 8.1   Labor Force Participation Rates by Gender and Household Structure, United States, 1900–2007

Male	1900	1920	1940	1960	1980	2000	2007
Two parents with children	97.4%	97.9%	96.3%	97.0%	94.4%	89.5%	92.5%
Two parents without children	91.8%	91.0%	89.0%	87.6%	82.2%	79.3%	79.5%
Female-headed household with children	94.0%	94.2%	94.4%	88.6%	81.9%	75.1%	78.0%
Other	93.1%	92.5%	88.8%	84.6%	82.6%	79.7%	81.4%
Total	94.6%	94.5%	92.3%	92.5%	87.8%	83.2%	84.5%
Female							
Two parents with children	4.1%	6.5%	10.4%	28.7%	52.8%	66.9%	68.5%
Two parents without children	31.9%	36.4%	41.3%	48.5%	61.0%	67.7%	68.7%
Female-headed household with children	44.7%	44.5%	40.6%	56.9%	66.9%	74.7%	77.7%
Other	49.0%	58.4%	61.8%	70.6%	74.1%	74.6%	74.6%
Total	20.7%	24.2%	29.2%	41.0%	60.4%	70.0%	71.5%

Source: Author's calculation from Steven Ruggles, J. Trent Alexander, Katie Genadek, Ronald Goeken, Matthew B. Schroeder, and Matthew Sobek, Integrated Public Use Microdata Series: Version 5.0 [Machine-readable database] (Minneapolis: University of Minnesota, 2010).

Taken together, these changes restructured the types of households in which Americans lived. At the beginning of the twentieth century, 60 percent of American households included two parents (a working man and an at-home woman) and children; by 2007 only 7 percent of American households fit this definition. Three types of households were prevalent by the beginning of the twenty-first century. First, two-parent, dual-earner households had increased to around 20 percent. Second, "empty nest" households (two adults over 50 and no children present) had increased from 6 to 17 percent. Finally, individuals living on their own had increased their share of households from 7 to 33 percent (Chart 8.2).

One group didn't change much during the century—female-household heads with children. In 1900 about 9 percent of households fit this description; by the beginning of

Chart 8.2   Household Structure, United States, 1900–2007

	1900	1920	1940	1960	1980	2000	2007
Two parent, spouse works, with children	2.0%	3.3%	4.8%	13.8%	19.3%	19.9%	19.6%
Two parent, spouse not working, with children	59.9%	56.4%	48.0%	35.7%	17.3%	9.8%	7.2%
Empty nest	5.9%	7.7%	10.6%	17.3%	16.6%	16.2%	17.2%
Other childless couple	10.3%	11.9%	12.9%	7.9%	7.7%	6.6%	5.7%
Female householder with children	8.6%	7.2%	7.5%	6.0%	8.8%	10.4%	10.8%
Single male	4.5%	4.1%	4.7%	5.6%	11.1%	14.3%	15.4%
Single female	2.7%	3.2%	5.4%	9.4%	15.3%	17.2%	17.8%
Other	6.2%	6.3%	6.1%	4.3%	3.9%	5.5%	6.3%
	100.0%	100.0%	100.0%	100.0%	100.0%	100.0%	100.0%

Source: Author's calculation from Steven Ruggles, J. Trent Alexander, Katie Genadek, Ronald Goeken, Matthew B. Schroeder, and Matthew Sobek, Integrated Public Use Microdata Series: Version 5.0 [Machine-readable database] (Minneapolis: University of Minnesota, 2010).

Chart 8.3   Marital Status of Female Householders, United States, 1900–2007

	1900	1920	1940	1960	1980	2000	2007
Married, spouse absent	11.2%	11.6%	17.4%	9.3%	3.0%	4.0%	5.0%
Separated	0.0%	0.0%	0.0%	16.6%	17.4%	12.1%	11.9%
Divorced	2.6%	4.1%	8.2%	19.4%	39.8%	39.6%	37.5%
Widowed	83.6%	82.4%	72.9%	51.9%	27.4%	18.3%	14.5%
Never married/single	2.7%	1.9%	1.5%	2.9%	12.4%	25.9%	31.1%
	100.0%	100.0%	100.0%	100.0%	100.0%	100.0%	100.0%

Source: Author's calculations from Steven Ruggles, J. Trent Alexander, Katie Genadek, Ronald Goeken, Matthew B. Schroeder, and Matthew Sobek, Integrated Public Use Microdata Series: Version 5.0 [Machine-readable database] (Minneapolis: University of Minnesota, 2010).

the twenty-first century, the number stood at 10 percent. Yet this stability hid a more politically significant change. Early in the twentieth century, the overwhelming majority of female household heads were widows; by the turn of the twenty-first century, the majority were divorced, separated, or never married (Chart 8.3).

The changing family and work experience of Americans had a number of important impacts on employment and public assistance. The older system of social insurance, designed for a society dominated by breadwinner families, no longer fit the more diverse and complex family economies of the early twenty-first century. More importantly, the public assistance system for children and their caretakers struggled with the changing status of women. Should women be expected to work? If so, under what conditions and how much?

UNEMPLOYMENT COMPENSATION

Work is the foundation of social welfare. While government programs seek to provide aid for those who are unable to work because of disability, old age, or lack of employment, public welfare assumes that most families will support themselves through the private economy.

As a result, the issue of unemployment is often the starting point for public welfare. During the nineteenth century, as the number of wage workers exploded, unemployment emerged as a novel social problem that puzzled social reformers. Workers attempted to address lack of work through union funds, labor cooperatives, and work sharing—none of which could deal with the volatility of the new economy and its impact on the unemployed. By the early twentieth century, the idea of social insurance emerged as the best solution to the problem of unemployment, but in the United States, it was not until the Great Depression that the federal government took on the task of developing a system of unemployment compensation.[1] In contrast to Old Age Insurance, which was developed as a federal program, the architects of the Social Security Act opted for a state-led system. As with many social programs, that early decision guided later development of the unemployment compensation system.[2]

[1] Alexander Keyssar, *Out of Work: The First Century of Unemployment in Massachusetts* (New York: Cambridge University Press, 1986).

[2] Michael B. Katz, *In the Shadow of the Poorhouse: A Social History of Welfare in America*, 10th anniversary ed. (New York: Basic Books, 1996), 185–212.

For much of the past generation, policymakers have allowed the effectiveness of the unemployment compensation system to decline. In particular, eligibility requirements and administrative decisions have resulted in a program that covers only a fraction of the unemployed. The program's design is inadequate to deal with the high unemployment of recent years or the long spells of unemployment experienced by many workers during the 2007–2009 recession.

At the same time, changing patterns of women's work reduced the pressure for innovation in the unemployment compensation system. When the system was created in the 1930s, few married women worked outside the home. Unemployment of the family's breadwinner was devastating, because the husband typically was the sole income earner. Two-earner families, which had became more common by the end of the twentieth century, were more resilient because they had multiple wage earners. Often, the employed member of a dual-earner family can increase their earnings when the partner becomes unemployed.

What Is Unemployment?

An unemployed worker is a member of the labor force who is currently not working but actively seeking work. It is useful to make a few distinctions in identifying where the unemployed fit into the entire working-age population. The most basic division is between members of the civilian labor force and those not in the labor force.[3] Persons not in the labor force can be divided into two groups: those not seeking employment and those who would seek employment if they believed they could successfully find work. The latter group is called "discouraged workers" because they are not part of the official unemployed but are influenced by the overall employment environment. The official unemployed hold a unique status. Although not currently employed, they are considered part of the labor force because they are seeking work.

The final category—employed members of the labor force—can be subdivided as well. Full-time workers are defined as those working 35 hours or more per week, while part-time workers are employed for less than 35 hours a week. Involuntary part-time workers are workers who have a part-time job but would like a full-time job if one were available.

In March 2010, for example, the civilian labor force included 154 million people of which 15 million were unemployed. Thus, the official unemployment rate was 9.7 percent. However, an additional nine million people were working part-time (involuntarily) for economic reasons. Finally, another million were out of the labor force (involuntarily) as "discouraged workers." Taken together, 25 million Americans desired a more favorable labor market status (Chart 8.4).

Unemployment is a highly *cyclical* phenomenon. Since 1970 when unemployment stood at 4 percent, it has risen as high as 11 percent (in 1982) and fallen below 4 percent in 2000. While unemployment in the 2007–09 recession did not rise as high as it had in 1981–82, the recent recession was notable for the speed of its increase, rising from 4.7 to 10.0 percent in 23 months (Figure 8.1).

Not all people have the same risk of suffering from unemployment. In 2007–09, the average unemployment rate was 6.5 percent. However, a number of groups had

---

[3]Members of the military are also part of the labor force. In the remainder of this chapter, however, the term "labor force" will refer to the civilian labor force.

Chart 8.4   Employment Status of Civilian Population, United States, March 2009–March 2010

Employment status	March 2009	January 2010	February 2010	March 2010	Change Feb–March 2010
Civilian non-institutional population	235,086	236,832	236,998	237,159	161
Civilian labor force	154,164	153,170	153,512	153,910	398
Participation rate	65.6	64.7	64.8	64.9	0.1
Employed	140,854	138,333	138,641	138,905	264
Employment-population ratio	59.9	58.4	58.5	58.6	0.1
Unemployed	13,310	14,837	14,871	15,005	134
Unemployment rate	8.6	9.7	9.7	9.7	0
Part time for economic reasons	9,023	8,316	8,791	9,054	263
Slack work or business conditions	6,839	5,873	6,185	6,177	-8
Could only find part-time work	1,847	2,295	2,212	2,388	176
Part time for noneconomic reasons	18,829	18,563	18,360	18,379	19
Persons not in the labor force (not seasonally adjusted)					
Discouraged workers	685	1,065	1,204	994	—
All figures, except percentages, in thousands					

Source: US Bureau of Labor Statistics, "The Employment Situation—March 2010," (Washington, DC: Department of Labor, 2010), http://www.bls.gov/news.release/archives/empsit_04022010.pdf.

much higher rates. Those without a high school diploma had an unemployment rate of 14.2 percent compared to a rate of only 2.1 percent among those with a graduate degree. Race also influenced likelihood of unemployment. African Americans' rate of 10 percent was twice the white rate of 5 percent (Chart 8.5).

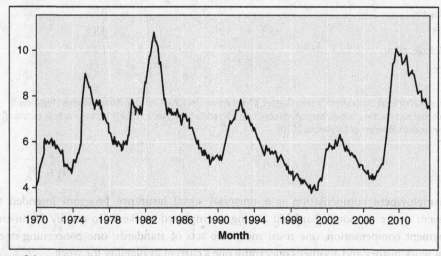

Figure 8.1

Civilian Unemployment Rate (Monthly), United States, 1970–2013

Although the overall economy recovered from the 2008–09 recession, the unemployment rate declined much more slowly.

Source: US Department of Labor, Bureau of Labor Statistics, http://data.bls.gov/pdq/SurveyOutputServlet.

Chart 8.5   Unemployment Rate by Selected Characteristics, United States, 2007–2009

Educational attainment	Unemployment rate
Less than HS grad	14.2%
HS grad	8.0%
Some college	5.6%
Bachelor's degree	3.3%
Post BA	2.1%
Region	
New England Division	6.0%
Middle Atlantic Division	5.9%
East North Central Division	7.6%
West North Central Division	5.7%
South Atlantic Division	6.1%
East South Central Division	7.5%
West South Central Division	5.2%
Mountain Division	5.6%
Pacific Division	7.6%
Metropolitan status	
Not identifiable	5.1%
Not in metro area	6.9%
Central city	7.0%
Outside central city	6.0%
Central city status unknown	6.6%
Race	
White	5.4%
Black	10.6%
Hispanic	8.5%
API	4.5%
Multiple, other	11.2%
Total	6.5%

Source: Author's calculation from Steven Ruggles, J. Trent Alexander, Katie Genadek, Ronald Goeken, Matthew B. Schroeder, and Matthew Sobek, Integrated Public Use Microdata Series: Version 5.0 [Machine-readable database] (Minneapolis: University of Minnesota, 2010).

Eligibility

Unemployment compensation is a universal social insurance program intended to prevent severe economic hardship among unemployed workers. To qualify for unemployment compensation, one must meet two sets of standards: one concerning one's past work history and another concerning one's current availability for work.

Work history

Eligibility for unemployment compensation varies from state to state. Generally speaking, one needs to have worked for an employer who is paying into the unemployment compensation fund for a certain number of quarters per year. In Pennsylvania, for example, a worker must have worked four out of the previous five quarters to qualify for unemployment compensation.

A variety of occupations, including the self-employed, are generally excluded from the unemployment compensation system. The trend toward reclassification of workers as "independent contractors" has expanded the number of workers not covered by the unemployment compensation system.[4] An increasing proportion of Americans find themselves working in the *informal* economy, in which wages are typically paid on a "cash-only" basis. One analyst estimated that in 1999–2000, this shadow economy accounted for $8.6 trillion in economic activity in the United States, nearly 9 percent of the entire economy.[5] As a result, workers with long work histories can find themselves ineligible for unemployment compensation.

A variety of trends—rise in episodic employment, increasing use of "independent contractors," expansion of the informal economy—have combined to reduce the proportion of the unemployed population that is eligible for unemployment compensation. In recent years, only about 35 percent of the official unemployed have been covered by the program.

The reason one leaves their previous job also may affect eligibility. Generally speaking, workers who leave a job voluntarily or are fired for cause are not eligible for unemployment insurance. Because employers are taxed based on the number of their former workers who file for unemployment compensation, employers often appeal cases. During the 2007–2010 recession, for example, employers appealed a higher proportion of cases—often using professional consultants—even in situations where the appeal had no merit, in the hope that the unemployed worker would not contest the case.[6] In some states, workers idled by strikes and lockouts are ineligible to collect unemployment compensation.

Current availability for work

To be eligible for unemployment compensation, one must conform to the three "As," that is, the worker must be *able* to work, *available* for work, and *actively* seeking employment. The extent to which recipients are required to demonstrate these qualities varies with the labor market situation. During periods of low unemployment, a recipient may be required to file weekly paperwork showing where they have applied for jobs. When unemployment is high, workers may not need to do so. In addition, the longer a worker collects unemployment, the more likely he is to face a need to document his job search. For example, a worker collecting *extended benefits* (EB, see below) may be required to accept a suitable job offer, although the definition of suitability varies from state to state.

Benefits

Generally, unemployment benefits are received weekly. In most states, the basic unemployment system provides 26 weeks of benefits. During periods of high unemployment,

---

[4]Steven Greenhouse, "U.S. Cracks Down on 'Contractors' as a Tax Dodge," *New York Times*, February 17, 2010, http://www.nytimes.com/2010/02/18/business/18workers.html?pagewanted=all.

[5]Friedrich Schneider, "Size and Measurement of the Informal Economy in 110 Countries around the World," paper presented at "Workshop of Australian National Tax Centre, ANU," Canberra, Australia, July 17, 2002.

[6]Jason DeParle, "Contesting Jobless Claims Becomes a Boom Industry," *New York Times*, April 2, 2010.

the unemployed can become eligible for an additional 13 weeks of extended benefits (EB). During periods of very high unemployment, Congress often passes emergency programs that provide benefits for a longer period. During 2009, for example, unemployed workers could qualify for nearly two years of benefits.

Benefit levels are typically tied to one's earnings in the previous year. For example, in Pennsylvania in 2013, the unemployment compensation system provided 52 percent of a covered worker's earnings up to the monthly ceiling of $4,754. If a worker earned more than this amount (the equivalent of $57,052 per year), their benefits would not increase, so the percentage of their wages replaced would drop.

Financing and Administration

State departments of labor run unemployment compensation programs. The federal government has two roles. It sets minimum standards for state programs, and it runs a trust fund that provides backup for state programs that face difficulties.

The unemployment compensation system is generally funded through employer taxes. Tax rates typically vary by *experience rating*, that is, the frequency with which the employer lays off members of its workforce. The tax rate can vary from 1 to over 5 percent of its taxable payroll, depending on the history of a firm.

The unemployment tax is *earmarked*, that is, used only to pay unemployment benefits, and is held in a state trust fund, out of which benefits are paid. In addition to the basic tax rate, employers nationwide pay an additional federal tax that goes into a federal trust fund. The federal fund is used to aid states when their trust funds face exhaustion due to an increase in unemployment.

Because in most states employers pay all unemployment compensation taxes, they have exercised a significant influence over the recent development of the systems. Combined with the conservative tilt in social policy since the 1980s, this has served to reduce the *horizontal* adequacy of the unemployment system, with a majority of the unemployed ineligible for benefits.

A broader issue relates to the *vertical* adequacy of the program. The unemployment system works best for workers in industries—like manufacturing and construction—in which cyclical or seasonal unemployment is common. A construction worker who is laid off for the winter or an autoworker who is laid off when sales are slow is well served by the system.

In the past generation, however, unemployment is more likely the result of the elimination of a job, rather than seasonal slowdown. Internationally, many advanced nations have recognized this new reality by changing the benefits for which the long-term unemployed are eligible. The Organization for Economic Cooperation and Development (OECD) studied the relationship of unemployment benefits for short- and long-term unemployed workers. It uses a measure called the net replacement rate (NRR), which estimates one's unemployment benefits as a percentage of one's wage before becoming unemployed. The most typical pattern is to shift workers from a program that offers relatively generous benefits to one that offers somewhat less generous benefits. For example, a newly unemployed worker in Germany with a spouse and two children will receive benefits equal to 59 percent of his wages when first unemployed, but only 46 percent of his wages after five years. The US unemployment compensation system is relatively generous by international standards for the recently unemployed; the NRR is 55 percent. However, the long-term unemployment

Chart 8.6   Net Replacement Rate (NRR), Initial and Long-Term (60th month) Unemployed, Two-Parent, Two-Children, One-Worker Families, 2008[1]

	Initial NRR 2008	Long-term (60th month) NRR 2008
OECD countries		
Australia	47	47
Austria	56	52
Canada	64	36
France	67	42
Germany	59	46
Hungary	61	43
Ireland	48	68
Italy	62	0
Japan	53	58
Korea	49	26
Norway	65	55
Poland	46	34
Portugal	78	33
Spain	61	28
Sweden	50	54
United Kingdom	45	45
United States	55	11

[1]Net replacement rate (NRR) is equal to the percent of previous wage provided through unemployment benefits.

Source: Organisation for Economic Cooperation and Development, www.oecd.org/els/social/workincentives.

benefits—consisting mostly of food stamps—are near the bottom among OECD nations; the NRR is only 11 percent (Chart 8.6).[7]

PUBLIC ASSISTANCE

As the OECD data suggest, many advanced nations have developed programs that integrate short- and long-term unemployment compensation into a single system. Programs for the long-term unemployed typically are less generous and include "workfare" requirements that provide incentives to find a job. In the United States, however, the gap between unemployment compensation and public assistance is greater than in most nations. Rather than trying to integrate the two systems, the United States provides workers who exhaust their unemployment benefits with few palatable alternatives.

Public assistance in the United States occupies a unique policy force field. The economic and political forces that influence welfare policy are far different from those

Assess your comprehension of "Public Assistance" by completing this quiz.

---

[7] OECD Directorate for Employment, Labour, and Social Affairs, "Benefits and Wages: Statistics," http://www.oecd.org/els/benefitsandwagesstatistics.htm.

shaping the unemployment compensation system. Concerns about family stability and race that have almost no presence in debates over unemployment have been central to the policy debate over welfare. The result is a system that does a poor job of promoting work, protecting families against poverty, or preparing workers for the new economy.[8]

Policy Force Field of Public Assistance

No issue in American social policy has been more contentious than public assistance or "welfare." Historically, welfare was intended to have little connection to economic forces. It was targeted to groups that were not expected to work and that would remain a relatively small share of the workforce. From the poor laws of the nineteenth century through mothers' pensions and Aid to Dependent Children (ADC), public assistance remained a program for those who were not expected to work.[9]

All of that changed after World War II. First, the share of public assistance recipients who were widows dropped, replaced increasingly by single, divorced, or separated mothers. Second, the job market for married women—which was virtually nonexistent before the war—grew sharply. Once the number of married women who were working began to increase, the expectation that welfare mothers would not work came into question. This undermined the rationale of welfare and shifted the debate about welfare to the issue of the system's impact on recipients' willingness to work.

The issue of work requirements—like so many others—was complicated by race. In the decades after the enactment of ADC, Southern states administered the program in ways that disadvantaged African Americans. By the 1950s, welfare recipients were stereotypically African American, and opponents frequently linked race, laziness, and immorality in their attacks on welfare.[10]

In reality, black women did have a special work disincentive due to the low wages they were able to earn in the labor market. The work disincentive associated with public assistance is based on the relationship between two figures: the amount one receives from the government and the amount one earns by working. If a woman can earn much more by working than by collecting welfare, public assistance will not cut into her incentive to work. If wages are very low, public assistance will be more attractive. In the 1960s, the average employed female head of household without a high school diploma earned much more than the average welfare payment if she were white, but much less if she were black. Only in the late 1960s and early 1970s, thanks largely to civil rights laws that attacked race and gender discrimination, did the average black woman finally earn wages that were higher than welfare payments (Figure 8.2).

The controversy over work disincentives was reinforced by a cultural clash over the impact of welfare on family stability. During the 1950s and 1960s, many states enacted "man in the house" and "suitable family" regulations as a means of denying welfare to single mothers. In arguing for progressive welfare reform, many social workers and other

---

[8]However, in recent years, some politicians have claimed that unemployment compensation does breed "dependency." See, for example, Thomas B. Edsall, "The Anti-Entitlement Strategy," *New York Time*, December 25, 2011, http://campaignstops.blogs.nytimes.com/2011/12/25/the-anti-entitlement-strategy/?scp=5&sq=republican%20unemployment%20compensation%20dependency&st=Search.

[9]Theda Skocpol, *Protecting Soldiers and Mothers: The Political Origins of Social Policy in the United States* (Cambridge: Belknap Press of Harvard University Press, 1992), 424–479.

[10]Ira Katznelson, *When Affirmative Action Was White: An Untold History of Racial Inequality in Twentieth-Century America* (New York and London: W.W. Norton and Company, 2005), 25–52.

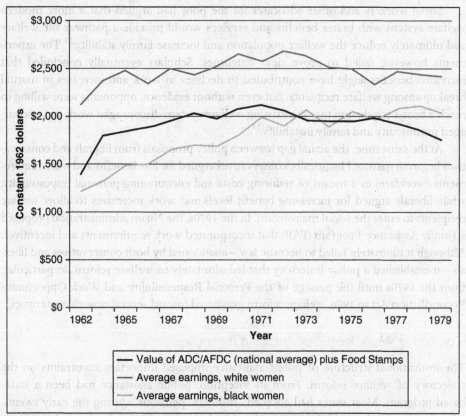

Figure 8.2
Comparison of Average Wages of Black and White Women with Less Than a High-School Education with the Average Combined Value of AFDC and Food Stamps, 1962–1979
Because of discrimination, black women rarely were able to earn more than the value of welfare benefits until the late 1970s.
Source: Author's calculation from Current Population Survey and Social Security, Annual Statistical Supplement.

welfare workers argued that Aid to Families with Dependent Children (AFDC as the program was renamed in the 1960s) should be expanded to include married couples living in poverty, suggesting that AFDC might discourage women on welfare from marrying. More potently, opponents of welfare viewed the program as responsible for increases in divorce and out-of-wedlock births.[11]

These two streams of criticism—welfare as work disincentive and welfare as family destroyer—found unanticipated support in a series of "income maintenance experiments" sponsored by the federal government during the late 1960s and early 1970s. These social experiments tested the effect of changes in welfare regulations by randomly assigning applicants to different programs and measuring how program characteristics affected a variety of outcomes, including work, earnings, and family stability.[12]

---

[11]A generation removed from the controversy, it is clear that social workers and welfare advocates had underestimated the role of gender conflict in poor families. Historically, many poor couples had remained together out of economic necessity. When the income maintenance experiments gave poor women a higher level of benefit without the stigma usually attached to welfare receipt, many poor women chose to get out of unhappy marriages. When the screws of economic scarcity were loosened slightly, many of those women chose to walk out.

[12]Alicia H. Munnell, ed., *Lessons from the Income Maintenance Experiments* (Boston: Federal Reserve Bank of Boston and the Brookings Institution, 1986).

Social workers and other advocates for the poor had argued that a more modern welfare system with better benefits and services would provide a pathway off welfare and ultimately reduce the welfare population and increase family stability.[13] The experiments however, failed to prove clear outcomes. Scholars eventually concluded that increased benefits *might* have contributed to declines in work and increases in marital breakup among welfare recipients. But even without evidence, opponents were willing to reach a broad conclusion that the existing welfare system discouraged work and encouraged promiscuity and family instability.[14]

At the same time, the actual gap between policy proposals from liberals and conservatives began to narrow. Historically, conservatives argued for low benefits and work requirements (workfare) as a means of reducing costs and encouraging personal responsibility, while liberals argued for increasing benefit levels and work incentives to allow welfare recipients to enter the social mainstream. In the 1970s, the Nixon administration proposed a Family Assistance Program (FAP) that incorporated work requirements and incentives. Although it ultimately failed to become law—abandoned by both conservatives and liberals—it established a policy trajectory that led ultimately to welfare reform. In particular, from the 1970s until the passage of the Personal Responsibility and Work Opportunity Reconciliation Act in 1996, welfare reform gravitated toward several new characteristics.

Combining Work Requirements and Incentives

The institutional structure of public assistance imposed important constraints on the trajectory of welfare reform. From its inception, public assistance had been a state-based program. Most states had adopted "mothers' pensions" during the early twentieth century, and the 1935 Social Security Act simply provided federal matching funds and new regulations for these state programs. During the welfare reform push of the early 1970s, the public assistance programs for the aged and for people with disabilities had been converted into a federal program—Supplemental Security Income; however, the controversy over work incentives, race, and family instability prevented AFDC from following that path.

Governors and state legislators continued to increase their ownership of welfare reform through the 1980s and 1990s. In contrast to the federal government, for which the cost of AFDC was always a minor budget item, welfare was a large part of state budgets. Also in contrast to the federal government, states had to balance their budgets. As a result, economic slowdowns that decreased state revenues and increased welfare rolls led states to adopt more restrictive welfare policies—within the constraints of federal oversight.

The simplest way for states to restrict welfare was to cut benefits, an aspect of welfare policy over which the states had wide latitude. Between the early 1970s and the 1990s, state cuts in benefits combined with inflation to reduce average welfare benefit levels across the nation. Although the nominal average family benefit increased from $191 to $378 per month between 1972 and 1994, corrected for inflation, this represented a 44 percent decline in benefits. In fact, states with the highest welfare benefits in 1972 tended to slash benefits by a higher percentage than low-benefit states. Formerly high-benefit states—including Illinois, Vermont, and New Jersey—cut average benefits by over 60 percent during that period.

---

[13]This argument and social workers' advocacy were behind the public welfare amendments of 1962.

[14]Charles Murray, *Losing Ground: American Social Policy, 1950–1980* (New York: Basic Books, 1984).

After Congress passed a significant welfare reform bill in 1988—the Family Support Act (FSA)—the states' role in reform expanded further. The FSA included increased federal funding for job training, the JOBS program, that required states to match the federal funding. Many states ignored the program—leaving more than a billion dollars of job-training funds unspent—but used a little-noted element of the bill to experiment with more radical reform. The *waiver* provision of the FSA allowed states to apply to the federal government for a waiver to disregard national regulations and implement new forms of welfare restrictions, including more stringent work requirements and connecting welfare payments to a number of behavioral requirements. By the time national welfare reform passed in 1996, 43 states had received waivers to replace AFDC with some variation.[15]

Welfare Reform and the Clinton Administration

Bill Clinton made welfare reform a central part of his presidential campaign in 1992. His proposals were based on policy analysis conducted by several Harvard University professors during the late 1980s. That research concluded that most welfare recipients spent relatively little time in the system, but that a significant minority of recipients collected benefits for years and that this small group represented a large share of total welfare spending.[16]

Based on this analysis, Clinton proposed a two-part approach to "end welfare as we know it."[17] First, the government should provide better support for working families by expanding the Earned Income Tax Credit. Second, public assistance should be restructured to push long-term recipients toward self-sufficiency. Clinton achieved both of these objectives, but not in the way he anticipated.

EARNED INCOME TAX CREDIT (EITC)

The earned income tax credit (EITC) is a *refundable* tax credit for working families with low income. It had its origins in the welfare reform debate of the 1970s. The Nixon administration proposed a *negative income tax* (NIT) as the basic structure for the welfare system. Under an NIT, rather than paying income taxes at the end of the year, low-income families would receive a check, a tax credit, from the government. At the time, reformers hoped that using the tax system—rather than a welfare bureaucracy—would reduce the stigma associated with welfare. Although Nixon's plan failed to win passage, Congress did add the EITC to the tax system. At the time, its size was quite modest, but in 1993 Congress supported a Clinton administration effort to expand the program. Today, approximately 24 million American households receive the EITC annually. Still, in a given year, an estimated 15 percent of families eligible for the EITC do not claim the benefit.

The EITC's great asset is its simplicity. In essence, it provides a government grant to supplement the wages of low-income workers. The credit is available only to families

---

[15]US Department of Health and Human Services, "Setting the Baseline: A Report on State Welfare Waivers," June 1997, http://aspe.hhs.gov/hsp/isp/waiver2/waivers.htm.

[16]Mary Jo Bane and David T. Ellwood, *Welfare Realities: From Rhetoric to Reform* (Cambridge: Harvard University Press, 1994).

[17]Richard L. Berke, "Clinton: Getting People off Welfare," *New York Times*, September 10, 1992; in a campaign ad initially broadcast on September 9, 1992, Clinton stated: "I have a plan to end welfare as we know it—to break the cycle of welfare dependency. We'll provide education, job training and child care, but then those that are able must go to work, either in the private sector or in public service"; references come from Demetrios James Caraley, "Ending Welfare as We Know It: A Reform Still in Progress," *Political Science Quarterly* 116, no. 4 (Winter 2001–2002): 527.

with a working adult. The size of a family's credit is based on the earnings of the household and the number of children. The size of the credit rises with a family's earnings until they reach a threshold after which the tax credit is phased out.

As the credit became larger and covered more families, adjustments have been made to how it is paid. Originally, a family would have to wait until it filed its tax return the following April to receive the EITC payment. This reduced its effectiveness, because it delayed access to the funds. It may also have encouraged some families to use the money for some big-ticket item rather than to cover essential expenses. Currently, families can receive the credit on a monthly basis.

The EITC has remained popular even though it has grown into the country's largest antipoverty program. As we noted earlier, tax expenditures tend to be supported by both liberals and conservatives, and the EITC is the best example of a tax expenditure that has a significant impact on the economic well-being of American families.

One irony of the EITC, however, is its impact on the official poverty rate. Because it operates through the tax system, it is not counted as part of the calculation of a family's official poverty status. However, the Supplemental Poverty Measure discussed in Chapter 4 incorporates EITC into its calculations.

TEMPORARY ASSISTANCE FOR NEEDY FAMILIES (TANF)

The expansion of the EITC was the first part of the Clinton administration's plan to "end welfare as we know it." However, the second element, the development of a more humane, work-oriented system of public assistance, fell victim to a variety of political and practical forces.

The passage of the Family Support Act in 1988 led to an increase in the number of families on AFDC, from 3.5 million in 1988 to 4.7 million in 1994. Much of this increase was fueled by the expansion of the AFDC-U program—extending benefits to two-parent families—included in the FSA.[18]

The greater influence of state governments associated with the expansion of state waivers combined with Republican successes in the 1994 midterm elections set the stage for the passage of the *Personal Responsibility and Work Opportunity Reconciliation Act* in 1996, which ended AFDC and replaced it with TANF. Although AFDC allowed a great deal of state-level policymaking, TANF provides a much greater level of state autonomy. Indeed, a number of states have virtually shut down their assistance programs. Nationally, the number of adults on AFDC/TANF fell from over 14 million in 1993 to 3.8 million in 2007, an overall decline of 72 percent. The number of recipients increased by a bit less than half a million between 2007 and 2011. Still, given the surge in unemployment, poverty, and dependence on food stamps during and after the recession, the AFDC/TANF increase was meager.

Among individual states, between 1993 and 2011, Wyoming reported a decrease in recipients from 18,238 to 607, a 96 percent decline. Among larger states, Illinois, Florida, Texas, and Georgia all reported declines of 80 percent or more in average number of recipients (Chart 8.7).[19]

---

[18]Rebecca M. Blank, "What Causes Public Assistance Caseloads to Grow?," working paper 6343 (Cambridge: National Bureau of Economic Research, 1997).

[19]National and state recipient data come from US Department of Health and Human Services, Administration for Children and Families, "TANF-Caseload Data," http://www.acf.hhs.gov/programs/ofa/data-reports/caseload/caseload_recent.html.

Chart 8.7 Average AFDC/TANF Caseloads by State, 1993–2011

	1993	2007	2011	1993–2007	2007–2011	1993–2011
US Totals	14,142,710	3,896,830	4,363,000	−72.4%	12.0%	−69.2%
Wyoming	18,238	487	607	−97.3%	24.6%	−96.7%
Louisiana	262,703	24,156	23,674	−90.8%	−2.0%	−91.0%
Georgia	398,329	43,414	36,911	−89.1%	−15.0%	−90.7%
Illinois	688,864	67,731	88,491	−90.2%	30.7%	−87.2%
North Carolina	334,761	47,048	43,544	−85.9%	−7.4%	−87.0%
Florida	694,535	75,282	93,913	−89.2%	24.7%	−86.5%
Idaho	21,295	2,389	2,881	−88.8%	20.6%	−86.5%
Texas	781,622	132,841	110,752	−83.0%	−16.6%	−85.8%
Oklahoma	138,059	19,831	19,865	−85.6%	0.2%	−85.6%
Mississippi	171,745	23,284	25,079	−86.4%	7.7%	−85.4%
West Virginia	118,995	22,294	23,189	−81.3%	4.0%	−80.5%
Connecticut	161,506	35,746	31,864	−77.9%	−10.9%	−80.3%
Arizona	196,539	77,912	39,937	−60.4%	−48.7%	−79.7%
Vermont	28,547	10,680	6,233	−62.6%	−41.6%	−78.2%
Puerto Rico	190,091	33,663	42,652	−82.3%	26.7%	−77.6%
Michigan	688,127	188,696	158,322	−72.6%	−16.1%	−77.0%
New York	1,196,589	265,087	279,238	−77.8%	5.3%	−76.7%
New Jersey	349,388	81,467	84,132	−76.7%	3.3%	−75.9%
North Dakota	18,518	5,202	4,495	−71.9%	−13.6%	−75.7%
Montana	34,596	7,999	8,551	−76.9%	6.9%	−75.3%
Arkansas	72,714	19,585	18,164	−73.1%	−7.3%	−75.0%
Rhode Island	61,727	19,654	15,573	−68.2%	−20.8%	−74.8%
Minnesota	191,466	62,976	48,789	−67.1%	−22.5%	−74.5%
Colorado	123,244	25,363	32,110	−79.4%	26.6%	−73.9%
Wisconsin	236,860	36,713	63,124	−84.5%	71.9%	−73.3%
Pennsylvania	607,870	145,868	162,563	−76.0%	11.4%	−73.3%
Utah	52,613	11,559	14,255	−78.0%	23.3%	−72.9%
Indiana	210,821	110,588	57,786	−47.5%	−47.7%	−72.6%
South Carolina	146,626	33,615	40,274	−77.1%	19.8%	−72.5%
Maryland	221,190	42,304	61,455	−80.9%	45.3%	−72.2%
Kentucky	224,833	59,820	62,798	−73.4%	5.0%	−72.1%
Alaska	36,388	8,435	10,196	−76.8%	20.9%	−72.0%
Ohio	718,701	167,620	215,221	−76.7%	28.4%	−70.1%
Massachusetts	325,431	91,049	99,337	−72.0%	9.1%	−69.5%
Nebraska	48,247	14,390	15,100	−70.2%	4.9%	−68.7%
Missouri	261,463	90,857	86,123	−65.3%	−5.2%	−67.1%
Virgin Islands	3,765	1,229	1,257	−67.4%	2.3%	−66.6%
South Dakota	20,104	5,972	6,824	−70.3%	14.3%	−66.1%
Dist. of Col.	66,706	13,895	22,734	−79.2%	63.6%	−65.9%

(Continued)

Chart 8.7   (Continued)

	1993	2007	2011	1993–2007	2007–2011	1993–2011
New Hampshire	29,483	10,323	10,414	−65.0%	0.9%	−64.7%
Virginia	194,326	65,649	73,289	−66.2%	11.6%	−62.3%
Maine	67,447	24,369	25,979	−63.9%	6.6%	−61.5%
Alabama	139,752	42,176	55,973	−69.8%	32.7%	−59.9%
Kansas	88,072	35,982	37,044	−59.1%	3.0%	−57.9%
Iowa	101,079	41,692	43,828	−58.8%	5.1%	−56.6%
Washington	288,076	117,271	139,358	−59.3%	18.8%	−51.6%
Hawaii	55,876	13,997	27,184	−75.0%	94.2%	−51.3%
Tennessee	310,872	153,591	152,957	−50.6%	−0.4%	−50.8%
New Mexico	95,392	33,918	50,793	−64.4%	49.8%	−46.8%
Delaware	27,672	9,071	15,496	−67.2%	70.8%	−44.0%
Guam	5,440	2,264	3,199	−58.4%	41.3%	−41.2%
California	2,462,489	1,160,638	1,462,880	−52.9%	26.0%	−40.6%
Oregon	117,697	41,823	79,016	−64.5%	88.9%	−32.9%
Nevada	35,223	17,366	27,578	−50.7%	58.8%	−21.7%

Source: US Department of Health and Human Services, http://www.acf.hhs.gov/programs/ofa/data-reports/caseload/caseload_recent.html.

One remarkable feature of TANF's caseload history was the program's relative *lack* of response to the recession that began in 2007. In fact, caseloads continued to decline in 2008 and 2009, even as unemployment climbed above 10 percent. There was also a striking divergence between states, with some states recording large increases between 2007 and 2011 while others recorded large decreases. Declines in caseloads after 2007 had more to do with efforts by the states to cut their budgets than with the economic well-being of their low-income residents. Arizona, for example, cut its welfare rolls by 49 percent between 2007 and 2011 and—thanks to the new "flexibility" in states' use of the block grant—used the savings to plug the state's budget gap.[20]

Eligibility

Because TANF is considered a transitional program, that is, recipients are expected to use it as part of a move to self-sufficiency, the program includes two sets of eligibility requirements: one for initial eligibility and a second for continuing eligibility.[21]

TANF is a selective, income-tested program. Generally speaking, to receive TANF, one must be a child or caretaker living in a family with low income. Some states use an estimate of gross income while others adjust income for determining eligibility. The eligibility standard is significantly lower than the federal poverty line. Some states include a disregard

[20]Jason DeParle, "Welfare Limits Left Poor Adrift as Recession Hit," *New York Times*, April 7, 2012, http://www.nytimes.com/2012/04/08/us/welfare-limits-left-poor-adrift-as-recession-hit.html?pagewanted=all.

[21]The following section draws on the Welfare Rules Database developed and maintained by the Urban Institute, www.anfdata.urban.org/wrd/.

for assets, usually including a car and several thousand dollars. States vary in their treatment of the income of other relatives or nonrelatives living in the household. Two-parent families are eligible in many states, but they typically have a set of requirements above those for one-parent families.

A relatively new element of eligibility is the effort by most states to *divert* families from applying for welfare. Some states offer families a modest lump sum of money to cope with an immediate crisis. If accepted, the family is ineligible for welfare for a number of months. In Georgia, for example, a family can receive a cash payment equal to four months of a welfare grant, but if accepted, it is ineligible to apply for TANF for a full year. In other states, applicants are required to conduct a job search either before they apply for welfare or while they are being considered.

To remain eligible for benefits, one must conform to a variety of asset, income, and earnings tests. One particularly important element of continuing eligibility for TANF relates to child support. All states require child support payments to a welfare recipient be assigned to the state. States vary in terms of whether they count child support toward a recipient's income, how much of child support they pass through to recipients, and how much they keep to offset welfare payments. In New York, for example, each month the first $50 of child support is passed on to the recipient, but all additional support is counted against the family's income in determining eligibility.

Eligibility is also influenced by the personal behavior of recipients. Two common behavior tests are requirements that dependent children attend school (required by 33 states) and that children are immunized (required by 26 states).

Recipients also face a variety of *time limits* in remaining eligible for TANF. The federal law includes a *five-year* lifetime limit on federal benefits, but many states have lifetime limits that are more stringent. States often have additional time limits for a particular spell on welfare. For example, in North Carolina, a family is eligible for 24 consecutive months, after which it is ineligible for three years.

Generally, recipients are required to enroll immediately in some work or job-training activity. Among the most common allowable activities are

(a) Job-related activities include one or more of the following: job-skills training, job-readiness activities, job development and placement, job search.

(b) Education and training (E&T) activities include one or more of the following: basic or remedial education, high school/GED, English as a second language, post-secondary education, on-the-job training.

(c) Employment activities include one or more of the following: unsubsidized job, work supplement/subsidized job, CWEP/AWEP, community service.[22]

The FSA of 1988 had encouraged welfare recipients to enroll in post-secondary educational institutions. Although allowed by some states, generally they have tilted away from allowing recipients to improve their educational credentials and toward identifying immediate employment, even if the wages of the job fall short of a self-sufficiency income. To remain eligible, recipients must devote between 20 and 40 hours a week to approved activities.

The decentralization of public assistance has made it more difficult to find national data on TANF. However, the federal Office of Family Assistance does issue occasional reports to Congress.

---

[22]US Administration for Children and Families, *Temporary Assistance for Needy Families: Eighth Annual Report to Congress* (Washington, DC: Department of Health and Human Services, 2009), Chapter 12, http://archive.acf.hhs.gov/programs/ofa/data-reports/annualreport8/chapter12/chap12.htm.

Since 1996, even mothers with very young children have been required to seek employment if they applied for TANF.

If recipients fail to meet these continuing eligibility requirements, they are subject to a variety of sanctions. Because of the number of continuing requirements, sanctioning has become an important element of TANF. Most sanctioning leads to a suspension of benefits for a period of time. Some states allow partial or total benefit cutoffs. Some states cut off the benefits only of adult members of the household, but in many states the entire family loses its benefits.

Benefits

The main benefit of TANF is a monthly cash payment. The value of AFDC payments declined sharply during the last 20 years of the program. For the most part, this decline has continued under TANF. Maximum benefits ranged from 19 percent of the federal poverty line in Alabama to 125 percent of the line in Hawaii. In 2008 the maximum benefit for a family of three in Alabama was $269 and in Hawaii was $1,802. The median figure for a family of three for all 50 states was $700 per month or 48 percent of the poverty line for that family size.

Yet even these figures give too generous a portrait of TANF benefit levels. Among women heads of households who reported any TANF income in 2008, the average monthly benefit was $389 for all families and $354 for three-person families.[23]

The maximum benefit can be reduced for a number of reasons, including adjustments for child support, earnings, and sanctions imposed because of noncompliance with

---

[23]Author's calculation from the Current Population Survey, March 2009 file.

work or behavioral requirements. One behavioral requirement that has directly affected benefit levels is the *family cap*, which restricts the benefits to a family if the mother gives birth to a child while collecting TANF. In 2008, 19 states included a family cap in their calculation of benefits.

Financing

The most important change in public assistance included in the 1996 law was the shift in financing. Before 1996, the federal government paid roughly half of state AFDC costs. Because AFDC was an *entitlement*, the federal government was obligated to provide funding on an open-ended basis, and states were required to provide AFDC to all applicants who met the eligibility standards. As we've noted, the second aspect of entitlement—the state's obligation to individual applicants—was often skirted by states' administrative practices.[24]

The 1996 law shifted federal spending on public assistance to a block grant based on a state's welfare spending in the years immediately before 1996. The block grant did not obligate the states to provide welfare to all eligible recipients. It also gave states the ability to spend federal funds for a variety of purposes other than assistance to individuals. For example, according to the 2006 official HHS report on TANF, of the $20 billion of federal funding available that year, states transferred 5 percent to the Social Service block grant and 9 percent to the Child Care and Development block grant. Of the remaining $17.6 billion , states spent $14.6 billion of which only $5.8 billion—41 percent—was spent on grants to individuals. The majority of block grants were spent on direct child care (14 percent), work activity (9 percent), and a variety of other benefits and services.[25]

When TANF was being debated in Congress, critics raised a concern that the block grant approach would allow states to cut their financial commitment to welfare. To address these concerns, the legislation called for a maintenance-of-effort (MOE) of state funding at its level in the mid-1990s. As with the block grant, however, the MOE payments did not need to be used for individual assistance payments.

One novel aspect of the financing of TANF is that it requires the states to meet certain standards with respect to the percent of recipients who are involved in work activities or face cuts in their block grants. However, in the original legislation, the calculation of this *participation rate* was so loose that no state faced a sanction, primarily because caseload reductions could be counted toward the participation rate. The 2005 reauthorization of TANF tightened these standards, although reducing the number of recipients remains a popular way of meeting participation rate requirements.

Administration

As the previous description of the program makes clear, federal administration of TANF consists largely of oversight of the block grant and its requirements with respect to participation rates and maintenance-of-effort. Federal oversight has become so scant, in fact, that it is difficult to track exactly what is happening at the national level. For the first five years after the enactment of TANF, the federal government issued annual reports on TANF. However, in recent years, the gap between federal "annual" reports has lengthened to three years, and available administrative data have become less complete.

[24]Article in Sheldon H. Danziger and Daniel H. Weinberg, eds., *Fighting Poverty: What Works and What Doesn't* (Cambridge: Harvard University Press, 1987).

[25]US Department of Health and Human Services, *Temporary Assistance for Needy Families Program (TANF), Seventh Annual Report to Congress*, December 2006, http://www.acf.hhs.gov/programs/ofa/data-reports/annualreport7/TANF_7th_Report_Final_101006.pdf.

TANF's "Success"

One lesson of politics is that the quicker one can declare a policy a "success," the better it is for its supporters. This certainly has been the case with TANF. TANF was enacted after an historical peak in the number of families on welfare. Before the legislation became law, welfare rolls had already started to decline, thanks to aggressive state action and the improving national economy. For the first six years, states enjoyed all of the benefits of the new welfare reality. An upswing in the labor market reduced poverty overall, the number of applicants for welfare decreased, and states had new flexibility in how they used federal funding. Together these facts allowed the supporters of welfare reform to declare success.

Since the early 2000s, however, welfare reform's success has been harder to track. Child poverty began to rise again, and the recession that began in late 2007 led to another spike in the poverty rate. The new style of public assistance, however, failed to respond to the economic realities of a collapsing economy. Overall, TANF rolls increased by less than 10 percent during the first two years of the recession. The gap between the number of families receiving food stamps—which increased by 40 percent during the recession—and TANF was one measure of how states used their new flexibility to ignore, rather than address, the economic needs of their residents.[26]

THE TRAINING CONUNDRUM

Assess your comprehension of "The Training Conundrum" by completing this quiz.

For the new public assistance system to function as intended, welfare must lead to work. Yet the history of job training efforts in the United States, as well as recent developments, clutter the path to self-sufficiency with many barriers. As with other aspects of social welfare, education and training opportunities in the United States are characterized by a striking dualism. Young people who are successful in the mainstream educational system—high school and four-year college—enjoy a system that provides them with the skills and opportunities to enter the labor force and succeed. However, youths and young adults who fall out of that system for one reason or another face uncertain prospects and very little help in righting themselves later (Figure 8.3).

Several policies around job training converged during the late 1990s. Welfare reform in 1996 increased pressure on states to put welfare recipients to work quickly. In 1998 the Workforce Investment Act (WIA) shifted the character of federal commitment to job training.

Like its predecessor, the Job Training Partnership Act, WIA placed implementation of job training programs into the hands of a local board with a private industry majority, renamed the Work Investment Board. The WIA mandates a *sequence of service* that requires applicants for job training to seek employment and enroll in basic skills classes before being allowed to enter training programs. The chief mechanism through which job training is provided is an *individual training account*, essentially a *voucher* that the recipient can use to seek appropriate training.

The WIA also restructured the market for training opportunities. The law and Department of Labor guidelines mandate a set of performance indicators focused on improving the wages of program participants. Although on the face of it this seems

---

[26]Robert Pear, "In a Tough Economy, Old Limits on Welfare," *New York Times*, April 10, 2010.

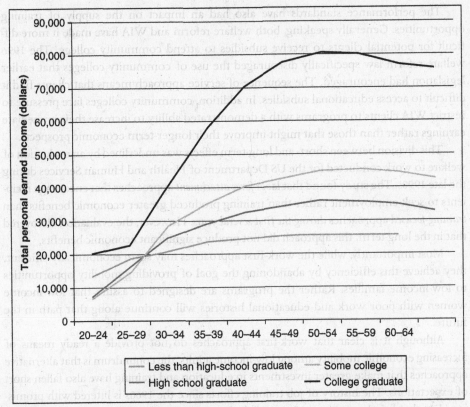

Figure 8.3

Average Annual Earnings by Age and Educational Attainment, United States, 2005–08
Although many Americans doubt the value of a college education, workers with a college degree still earn much more than other workers.

Source: Author's calculations from Steven Ruggles, J. Trent Alexander, Katie Genadek, Ronald Goeken, Matthew B. Schroeder, and Matthew Sobek, Integrated Public Use Microdata Series: Version 5.0 [Machine-readable database] (Minneapolis: University of Minnesota, 2010).

sensible, the policy has had a number of unanticipated impacts on the delivery of job training. To begin, because the performance standards do not take into consideration the background of participants, programs that serve clients with significant disadvantages appear to perform worse than those that focus on easier-to-serve clients. As a result, programs have an incentive to "cream" the more advantaged clients in order to boost their performance indicators. This probably explains why the proportion of low-income people served by WIA programs has declined.[27]

Like most TANF programs, WIA programs have tended to focus increasingly on "work first" strategies in which clients are required to seek out employment before they receive any services. Both the cost and benefits of these programs are quite low. Poorly educated clients with little experience typically find low-wage jobs that barely increase their income, but because the cost of the program is so low, these small benefits appear to outweigh the cost of the program. Although more expensive interventions may yield more favorable outcomes, their expense may be determined to exceed their benefits.

---

[27]Harry J. Holzer and Margy Waller, *The Workforce Investment Act: Reauthorization to Address the "Skills Gap"* (Washington, DC: The Brookings Institution, December 2003).

The performance standards have also had an impact on the supply of training opportunities. Generally speaking, both welfare reform and WIA have made it more difficult for potential clients to receive subsidies to attend community college. The 1996 welfare reform law specifically discouraged the use of community colleges that earlier legislation had encouraged. The sequence-of-service approach means that clients find it difficult to access educational subsidies. In addition, community colleges face pressure to restrict WIA clients to programs with a demonstrated ability to increase their immediate earnings rather than those that might improve their longer-term economic prospects.

This division between short- and long-term effects was underlined by an evaluation of welfare to work conducted for the US Department of Health and Human Services during the late 1990s. The study found that *labor force attachment* approaches that encourage recipients to seek employment rather than training produced greater economic benefits than *training-focused* approaches *during the first several years*. However, the evaluation discovered that in the long-term, this approach did not produce significant economic benefits.

Most importantly, while the work-first approaches may seem economically efficient, they achieve this efficiency by abandoning the goal of providing mobility opportunities to low-income families. Rather the programs are designed to assure that low-income women with poor work and educational histories will continue along that path in the future.

Although it is clear that work-first approaches do not provide a ready means of increasing economic mobility among low-income adults, the conundrum is that alternative approaches that make greater investments in education and training have also fallen short of expectations. The history of job training efforts since the 1960s is littered with promising ideas that failed to perform. Some of the most intense approaches—like Job Corps, a residential program that provides intensive services over many months—have been shown to perform well for some populations, but many other high-cost programs have not.

> In all, there are many examples of publicly funded training in the United States that are effective and promising, as well as cost-effective. But the overall impacts on the US workforce will continue to be very modest, as long as federal policymakers continue to limit funding as much as they have in recent years.[28]

With welfare-to-work and job-training programs committed to low-cost, low-impact approaches, it is not surprising that the majority of low-income workers have abandoned these programs, instead developing their own "programs" of economic mobility. Unfortunately, when they do so, they enter a sector in which predatory behavior by for-profit companies is often the norm.

Proprietary or for-profit educational institutions have focused on those parts of the market in which profits are most secure. Because the government guarantees student loans and grants for low-income students, these institutions are able to enroll students in programs without concern for whether the program will benefit the student financially or if they will be able to repay their loans. It is not unusual for programs in car mechanics or culinary arts to leave students tens of thousands of dollars in debt but without increased earning power. One student enrolled in a culinary arts program dropped out when he discovered that those ahead of him were taking minimum wage jobs as busboys and dishwashers.[29]

---

[28]Holzer and Waller, "The Workforce Investment Act."

[29]Peter S. Goodman, "The New Poor: In Hard Times, Lured into Trade School and Debt," *New York Times*, March 14, 2010.

In an effort to curb abuses by for-profit schools, Congress passed an overhaul of the student loan program as part of the health care reform law. Efforts to monitor misuse of student loans provoked a massive lobbying effort to limit the regulations associated with the law. Although the regulations did impose new oversight of loan abuse, they did so "on a much less ambitious scale than the administration first intended, relaxing the initial standards for determining which schools would be stripped of federal financing."[30]

The alternative to for-profit educational institutions—the community college system—faces its own challenges. As noted, welfare reform and WIA imposed constraints that have reduced access to its programs. Community college enrollment remained relatively flat during the decade after the passage of welfare reform but increased in 2007 and 2008 as the unemployment rate jumped. In 2008, 3.4 million Americans between the ages of 18 and 24 were enrolled in a two-year college.

The Health Care and Education Reconciliation Act of 2010, in addition to its health care and student loan titles, included additional funding for community college construction and modernization. However, the bulk of community college funding comes from state government, and the recession put pressure on states to reduce that funding. In California, for example, enrollments in community colleges exploded as students looked for low-priced courses, but state budget cuts led to declines in course offerings and support services even as the need increased.[31] Community college dropout rates raised doubts as well about the fit between the opportunities afforded by these institutions and the needs and interests of their students.

CONCLUSION

In the past 15 years, the federal government has begun an ambitious effort to integrate three systems that are central to Americans' social welfare: employment, education, and public assistance. As with many other challenges, ideology and institutional inertia have played important roles in the trajectory and success of these efforts.

A relatively neglected element of the social welfare system—unemployment compensation—played a central role during the recession of 2007–10. Congress stepped in as rising unemployment placed higher demands on the system, eventually extending the program to prevent exhaustion of benefits for the long-term unemployed. Still, the horizontal adequacy of the system came up short, as a majority of the unemployed did not benefit from the system.

The recession identified shortcomings in the public assistance system newly reformed in 1996. As unemployment mounted and a majority of the unemployed did not qualify for insurance benefits, TANF barely responded. After falling sharply during the previous decade, the intake of recipients failed to respond to the uptick in need, leaving many poor families dependent solely on nutritional programs and charity.

The job training system—reformed by Congress in the late 1990s—was also inadequate to meet the new demands. Declining funds, "creaming," and privatization

[30]Eric Lichtblau, "With Lobbying Blitz, For-Profit Colleges Diluted New Rules," *New York Times*, December 9, 2011, http://www.nytimes.com/2011/12/10/us/politics/for-profit-college-rules-scaled-back-after-lobbying.html?pagewanted=all.

[31]Katharine Mieszkowski, "Pressure of New Students and Old Weigh on Community Colleges," *New York Times*, April 8, 2010, http://www.nytimes.com/2010/04/09/education/09sfcollege.html?pagewanted=all&_r=0.

created a system that often turned its back on the poorest applicants in the search for better "performance indicators." Many community colleges sought to take up the slack but were hampered by a flood of new students and a trickle of funding.

POLICY PRACTICE: DISCRETION AND SANCTIONING

Policy doesn't always flow from the top down. As we've seen in this chapter, agents lower in the pecking order sometimes can begin making policy and then force those higher up to adapt to it. The role of state governments in transforming public assistance after the 1970s is a dramatic example.

Practitioners too can play a role in policymaking. In the 1960s, Michael Lipsky coined the term "street-level bureaucrat" to describe how frontline practitioners—like teachers, policemen, and social workers—represent the place where "policy" meets the people affected by policy. For Lipsky, this interface of policy and people provided an opportunity to consider the contradiction between social control and "helping" in the lives of professionals and their clients. Yet it also points to the role of *discretion* in the implementation of policy, and how that discretion itself can constitute policy.

The issue of discretion has become increasingly relevant since the passage of welfare reform. The number of requirements to continue eligibility has expanded the role of frontline workers in determining who receives benefits and who is *sanctioned* for violating those rules.[32]

Social workers' personal involvement in the public assistance system has declined over the years, even though many of their clients continue to depend on the benefits. Before the 1970s, social workers often served as caseworkers for public assistance clients. During this era, the caseworker's job integrated two distinct functions: income maintenance eligibility and the delivery of services. The boundary between the two was often hazy. If a caseworker visited a welfare family, was he there to determine eligibility or to dispense helpful advice and services?

This ambiguity played a role in the professionalization of social work during the 1960s. The public welfare amendments of 1962 mandated that AFDC clients should receive services and that these services would—over time—increase self-sufficiency and decrease the welfare rolls. Although the amendments failed at these goals, they did encourage social workers to examine their professional relationship to public assistance clients. A number of social workers argued that the integration of income maintenance and social service had a tendency to add a coercive element to the client/worker relationship and therefore limit the client's autonomy.

Policy Practice

Practice Behavior Example: Understand that policy affects service delivery and actively engage in policy practice.

Critical Thinking Question: How can social workers use their professional discretion to influence the implementation of policies? Is this opportunity more likely to be present in some settings than others?

Professional Identity

Practice Behavior Example: Advocate for client access to the services of social work.

Critical Thinking Question: In recent years, social workers have been criticized for advocacy of the "separation of services" during the 1960s and 1970s. How might social workers today view the ethics of this policy innovation?

---

[32]Michael Lipsky, *Street-Level Bureaucracy: Dilemmas of the Individual in Public Service*, 30th anniversary ed. (New York: Russell Sage Foundation, 2010).

Social workers generally supported the move toward *separation*, although little evidence suggested that clients actually felt coerced by social workers in this regard. It is possible that a simpler—economic—logic also facilitated the move to the separation of services. The determination of eligibility and calculation of benefits were relatively simple tasks that did not require an advanced degree in social work or a related field. As a result, welfare administrators could support separation of services, not for its impact on client autonomy but because it meant workers who were less professionalized and less expensive than social workers could do much of public assistance administration.[33]

While public assistance remained an entitlement, there was little reason to revisit this division. As long as welfare was a right—if one was eligible, the state had to provide aid—the determination of eligibility and benefits remained a straightforward technical action that required little discretion or professional judgment. However, during the 1990s, state waivers and the passage of federal welfare reform changed the situation. The determination of welfare eligibility was no longer a narrow, technical function. Workers were asked to make determinations about whether clients were complying with the range of new requirements tied to continued eligibility.

Most importantly, public assistance workers were now responsible for determining if recipients were to be sanctioned for failure to meet one or more requirements. While some of the behavioral requirements—school attendance or immunization, for example—are possible grounds for sanctioning, the vast majority of sanctions relate to work requirements.

On the face of it, sanctions can be seen as a means of "encouraging" clients to seek self-sufficiency. According to this logic, the moral hazard of welfare—recipients receive benefits without working—can be counteracted by removing the benefits if they refuse to work. Yet the language of "encouragement" hides a more naked interest of the state: sanctioning workers and eventually dropping them from the rolls allows the state to meet its "participation rate." In the original legislation, this rate is calculated by dividing the number of TANF recipients in an approved work activity by the total number of eligible recipients. By reducing the size of the denominator (the total number of recipients), sanctions increase the participation rate without increasing the number of recipients actually working. For example, when Texas instituted a tougher sanction policy, it increased its participation rate by reducing the number of welfare recipients, not by increasing those at work.[34] Another study of Texas found that when the state instituted tougher policies, frontline workers tended to focus on narrow clerical tasks, like filling out a form correctly, rather than the presumed goals of the sanction—that is, "encouraging" the client to work.[35]

In many cases, the increased discretion provided to workers is used to advance organizational objectives, not to benefit clients. Yet in other cases, local welfare departments have used discretion to reintegrate social work services into the eligibility

---

[33]George Hoshino, "Separating Maintenance from Social Services," *Public Welfare 30 (1972)*, however, argues that states resisted the move toward separation because they had used the 75 percent match provision around social service spending to expand the range of state services paid for by federal funds.

[34]Kauff et al., *Using Work-Oriented Sanctions to Increase TANF Program Participation* (Washington, DC: Mathematica Policy Research, September 2007).

[35]Vicki Lens, "Implementing Full and Partial Work Sanctions: The Case of Texas," *American Review of Public Administration* 39, no. 3 (May 2009): 299.

process. For example, after the reauthorization of TANF, Utah instituted a two-phase *problem-solving process:*

> The first phase is a meeting between the client, case manager, and a social worker. The second is a case conference with a wider variety of staff and partners such as child welfare agency staff, employment service providers, probation officers, and mental health therapists. Including these individuals provides different perspectives on how best to assist the client in resolving participation issues and identify available supports. It also ensures that several people review a case before it is sanctioned off TANF, providing a check on the decisions of case managers who have substantial discretion in initiating the sanction process.[36]

Suffolk County, New York, instituted a similar mediation session in which a third party works with the case manager and client to resolve differences.

A more ambiguous case of street-level bureaucrats making policy comes from California. There, noncompliant clients at risk of being sanctioned are required to attend a meeting to determine if good cause exists or to develop a plan to bring them back into compliance. The client is also informed that if they fail to attend the meeting, a *home visit* will occur the following day. The researchers concluded that many clients interpreted the home visit as a type of threat that shocked clients into complying. At the same time, the greater discretion given the home visitor often led to resolution of cases in ways that actually had an adverse effect on the state's participation rate, for example, by identifying good cause for the client's nonparticipation.

These examples are more likely the exception than the rule. In most states, the discretion given case managers is probably used to advance agency objectives (increasing work participation rates), often at the expense of clients' economic well-being. However, the examples from Utah, New York, and California raise the possibility that social workers will be involved in the reintegration of services and eligibility/benefit determination. Whether that provides an opportunity to improve the options available to low-income families or simply adds another coercive element to their lives will be up to the street-level bureaucrats who do their part to make policy from the bottom up.

Engage, Assess, Intervene, Evaluate

Practice Behavior Example: Develop, analyze, advocate, and provide leadership for policies and services.

Critical Thinking Question: What skills do social workers need to develop to provide organization-level leadership in adapting policies to better serve their clients?

Assess your analysis and evaluation of the chapter's content by completing the Chapter Review.

---

[36]Kauff et al., "Using Work-Oriented Sanctions," xxi.

9

The Challenge of Social Justice

INTRODUCTION

Political theorists have long recognized that majority rule can often lead to minority oppression. Plato saw democracy as always at risk of degenerating into tyranny. In his *Democracy in America*, based on his US travels during the 1830s, Alexis de Tocqueville raised the specter of the "tyranny of the majority" and the need for "self-interest rightly understood" as the only means for holding that tyranny in check.[1]

In this chapter we examine how democracy has failed several groups historically excluded from enjoying the full benefits of American society. African Americans—as the only group ever enslaved—certainly demand our attention in this regard. Although the civil rights movement of the 1960s and 1970s brought an end to the "Jim Crow" system of racial oppression, African Americans still find themselves marginalized in many areas of American life. More importantly, a number of scholars have argued that the emergence of *mass imprisonment* represents a new system of racial oppression, which has taken over from Jim Crow as a means of perpetuating the marginality of African Americans.

It's difficult to talk about the majority of the population as marginal. Still, women's changing role in the labor force and resulting changes in family life have highlighted the many ways that their lives are still restricted. In particular, the issue of *violence against women* continues to stand as a major barrier to their full enjoyment of life in American society.

[1] Alexis de Tocqueville, *Democracy in America* (New York: AA Knopf, 1945). Originally published as *De la democratie en Amerique* (Brussels: L. Hauman et Cie, 1835).

The struggle of individual rights and collective responsibility has played out in unexpected ways for people with disabilities. For most of the twentieth century, social welfare discussions of the issue focused on the need to accept collective responsibility for people with disabilities, particularly by adopting programs to reduce their poverty and provide rehabilitation services. In the past generation, spurred to a great extent by the mobilization of people with disabilities themselves, *the disability rights movement*—their struggle to secure individual rights to opportunity, access, and mobility—has taken precedence over a charity or social-welfare approach.

Lesbian, gay, bisexual, and transgender (LGBT) persons represent the newest stratum of the population to demand broader rights. Not very long ago, LGBT was viewed not as a status but as a condition to be treated. Only in 1973 was homosexuality removed from the DSM-II. In contrast to African Americans, women, and people with disabilities, gays aren't clearly economically disadvantaged. In contrast to the other forms of oppression discussed in this chapter, a large proportion of Americans see discrimination against LGBT persons as justifiable. The current focus of this struggle has been the controversy over *same-sex marriage*.

The pursuit of justice is central to the professional identity of social workers. Ironically, as movements among marginalized groups have become more militant and focused on civil rights, social workers and other "helpers" have often been cast as paternalistic (or, alternatively, maternalistic). That is to say, their concern and charity are seen as part of the problem.

More recently, some of the limits of the civil rights approach have become clearer, especially as state and federal courts have become more conservative and less willing to support the expansion of rights. This has led activists in a number of fields to reconsider the role of counseling, services, and income support programs in continuing to improve the standing of groups in our society. The arc of the moral universe is indeed long. It is social work's commitment that it will bend toward justice.[2]

MASS IMPRISONMENT

African Americans have found themselves subjected to several systems of racial oppression during the first 350 years of their presence in North America. The civil rights movement represented the triumph over the Jim Crow system of racial segregation. But recently a number of scholars have suggested that mass imprisonment represents the construction of a new system of racial oppression. Loïc Wacquant argues that since the seventeenth century African Americans have experienced four separate systems of oppression. He suggests that "the task of *defining, confining, and controlling* African Americans in the United States has been successively shouldered by four 'peculiar institutions': slavery, the Jim Crow system, the urban ghetto, and … the expanding carceral system." For Wacquant, the first three of these institutions served two purposes: "to recruit, organize, and extract labor out of African Americans" and "to demarcate

---

[2]The sentence—"The arc of the moral universe is long but it bends toward justice."—is usually identified with Martin Luther King, Jr., who incorporated it into a number of articles and speeches, including a speech at Wesleyan University in 1964. However, its origins date to the early nineteenth century, when Theodore Parker, a Unitarian minister, incorporated its key phrases in a sermon. President Obama has frequently use the quotation, which he usually attributes to Dr. King. See Jamie Stiehm, "Oval Office Rug Gets History Wrong," *Washington Post*, September 4, 2010, http://www.washingtonpost.com/wp-dyn/content/article/2010/09/03/AR2010090305100.html.

and ultimately seclude them so that they would not 'contaminate' the surrounding white society that viewed [African Americans as] … inferior and vile." For Wacquant, stratification within the black community—the rise of a significant black middle and upper class—required a new mechanism of racial oppression, which included mass imprisonment.[3]

According to Michelle Alexander, "what has changed since the collapse of Jim Crow has less to do with the basic structure of our society than with the language we use to justify it." Alexander argues that we now use the criminal justice system to restrict the rights of poor African Americans to social welfare assistance, the right to vote, and employment.[4]

It would be easy to dismiss Wacquant's and Alexander's arguments as hyperbolae to make a point about the injustice of the criminal justice system. However, as we look more closely at the facts of mass imprisonment, their observations become more convincing as an accurate representation of the contemporary situation.

The rise of mass imprisonment is particularly important for social work. Not so many years ago, criminal justice was an important field for the profession. Social workers worked with juveniles and other at-risk populations to prevent crime, worked with clients within the criminal justice system, and worked with offenders upon their release. The War on Poverty in the 1960s, in fact, began as an initiative in the US Department of Justice aimed at reducing juvenile delinquency.

The ideas that linked social work to the criminal justice system were *prevention* and *rehabilitation*. First, social workers believed that the causes of criminality were often found in the environment, and that if you changed the environment, you could divert people—especially young people—from criminal activity. Second, social workers believed that once a person was caught up in the criminal justice system, it was possible to change their behavior in a way that would allow them to leave the system and become a successful member of the wider society.

Generally, of course, social workers continue to believe in prevention and rehabilitation, and many continue to work with at-risk populations, prisoners, and former prisoners. In the meantime, however, the criminal justice system has taken a sharp turn away from these beliefs. Instead, the system has increasingly defined criminality as a persistent characteristic of individuals and groups and implemented policies that treat such people as a group to be isolated from the rest of society to protect "law-abiding citizens" from their predations.

Professional Identity

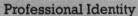

Practice Behavior Example: Know the profession's history.

Critical Thinking Question: How can we explain the declining influence of social work in the criminal justice system? To what extent was it a result of changes in the wider society, criminal justice policy, and ideas about the profession?

One outcome of this change in ideology has been the explosion in both the number and percentage of Americans in prison, on probation, or on parole. As the proportion of the adult population in prison rose above 1 percent, the criminal justice system became a system of mass imprisonment that was no longer simply about apprehending and punishing individual criminals. As David Garland has noted, mass imprisonment is characterized by "a rate of imprisonment…that is markedly above the historical and comparative norm for societies of this type…[Imprisonment] ceases to be the incarceration

[3]Loïc Wacquant, "Deadly Symbiosis: When Ghetto and Prison Meet and Mesh," *Punishment and Society* 3 (2001): 95–133.

[4]Michelle Alexander, *The New Jim Crow: Mass Incarceration in the Age of Colorblindness* (New York: New Press, 2010), 1–2.

of individual offenders and becomes the systematic imprisonment of whole groups of the population."[5]

What are the causes of this dramatic shift in our use of the criminal justice system? One might argue that it is a simple case of cause and effect. As crime has gone up, society has responded by using more of its resources to apprehend and punish the perpetrators. However, this type of explanation does not fit the facts. Although the United States did experience a spike in crime during the 1960s and 1970s—an increase correlated with the years the baby boom generation reached the age when men are most likely to commit crimes—by the 1980s, rates of victimization and crime began a decline that has continued for a generation. So a simple cause-and-effect explanation will not work.

Other commentators see the rise of mass imprisonment as a reaction to fundamental changes in our society. Changes in work and family life, this theory suggests, have had an impact on the structure of social order and have exacerbated anxiety about the stability of our world. Among the more proximate causes are

- anxieties about crime and violence,
- demand for public protection,
- giving priority to victims over offenders,
- political populism,
- declining faith in established ways of reinforcing social order, and
- disregard for the status of the "undeserving poor."[6]

In other words, this perspective suggests that a set of social anxieties generated by the sweep of social change found an object in criminality. If we were unsure about the nature of our relationships and status at home or at work, we could gain a sense of order by identifying a stratum of society—the criminal class—that was the cause of our distress and develop effective means of keeping its members away from us.

Once mass imprisonment was established, it generated its own momentum. What some have called the "penal-industrial complex" obviously does great harm to many, but it also has its beneficiaries. The system provides employment for tens of thousands. Many prisons are located in declining and depressed rural areas where they provide virtually the only source of employment growth. Because—for the census—prisoners are usually counted as living at the penal facility, conservative rural politicians benefit from the population increases in their districts without having to worry that these "constituents" might actually be able to vote. Finally, increasing privatization has spread the economic benefits of this growth industry to entrepreneurs and investors.[7]

As with the post-reform welfare system, social workers find themselves connected to a system with which they share few values. However, the consequences of that system—spouses and children separated from their partners and parents, ex-offenders unable to find employment and means of survival—have become an increasing reason why people seek services. Thus, although no longer integrated systems, the workings of criminal justice continue to impact the lives of social workers and their clients.

---

[5]David Garland, "Introduction: The Meaning of Mass Imprisonment," *Punishment & Society* 3, no. 1 (January 2001): 5–6.

[6]David Garland, "Epilogue: The New Iron Cage," *Punishment & Society* 3, no. 1 (January 2001): 197.

[7]Eric Schlosser, "The Prison-Industrial Complex" *The Atlantic* (December 1998), online ed., http://www.theatlantic.com/magazine/archive/1998/12/the-prison-industrial-complex/4669/.

Trends in Victimization, Arrests, and Imprisonment

We talk about crime rates as if we actually know the number of crimes committed, by whom, and where. The reality is quite different. For the most part, what we know about crime comes from police reports. If a crime occurs and is reported, eventually it will turn up in police records and be reported to the Federal Bureau of Investigation (FBI) as part of the Uniform Crime Report (UCR). Clearly, many crimes don't end up in these reports, especially if victims decide not to report the crime. Indeed, one paradox of crime fighting is that an increase in the number of police in a neighborhood sometimes leads to an *increase in reported crime*. Alternatively, cuts to a city's police force often lead to a decline in reported crime.

Because crime statistics are so notoriously inaccurate, a more reliable estimate of the experience of crime is a *victimization survey*, like the National Crime Victimization Survey conducted since 1973 by the Bureau of Justice Statistics.[8] These data show that, with a few exceptions, rates of serious violent crime have declined significantly since the survey was first conducted. The highest rate for serious violent crimes was reached in 1974 when 2.3 percent of the adult population reported experiencing an incident. The recessions of the late 1970s were associated with a minor increase between 1978 and 1981, which was followed by a decline from 2.3 percent in 1981 to 1.7 percent in 1990. After a small increase in the early 1990s, the serious violent crime victimization rate fell below 0.7 percent in the early 2000s. The recession that began in 2007 was again associated with an increase in victimization.

During the 1970s and 1980s, the United States focused new resources for the "war on crime." As a result, even as victimization rates were declining by more than a third between 1974 and 1990, the FBI's Uniform Crime Reports (UCR) were showing an *increase* in reported serious violent crime from 0.5 to 0.8 percent. After 1990, both indexes declined sharply, although the victimization survey rate fell more quickly than the figures reported by the FBI.

Who is likely to be a victim of crime? In 2010, the violent victimization rate for the entire population stood at 1.5 percent.[9] Men (1.6 percent) had a slightly higher risk of victimization than women (1.4 percent). Among ethnic groups, risk among American Indians and Alaskan Natives (4.2 percent) was about three times the national average. Among larger ethnic groups, African Americans' rate (2.1 percent) was 0.6 percentage points above the national average. Hispanics had roughly the same risk as the population as a whole, while the rates for non-Hispanic whites and Asian Pacific Islanders were below the national average. Interestingly, multiracial individuals reported a victimization rate of 5.3 percent, well above the African American figure.[10] Victimization varied with age as well. Persons 18 to 20 years of age had the highest risk (3.4 percent) followed by those 21 to 24 years of age (2.7 percent). Rates declined rapidly among older age groups (Chart 9.1).

These data tell an important story. Americans at the beginning of the twenty-first century were much less likely to experience serious crimes than they had been a generation earlier. Yet most Americans are unaware of this trend, which is so fundamental to

[8]Janet L. Lauritsen and Karen Heimer, "Violent Victimization among Males and Economic Conditions: The Vulnerability of Race and Ethnic Minorities," *Criminology and Public Policy* 9, no. 4 (2010): 665–692.
[9]The violent victimization rate is different from the "serious violent" victimization rate cited earlier.
[10]Jennifer L. Truman, *Criminal Victimization, 2010* (Washington, DC: Bureau of Justice Statistics, 2011), http://www.bjs.gov/content/pub/pdf/cv10.pdf.

Chart 9.1 Demographic Characteristics of Crime Victims, 2010

Demographic characteristic of victim		Percent of total population	Total	Rape/ sexual assault	Robbery	Total assault	Aggravated assault	Simple assault
	Total	100	14.9	0.7	1.9	12.3	2.8	9.5
Sex								
	Male	48.8	15.7	0.1	2.4	13.1	3.4	9.7
	Female	51.2	14.2	1.3	1.4	11.5	2.3	9.2
Race/Hispanic origin								
	White*	67.9	13.6	0.7	1.4	11.6	2.6	9
	Black	11.9	20.8	1.1	3.6	16.1	4.7	11.4
	Hispanic	14	15.6	0.8	2.7	12	2.3	9.8
	American Indian or Alaskan Native	0.5	42.2	—	4.3	37.9	19.5	18.3
	Asian or Pacific Islander	4.7	6.3	0.6	1.1	4.5	0.5	4
	Two or more races	1	52.6	1.2	8	43.5	8.5	34.9
Age								
	12–14	4.7	27.5	2.7	0.7	24.1	5.8	18.3
	15–17	4.8	23	1.7	2.7	18.6	3.9	14.7
	18–20	5.1	33.9	1.1	5.9	26.9	6.9	20
	21–24	6.5	26.9	1.5	3.7	21.7	8	13.7
	25–34	16.3	18.8	1.3	2.5	15	3.3	11.7
	35–49	24.7	12.6	0.6	1.5	10.4	1.9	8.6
	50–64	22.7	10.9	—	1.3	9.7	2.1	7.6
	65 or older	15.1	2.4	0.1	0.6	1.7	0.2	1.5

Source: National Crime Victimization Survey, 2010. Adapted from Jennifer L. Truman, *Criminal Victimization, 2010* (Washington, DC: Bureau of Justice Statistics, 2011), Table 9.

social well-being. One reason is that the actual reduction in crime has not been accompanied by a reduction in the fear of crime. Since the 1960s, the Gallup organization has asked Americans if there is an area within a mile of their house where they are afraid to walk. That index reached a high in the early 1980s at 48 percent. The figure declined to a low of 30 percent in 2002 but rose to 38 percent in 2011. Although crime was a fraction of what it had been in the 1970s, nearly 4 in 10 Americans still fear walking alone at night.[11]

Another reason that the good news on crime has not registered with the general public is because it was not echoed in the number of arrests and imprisonments. While the number of victims and reports of violent crimes were falling after 1973, the number

[11]Lydia Saad, "Nearly 4 in 10 Americans Still Fear Walking Alone at Night," Gallup Wellbeing, November 5, 2010, http://www.gallup.com/poll/144272/nearly-americans-fear-walking-alone-night. aspx; *Sourcebook of Criminal Justice Statistics,* Table 2.37.2011, http://www.albany.edu/sourcebook/pdf/t2372011.pdf.

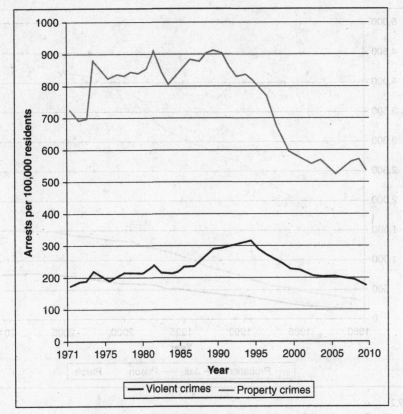

Figure 9.1
Arrests for Violent and Property Crimes, 1971–2010
After rising for two decades, rates of reported crime have been falling since the 1990s.

Source: Sourcebook of Criminal Justice Statistics, http://www.albany.edu/sourcebook/csv/t422010.csv.

of arrests for violent crime actually increased from 187 per 100,000 in 1973 to 218 in 2002. Although the arrest figure has fallen in recent years, only in 2010 did it fall below the level of the early 1970s. Police departments continued to arrest people in high numbers, even as the number of violent crimes committed declined (Figure 9.1).

The rapid decline in actual crimes and the more or less stable arrest figures are striking, but that disconnect pales by comparison with the *corrections supervision* figures. Here we draw a distinction between four different ways that a person can come under corrections supervision:

- *Probation*—One has been convicted of a crime, but rather than serving a prison sentence, one is allowed to remain in the community with restrictions on one's behavior and other requirements.
- *Jail*—Typically administered by counties, jails hold prisoners who are either awaiting trial or transfer.
- *Prison*—Typically administered by states or the federal government, prisons are where most persons serve their sentences.
- *Parole*—After serving part of one's sentence, prisoners are often granted release, again with restrictions on their behavior and other requirements.

Regardless of what happened in terms of actual crimes and arrests, the American prison and supervision populations continued to grow. In the late 1970s, after decades

Chapter 9

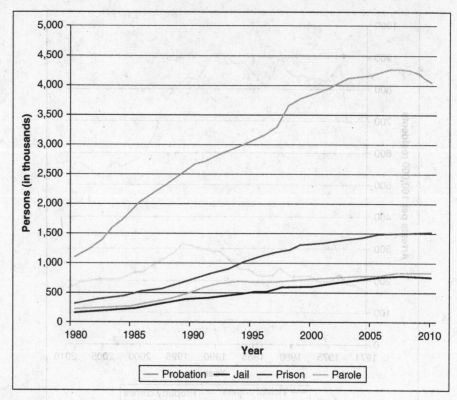

Figure 9.2
Adults under Correctional Supervision, by Type, 1980–2010
Although crime rates have dropped since the 1990s, the share of the population either jailed or under correctional supervision has continued to grow.

Source: Sourcebook of Criminal Justice Statistics, http://www.albany.edu/sourcebook/csv/t6652009.csv.

during which this population remained fairly stable at around 125 per 100,000 inhabitants, the rate began increasing and has not stopped since. By the late 2000s, more than 2.27 million Americans were serving time in prisons and jails. Yet this figure—more than 1 percent of the adult population—was dwarfed by the explosion in probation. By the late 2000s, more than 4.2 million Americans were serving probation. Between 2007 and 2010, the figure declined for the first time in a generation (Figure 9.2).

Probation in many ways is preferable to prison, yet it's easy to underestimate its implications for a person's future life chances. A first-time felony conviction (even if it carries no prison time) can effectively bar a person from getting a job, living in public housing, or collecting government benefits. If one has children, they are often taken away for "neglect" and—thanks to the new emphasis on permanency—the mother can lose her parental rights. As Michelle Alexander has pointed out, plea bargains that force arrestees to waive their right to a trial in exchange for probation have now become a key part of the penal-industrial complex. She believes that if those arrested stopped accepting plea bargains, the current system would quickly break down.[12]

In other words, rather than representing a type of leniency, probation now functions as a way for the criminal justice system to increase its productivity. By accelerating the

[12]Michelle Alexander, *The New Jim Crow: Mass Incarceration in the Age of Colorblindness* (New York: New Press, 2010).

speed with which it can process its "raw material" (i.e., people arrested for crimes) the system turns out a larger and larger share of the population that has had many of its basic rights—as citizens, parents, and voters—extracted.

The imprisonment rates in the United States stand out in international comparisons. Although the crime rate in the United States is now *below* international averages, the imprisonment rate here is five or six times that of other *high imprisonment societies*. According to a 2012 report, 10 million people are held in prisons throughout the entire world. The rate of incarceration in the United States (743 per 100,000) is 30 percent higher than the rate in Russia (568 per 100,000) and eight times higher than the median rate for Western Europe (96 per 100,000).[13] This means that—worldwide—22 percent of the world's prisoners live in the United States.

The Color of Prison

If the prison population were 1 percent of all social groups, the issue of mass imprisonment might have gained wider attention. In reality, however, imprisonment is concentrated in relatively few social groups. In 2010, of the 1.4 million men in state or federal correctional facilities, 558,700 or 38 percent were non-Hispanic blacks. Compared to 0.46 percent of the white population, 3.1 percent of black men are under correctional authority.[14]

While these figures are startling enough, even these data understate the disparity, according to an in-depth analysis of the likelihood of imprisonment conducted by Bruce Western of Harvard University. Western computed the annual risk of imprisonment for different race and ethnic groups and by different levels of educational attainment. He then estimated, for people born before and during the era of mass imprisonment, the cumulative likelihood that a person with particular characteristics would end up in prison at some point during their life.

A white male born between 1945 and 1949 with at least some college education, Western found, had only a 0.5 percent chance of ever going to prison. The same person born 20 years later saw his chances of prison time increase, but they were still under 1 percent. Rates for white men increased markedly if they had less education. For a white high school dropout, the chance of going to prison increased from 4 percent for someone born in the late 1940s to 11 percent for someone born in the late 1960s.

Even before the era of mass imprisonment, a black male with some college had a 6 percent chance of entering prison at some point in his life—a rate much higher than that of a white high school dropout. But the risk of imprisonment truly soared for black males without a high school diploma. A black high school dropout born in the late 1940s had a one-in-six chance of going to prison (17 percent). Twenty years later, his risk stood at 59 percent. In other words, for this group, *going to prison had become one of the most common life events.*[15]

---

[13]Roy Walmsley, *World Prison Population List* (London: International Center for Prison Studies, 2010), http://www.idcr.org.uk/wp-content/uploads/2010/09/WPPL-9-22.pdf.

[14]*Sourcebook of Criminal Justice Statistics*, Table 6.33.2010, http://www.albany.edu/sourcebook/pdf/t6332010.pdf.

[15]Bruce Western, *Punishment and Inequality in America* (New York: Russell Sage Foundation, 2006), 26–29. "Black men in their early thirties in 1999 without college were more than twice as likely to have served time in prison than to have served in the military. By 1999, imprisonment had become a common life event for black men that sharply distinguished them from white men" (p. 28).

The impact of mass imprisonment on African Americans has led some commentators to assert that mass imprisonment represents a racial caste system. As we noted, Loïc Wacquant and Michelle Alexander have argued that mass imprisonment arose after the older system of racial stratification—Jim Crow—gave way, and that it represents a new set of social mechanisms for assuring that a large part of the African American population loses the benefits of American citizenship.

The Rise of Mass Imprisonment

The origins of mass imprisonment date back to the 1960s. At the time, prison populations had been relatively stable for several decades. For most of the previous two decades, the practice of criminal justice had stressed its potential as a means of rehabilitation, which would allow the prisoner to reenter society as a productive citizen. Indeterminate sentences gave judges wide discretion in individualizing punishment and, once inside the criminal justice system, perpetrators would often encounter helping professionals, including social workers. However, the rehabilitative idea had come under challenge. Although states continued to invest in rehabilitation, increasingly, social scientists and observers came to question its efficacy. The perception that rehabilitation failed set the stage for new ideas to influence criminal justice policy after the 1960s.[16]

The civil rights movement can be seen as a kind of watershed in the history of crime and punishment. The movement itself employed civil disobedience as a strategy against Jim Crow, which raised the issue of whether unjust laws needed to be observed. More importantly, the civil unrest that swept American cities after 1964 raised a specter of black lawlessness that shook white America. After riots in several cities in 1964, Republican Presidential Candidate Barry Goldwater drew a connection between the liberal social policies of the Johnson administration and the riots: "Choose the way of [the Johnson] administration and you have the way of mobs in the street."[17] However, it was Richard Nixon who, in his 1968 presidential campaign, convincingly linked lawlessness, black protest, and the threat to the "silent majority" of white Americans. Although the "war on crime" initiated by Nixon seems mild by today's standards, his invoking of the threat of African Americans was critical to setting the trajectory of imprisonment over the next generation.

During the 1970s, the faith in rehabilitation was replaced by a more punitive approach to criminal justice. The "war on crime" of the 1968 presidential campaign was quickly followed by the "war on drugs" in 1971. The Reagan administration assured that these wars would swell the prisons when it persuaded Congress to agree to federal mandatory sentencing for drug offenses. In terms of actually expanding the prison population, however, a more critical role was played at the state level. Although Republicans led the charge for stiffer mandatory sentences, longer sentences, and prison expansion; by the 1990s, "law and order" had become an area of competition between the parties as each used the issue to bid for popular support.[18] The passage of "three strike" laws—for which three felony convictions carried automatic sentences of 25 years to life imprisonment—provided a new means through which the accumulation of several relatively

---

[16]David Garland, *The Culture of Control: Crime and Social Order in Contemporary Society* (Chicago: University of Chicago Press, 2001), 53–74.

[17]Barry Goldwater, "Peace through Strength," in *Vital Speeches of the Day*, vol. 30 (New York: City News, 1964), 744. Quoted in Michelle Alexander, *The New Jim Crow: Mass Incarceration in the Age of Colorblindness* (New York: New Press, 2010), 41.

[18]Western, *Punishment and Inequality*, 59–61.

minor offenses could lead to long prison sentences. By 2000, nearly half the states had passed three-strike laws and limits on parole for mandatory sentences.[19]

As state and federal legislators advocated longer sentences, the courts broadened the ability of the police to apprehend suspects. During the 1950s and 1960s, a series of land-mark Supreme Court cases expanded the rights to legal representation and protections against illegal searches and seizures for those who were apprehended; however, as the war on drugs and crime expanded, the courts proved willing to play their part. The Fourth Amendment to the US Constitution, which protected Americans from searches and seizures without probable cause, came under particular attack as the Supreme Court pro-vided law enforcement with new ability to circumvent these protections. As a result, the use of "stop and frisk" tactics by the police became increasingly common after the 1990s.[20]

We will be long in paying for the cost of mass imprisonment. The cost must be mea-sured in the lives of those caught up in the criminal justice system—who have lost their right to vote, faced discrimination in employment, lost eligibility for public benefits, and lost years of their lives. It will be measured as well in the funds devoted to maintaining an aging population of long-term prisoners instead of investing in human potential. It will be measured in the lives of spouses, partners, and children whose material and emotional lives have been harmed by the indiscriminant use of prisons as a response to social inequality. Finally, we all will pay the cost, because damaging the citizenship rights of a portion of the population inevitably harms the ideal of citizenship for everyone. The proliferation of "voter ID" laws after 2010 is but one example of how curtailing civil rights can easily become seen not as deviant but the norm.[21]

> **Assess your comprehension of "Mass Imprisonment" by completing this quiz.**

GENDER AND VIOLENCE

Women's oppression is complicated by the fact that a majority of women share house-holds with men. Because of the family connection, in many areas of social policy, rela-tionships between men and women have been viewed as essentially a private matter into which the state should not intrude. Until the 1970s, for example, police standard oper-ating procedure for domestic violence incidents viewed arrest as a last resort. Instead, policemen were supposed to encourage the aggressor to "take a walk around the block" to cool off.[22] Mimi Abramovitz referred to this bias as the *family ethic*, the idea that wom-en's status in all areas should be seen through their normative roles as mother and wife.[23]

In the workplace, issues like "equal pay for equal work" and discrimination in hir-ing and promotion were framed by women's presumed economic dependence on men.

---

[19]Western, *Punishment and Inequality*, 65.

[20]Russ Buettner and William Glaberson, "Courts Putting Stop-and-Frisk Policy on Trial," *New York Times*, July 10, 2012, http://www.nytimes.com/2012/07/11/nyregion/courts-putting-stop-and-frisk-policy-on-trial.html.

[21]Alexander Keyssar, *The Right to Vote: The Contested History of Democracy in the United States*, revised ed. (New York: Basic Books, 2009).

[22]Emily J. Sack, "Battered Women and the State: The Struggle for the Future of Domestic Violence Policy," *Wisconsin Law Review* (2004): 1657–1740. Quotation on p. 1662.

[23]Mimi Abramovitz, *Regulating the Lives of Women: Social Welfare Policy from Colonial Times to the Present* (Boston: South End Press, 1989), 36–40.

Title VII of the Civil Rights Act of 1964 (P.L. 88–352)

(a) Employer practices
It shall be an unlawful employment practice for an employer

  (1) to fail or refuse to hire or to discharge any individual, or otherwise to discriminate against any individual with respect to his compensation, terms, conditions, or privileges of employment, because of such individual's race, color, religion, sex, or national origin; or

  (2) to limit, segregate, or classify his employees or applicants for employment in any way which would deprive or tend to deprive any individual of employment opportunities or otherwise adversely affect his status as an employee, because of such individual's race, color, religion, sex, or national origin.

http://www.eeoc.gov/laws/statutes/titlevii.cfm

For example, although women were actively recruited into the labor force during World War II, at the war's end they were unceremoniously forced out of jobs to make room for returning males.[24]

In education as well, women faced unequal treatment. Parents often saw girls' education as less important than boys'. Many fields excluded women from study. Women athletes, when they weren't dealing with the presumption that they were lesbians, had to cope with shoddy facilities and lack of recognition.

Moreover, the tactics of the feminist movement of the late nineteenth and early twentieth century complicated the issue of women's unequal treatment. In their drive to secure the vote, women's groups made a tactical decision to appeal to female social roles to assure men that they would act as a conservative force in politics. Likewise, in social welfare, *maternalism* appealed to women's traditional role to justify their entry into the public sphere and their advocacy of policies to protect women and children from exploitation.[25]

Women's "natural" dependence on men was so obvious that their inclusion in the Civil Rights Laws of the 1960s happened virtually by accident. The critical sections of the 1964 Civil Rights Act did not include "sex" among the enumerated classes. Indeed, many leading women's groups, including the President's Commission on the Status of Women and the Women's Bureau, opposed women's inclusion in Title VII. The amendment to add "sex" was proposed by Representative Howard Smith of Virginia, most likely in the hope that its inclusion would hurt the bill's prospects. Indeed, a supporter of the broader bill, Representative Edith Green of Oregon, appealed to members to reject the amendment, noting that "race discrimination was a more serious problem than sex discrimination and that further study was needed because of the biological differences between men and women."[26]

Whatever the motives of Congress, "sex" remained in the bill and served as a spark for the legal recognition of women's rights. Given the equivocal support for the Title VII amendment, it is remarkable that within a decade Congress would pass an Equal Right

---

[24]Mark J. Stern and June Axinn, *Social Welfare: A History of the American Response to Need* (Boston: Pearson Education Press, 2011), Chapter 7.

[25]Gwendolyn Mink, *The Wages of Motherhood: Inequality in the Welfare State, 1917–1942* (Ithaca: Cornell University Press, 1996).

[26]Michael Evan Gold, "A Tale of Two Amendments: The Reasons Congress Added Sex to Title VII and Their Implication for the Issue of Comparable Worth," *Duquesne Law Review,* 19 (1981): 453–477, http://digitalcommons.ilr.cornell.edu/cbpubs/11/.

Amendment (ERA) to the Constitution and send it to the states for ratification. While the failure of the ERA to win ratification was seen as an early victory for the New Right in American politics, its history underlines how quickly the idea of gender equality entered social policy discussions.[27]

Although women's struggles for equality in employment and education have paralleled those of racial minorities, a unique dimension of struggle has been *interpersonal violence* (IPV). Women are more at risk of violence from persons they know. There is evidence that the risk of violence, particularly partner violence, plays a significant role in preventing women from asserting their rights both within their relationships and in the public sphere.

Until the 1970s, domestic violence was generally treated as a private matter between men and women. Police and courts were extremely reluctant to intervene in nonfatal domestic disputes. The feminist movement of the late 1960s and early 1970s—with its emphasis on women's rights, self-help, and participatory organizations—set the stage for battered women to speak out and seek help. Grassroots women's organizations took the lead in developing services for battered women. After the 1970s, policies changed rapidly as states adopted mandatory arrests and "no drop" prosecutions to overcome barriers to addressing the problem. In 1994, Congress gave its support to these efforts by passing the Violence Against Women Act, which provided grants to states for improving law enforcement and to government and nongovernmental organizations for providing services.

Diversity in Practice

Practice Behavior Example: Understand the dimensions of diversity as the intersectionality of multiple factors including age, class, color, culture, disability, ethnicity, gender, gender identity and expression, immigration status, political ideology, race, religion, sex, and sexual orientation.

Critical Thinking Question: How did the intersectionality of multiple factors contribute to traditional approaches to domestic violence? Did changes in these factors play a role in the shift in policies after the 1970s?

Ironically, the shift in the legal and service status of interpersonal violence may have been too successful, in that it triggered unanticipated backlash. First, policy shifts mobilized a number of groups in opposition, supported by the claim that the courts had been taken over by feminist ideology. At the same time, law enforcement's support of women's rights created an uneasy alliance between the police, prosecutors, and advocates, which occasionally caused women's groups to question policy. Antifeminists often used the equivocation on the part of women's rights advocates as a rationale for undermining policy initiatives.[28]

In recent years, advocates have recognized that the most effective way to reduce violence and allow women to resume their lives is a combination of law enforcement and social service strategies. Certainly, women need the protection provided by the criminal justice system, but they also need help in finding employment, housing, and child care and in processing the impact of violence. As a result, social work and other helping professions have become an important part of the policy response to interpersonal violence.

Prevalence of Interpersonal Violence

A variety of surveys can be used to estimate the frequency with which women experience interpersonal violence (IPV). As noted earlier in this chapter, there is a large gap between victimization and crime reports for all crimes, and there is reason to believe that this is especially true for interpersonal violence. The two most widely used surveys—the

[27]Donald G. Mathews and Jane Sherron DeHart, *Sex, Gender, and the Politics of ERA: A State and the Nation* (New York: Oxford University Press, 1990).
[28]Sack, "Battered Women and the State," 1660.

Chart 9.2 Relationship of Assailant to Victim by Crime, 2010

Relationship to victim			Violent crime		Rape/sexual assault		Robbery		Aggravated assault		Simple assault	
			Number	%	Number	%	Number	%	Number	%	Number	%
Male victims												
	Total		1,956,320	100	15,020	100	302,400	100	420,460	100	1,218,440	100
	Nonstranger		781,300	40	11,730	78	51,780	17	208,020	49	509,770	42
		Intimate/a	101,530	5	—	—	22,110	7	29,290	7	50,140	4
		Other relative	111,680	6	—	—	1,900	1	41,710	10	68,070	6
		Friend/acquaintance	568,090	29	11,730	78	27,780	9	137,020	33	391,560	32
	Stranger		934,520	48	1,220	8	216,330	72	154,680	37	562,290	46
	Unknown/b		240,500	12	2,070	14	34,280	11	57,760	14	146,380	12
Female victims												
	Total		1,854,980	100	169,370	100	176,270	100	304,720	100	1,204,620	100
	Nonstranger		1,182,330	64	124,030	73	76,140	43	163,150	54	819,010	68
		Intimate/a	407,700	22	29,010	17	36,540	21	71,640	24	270,510	22
		Other relative	162,510	9	12,920	8	18,540	11	14,510	5	116,530	10
		Friend/acquaintance	612,130	33	82,100	48	21,070	12	76,990	25	431,970	36
	Stranger		562,580	30	41,950	25	93,760	53	114,460	38	312,410	26
	Unknown/b		110,070	6	3,390	2	6,360	4	27,110	9	73,210	6

Source: National Crime Victimization Survey, 2010. Adapted from Jennifer L. Truman, *Criminal Victimization, 2010* (Washington, DC: Bureau of Justice Statistics, 2011), Table 5.

National Crime Victimization Survey and the Violence Against Women Survey—report that the vast majority of victims of IPV are women.

The 2010 National Crime Victimization Survey estimated that about 100,000 men and 400,000 women were victims of violent crime. This represents rates of 0.8 per thousand men and 3.1 per thousand women. Of the women, 342,000 experienced either simple or aggravated assault, and another 29,000 experienced rape or sexual assault.[29]

NCVS data estimate that rates of IPV have dropped over the past two decades. In 1993, the rates for men and women were 1.6 and 9.8 per thousand respectively. This means that the risk of IPV has dropped by 50 percent among men and 68 percent among women between 1993 and 2010 (Chart 9.2).

Black and Hispanic women are more at risk of IPV than white women. In 2005, the rates for black and Hispanic women were 28 and 31 percent above the rate for all women. Although rates have dropped among all ethnic groups, they have dropped more slowly among black and Hispanic women than among non-Hispanic white women.

The National Violence Against Women Survey (NVAWS) in 2000 estimated much higher rates of violence. It estimated that in that year 1.3 million women and 835,000 men were physically assaulted by an intimate partner. Although the gap between men and women was not as large as in the NCVS, the NVAWS indicated that women were more likely to be injured as a result of the violence. Based on the survey, researchers estimated that the lifetime risk of IPV was 25 percent among women and 8 percent among men.[30]

Read "Measuring Intimate Partner (Domestic) Violence" on the debate over the prevalence of different forms of IPV.

A third source of information, the National Family Violence Survey (NFVS), estimated much higher rates of assault and nearly equal rates between men and women, a finding that has provoked skepticism. National Institute of Justice researchers have been among the skeptics because they believe that "collecting various types of counts from men and women does not yield an accurate understanding of battering and serious injury." In particular, critics have suggested that the NFVS includes many minor incidents—like pushing and shoving—that wouldn't be detected by the other surveys.[31]

State and Local Policy Changes in Addressing Interpersonal Violence

Many of the policy innovations concerning interpersonal violence, especially regarding police and prosecution, have occurred at the state and local levels of government. As we've noted, before the 1970s, police normally did not intervene in domestic disputes unless the woman was in serious danger. Prosecutors would not proceed with cases against batterers unless the victims were willing to testify against them. Typically, even though domestic violence cases were rare, 50 to 80 percent were dropped. The possibility that the abuser might coerce the victim into dropping a case rarely entered into decisions about prosecution, which effectively encouraged intimidation. Courts rarely issued restraining orders, except in the case of divorce or separation.[32]

---

[29]Truman, *Criminal Victimization, 2010.*

[30]Patricia Tjaden and Nancy Thoennes, "Full Report of the Prevalence, Incidence, and Consequences of Violence Against Women," (Washington, DC: National Institute of Justice, 2000), https://www.ncjrs.gov/pdffiles1/nij/183781.pdf. See also, National Institute of Justice, "How Widespread Is Intimate Partner Violence?" http://www.nij.gov/nij/topics/crime/intimate-partner-violence/extent.htm#note1.

[31]Richard J. Gelles, "Estimating the Incidence and Prevalence of Violence Against Women: National Data Systems and Sources," *Violence Against Women* 6 (2000): 784–804.

[32]Angela Corsilles, "No-Drop Policies in the Prosecution of Domestic Violence Cases: Guarantee to Action or Dangerous Solution?" *Fordham Law Review* 63 (1994): 853–857.

The first step in the policy shift began with grassroots feminist efforts to identify domestic violence as an element of women's oppression. These efforts typically viewed the police and courts as part of the oppressive structure and preferred taking direct action to ameliorate women's risks, including establishing safe houses and women's shelters.[33]

Given these origins, women's advocates often greeted the move to reform police and court practices with ambivalence. Could these male-dominated institutions really serve women's interests? If so, what kinds of compromises would be necessary? As advocates overcame these concerns, they pursued three types of reform: civil protection orders, mandatory arrest policies, and "no drop" prosecution policies.

Civil protection orders

The first significant change in public policy was the adoption of protection orders. These orders typically included stipulations—"including prohibiting all contact with the victim, requiring the subject of the order to vacate any residence in which he and the victim resided together"—and set conditions concerning custody and visitation rights. State legislatures began passing these laws in the mid-1970s, and by the mid-1990s they had become universal.[34]

Changes in arrest policy

After women's advocates successfully sued a number of police departments over their domestic violence policies, many jurisdictions began to change policies regarding police behavior in domestic disputes. Previously, police were often prohibited from making arrests without a warrant unless there was "probable cause" that a felony had been committed. New laws allowed police action in the case of less serious crimes. By the middle of the 1980s, many states and cities had adopted *mandatory arrest* policies, which led to a significant increase in the number of arrests for domestic violence.

As we've noted elsewhere in this book, one way that practitioners can influence policy relates to their discretion. In the case of mandatory arrest, reform was enacted because of a perception that police officers were "making policy" by showing leniency toward abusers when they encountered situations with evidence of interpersonal violence.[35]

Prosecution

Once an abuser is arrested, the disposition of the case is turned over to the courts. Before the 1970s, cases were frequently not prosecuted because either the victim was dissuaded from testifying or the prosecution, for whatever reason, decided not to continue the case. As with arrests, changes in state laws during the 1980s and 1990s removed some of prosecutor's discretion in dealing with these cases.

One of the major innovations—"no drop" policies—raised difficult questions about victims' autonomy. The crux of "no drop" prosecution was that the prosecutor's decision to proceed with a case should not be influenced by the victim's willingness to proceed. The rationale for these policies was to increase the number of prosecutions, which in turn would encourage police to be more aggressive in making arrests. Prosecutors also

---

[33]Elizabeth Pleck, *Domestic Tyranny: The Making of Social Policy Against Family Violence From Colonial Times to the Present* (New York: Oxford University Press, 1987), 184–200.

[34]Sack, "Battered Women and the State," 1667.

[35]Sack, "Battered Women and the State," 1670.

adopted policies, including collaborating with advocacy groups in developing specialized services, to encourage victims to stay with cases.

Although these policy innovations improved legal efforts to reduce domestic violence, they were not uniformly applied. In some places, both the police and courts adopted "evenhanded" policies where abuser and victim were each treated as a risk to the other and both parties faced arrest or mutual protection orders. Women's advocates, while welcoming more aggressive policing and prosecution, were concerned that "no drop" policies—which allowed cases to proceed without the victim's consent—might steal autonomy from victims who had already been violated.

Violence Against Women Act (VAWA) of 1994

Although most legal protection for victims of domestic violence was initiated at the state level, the federal government entered the field in 1994 with the passage of the Violence Against Women Act (VAWA), Title IV of the Violent Crime Control and Law Enforcement Act of 1994.

VAWA funded a number of federal initiatives. It changed some sentencing and evidence rules in the federal courts' treatment of sex crimes. It provided grants to law enforcement and prosecutors to improve their pursuit of domestic violence cases and stipulated that to qualify for a grant the grantee had to adopt particular policies. The act provided funding through the US Department of Transportation to make public transit safer. Finally, it provided federal funding to support victim services, shelters, safe houses, youth education, and a national hotline.

In 2012 VAWA was due to be reauthorized. However, a dispute broke out between the House and Senate over three issues: 1) allowing Indian tribal courts to try certain cases of domestic violence; 2) expanding the number of temporary visas for immigrant victims of abuse; and 3) extending protection to cover lesbian, gay, bisexual, and transgender victims of abuse. The Senate—by a large bipartisan majority— supported all three, while the Republican-controlled House bill rejected all three in a party-line vote. In early, 2013, Congress finally passed and President Obama signed the reauthorization legislation.[36]

Assess your comprehension of "Gender and Violence" by completing this quiz.

DISABILITY AND DEPENDENCE

People with disabilities have long been considered part of the "deserving poor." Yet we should note that this categorization frames them as both "deserving" and "poor." Indeed, in spite of the passage of significant social welfare entitlements between the 1950s and 1970s, 27 percent of people with self-care disability had an income below the federal poverty line in 2009.[37]

The nature of the "deserving-ness," however, has been an issue for people with disabilities. It derived to a great extent from a perception that people with disabilities had a limited capacity for independence and needed a paternalistic welfare system to

---

[36]Robert Pear, "House Vote Sets Up Battle on Domestic Violence Bill," *New York Times*, May 16, 2012, http://www.nytimes.com/2012/05/17/us/politics/house-passes-domestic-violence-bill.html.

[37]Author's calculation from Steven Ruggles, J. Trent Alexander, Katie Genadek, Ronald Goeken, Matthew B. Schoeder, and Matthew Sobek, *Integrated Public Use Microdata Series: Version 5.0.* (Minneapolis: University of Minnesota, 2010).

meet their needs. As with other aspects of the welfare system, that charitable impulse inevitably threatens the ability of people with disabilities to exercise autonomy over their work, family, and private lives.

Many of the programs directed at people with disabilities are covered in other sections of this book. Chapter 10 covers the two income support programs—Social Security Old Age, Survivors, and Disability Insurance and Supplemental Security Income—because older Americans also qualify for these programs. Chapter 7 discusses the two major health programs—Medicare and Medicaid—as a part of the broader discussion of health care policy.

In this section, we focus on the role of the disability rights movement in challenging the paternalistic social welfare paradigm and the resulting federal legislation that culminated in the Americans with Disabilities Act of 1990. We then assess the extent to which the newer "civil rights" paradigm has had the effect anticipated by its supporters. Finally, we discuss the renewed interest in a social welfare approach to the well-being of people with disabilities.

The relationship between disability and medical science is ironic. Historically, doctors were fairly limited in their ability to treat most conditions. As a result, when people experienced a serious illness, they usually died. As medicine has developed ways of preventing death (or rather promoting longevity), it has contributed to an increase in the number of people with disabilities. Many traumas like spinal cord injuries that used to be fatal have instead resulted in chronic conditions. Diseases like cancer and diabetes that typically were short-lived and deadly are now conditions that people learn to live with.

Government first paid attention to people with disabilities typically as the result of war. Although in past wars most soldiers wounded or sickened soon died, through the twentieth century, a larger proportion did not perish on the battlefield and instead became part of the disabled population. Veterans' programs began during the earliest days of the Republic, with injured veterans and the dependents of those who died typically being the first to receive aid. As we noted in Chapter 7, the veterans health system is emblematic of the willingness of government to make provisions for citizens who have served in the armed forces.

In contrast, the problems of people with disabilities as a class rarely attracted significant attention. The primary policy response was to hide them. Although the rise of institutions during the nineteenth century affected many populations—criminals, delinquent children, orphans, and the poor—people with disabilities comprised a large share of the inmates of institutions. People with mental disabilities, in particular, filled the "insane asylums" that persisted until the middle of the twentieth century.

Immediately following World War II, the large number of injured veterans pushed the issue of rehabilitation onto the national agenda. Similarly, as the problems of older Americans became more prominent, people with disabilities were often included in program expansion. For example, the original movement toward Social Security Disability Insurance in the 1950s was a "disability freeze" in 1954, which allowed disabled workers to collect Social Security old-age benefits as if they had continued to contribute to the program after they became disabled. Disability Insurance was added in 1956.

Even a watershed moment in the history of disability policy—like the passage of Section 504 of the Rehabilitation Act of 1973, which provided the first guarantee of nondiscrimination for people with disabilities—grew more out of the expansive language associated with the civil rights movement than a specific focus on people with disabilities. The first effort to articulate the civil rights of people with disabilities was a Senate bill in 1972 that would have amended the Civil Rights Act of 1964 to add "physical and mental handicap" to its protected classes. That strategy failed; the bill never even received a hearing. Indeed, even many supporters of civil rights worried that broadening the protections under the 1964 act might lead to weakening the existing ones.[38]

The idea of a civil rights guarantee, however, was kept alive by the need for Congress to renew the federal vocational rehabilitation program. The reauthorization of the Rehabilitation Act expanded eligibility to include persons with more severe disabilities and created new programs for particular groups. Still, the bill originally did not include any civil rights guarantee. In fact, the inclusion of what became Section 504 was the result of a meeting of Congressional staffers with no input from legislators. "It appears that most members of Congress either were unaware that Section 504 was included in the act," according to Richard Scotch, "or saw the section as little more than a platitude, a statement of a desired goal with little potential for causing institutional change."[39] Even though the act itself was ultimately passed by Congress three times and vetoed in both 1972 and 1973, neither Congress nor the president had much to say about Section 504. The simplicity of the language belied its significance:

> No otherwise qualified handicapped individual in the United States, as defined in Section 7(6), shall, solely by reason of his handicap, be excluded from the participation in, be denied the benefits of, or be subjected to discrimination under any program or activity receiving Federal financial assistance.[40]

Yet despite its simplicity, the passage of Section 504 had wide-ranging implications for disability policy for the next 40 years.

Congress has often passed broad guarantees like Section 504 that have ended up simply becoming a "scrap of paper" with little real impact. After all, the Civil War amendments to the Constitution were supposed to guarantee the citizenship rights of African Americans, something that was not accomplished for another century. Section 504 was different for two reasons: the disability rights movement and the battle over federal regulations.

As discussed in Chapter 1, we can think of policy as the function of two "worlds" of policy—the little world of official policymaking and the big world of political economy. Both of these worlds contributed to the making of disability policy after 1973.

The Disability Rights Movement

The disability rights movement began as a series of movements as people who shared a common physical or mental limitation (and their parents, families, friends, and advocates) organized to demand better conditions or recognition.

The beginnings of grassroots organizing grew out of parents' efforts on behalf of children with disabilities during the 1950s. However, in the 1960s the strategies and tactics of the civil rights movement captured the imagination of adults with disabilities. One of those strands began in California in the late 1960s when Ed Roberts, a victim

[38]Richard K. Scotch, *From Good Will to Civil Rights: Transforming Federal Disability Policy*, 2nd ed., e-book ed. (Philadelphia: Temple University Press, 2001), location 415–17.
[39]Scotch, *From Good Will to Civil Rights*, location 531.
[40]Title 45 Code of Federal Regulations Part 84, http://ecfr.gpoaccess.gov/cgi/t/text/text-idx?c=ecfr; sid=ba99912314cc73eb73bea70a4d300161;rgn=div5;view=text;node=45%3A1.0.1.1.43;idno=45;cc= ecfr. See also, http://ecfr.gpoaccess.gov/cgi/t/text/text-idx?c=ecfr;sid=ba99912314cc73eb73bea70a 4d300161;rgn=div5;view=text;node=45%3A1.0.1.1.43;idno=45;cc=ecfr. See also, US Department of Health and Human Services, Office for Civil Rights, "Fact Sheet: Your Rights Under Section 504 of the Rehabilitation Act," http://www.hhs.gov/ocr/civilrights/resources/factsheets/504.pdf.

Eunice Fiorito, Social Worker, and the Emergence of Disability Rights

The development of coalitions [of different disability organizations] was encouraged when individuals attending the PCEH conference in 1972 were outraged by President Nixon's veto [of the Rehabilitation Act]. One person involved was Eunice Fiorito, a blind social worker from New York City, an organizer of a local cross-disability group called Disabled in Action, and the first director of the New York City Mayor's Office for the Handicapped. She described the first demonstration:

In 1972 we planned a demonstration at the Lincoln Monument. We all came out of the President's Committee the night of the big banquet, all of the kids had this march and demonstration and then had this all-night vigil over at the Lincoln Monument. I went to the banquet in my very formal outfit and then [demonstrated] in the rain for about six hours.

—From Richard Scotch, *From Good Will to Civil Rights*

of the polio epidemic of the early 1950s, attempted to get an education. After two years at a community college, Roberts requested funding from the state rehabilitation department to attend a four-year college but was turned down because the department ruled it was not feasible that he could ever work. After fighting the state and the University of California—a dean suggested that "we've tried cripples before and it didn't work"—Roberts was instrumental in getting the university to create a residence for severely disabled students. Eventually, this effort led to the creation of the Center for Independent Living (CIL) in 1972. The CIL represented both a significant innovation in providing a range of services and accommodations that allowed people with disabilities to live independently and a radical rethinking of the psychology of people with disabilities. In the East, groups like Disabled in Action (DIA) adopted the tactics of protest and civil disobedience to dramatize the denial of rights and funding to people with disabilities.[41]

The passage of Section 504 provided the disability rights movement with a clear objective: make sure that its promise of access and rights were fulfilled. Attendees at the President's Committee on Employment of the Handicapped (PCEH) organized a demonstration to protest Nixon's veto of the original bill. Although the PCEH, founded in 1948, was seen as a conservative voice for the handicapped, it allowed groups organized around particular disabilities to examine their common concerns. It helped form the American Coalition of Citizens with Disability, which would influence policy over the next several decades.

From Section 504 to the Americans with Disability Act

But other forces associated with the little world of insider policy brought different concerns to the table. As we noted in Chapter 3, once a bill becomes law, the executive branch must translate its general language into specific regulations that can be used to enforce the law. The task of writing the regulations is assigned to a particular department of government or a task force drawn from several departments. The translation process is particularly critical when the law itself is expansive, like Section 504. Regulation writing in the case of Section 504 was assigned to the Department of Health, Education, and Welfare (HEW, which became the Department of Health and Human Services after the

---

[41]Joseph P. Shapiro, *No Pity: People with Disabilities Forging a New Civil Rights Movement* (New York: Times Books, 1993), 53–58.

Department of Education was established). The Secretary of the Department, Casper Weinberger, decided to assign enforcement to the Office of Civil Rights (OCR), a "decision [that] was to have important consequences for the substance of the regulation." Dominated by lawyers who assumed an adversarial relationship with the institutions to be regulated, the OCR staff members "were generally unwilling to rely upon voluntary cooperation and the avowed good intentions of those whose discriminatory behavior they were trying to change."[42]

One immediate impact of the regulatory process was to change the definition of persons covered by the law. Originally, the Rehabilitation Act defined a "handicapped individual" as someone who has a disability but "can reasonably be expected to benefit in terms of employability from vocational rehabilitation services."[43] This idea—that public policy should focus only on people with disabilities who could become employable—had been used in the past to deny services (to say nothing of civil rights) to people whose disabilities were deemed by officials to be too severe. Ultimately, the concern of the civil rights office about the narrowness of the definition led to the passage of amendments to the act in 1974; the amendments dropped the employability standard and reaffirmed (in its legislative history) that Section 504 should be backed with explicit enforcement regulations.

Most importantly, rule-making for Section 504 also articulated the idea that discrimination against people with disabilities would not be redressed simply by equal treatment. Rather, organizations receiving funding from the government would need to make *accommodations* that would allow people with disabilities to participate fully, including the removal of physical barriers.

The drafting of the regulations associated with Section 504 occurred at a complex moment in American politics. President Nixon had been forced to resign in August 1974. His successor, Gerald Ford, was a traditional fiscal conservative. He was soon faced with two unpleasant realities: a Democratic landslide in the 1974 elections and a severe recession that increased unemployment and the federal budget deficit. As a result, the Ford administration was alarmed by the potential costs associated with Section 504 at the same time that he was being pushed toward more liberal policies by Congress and to the right by a challenge from Ronald Reagan for the 1976 Republican nomination.

The Ford administration ultimately delayed issuing the new regulations, and the incoming Carter administration issued them only after a series of demonstrations by disability rights advocates, including sit-ins at HEW headquarters in Washington, DC, and San Francisco. The cross-group organizing associated with the regulation process created a potent network of people with disabilities willing to use a variety of tactics to advocate their position.

The movement gained an unusual ally during the 1980s when Vice President George H. W. Bush was appointed to head a task force on "regulatory relief." Originally, the expectation was that Bush's task force would use its influence to weaken enforcement of Section 504. Ultimately this effort failed. Instead, the Reagan administration's National Council on the Handicapped in its 1986 report, *Toward Independence*, recommended a more comprehensive approach to the rights of people with disabilities, a vision that ultimately led to the passage of the Americans with Disabilities Act and its enthusiastic support from President George Bush in 1990.

---

[42]Scotch, *From Good Will to Civil Rights*, location 618.

[43]Scotch, *From Good Will to Civil Rights*, location 644.

The Americans with Disabilities Act addressed discrimination in four areas:

- Private employers with more than 15 employees must make "reasonable accommodation" for qualified individuals to encourage their employment.
- State and local governments (not covered by Section 504), including transit agencies, were required to remove barriers.
- Public accommodations, including restaurants, hotels, private schools, and public spaces, were required to make reasonable modifications.
- Telecommunications services were required to take action to make them accessible to the hearing-impaired.

Since its passage, the Americans with Disabilities Act (ADA) has resulted in significant changes to the expectations and realities of people with disabilities. As with other civil rights innovations, changes required to conform to the law have benefited many other populations. The curb cuts once rare in American cities now facilitate mobility not only for people in wheelchairs, but for parents with strollers and people of all ages with physical limitations that don't reach the threshold of a disability. At the same time, the mandate to provide reasonable accommodations has expanded the range of conditions that are covered by the act.

Still, the ADA has not been an unqualified success. Perhaps the greatest disappointment for advocates has been its lack of impact on the employment of people with disabilities. Some have suggested that fear of the cost of accommodation has worked to dissuade employers from hiring people with disabilities on other grounds. A more likely barrier to the employment of people with disabilities has been the nature of the health care system. In accepting employment, workers risk losing their entitlement to Medicaid and Medicare. If the potential job has inadequate health insurance or if they become unemployed, months or years could pass before they regain eligibility for the government programs. The Ticket to Work and Work Incentive Improvement Act of 1999 extended the period during which a worker could

THE WASHINGTON POST / GETTY IMAGES

Accessible transportation has increased the ability of people with disabilities to lead independent lives.

retain Medicare, but employment still carries the risk that Social Security might determine that a person is no longer disabled and cause them to lose both their cash and health benefits.[44]

In the meantime, the disability rights movement has addressed ongoing challenges facing people with disabilities while raising troubling new questions. The successes of the disability rights movement were based on bridging a number of contradictions in beliefs about disability. Those involved in the movement believe that the category of "disability" is *socially constructed*. Many people have physical and psychological *impairments*, but only some of these impairments are turned into *disabilities* by the ways in which society either accommodates them or not. Yet, this *universal* view of disability is in conflict with the common view of people with disabilities as a distinct, identifiable group of individuals.[45]

Two other aspects of the disability rights movement ideology are more challenging to social work. First, the movement has a generally skeptical, if not hostile, view of professionals. Second, it rejects the view of people with disabilities as needing "welfare." In both cases, members of the movement see "help" as a means of asserting control over people with disabilities and relegating them to an inferior social status.[46] Yet these beliefs contradict the reality of many people with disabilities who need professional aid to achieve independence and who, without social welfare programs, would live in dire poverty.

The movement's ideology also minimizes the extent to which support for the ADA and programs for people with disabilities derives from more traditional views of disability. To a great extent, expansion of the rights of people with disabilities is based on the older "social welfare" view of them as a group in need of protection. At the same time, many conservatives supported the new "civil rights" attitude because the promise of "independence" would reduce social responsibility. Although hardly universal, one concern is that this view could lead to an attack on cash programs for people with disabilities on the assumption that welfare breeds dependency.[47]

Indeed, the limits of the ADA's success have led some disability rights activists to suggest that we are entering an era in which the older "social welfare" attitude and the newer "civil rights" attitude need to coexist. Just as domestic violence policy has come to recognize that a legal approach must be complemented with counseling and services, many commentators are coming to see that regulations and lawsuits alone will not allow people with disabilities to overcome the structural barriers they face in attaining full social integration.[48] Rather, future success of the disability movement will depend on resolution of the continuing dilemma between charity and rights.

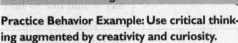

Critical Thinking

Practice Behavior Example: Use critical thinking augmented by creativity and curiosity.

Critical Thinking Question: The disability rights movement has provoked debate about the role of charity and rights in driving social policy. How is the tension between charity and rights present in other fields of practice?

Assess your comprehension of "Disability and Dependence" by completing this quiz.

[44]Samuel R. Bagenstos, "The Future of Disability Law," *Yale Law Journal* 114, no. 1 (October 2004): 5.

[45]Samuel R. Bagenstos, *Law and the Contradictions of the Disability Rights Movement* (New Haven: Yale University Press, 2009), 20–21.

[46]Bagenstos, *Law and the Contradictions of the Disability Rights Movement*, 21–32.

[47]Eduardo Porter, "Disability Insurance Causes Pain," *New York Times*, April 24, 2012, http://www.nytimes.com/2012/04/25/business/economy/disability-insurance-causes-pain.html?pagewanted=all.

[48]Bagenstos, *Law and the Contradictions of the Disability Rights Movement*, 116–131.

MARRIAGE EQUALITY: THE LAST DISCRIMINATION?

Although African Americans, women, and people with disabilities have had to struggle to win their rights, by the beginning of the twenty-first century, relatively few people questioned the idea that "equal protection" should apply to these groups. Not so for lesbians, gays, bisexuals, and transgender (LGBT) people. Major social, religious, and political institutions continue to look at these sexual orientations as deviant, a threat, or a sin. The struggle for LGBT civil rights in the early twenty-first century centered on the issue of marriage equality or "gay marriage."

Ironically, marriage equality was a battle that many in the LGBT activist community would like to have avoided. During the 1980s and 1990s, LGBT people had made slow progress on issues like domestic partner recognition by employers and health care providers. Although the Supreme Court upheld "antisodomy" laws in the 1980s, in 2003 the court reversed itself and recognized that the right to privacy extended to relationships between consenting adults, whatever their gender.

Indeed, many LGBT activists saw marriage itself as an element of a patriarchal social structure that had oppressed gay people for generations. They hoped to challenge marriage rather than expand it to include gays. The pressure for same-sex marriage, rather, came from the "homosexual rank and file, the man and woman in the street and in the pew."[49] In the early 1990s, several Hawaiian gay couples sued for the right to marry and, surprisingly, won a victory in the state's supreme court. The victory was short-lived, however, when a referendum passed an amendment to the state constitution outlawing marriage equality.

As with many of the rights battles discussed in this chapter, grassroots mobilization and legal decisions were often ahead of public opinion. In November 2012, voters in Maryland, Washington, and Maine supported marriage equality, reversing an earlier pattern by which many states' voters had reversed decisions taken by state courts and legislatures, including California in 2008 (Proposition 8 or Prop 8).[50] One troubling phenomenon has been a gap between public opinion polls and actual voting, with marriage equality gaining support in public opinion polls that does not materialize on election day, for example, in Maine in 2009. Advocates often attribute the gap between polls and elections to the use of outside money to mount public relations campaigns that paint same-sex marriage as threatening to other social institutions.

Still, evidence suggested that in much of the country attitudes were changing. Between 2001 and 2012, the proportion of adults who supported marriage equality rose from 35 to 48 percent, while the percent opposing it fell from 57 percent to 44 percent. Race, age, and geography sharply divided the population. African Americans, particularly religiously active African Americans, were much less likely to support marriage equality than the rest of the population. According to a Pew Research Center poll, black Protestants' views of gay marriage have changed even more slowly than white evangelical

---

[49]Jonathan Rauch, *Gay Marriage* (New York: Times Books, 2004). Quoted in Michael B. Katz and Mark J. Stern, *One Nation Divisible: What America Was and What It Is Becoming* (New York: Russell Sage Foundation Press, 2006), 203.

[50]Frank Bruni, "Hopeful News From Maryland," *New York Times*, August 2, 2012, http://bruni.blogs.nytimes.com/2012/08/02/hopeful-news-from-maryland/.

Protestants.[51] Indeed, the large African American turnout for Barack Obama in 2008 may have contributed to the passage of Proposition 8.

During the first years of the twenty-first century, attitudes toward marriage equality were changing among all age groups, but generational differences persisted. In 2012 only a minority of cohorts born before 1965 supported gay marriage, while a majority of younger adults did. This generation gap is one reason why those who support marriage equality are optimistic about its prospects in the long run.

The geography of marriage equality, on the other hand, paints a picture of cultural divides that are growing. The South, the Great Plains, and the interior West states generally have passed state constitutional amendments banning same-sex marriage. Several states in the Middle Atlantic region—New York, New Jersey, Delaware, and Maryland—have broad support for civil unions, have marriage equality laws, or are considering them. Only New England is now predominantly a region that recognizes marriage equality.

California represents the extreme political divide. In May 2008 the state supreme court decided by a 4-3 vote that the ban on same-sex marriage constituted illegal discrimination, but in November 2008, Proposition 8—a ban on same-sex marriage—was supported by 52 percent of voters. After the state courts ratified the Prop 8 outcome, a case was brought in federal court. Both a circuit court decision in August 2011 and an appeals court in February 2012 rejected Prop 8.

The federal policy on marriage equality was the Defense of Marriage Act (DOMA), signed by President Clinton in 1996 after passing both houses of Congress with large bipartisan majorities. DOMA established a federal definition of marriage as a legal union between one man and one women and that a spouse had to be of the opposite sex. As a result, DOMA resulted in same-sex partners and spouses having no claim to federal spousal benefits. The law also established that no state had to recognize a same-sex marriage recognized by another state.[52]

The Obama administration determined that DOMA was unconstitutional and announced that it would no longer defend it in court.[53] In May 2012, a federal appeals court in Boston declared parts of DOMA unconstitutional, and the Supreme Court ratified that decision in 2013.

The battle over marriage equality underlines the challenges of reconciling democratic values with civil rights. If they had had to wait for support by the majority, African Americans, women, and people with disabilities would never have attained legal equality. At the same time, without grassroots movements, new policies on domestic violence and disability rights would not have been translated into real changes in people's lives.

The battle over marriage equality was not on the agenda of LGBT advocates until *after* average gay and lesbian couples decided that it was important to them, their children, and their communities. Ultimately, it will be their determination—not that of any state or federal court or the vote on any state referendum—that will decide the issue.

State laws around marriage equality and other forms of discrimination are changing rapidly. Check the Human Rights Campaign's "Maps of State Laws and Policies" for current information.

Assess your comprehension of "Marriage Equality: The Last Discrimination?" by completing this quiz.

[51]Pew Forum on Religion and Public Life, "Changing Attitudes on Gay Marriage," http://features.pewforum.org/same-sex-marriage-attitudes/. Between 2001 and 2012, support for gay marriage increased from 30 to 35 percent among black Protestants and from 13 to 19 percent among white Evangelical Protestants.

[52]PL 104–199, http://thomas.loc.gov/cgi-bin/bdquery/z?d104:HR03396:|TOM:/bss/d104query.html|.

[53]Charlie Savage and Sheryl Gay Stolberg, "In Shift, US Says Marriage Act Blocks Gay Rights," *New York Times*, February 23, 2011, http://www.nytimes.com/2011/02/24/us/24marriage.html?pagewanted=all.

CONCLUSION

This chapter has focused on issues of social justice affecting African Americans and Latinos, women, people with disabilities, and LGBT people. The chapter is part of the text's section on human needs. Social justice contrasts with the other human needs covered in this section—food, shelter, employment, and health care. In a fundamental way, however, it is the starting point for an understanding of our society's response to these other needs.

In Chapter 4 we discussed the capabilities approach, which argues that our understanding of human well-being must begin with an idea of freedom. People should possess the freedom to live and act in the ways that they choose. Although Martha Nussbaum goes on to enumerate particular dimensions of well-being that should be protected, these particular capabilities are a product of the more general imperative of human freedom.

Human Rights and Justice

Practice Behavior Example: Incorporate social justice practices in organizations, institutions, and society to ensure that these basic human rights are distributed equitably and without prejudice.

Critical Thinking Question: Can you identify instances where a social welfare organization has been slow to adapt to changing standards of social justice?

Ultimately, social welfare is based on two fundamental sets of rights. As members of a national community, one enjoys the rights of *citizenship*. As a human being, one enjoys the rights of *personhood*. In some ways, the two are in conflict; noncitizens often find themselves excluded from the world of citizenship rights. Yet, in a more fundamental way, the two types of rights must reinforce one another.

The quests for social justice discussed in this chapter share a common interest in closing the gap between citizenship and human rights. Although the battleground is often defined in terms of a more comprehensive view of citizenship, the argument is really about whether or not we will deny people's personhood because of their race, gender, ability, or sexual orientation.

Yet, for social work, this may not be enough. A victim of interpersonal violence, a person with a disability struggling with mobility, a former prisoner looking for a job, or a gay couple adjusting to a new neighborhood have issues that go beyond an assertion of their rights. They need help negotiating the large and small decisions that lie between the potential of a life they have reason to value and its actualization. Increasingly, society is coming to see that social services are the essential complement to the rights won by formerly marginalized groups.

At the same time, it is the responsibility of social workers to see the struggle for those rights as an essential element of their professional lives. Mass imprisonment is the most profound reality challenging the well-being of younger Americans, our neighborhoods and communities, and contemporary American society. We can look at contemporary social movements and congratulate ourselves for all of the "progress" we've made in addressing human rights. Yet, in many ways, that "progress" is overshadowed by the resurrection of mass imprisonment as a new system of racial control.

Test your understanding and analysis of this chapter by completing the Chapter Review.

10

Providing Income and Services to Older Americans

DAVID HURN / MAGNUM PHOTOS

INTRODUCTION

Older adults are a special population that we all aspire to join one day. Yet, despite the universal appeal of a long and productive life, the actual circumstances of older Americans have rarely been enviable. Like many other special populations, they are often subject to economic marginalization, discrimination, and stereotyping.

No population has benefited more from the expansion of social welfare than older adults. Before the creation of federal social welfare programs in the 1930s, a majority of older Americans were desperately poor. They were often seen as economically redundant, slow-witted, confused, and a drag on the economy. Since the 1930s, Social Security and government-financed pension programs have insured the material well-being of a majority of older Americans, Medicare has provided access to good health care, and services for older adults have expanded.

Ironically, the success of these programs has generated a new set of stereotypes of older adults. Where once they were criticized for staying too long in the labor force, they are now condemned for collecting Social Security too long while younger workers have to sweat to make ends meet. Where other populations are often diagnosed with depression, older adults are more likely to be seen as "just old."[1] Such stereotypes affect the thinking of older adults as well.

---

[1]Susan Ruppel, William Jenkins, Jan Griffen, and Judy Kizer, "Are They Depressed or Just Old? A Study of Perceptions about the Elderly Suffering from Depression," *North American Journal of Psychology* 12, no. 1 (2010): 31–42.

Elderly who hold stereotypical views of older people are likely to have low scores on a number of quality-of-life measures.[2]

One thing that is clear is that a larger share of Americans will be elderly in the coming decades. Higher life expectancy—tied to improvements in health—combined with the aging of the "baby boom" generation will lead to an increase in the average age of the population.

This chapter examines the social welfare of older Americans. It focuses on two elements: income support and social services. Older adults enjoy a number of universal and selective income programs that have done much to reduce their poverty rate over the past generation. In addition, the federal and state governments have enacted a variety of programs focused on older Americans' service needs. In contrast to other stories we tell in this book, many programs for older adults have been successful in achieving their goals.

Again, success has its costs. The perception that older adults are now "affluent" has led to calls that their programs be cut—or at least "reformed" in ways that will reduce their effectiveness. Employing more stealth, other policy trajectories have tended to tilt the benefits of programs toward more affluent groups, simultaneously increasing their cost and making them less effective.

Most worrisome, the very size of programs for older adults makes them inviting targets for budget cutters. Although some changes in the systems for income support and services may be inevitable, social workers must be knowledgeable enough to differentiate true improvements from efforts to undermine programs masquerading as proposals to "reform" them.

THE STATUS OF OLDER AMERICANS BEFORE THE 1970s

Older Americans experienced two major changes in their social and economic status during the twentieth century. During the first third of the century, many were economically marginal—often desperately trying to hold onto jobs that were physically taxing and forced to live with their children to stay out of the poorhouse. Public and corporate policy that institutionalized retirement during the middle of the century improved the economic well-being of older adults but still left them with a higher-than-average risk of poverty. However, the adoption of uniform retirement policies standardized the life cycle of older adults to an unprecedented degree. Finally, after the 1970s, older adults achieved a "retirement wage" that allowed them to support themselves and remain in their own household—greatly expanding the *empty nest* household form. The last four decades also led to a decline in the uniformity of old age, as the age of retirement became less standardized.

These patterns of change occurred as the older adult population grew rapidly. In 1900, only 4 percent of Americans were over the age of 65, and another 14 percent were between 50 and 64. By 1960, these numbers had increased to 9 and 20 percent. The proportions remained relatively stable for the next 25 years as the baby boom swelled

---

[2]C. Sanchez Palacios, M. V. Trianes Tores, and M. J. Blanca Mena, "Negative Aging Stereotypes and Their Relation with Psychosocial Variables in the Elderly Population," *Archives of Gerontology and Geriatrics* 48, no. 3 (May 2009): 385–390.

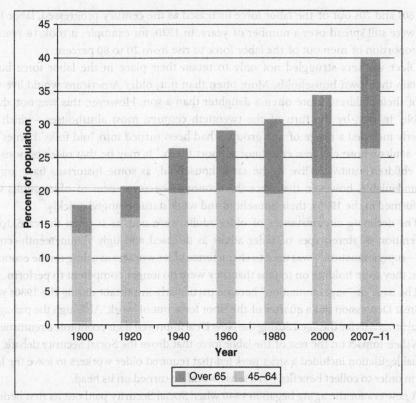

Figure 10.1
Proportion of US Population over 45 Years of Age, 1900–2011
The proportion of older Americans has grown steadily over the past century and will accelerate in
the coming decades.

Source: Author's calculations from Steven Ruggles, J. Trent Alexander, Katie Genadek, Ronald Goeken, Matthew
B. Schroeder, and Matthew Sobek, *Integrated Public Use Microdata Series: Version 5.0* [Machine-readable database]
(Minneapolis: University of Minnesota, 2010).

the younger population. After 1990, however, the proportions
increased again, reaching 13 percent for those over 65 and 27 percent for those between 45 and 64 by 2007–11. (Figure 10.1).

Early in the twentieth century, the lives of the aged were
framed by two common experiences: a slow exit from the labor
force and an inability to maintain an independent household.[3]
In an economy with few pensions and no Social Security, most
older workers had little choice but to hold onto their job as long as
possible. Often when a worker was too ill to hold down a physically
demanding job, he was able to transfer to a less demanding one—
night watchman appears to have been a common occupation for
older workers—but it invariably provided a lower income.

As a result, there was no standard retirement age early in the
century. In 1920, 83 percent of men at age 64 were still in the labor force, and this figure
fell only to 64 percent among men in their early 70s. Although the proportion of men in

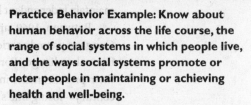

Human Behavior

**Practice Behavior Example: Know about
human behavior across the life course, the
range of social systems in which people live,
and the ways social systems promote or
deter people in maintaining or achieving
health and well-being.**

Critical Thinking Question: Depression is a common
problem among older adults. How might changes in
one's work and household statuses—in the past and
today—impact one's mental health?

---

[3]The following section draws on Michael B. Katz and Mark J. Stern, *One Nation Divisible: What America
Was and What It Is Becoming* (New York: Russell Sage Foundation, 2006), 141–153.

their 60s and 70s out of the labor force increased as the century progressed, labor force exits were still spread over a number of years. In 1920, for example, it took 18 years for the proportion of men out of the labor force to rise from 20 to 80 percent.

Older workers struggled not only to retain their place in the labor force but to maintain their own households. More often than not, older Americans would live with one of their children, more often a daughter than a son. However, this was not always possible. In fact, by the turn of the twentieth century, most almshouses—which had formerly included a range of age groups—had been turned into "old folks' homes" for older adults whose children could not support them.[4] It may be that older persons and their children *wanted* to live in the same household, as some historians have argued. It is undeniable, however, that once the economic circumstances of older adults were transformed in the 1930s, their household and work status changed quickly.

The declining circumstances of older adults were tied, as is often the case, to the proliferation of stereotypes of older adults as diseased and ugly. A nineteenth-century term—superannuation—was used to characterize older workers as a drag on the economy; that is, they were holding on to jobs that they were no longer competent to perform.

The issue of "superannuation" became particularly important during the 1930s when the Great Depression put a quarter of the labor force out of work. Although the passage of federal programs for the aged during the New Deal improved their economic circumstances, it was their impact on the rest of the labor force that drove the Social Security debate. The original legislation included a strict *work test* that required older workers to leave the labor force in order to collect benefits—in a sense workfare turned on its head.

A new era for the aging began in 1940 when Social Security paid out its first benefits. Yet the next three decades represented a transitional period. While the work life of older workers was transformed, their economic circumstances remained difficult. As we saw in Chapter 4, when the government began to measure "official" poverty in the 1960s, the poverty rate of those over 65 years of age was twice the national average.

Social Security imposed a new standardization on the employment history of older workers. Where previously retirement had been the result of older workers slowly losing a grip on their jobs, it now became a date fixed by corporate and government policy. By 1960 a large share of workers left the workforce around age 65.

However, Social Security still did not provide a retirement wage, and poverty among the older Americans remained high. As a result, older adults continued to lose their ability to maintain independent households, so they were likely to move in with one of their children.

Between 1969 and 1973, the contemporary Social Security system took shape. Congress passed a series of benefit increases. Low-income workers, in particular, benefited from the change. For these workers, retirement benefits equaled up to 90 percent of their preretirement income. The features that defined old age at the beginning of the century—losing one's job, living with one's children, poverty—had come to an end.

The most important element of this transition was the decline of poverty among older Americans. By the 1980s, the poverty rate of persons over the age of 65 was actually lower than that of the rest of the population. At the same time, older Americans were increasingly likely to remain in their own households. Disability, more than poverty, became the most common reason that older persons would have to live in an institution or with others.

---

[4]Michael B. Katz, *In the Shadow of the Poorhouse: Social History of Welfare in America*, 10th anniversary ed. (New York: Basic Books, 1996), 88–116.

One consequence of these changes was the explosion of older Americans living alone. Though not necessarily a problem, the lack of social connections and services could pose a real risk for those with limited financial resources. During heat waves, for example, a disproportionate number of fatalities are older persons living by themselves.[5]

During the final decades of the twentieth century, the aging—like other age groups—pushed back against the standardization of their life cycle. Resistance was most apparent around the issue of retirement. A variety of age discrimination laws ended mandatory retirement for most occupations. A loosening of the earnings tests for Social Security benefits allowed workers to earn more and still collect benefits. As a result, retirement age has become less clearly demarcated.

Assess your comprehension of "The Status of Older Americans before the 1970s" by completing this quiz.

INCOME SUPPORTS FOR OLDER AMERICANS

Federal income supports for older Americans are generally seen as one of the major successes of the American social welfare system. In contrast to most groups, a large share of older adults who might otherwise live in poverty are lifted above the poverty line by a combination of Old Age, Survivors, and Disability Insurance (OASDI) and Supplemental Security Income (SSI). Yet even these programs face contradictory pressures. On the one hand, the perception that Social Security will "go broke" is now widely believed by many younger Americans who have become increasingly skeptical about current policy. On the other hand, as we found in Chapter 4, a more accurate poverty line like the Supplemental Poverty Measure would raise the poverty rate of older Americans more than any other group. Nevertheless, OASDI and SSI continue to function effectively in ensuring older Americans'—and many other groups'—Social Security.

At the same time, many—but not all—older Americans receive pension income. These "private" programs are made possible through a very generous set of tax *expenditures* for corporations and individuals. In contrast to the fully public programs, pensions benefit the well-off older adults much more than those living on a limited income. Because pensions have grown more rapidly than the public programs, overall policy now encourages increasing income inequality among older Americans. This challenge to social justice—more than Social Security "going broke"—should be a major concern for social workers and other helping professionals.

Old Age, Survivors, and Disability Insurance (OASDI)[6]

At the table in the kitchen, there were three bowls of porridge. Goldilocks was hungry. She tasted the porridge from the first bowl. "This porridge is too hot!" she exclaimed. So, she tasted the porridge from the second bowl. "This porridge is too cold," she said. So, she tasted the last bowl of porridge. "Ahhh, this porridge is just right," she said happily and she ate it all up.[7]

[5]Eric Klinenberg, *Heat Wave: A Social Autopsy of Disaster in Chicago* (Chicago: University of Chicago Press, 2002).
[6]This section describes the primary insurance program for older Americans, workers' survivors, and people with disability. To avoid repetition, we describe the entire program here, even though older adults are only one of the groups that receive benefits from the program.
[7]http://www.dltk-teach.com/rhymes/goldilocks_story.htm.

Critics of Social Security are a bit like Goldilocks. Over the years, they have charged that it's unfair to well-off people and to poor people. It benefits older adults at the expense of children and younger workers. It's a "bad deal" because we'd get a better return if we had private retirement accounts. It is unfair to minorities and immigrants.

Social Security is easy to mischaracterize because it does so many things to benefit so many groups. If we look at the program from only one perspective, it seems "too hot" or "too cold." Fashioning a program that is "just right" remains an ongoing challenge for policymakers.

OASDI is the nation's largest and most important social welfare program. In 2009, the program had over 50 million beneficiaries and paid out more than $600 billion in benefits—fully 5 percent of the national income.

History and current structure

The original Social Security Act in 1935 covered only older workers. However, before any benefits were paid, Congress had added survivors' insurance for the dependents of covered workers. In the 1950s, people with disabilities were added to the program.

The architects of the program—many of whom were involved in its administration for the first four decades—designed Social Security to avoid many of the controversies that plagued other New Deal programs. They combined a set of benefits and a set of earmarked taxes to protect the program from future efforts of dismantle it. In doing so, they chose a conservative approach that provided relatively modest benefits.

Over time, the program expanded. During its earliest decades, the growth of the trust funds provided a basis for expanding eligibility and benefits. The final burst of expansion between 1969 and 1973, however, quickly created a fiscal problem for the program. A reform bill in 1983 sought to restore its fiscal balance. While still not "just right," the basic framework of Social Security has not changed significantly in the past 30 years.

Eligibility[8]

OASDI is a contributory social insurance program. It is universal, meaning that there is no income test. To be eligible, one must have paid payroll taxes for the equivalent of 10 years. When the program began, significant parts of the labor force were not covered, including agricultural, domestic, and government employees. Today, the program covers virtually the entire labor force—with the exception of railroad workers whose plan predates OASDI. The program covers three classes of beneficiaries:

- *Retired workers*—Based on one's year of birth, a worker's full retirement age (FRA) may range from 65 to 67. Retired workers can qualify for reduced *early retirement* benefits between the age of 62 and their FRA.
- *Covered workers' dependents and survivors*—When a worker dies, his children qualify for survivor benefits until they reach the age of 18 or when they graduate from high school, whichever occurs last. Widows and widowers are covered while they are caring for covered children and until they reach 62 (for reduced benefits) or their FRA. A retired worker's spouse qualifies for benefits when he reaches FRA or 62 for early retirement. A spouse who is older than the worker may qualify for benefits before the covered worker retires. Finally, retired or disabled workers' children are covered using the same rules that cover surviving children.

---

[8]Social Security Administration, *Annual Statistical Supplement 2011*, http://www.ssa.gov/policy/docs/statcomps/supplement/.

- *Workers who become disabled*—People with disabilities qualify for benefits if they are incapable of substantial gainful activity, a status that is subject to periodic review. Because disability—defined by gainful activity—is a more ambiguous status than old age, it has generated a number of controversies during the history of the program.

The number of beneficiaries of disability insurance increased from less than 1 million in 1965 to 2.9 million in 1980. Concerned by the rapid increase in the size of the program, Congress authorized a review of existing cases with an eye toward identifying beneficiaries who were ineligible. The Reagan administration, which inherited the task when it took office in 1981, pursued the review with great enthusiasm, increasing what had originally been seen as a possible $10 million savings into a $3.5 billion savings. Using procedures that had long been used against welfare clients—essentially cutting off benefits and forcing eligible recipients to appeal—the review created a storm of protest that led to its suspension in 1983 and a new law that clarified grounds for review of existing cases in 1984.[9]

Eligibility for disability insurance (DI) requires recent contributions to the system. Those over the age of 31 claiming DI are required to have made contributions in 20 of the previous 40 quarters (roughly 5 of the previous 10 years). Younger workers are also required to have made contributions in about half of the quarters since they turned 21.

Benefits

The primary benefits paid by OASDI are monthly cash payments tied to the insured worker's contribution to the system during his work life. The calculation of benefits is a two-part procedure. First, the Social Security Administration uses its records of a beneficiary's wages to calculate an Averaged Indexed Monthly Earnings (AIME), essentially a calculation of average earnings over the worker's lifetime corrected for inflation.[10] The AIME is then used to calculate a Primary Insurance Amount (PIA), essentially what a monthly benefit would be when a worker reached his full retirement age (FRA). The calculation of PIA is one of the keys to the system. For a worker who turned 62 in 2009, the formula for converting one's AIME into one's PIA was

- 90 percent of the first $744 of AIME, plus
- 32 percent of the next $3,739 of AIME, plus
- 15 percent of AIME over $4,483.

As this formula shows, very low-wage workers—with an AIME under $744—earn a PIA that is equal to 90 percent of their AIME. Modest earning workers whose AIME was less than $4,400 (or about $50,000 per year) get 90 percent of the first $744 of their AIME and 32 percent of the remainder. Someone with an AIME over $4,400 would see their PIA go up by only 15 cents for each dollar of additional earnings.[11]

The following table shows what would happen to someone born in 1951 who earned a particular wage in 2010, based on the assumption that they had earned this amount (indexed for inflation) from the time they entered the workforce in 1973. A worker who

[9]Mark J. Stern and June Axinn, *Social Welfare: A History of the American Response to Need* (Boston: Pearson Educational, 2011), 292.
[10]In contrast to other inflation corrections, the AIME is corrected for average wages rather than prices.
[11]The two *bend points* where the AIME percentage changes are indexed to inflation and change from year to year.

Chart 10.1   OASDI Replacement Rates for Retired Workers with Different Earnings Histories, 2010

	Earnings in 2010	AIME	PIA	Annual benefit	Replacement of 2010 earnings
Low wage	18,601	1,550	937	11,244	60.4%
Average wage	41,335	3,444	1,543	18,516	44.8%
High wage	66,136	5,511	2,048	24,576	37.2%
Max wage	106,800	8,569	2,506	30,072	28.2%

Source: Author's calculation (based on monthly rate) using Social Security Administration's benefit calculator, http://www.ssa.gov/estimator/.

earned only $18,600 in 2010 would have an AIME of $1,550 and a PIA of $937, equal to 60 percent of his 2010 earnings. For the average-wage worker, earning about $41,000 in 2010, his PIA is 45 percent of his 2010 earnings. For high-wage workers, who gain only 15 percent of the increase in their wages, the PIA drops to less than 30 percent of 2010 earnings (Chart 10.1).

Bear in mind that this is the simplest calculation of PIA. A variety of other life circumstances—years out of the labor force, a period of disability, change in one's marital status, the age of retirement—can influence one's benefits.

These formulas are the key "Goldilocks" element of OASDI. The program seeks to reconcile two elements of social justice: equity and equality. Because Social Security is a contributory program, it seeks to tie benefits to contributions. At the same time, the program seeks to address the poverty risks of low-income workers by assuring that they have adequate income when they reach retirement. Getting the balance between those two objectives is the great challenge of retirement planning.[12]

Retired workers

When Social Security was enacted, retirement age was set at 65. As we've noted, the program originally included a strict work test as a means of forcing workers out of the labor force if they wished to collect benefits. Since then, policies concerning both age of retirement and the earnings test have changed significantly.

Early retirement at age 62 was instituted in 1961. Persons retiring in the 2010s receive a 25 percent reduction in their PIA if they retire at 62; this amount is prorated for those who retire between 62 and their FRA. As one means of addressing the system's fiscal problems in the 1980s, Congress passed a phased-in increase in the FRA. For those born between 1943 and 1960, FRA is 66; for those born after 1960, it is 67.

Again, in response to concerns about the fiscal health of the system, Congress liberalized the earnings test several times. In 1939, any earnings above $15 per month disqualified you from receiving benefits, and as late as 1960, earning $100 per month led to a cut in one's full monthly check. Beginning that year, beneficiaries faced a percentage reduction in their benefits. Currently, once a beneficiary reaches FRA, there is no

[12]Neil Gilbert and Paul Terrell, *Dimensions of Social Welfare Policy*, 7th ed. (Boston: Allyn and Bacon, 2009), 79–83.

earnings test (although if one delays collecting benefits after FRA, one's monthly benefits continue to increase). Below that age, a certain amount of earnings (just over $14,000 in 2009) are exempt and then one's benefits are reduced by one dollar for each three dollars of additional earnings.

The effect of these changes has been to reduce the pressure of older Americans to retire in order to collect Social Security. Given that this was one of the primary purposes of Social Security in the 1930s, one may ask if the issue of "superannuation" could make a comeback. If the baby boom generation holds on to their jobs while still collecting Social Security, one could imagine a point in the future when the continuing presence of older workers in the labor force (and its impact on the opportunities available to younger workers) regains the attention of policymakers, especially during a period of high unemployment.

Dependents and survivors

Dependents and survivors present a variety of situations in which the level of benefits is other than PIA. Benefits vary depending on the age of dependents, their work history, and their marital status.

The status of spouses—more often women than men—has been affected both by changes in work patterns and the formation and dissolution of families. In the 1940s, it was assumed that most eligible workers would be male, and that a majority of women would receive spousal benefits, which are equal to half of the worker's PIA. If a spouse became eligible for her own benefits, she could choose either her benefits or one-half of her spouse's benefits. As women's labor force participation has increased, however, the need to choose one or the other unfairly disadvantaged many women. If they had been out of the labor force for significant periods of time, their benefit was often less than one-half of their husband's. Advocates suggested that it was inequitable for these women essentially to receive no benefit for their time in the labor force.

During the 1980s, a number of proposals to remedy this feature of the system were given consideration, the most popular of which was *earnings sharing*. Through earnings sharing, one's benefit would be based on the pooled earnings of both spouses, rather than separately for each spouse. However, moving to such a system would disadvantage single-earner families, which were more likely to have lower retirement incomes.[13] As the share of women with continuous labor force attachment has grown, the scope of this problem has been reduced.

As divorce has become more common, the treatment of divorced spouses has taken on greater significance. A divorced spouse is eligible for spousal benefits if he or she has been married for more than 10 years and has not remarried. Although many will remarry or qualify for their own retirement benefit, these rules can leave a proportion of long-married persons—usually women—trying to support a single-person household on one-half of their former spouse's benefits.

Disability

Once eligibility for DI is established, benefits are based on the AIME and PIA, as with retirement benefits. However, the years used for calculating the AIME vary based on when the person worked and when he became disabled.

---

[13]Melissa M. Favreault and C. Eugene Steuerle, *Social Security Spouse and Survivor Benefits for the Modern Family* (Washington, DC: Urban Institute, 2007).

Inflation protection

Since the mid-1970s, OASDI benefits have been indexed, that is, corrected for inflation. Each year, the Social Security Administration uses the consumer price index (CPI)[14] to calculate the rate of inflation over the previous year. Current beneficiaries then have their monthly checks increased by this amount. The indexation also affects the maximum earnings covered by the payroll tax, the "bend points" for calculating the PIA, and the maximum earnings disregarded for retirees, among other figures.

The 1983 reform bill included an alternative calculation of the indexing factor when the trust fund balances fall below a certain level. This "stabilizer" procedure has not been used since 1983 but may come into play as the trust fund amounts drop in the coming decades.

The indexation of OASDI is both one of its most important features and one of its most problematic. Even a moderate amount of inflation can, over time, decrease the buying power of one's income. For example, a 5 percent inflation rate over 10 years would lead to nearly a 40 percent decline in the value of a given income. Unlike private pensions, which generally are not indexed for inflation, the system provides beneficiaries with an important hedge against inflation.

Yet at the same time that indexation provides a level of predictability for retirees, it introduces unpredictability in the projection of future benefit levels. The rapid inflation of the 1970s was a major contributor to the fiscal difficulties of the system before the 1983 law. Since 1983, public policy has kept inflation low—a policy that carries its own risks for the economy—so the system has remained relatively stable. However, it is possible that in the coming years government might find itself willing to tolerate higher inflation—for example, as a means of reducing the size of the federal budget deficit. If so, it will need to take into consideration how higher inflation would affect OASDI benefits.[15]

Administration and financing

OASDI (and SSI) are unique public programs because they are fully funded and administered by the federal government. While the vast majority of other social welfare programs are administered by states, counties, or cities, OASDI claims and problems are handled by over 1,300 field offices that report to 10 regional offices and ultimately to the Social Security Administration (SSA) headquarters in Baltimore. Governance of the system is provided by the SSA commissioner, appointed by the president to a six-year term, and a bipartisan advisory board.

OASDI is funded by a share of the FICA tax that is collected from virtually all workers' payroll checks. The FICA tax of 7.65 percent is divided up and deposited in three different trust funds: an old age and survivors fund, a disability insurance fund, and a Medicare (or HI) fund. Each month a share of the trust funds are used to pay benefits. The remainder is invested in government securities.

The purpose of the trust funds is to act as a buffer between the taxes collected and benefits paid. Since the 1930s, policy around the trust funds has gone through a number of changes. When the program started, it was run on a full-reserve basis, that is, the intention was to have enough money in the trust fund to pay all current and future claims

---

[14]Technically, the SSA uses the CPI-W, the consumer price index for urban wage earners and clerical workers.

[15]Paul Krugman, "Unemployment and Inflation," *New York Times*, April 8, 2012, http://krugman.blogs.nytimes.com/2012/04/08/unemployment-and-inflation/.

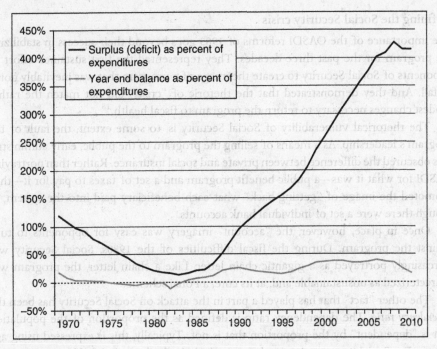

Figure 10.2
Year-End Balance and Surplus (Deficit) of Old Age and Survivors Insurance Trust Fund, as Percent of Annual Expenditures, 1969–2010
Since the 1980s, increased payroll taxes and later retirement ages have allowed the Social Security trust funds to increase rapidly.

Source: Social Security Administration, Annual Statistical Supplement 2011, Table 4.A1.

against the system. However, that policy became untenable as the claims against the system expanded. During the 1960s and 1970s, the program increasingly ran on a "pay as you go" basis that relied on current workers' payroll taxes to pay current retirees' benefits. In a "pay as you go" system, the required trust fund is needed only to pay a few months of benefits so that the system doesn't encounter a cash-flow problem.

This system was tested by the rapid expansion of benefits between 1969 and 1972. The problem was exacerbated by a mistake in the benefit formula that provided some workers with benefits that exceeded their final paycheck. As a result, the balance of revenues to expenditures fell from a surplus of 20 percent to a 12 percent deficit in 1982.[16]

Congress made revisions in the formula and allowed transfers between the OASI and DI trust funds in 1978, but economic stagnation between 1979 and 1982 once again provoked a decline in the trust fund balance. The Reagan administration attempted to use the problem as a rationale for major restructuring of the program, a move that was quickly rejected by Congress. Eventually, a bipartisan commission appointed by the president and Congress fashioned a proposal of modest changes in the system and staged increases in the retirement age to 67. Combined with generally good economic conditions between the mid-1980s and 2007, these shifts have allowed for a substantial increase in the trust fund balances to help cushion the retirement of the baby boom generation over the next two decades (Figure 10.2).[17]

---

[16]June Axinn and Mark J. Stern, *Dependency and Poverty: Old Problems in a New World* (Lexington, MA: Lexington Books, 1988), 127–153.

[17]Paul Light, *Artful Work: The Politics of Social Security Reform* (New York: Random House, 1985).

Defining the Social Security crisis

The importance of the OASDI reforms of 1983 goes beyond their success in stabilizing the program for the past three decades. They represented the first sustained effort of opponents of Social Security to create the image of a program that was inevitably going to fail. And they demonstrated that the rhetoric of "crisis" did not match the rather modest changes necessary to return the program to fiscal health.[18]

The rhetorical vulnerability of Social Security is, to some extent, the fault of the program's leadership. As a means of selling the program to the public, early administrators obscured the difference between private and social insurance. Rather than portraying OASDI for what it was—a public benefit program and a set of taxes to pay for it—they promoted the image of "getting back" what each beneficiary paid into the system, as though there were a set of individual bank accounts.

Once in place, however, the "account" imagery was easy for opponents to turn against the program. During the fiscal difficulties of the 1980s, Social Security was increasingly portrayed as a gigantic chain letter. Like a chain letter, the program was characterized as unsustainable and, at its core, a Ponzi scheme.

The other "fact" that has played a part in the attack on Social Security has been the *dependency ratio*. The dependency ratio is defined as the proportion of the population that is "dependent" by the proportion that is not. Typically, this is expressed using age groups. For Social Security, the starting point is typically the ratio of older Americans to persons between the ages of 18 and 64. The graph of this relationship appears to make a clear case for a looming crisis (Figure 10.3).

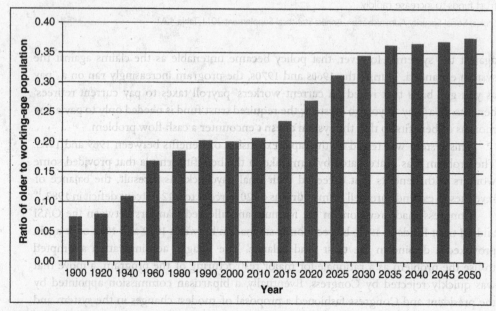

Figure 10.3
Age Support Ratio, 1900–2050
If we focus on the ratio of older Americans to the working-age population, it appears that dependency is a major challenge for the coming decades.

Note: Population over the age of 65 as percent of population 18–64 years of age.

Source: Based on US Census population projections, http://www.census.gov/population/projections/data/national/2009.html.

---

[18]Axinn and Stern, *Dependency and Poverty*, 135–144.

In his 2005 State of the Union address, President George W. Bush made this case:

> Social Security was created decades ago, for a very different era. In those days
> people did not live as long, benefits were much lower than they are today, and a
> half century ago, about 16 workers paid into the system for each person drawing
> benefits. Our society has changed in ways the founders of Social Security could
> not have foreseen. In today's world, people are living longer and therefore drawing
> benefits longer—and those benefits are scheduled to rise dramatically over the next
> few decades. And instead of 16 workers paying in for every beneficiary, right now
> it's only about 3 workers—and over the next few decades, that number will fall to
> just 2 workers per beneficiary. With each passing year, fewer workers are paying
> ever-higher benefits to an ever-larger number of retirees.[19]

Yet, the argument that "demography is destiny" rests on a number of shaky propo-
sitions. First, the *total dependency ratio* would need to take into consideration both the
increase in older Americans and the decrease in young Americans (under 18). This graph
looks a good deal less scary. In fact, at no point during the next 40 years does the estimated
total dependency ratio approach the figures for 1900 or 1960 (Figure 10.4).

In addition, the logic of the dependency ratio ignores the centrality of *productivity* to
social support. The hallmark of modern societies is the increase in the amount of goods
and services that can be produced by each worker. Two centuries ago, a huge proportion
of Americans had to spend all of their time raising food just to keep us from starving.
A century ago, after the industrial revolution, much of that labor was able to switch from
food production to goods production because of improvements in agricultural productivity. Today, much of that labor has switched from goods production to services because
of increases in goods productivity. Just since 1992, the amount produced by one hour of
labor has increased by 40 percent.[20] At that rate, productivity in 2050 will be more than
twice what it was in 1992. There may be fewer active workers for each retiree in the coming decades, but those workers will be able to produce much more than is possible today.

This is not to say that there is no problem with Social Security. Sometime in the
future, Congress will need to consider changes in the tax basis and perhaps the retirement age. But as in 1983, the changes should amount to a "midcourse correction" rather
than a response to collapse and cataclysm as suggested by Bush and others.

Although conservatives failed to use the problems of the 1980s to restructure OASDI,
that did not deter them from trying to do so. George W. Bush's proposals during 2005
were the largest concerted effort since 1983 to *reform* Social Security out of existence. In
contrast to earlier attacks, the Bush administration portrayed its proposals as an effort to
"save" the program from inevitable collapse.

> Today, more than 45 million Americans receive Social Security benefits, and millions
> more are nearing retirement—and for them the system is strong and fiscally sound.
> I have a message for every American who is 55 or older: Do not let anyone mislead
> you. For you, the Social Security system will not change in any way.[21]

[19]George W. Bush, State of the Union Address 2005, http://www.washingtonpost.com/wp-srv/
politics/transcripts/bushtext_020205.html.

[20]*Economic Report of the President 2012*, Table B-50, http://www.gpo.gov/fdsys/pkg/ERP-2012/pdf/
ERP-2012-table50.pdf.

[21]George W. Bush, State of the Union Address 2005, http://www.washingtonpost.com/wp-srv/
politics/transcripts/bushtext_020205.html.

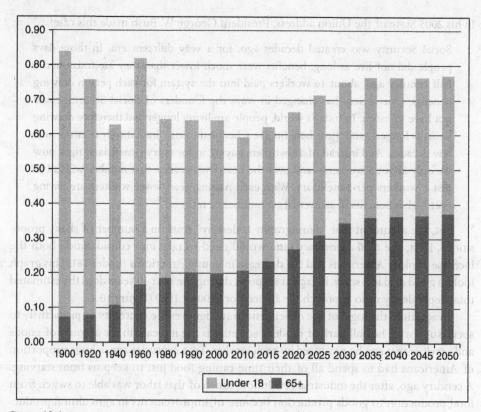

Figure 10.4
Total Age Dependency Ratio by Year, United States, 1900–2050
When children are taken into consideration, the dependency ratios of the coming decades will remain much lower than those of the mid-twentieth century.

Note: Population 0–17 years old and 65 years and over as percent of population 18–64.

Source: Based on US Census population projections, http://www.census.gov/population/projections/data/national/2009.html.

To "save" the program, Bush proposed transforming Social Security for younger workers into a private retirement account similar to defined-contribution private plans, like those we will discuss later in this chapter. However, the funding for these private accounts would come from diverting a large share of payroll taxes from the OASDI trust funds. As a result, rather than solving the trust fund balance problem, it would have accelerated its decline.

The current projections by the trustees of the program suggest that under the most common assumptions, the trust funds are likely to be exhausted some time in the next 25 years. Under the moderate assumption, the fund will be exhausted around 2037. Yet, as the optimistic projection (I) suggests, the run on the trust funds caused by baby boomers will last for only 20 years after that. As in the past, it seems clear that the public is willing to support tax increases to keep the program operating. Indeed, the recession of 2007–2009 appears to have strengthened public support for the program. According to a 2010 Gallup poll, the proportion of Americans who believe that OASDI will be their major source of retirement income increased from 27 to 34 percent between 2007 and 2010 (Figure 10.5).[22]

---

[22]Jeffrey Jones, "Americans Shift Expectations about Retirement Funding," April 29, 2010, accessed May 7, 2010, http://www.gallup.com/poll/127592/.

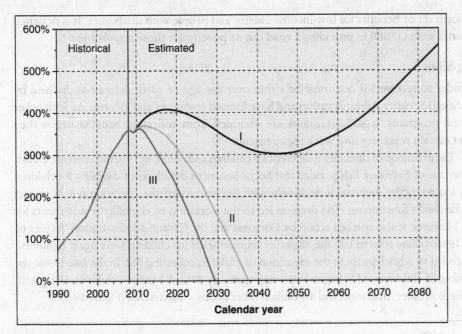

Figure 10.5
Projected Balance of Social Security Trust Fund, 2010
Although current payroll taxes are not sufficient to sustain Old Age Insurance through the rest of the century, the program will require only minor reforms to remain sustainable.

Source: 2012 Report of the Trustees of the Federal Old Age and Survivors and Disability Trust Funds, http://www.ssa.gov/oact/tr/2012/tr2012.pdf.

A *crisis* is not an objective condition. It is a judgment by one or more people that a situation requires radical action to bring about change. Although for the past 30 years conservatives have sought to label the challenges of the Social Security system a crisis, most of the public views the issue in less drastic terms. Certainly the program in the future won't be identical to what exists today, but that statement applies to virtually every aspect of American life. However, the changes that the future is likely to bring to Social Security—increase in taxes, change in the income covered by taxes, possibly an increase in the retirement age—are likely to build on past policy rather than attempt to restructure the basic retirement system.

> Given the declining value of other forms of retirement income, some commentators have suggested that we need to <u>increase Social Security benefits</u>.

Supplemental Security Income

Although OASDI has been a very successful program that provides the primary protection against poverty for older Americans, a significant share of older adults cannot escape poverty based on their Social Security check alone. Furthermore, those with low or no Social Security payments are unlikely to have significant income from other sources. As a result, since its inception, the Social Security system has included an *income-tested public assistance program* as a complement to OASDI. From the 1930s until the 1970s, this program—Old Age Assistance—was a state-administered program with federal matching funds. For most of this period, benefits were low and the program's antipoverty effectiveness was low.

As part of the welfare reform effort of the 1970s, Congress *federalized* OAA and the assistance program for people with disabilities (including a separate program for blind persons). The resulting program—Supplemental Security Income (SSI)—provides a uniform set of benefits for low-income elderly and people with disabilities. It is designed to work with OASDI in providing a road out of poverty for these populations.

Eligibility

In order to receive SSI one must be either over the age of 65 or defined as disabled by the Social Security Administration and have limited resources and income. As with other federal programs, legal immigrants are excluded from collecting benefits unless they meet certain residency and work requirements.

The definition of disability is different for children and adults. In 1990 the Supreme Court, in the case of *Sullivan v. Zebley*, ruled that Social Security's definition of disability for children was too restrictive, because it dealt only with the severity of the condition not its impact on the child's functioning. The decision led to the relaxation of eligibility requirements for SSI. However, it also sparked action by Congress and the Clinton administration. As part of the 1996 welfare reform bill, the eligibility requirements for children were again tightened, which led to a brief pause in the expansion of children collecting SSI. In the late 1990s, the number of children on SSI began increasing again. By 2012, 1.3 million children, along with 2.1 million older Americans and 4.9 million other adults, collected SSI (Figure 10.6).[23]

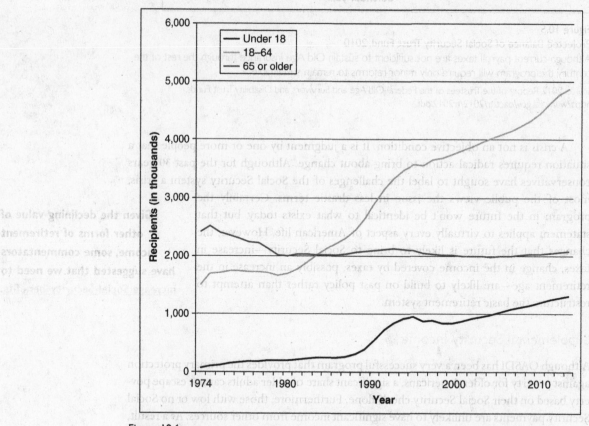

Figure 10.6
SSI Recipients by Age, United States, 1974–2012
Most of the growth in the SSI program has been among recipients under the age of 65.
Source: Based on Social Security Administration, 2013 Annual Statistical Summary, http://www.ssa.gov/policy/docs/statcomps/supplement/2013/7a.html.

[23]Social Security Administration, Annual Statistical Supplement 2011, Table 7.A8, http://www.ssa.gov/policy/docs/statcomps/supplement/2011/7a.html.

As its name implies, SSI was created as a *supplement* to OASDI. However, a number of categories of people do not qualify for OASDI but rely on SSI as their primary federal benefit. Children with disabilities are one of the largest groups. Among adults, people with disabilities who have not worked long enough to qualify for disability insurance are a significant category. Finally, older Americans who qualify for neither retirement nor survivors' benefits—many of whom are immigrants who entered the United States at an older age—often have SSI as a major source of income.

Benefits

Maximum SSI benefits for an individual in 2013 were $710 per month. For a couple, the maximum was $1,066. Like OASDI, SSI benefits are indexed to inflation.

An individual's SSI monthly benefit can be reduced in a number of ways. Most obviously, if one qualifies for OASDI or any other unearned income, one's benefits are reduced by the full amount (the first $20 per month are excluded). Earnings also reduce one's benefits, although a larger share of earned income does not count against one's benefit amount (the first $65 plus one-half of remaining earned income). As a result, older Americans collecting SSI benefits received an average of just over $371 per month in 2012.

Federal SSI benefits are supplemented by state funds in most of the United States. In some states, this supplement is administered by Social Security and automatically paid to anyone who receives SSI. In other states, the benefit is administered by the state, and eligible individuals must apply separately. The average monthly state supplement in 2012 ranged from less than $3 in Utah to $363 in Pennsylvania.

Administration and financing

SSI is not a contributory program. The funding for the program is authorized by Congress and paid out of general revenues.

The Social Security Administration is responsible for administration of most SSI programs, which are housed at the same offices that oversee OASDI. However, federal and state governments coordinate on the delivery of the state supplement.

Public Subsidies and "Private" Pensions

Social Security was never designed to be the sole means of support of older Americans. Earnings and investment or pension income are important elements of the income support of older Americans.

Since the Social Security reforms of the 1970s, federal public policy has been much more active with respect to "private" pensions than with Social Security and SSI. In particular, changes in the structure of private pensions have led to shifts in who receives a pension and the amount of pension income.

Pensions were an important element of what was called the *welfare capitalism* movement of the 1920s. During that era, a number of private companies claimed that private industry—not government—could provide for the well-being of its employees. They instituted a variety of programs—unemployment protection, pensions, recreational activities, and other services—to expand the benefits offered and to reduce the attraction of unions. Most of these schemes, however, fell apart during the early years of the Great Depression.

The next great expansion of pensions occurred during the 1940s. During World War II, most industries accepted a wage-and-price freeze as a means of subduing inflation. However, in the face of more militant unions and increased competition for workers because of low unemployment, employers turned to "fringe benefits," including pensions, as an alternative to wage increases.[24]

Two other events during the 1940s gave this shift toward fringe benefits a boost. First, the Revenue Act of 1942 allowed companies to deduct payments to pension funds as a business expense, turning them into tax expenditures. Second, the Supreme Court ruled that fringe benefits were a legitimate item for collective bargaining between unions and corporations.

As a result, pensions expanded rapidly in the mass production, unionized industries that were the core of the American economy in the 1950s. For the most part, these were *defined-benefit* pensions in which the company agreed to pay a lifetime pension of a certain amount to employees who had worked there for a certain number of years.[25]

However, during the late 1960s and early 1970s, a number of problems undermined employers' and employees' faith in defined-benefit plans. First, pensions typically were not *portable*—that is, they could not be taken from company to company. Originally this had been seen as a positive attribute because it fostered "loyalty" to a company. But as the pace of economic change sped up in the 1970s, the lack of portability was viewed as a trap that bound an employee to a company when both might benefit if he moved to another job. Despite the lack of evidence supporting this belief, employers began shedding defined-benefit plans.[26]

One aspect of this economic instability was plant closings and bankruptcies. In 1963 the Studebaker auto company closed its South Bend, Indiana, plant. Although the workers were covered by a joint company-union pension plan, with the plant closing, the funds set aside for the pension were insufficient to cover workers who were approaching retirement age. As a result, several thousand workers lost the pensions they had been promised.[27]

The final blow of the 1970s was inflation. The same decline in the value of money that led to the indexation of Social Security was devastating to the value of pensions. A pension that might have seemed comfortable when a worker first retired could have lost 50 percent of its value in a decade.[28]

These factors led to two policy responses: the passage of stricter federal oversight of pensions and an increase in defined-contribution pension plans in which workers and companies each made contributions into an individual account for each worker.

The Employee Retirement Income Security Act of 1974 (ERISA) established a new level of federal oversight of private pensions. It set new standards for the reserves that

[24]Nelson Lichtenstein, *Labor's War At Home: The CIO in World War II* (Philadelphia, Temple University Press, 2003), 136–156, 226–240.

[25]US Department of Labor, "Retirement Plans, Benefits, and Savings: Types of Retirement Plans," http://www.dol.gov/dol/topic/retirement/typesofplans.htm.

[26]Alan Gustman and Thomas Steinmeier, "Pension Portability and Labor Mobility: Evidence from the Survey of Income and Program Participation," NBER Working Paper #3525 (December 1990), http://www.nber.org/papers/w3525.pdf?new_window=1.

[27]John Bodnar, "Power and Memory in Oral History: Workers and Managers at Studebaker," *Journal of American History* 75, no. 4 (March 1989): 1201–1221; Jeffrey R. Brown, "Guaranteed Trouble: The Economic Effects of the Pension Benefit Guaranty Corporation," *Journal of Economic Perspectives* 22, no. 1 (Winter 2008): 177–198.

[28]Leora Friedberg and Anthony Webb, "Retirement and the Evolution of Pension Structure," *Journal of Human Resources* 40, no. 2 (Spring 2005): 281–308.

companies were required to maintain to pay for pensions. In addition, it established a system of pension insurance, the Pension Benefit Guaranty Corporation, to cover pensions for companies that go out of business or for other reasons discontinue their pension plans. An unanticipated element of ERISA that had far-reaching implications was its *preemption* clause, which essentially established that no state government could pass legislation governing private company pensions or (as it turned out) self-insured health care plans.[29]

Currently, within limits, the worker can choose a variety of investment strategies for the account. When a worker retires, the accumulated balance of the account can be converted into an annuity or other financial instrument for providing the worker with income. Although we think of these as *private* pensions, in fact, government is deeply involved in their financing. Defined-benefit pensions that are integrated with Social Security provide companies with a very favorable tax status. In addition, both company and individual contributions to defined-contribution plans are tax-deferred until funds are withdrawn from the account.

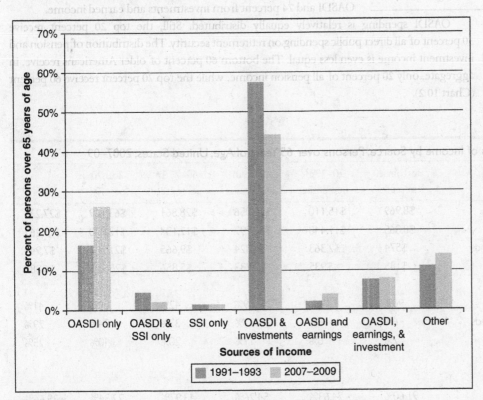

Figure 10.7

Sources of Income, Americans over the Age of 65, 1991–93 and 2007–09

The proportion of older Americans dependent solely on Social Security increased rapidly during the 1990s and 2000s.

Note: OASDI = Old age, survivors, and disability insurance; SSI = Supplemental Security Income.

Source: Author's calculations from Steven Ruggles, J. Trent Alexander, Katie Genadek, Ronald Goeken, Matthew B. Schroeder, and Matthew Sobek, *Integrated Public Use Microdata Series: Version 5.0* [Machine-readable database] (Minneapolis: University of Minnesota, 2010).

---

[29]Jacob Hacker, *The Divided Welfare State: The Battle over Public and Private Social Benefits in the United States* (New York: Cambridge University Press, 2002), 124–179.

Inequality and "Private" Pensions

The policy trajectories of Social Security and private pensions have moved in opposite directions. Since the 1980s, virtually the entire focus of OASDI policymaking has been on cutbacks that will be necessary to sustain the program through the middle of the twenty-first century. At the same time, Congress has continued to add to the tax breaks provided for private pensions. Although Social Security remains politically popular, there is virtually no serious policy discussion of program expansion to provide more reliable incomes to women, domestic workers, and other groups who continue to struggle with poverty in old age.

The *distributional* implications of this policy split are important (Figure 10.7). Most low-income Americans over the age of 65 receive very little income from investments. In 2007–09, among elderly in the lowest fifth of the income distribution, 90 percent of their income came from public sources and less than 6 percent from pensions and investment. Among elderly in the top fifth, 20 percent came from OASDI and 74 percent from investments and earned income.

OASDI spending is relatively equally distributed. Still, the top 20 percent receive 30 percent of all direct public spending on retirement security. The distribution of pension and investment income is even less equal. The bottom 60 percent of older Americans receive, in aggregate, only 20 percent of all pension income, while the top 20 percent receive 60 percent (Chart 10.2).

Human Rights and Justice

Practice Behavior Example: Understand the forms and mechanisms of oppression and discrimination.

Critical Thinking Question: Over the past generation, the federal government has rapidly expanded "private" retirement benefits while Social Security payments have only been adjusted for inflation. How have these policy choices contributed to increasing inequality?

Chart 10.2   Distribution of Income by Source, Persons over 65 Years of Age, United States, 2007–09

	Bottom 20 percent	20–39th percentile	40–59th percentile	60–79th percentile	Top 20 percent	Total
Total income	$8,969	$15,110	$20,056	$28,861	$63,169	$27,236
OASDI + SSI	$8,065	$11,448	$11,792	$12,134	$12,870	$11,262
Retirement, interest, dividends	$574	$2,363	$5,324	$9,665	$21,786	$7,943
Earnings	$185	$935	$2,233	$5,856	$25,221	$6,887
Percent						
OASDI + SSI	90%	76%	59%	42%	20%	41%
Retirement, interest, dividends	6%	16%	27%	33%	34%	29%
Earnings	2%	6%	11%	20%	40%	25%
Aggregate income						
Percent within group						
OASDI + SSI	91.60%	74.63%	54.26%	43.97%	22.34%	39.66%
Investment, pension	5.21%	15.00%	30.09%	36.65%	32.39%	29.38%
Earnings	1.80%	7.75%	11.78%	15.79%	40.49%	26.44%
Percent by category						
OASDI + SSI	19.54%	19.81%	19.54%	28.89%	30.65%	100.00%
Investment, pension	1.50%	5.38%	14.63%	32.50%	60.00%	100.00%
Earnings	0.58%	3.09%	6.36%	15.56%	83.33%	100.00%

Source: Author's calculation from Steven Ruggles, J. Trent Alexander, Katie Genadek, Ronald Goeken, Matthew B. Schroeder, and Matthew Sobek, *Integrated Public Use Microdata Series: Version 5.0* [Machine-readable database] (Minneapolis: University of Minnesota, 2010).

Of course, if pension income were really private income, we could argue that the well-off elderly earned this income. Pension income, however, is not purely private. All taxpayers foot the bill for a large share of pensions because of the tax expenditures associated with them. If a direct subsidy were distributed so unevenly, there would be widespread outrage. However, because these tax breaks are supported by both major parties, they remain popular even though a relatively small proportion of the population receives a large share of the benefits.

Assess your comprehension of "Income Supports for Older Americans" by completing this quiz.

OLDER AMERICANS ACT

Until the 1960s, most policy attention to the aging focused on the increased dependency of individuals as they age and their decline in physical and mental well-being. As we noted, Social Security was originally designed to encourage older workers to leave the workforce because of their supposed declining ability. However, as part of the Johnson administration's Great Society programs, a second policy goal emerged—providing older Americans with the opportunity to lead full and satisfying lives.

One policy response to this new concern was civil rights legislation to outlaw age discrimination in the workplace.[30] Another important outcome was the passage and continuing reauthorization of the Older Americans Act, originally signed into law in 1965.[31] Although the act focused on the special needs of older people, it also focused broadly on developing knowledge to improve their health and happiness and assuring that retirees lead lives characterized by "health, honor, [and] dignity."[32]

Excerpt from the Older Americans Act

The Congress hereby finds and declares that, in keeping with the traditional American concept of the inherent dignity of the individual in our democratic society, the older people of our Nation are entitled to, and it is the joint and several duty and responsibility of the governments of the United States, of the several States and their political subdivisions, and of Indian tribes to assist our older people to secure equal opportunity to the full and free enjoyment of the following objectives:

1. An adequate income in retirement in accordance with the American standard of living.

2. The best possible physical and mental health which science can make available and without regard to economic status.

3. Suitable housing, independently selected, designed and located with reference to special needs and available at costs which older citizens can afford.

4. Full restorative services for those who require institutional care.

5. Opportunity for employment with no discriminatory personnel practices because of age.

6. Retirement in health, honor, dignity—after years of contribution to the economy.

7. Pursuit of meaningful activity within the widest range of civic, cultural, and recreational opportunities.

8. Efficient community services which provide social assistance in a coordinated manner and which are readily available when needed.

9. Immediate benefit from proven research knowledge, which can sustain and improve health and happiness.

10. Freedom, independence, and the free exercise of individual initiative in planning and managing their own lives.

---

[30]US Equal Employment Opportunity Commission, "Age Discrimination," http://www.eeoc.gov/laws/types/age.cfm.

[31]US Department of Health and Human Services, Administration on Aging, "Unofficial Compilation of Older Americans Act, as Amended in 2006," http://www.aoa.gov/AoA_programs/OAA/oaa_full.asp.

[32]National Health Policy Forum, "The Basics: Older Americans Act of 1965," http://www.hadpg.org/docs/Policy/Basics_OlderAmericansAct_07-09-10.pdf.

The act established the Administration on Aging within the Department of Health, Education, and Welfare (now Health and Human Services) to administer the programs it created. The 1965 act required states to establish agencies on aging in order to qualify for federal funding. When the act was reauthorized in 1973, however, Congress called for the development of what came to be called the *area agencies for aging* (AAA). There are now more than 600 AAAs in the nation that are most directly involved in delivering the range of services funded by the federal government.

Since the establishment of the AAAs, the development of programs for older Americans has taken a trajectory quite different from those serving other populations. For the most part, federal policy since the 1980s has shifted responsibility for planning and delivery of social services to the states, what is commonly called *devolution*. As we saw in our discussion of public assistance, this has led each state to develop its own unique approach to policymaking. In contrast, the federal Administration on Aging has actively developed a network of state and local area agencies on aging, with a focus on comprehensive planning and coordination.[33]

The Older Americans Act funds a wide range of services for older adults, with a primary focus on supportive services, nutritional services—like "Meals on Wheels," which delivers meals to older individuals and couples—and health promotion. Recent reauthorizations of the law have given increased attention to support for family caregivers. With the increase in the "very old" population in recent years, policymakers have recognized that family and community members who provide uncompensated care for older adults are a critical part of older Americans' support system. Support for these caregivers—through the provision of *respite care* or short-term relief for family members—has come to be viewed as an essential element of these support systems.

Practice Context

Practice Behavior Example: Continuously discover, appraise, and attend to changing locales, populations, scientific and technological developments, and emerging societal trends to provide relevant services.

Critical Thinking Question: The Older Americans Act mandated a national system of service provision for older adults. How has this contributed to older Americans receiving relevant services? Can you contrast this system to the services received by other populations?

Assess your comprehension of "Older Americans Act" by completing this quiz.

The Older American Act funds a variety of program, like Meals on Wheels, that enhance the lives of older Americans.

[33]US Health and Human Services, Administration on Aging, "National Aging Network," http://www.aoa.gov/AOARoot/AoA_Programs/OAA/Aging_Network/Index.aspx.

POLICY PRACTICE: WOMEN'S UNPAID LABOR

During the early years of the women's movement, a popular demand was "wages for housework." Advocates argued that women should be compensated for the unpaid work they do for their partners and children, and that if this work were compensated, it would be more valued by society. The "wages for housework" campaign never made much headway, but the expansion of America's very old population has brought us back to the issue in a new, less strident guise—family caregiving (Figure 10.8).

While the issue of family caregiving is complex, the demographic realities that drive it are straightforward. The most rapidly increasing share of the population is people over the age of 85. While this group has benefited from all the improvements in health and well-being of the past generation, its members are still much more likely than the general population to be disabled or suffer from chronic medical conditions.

WAGES FOR HOUSEWORK FOR ALL WOMEN MEANS

THE POWER TO DECIDE WHETHER OR NOT WE WANT TO HAVE CHILDREN

THE POWER TO DEMAND SERVICES TO CUT DOWN ON HOUSEWORK AND THIS MEANS FIRST OF ALL FREE DAYCARE CENTERS OPEN ALL DAY LONG AND IN OUR NEIGHBORHOOD

THE POWER TO TAKE A VACATION FROM HOUSEWORK, INCLUDING FROM OUR CHILDREN

THE POWER TO REFUSE THE DOUBLE SHIFT OF A SECOND JOB, WHICH IS NOW OUR ONLY ALTERNATIVE TO WORKING FOR NOTHING

THE POWER TO DEMAND FREE MEDICAL CARE, INCLUDING FREE CHILD BIRTH, AND METHODS OF CONTRACEPTION THAT DON'T RUIN OUR BODIES AND OUR SEXUALITY AS WELL.

Figure 10.8
Wages for Housework Pamphlet
This pamphlet, produced by the New York Wages for Housework Committee in 1975, seemed radical at the time. However, the social welfare system now acknowledges the critical role played by kinship care in sustaining older adults and people with disabilities.

Source: New York Wages for Housework Committee, 1975. Thanks to Silvia Federici, an original member of the Committee. Barnard Center for Research on Women, http://www.barnard.edu/crow/archive/sexualhealth.htm.

At the same time, the social networks that support older adults are less robust than they used to be. Because most older Americans remain *economically independent* much longer than in past generations, by the time they are in need of services and support, their immediate relatives are often less able to aid them. The older person may have moved to a different region while his health was better, he may have few or no surviving children, or his children may already be retired or sick by the time he needs the additional help.

For those children or grandchildren who are able to help, the burden may seem overwhelming. An older person who needs constant help with feeding, dressing, and personal care; transportation to doctor visits; and support for the rest of daily life can quickly become virtually a full-time job to a caretaker. While many willingly assume these responsibilities, after a few months or years, the stress of the "job" may take its toll and lead the caretaker to give up and place the older relative in institutional care.

Although public policy is concerned with the independence and dignity of older Americans, a less flowery motivation drives the interest in family caregivers: dollars and cents. With the average cost of care in a nursing home now at several thousand dollars a month, the dollar benefit to the government for maintaining an older person at home is gigantic. A study of the economic value generated by family caregivers between 2000 and 2002—*just in the final year of life*—estimated the total value as $31,000 per older person and $1.5 billion for the country as a whole.[34] State and area agencies on aging have recognized this trade-off. The reauthorization of the Older Americans Act included additional funding to encourage local agencies to expand their services to family caregivers.

At the same time, the economic considerations are complex. Although many, perhaps most, family caregivers undertake this work because of a sense of obligation, many families have no financially conceivable option. Program administrators fear that if the alternatives to going it alone are too attractive, many more families will avail themselves of the services. Ultimately, one could imagine families whose relatives were not at risk of entering a nursing home would qualify for a set of new benefits around skilled nursing care, home health care, and respite services.

Family caregiving will never fulfill the feminist hope of "wages for housework." However, it does provide an example of how the informal actions of ordinary families can have a decisive impact on the formulation and implementation of social welfare policy.

Family caregiving also provides an example where practitioners, including social workers, can have an impact on policy implementation. Ultimately, professional judgments and values play a decisive role in deciding what supports can help caregivers and recipients of care maintain their independence and well-being. In managed care settings, this may require social workers to advocate for clients and to resist efforts to cut costs. At the same time, often by promoting the efficacy of clients, social workers can improve the overall efficiency of the care systems. In short, social work practitioners at times may support top-down policy prescriptions and at other times resist them. However, a clear focus on the values and principles that drive one's practice and the incorporation of existing intervention knowledge can play an important part in determining the trajectory of family caregiver policy.

Engage, Assess, Intervene, Evaluate

Practice Behavior Example: Implement prevention interventions that enhance client capacities.

Critical Thinking Question: Explain how promoting family caregiving can enhance clients' capacities while advancing organizational and policy goals.

Test your understanding and analysis of this chapter by completing the Chapter Review.

---

[34]YongJoo Rhee, Howard Degenholtz, Anthony T. Sasso, and Linda Emanuel, "Estimating the Quantity and Economic Value of Family Caregiving for Community-Dwelling Older Persons in the Last Year of Life," *Journal of the American Geriatrics Society* 57, no. 9 (September 2009): 1654–1659.

11

The Next Generation

Education and Child Welfare

INTRODUCTION

Rearing of children is seen as the ultimate *private* activity. Yet throughout American history, public policy has played an important role in the process. This chapter reviews the changing structure of American families and its implications for political support of children's programs. The philosopher Robert Goodin believes that the foundation for social welfare lies in a moral imperative to protect the vulnerable. He argues further that this responsibility goes beyond simply protecting the vulnerable from harm. We must also consider our ability to address conditions that prevent their exposure to harm. "If people can be said to be vulnerable to harms from men or from nature, from actions or from omissions," Goodin notes, "then protecting the vulnerable must amount to protecting them from *all* these sorts of threatened harm."[1]

Children certainly stand out as one of society's most vulnerable populations. Although most of us would agree that we owe them protection, the scope of that responsibility is very much open to question. Is our responsibility simply to protect the young against imminent harm—as in the case of physical abuse—or do we have a broader responsibility to address those conditions that increase their risk of harm or exploitation?

As we shall see, the way Americans treat their children splits in two the answer to these questions. When Americans speak about *their* children—that is, their biological or adopted children—they tend to use an expansive lens to address their responsibility.

---

[1]Robert E. Goodin, *Protecting the Vulnerable: A Reanalysis of Our Social Responsibilities* (Chicago: University of Chicago Press, 1985), 110.

However, when they talk about "other people's children," to use a phrase coined by Lazerson and Grubb, their sense of responsibility tends to be short-circuited and circumscribed.[2]

This division in our sense of responsibility has grown as the demographic realities of child-rearing have changed. Increasingly, a larger share of children are living in a smaller share of American households. The amount of time that adolescents and "adultolescents" are at least partially dependent on their parents for financial support has increased. As a result, at any one time, a large proportion of the population is unconcerned about "other people's children."

These unique concerns about children are mixed as well with more general concerns. The same suspicions about government action that influence the entire social welfare system are particularly acute when it comes to children. Few of us object when government pays for our aging parents' support or health care, but we worry about it exceeding its authority when it looks over our shoulder at how we raise our children. An enduring image of social workers in the popular media is that of a child protective worker showing up at the door to investigate a complaint about a child's treatment.

This chapter first examines the American household structure and changing geography of domestic life. We then examine the impact of increasing economic inequality on American children and the debate over poverty and female-headed households. Finally, we turn to universal and targeted programs that focus on children.

TWO PERSPECTIVES ON CHILDREN'S POLICY

Imagine two different societies. In one, children are seen as a national resource because they provide the nation's future citizens. As a result, government takes an active interest in every aspect of their development to assure that those citizens are healthy, adjusted, and loyal. In the other, children are seen as purely the private concern of their parents. The state is viewed as an outsider; its only role is to assure that parents do not commit crimes, like physical abuse, against their children. In that society, children are seen simply as little adults with no additional claims on society. How would these societies differ?

In the *socialized child-rearing* society, government would take an active interest in who got pregnant and when. Teen pregnancy would probably be discouraged with education campaigns, extensive availability of birth control methods, and abortion services. In contrast, women seen as desirable mothers because they are healthy and have the resources to support children would be encouraged to bear children through a set of financial incentives. Home health workers might visit these women regularly to encourage them to get pregnant and explain the psychological and social benefits of parenthood. High-government officials would use projections of the future economic and military needs of the society to determine the extent of these *pronatal* policies.

Government would institute a system of children's allowances to assure that no child lives in poverty. These allowances would have to include both a universal element that all parents receive and a selective element that would increase payments to low-income and single parents. The tax system would be used to target these payments while assuring that they are seen as a right of citizenship.

---

[2]The phrase "other people's children" comes from W. Norton Grubb and Marvin Lazerson, *Broken Promises: How Americans Fail Their Children* (Chicago: University of Chicago Press, 1988).

Government would guarantee health care for expectant mothers and their babies, who would have free access to prenatal and neonatal care. Mothers who did not take advantage of these services would receive letters and perhaps a visit from a home heath worker to make sure she was taking her vitamins. If a pregnant woman were seen as "unfit" for parenthood, arrangements would be made to provide extra services or, in an extreme case, to remove the child from her at birth. In certain cases, a home health worker might advise a woman to terminate her pregnancy.

The society might decide that parents should stay home with their infants and young children and provide one or two years of fully paid parental leave per child. Or perhaps it would opt to provide full-time, low-cost child care. Ideally, parents would have a choice about whether to avail themselves of leave or child care services. If parents chose to keep the child home, a social worker would visit the family frequently to assure that the child's home environment provided a sufficient amount of stimulation and that the parents were looking after her developmental needs in the optimal way.

Public schools would be required for all citizens, because private schools would be seen as encouraging exclusiveness and social division. Diversity of curriculum might be encouraged to respect the cultural and individual diversity of the population, but all schools would receive the same resources, and an extensive system of testing would be used to evaluate the effectiveness of the education. Schools that were shown to be ineffective would be closed; educational models that were shown to produce good results would be replicated. As children got older, projections of labor force needs would be used to channel children into different academic and vocational tracks so that the economy in the future would have the right number of gardeners, carpenters, and accountants. Perhaps aptitude tests would be used to more finely match children's capabilities to future job opportunities.

Now imagine the purely privatized child-rearing society. The decision to have a child would be made in private by the individuals and couples involved. Contraceptives and abortion might be available but would be priced at market rates so that women were free to make their own decisions.

Health care would be available through the market. Well-off families would be able to purchase the services they need and take time off work when necessary, but low-income families would have to make decisions about when to work and when not to. The chief mechanism for intervening in family life would be the police force, which would respond to reports of crimes against children. Professionals might have a responsibility to report incidents of abuse and neglect but would be trained to err on the side of inaction to respect the child-rearing philosophies of individual parents.

Government might require parents to send their children to school but generally would take a hands-off policy toward education. While a subsidy might be available for poor parents so they could afford low-cost schools, government would resist establishing public schools and the inevitable need to decide what children should learn.

Children whose parents had died, were incapable of carrying out their duties, or had been found to commit a felony against their children would be placed with a relative. An extensive set of child responsibility laws would require grandparents, siblings, cousins or more distant relatives to bear financial responsibility for these children. The designated relatives would either accept the child into their household or be required to pay for her upkeep in a foster family or institution.

Obviously, most Americans would find elements of both of these systems objectionable. Either extreme—surrendering control of one's children to state supervision or eliminating government's role as much as possible—strikes us as inappropriate.

The point is that children's unique status in society offers us no absolutely clear, unambiguous policy path. We believe that parents should bear primary responsibility for their children, but we also know that children's vulnerability and society's interest in rearing healthy, well-adjusted adults must play a role in social policy.

HOW AMERICANS RAISE THEIR CHILDREN

The American family has experienced profound changes over the last half century and continues that transformation today. Just in the past decade, the impact of recession on the transition from childhood to adulthood and the legalization in many states of same-sex marriage are changing how Americans think about marriage and child-rearing.

Changing Importance of Age and the Life Cycle

Most Americans don't think twice about the importance of age. Our birthdays, when we start and leave school, when we get a job, when we marry, when we retire—all are influenced by our "age consciousness," our certainty that age matters. Yet before the twentieth century, Americans were only vaguely aware of their age. This vagueness was captured by the census. When asked their age, Americans were much more likely to report certain figures than others. For example, the most popular answer tended to be a figure that ended in zero—30, 40, 50—suggesting that those residents didn't spend much time tracking their age. In fact, in 1900 more than 14 percent of adults chose this option (where we would expect only 10 percent to do so). The only other ages more popular than we would expect were ones ending in five—such as 35, 45, or 55. Most of this "age heaping" had been eliminated by the beginning of the twentieth century, as a larger and larger share of the population listed an exact age for themselves.

The reason why people increasingly knew their age was that it had become important. More and more life activities were tied to a particular age, with two government-regulated activities—going to school and retiring—taking the lead in standardizing the life cycle.

The past century also witnessed a dramatic change in the distribution of the population across the life cycle. A number of changes we will discuss below—delayed marriage, lower fertility rates, and rising life expectancy—combined to reshape what demographers call the "age pyramid." In 1900 it was indeed a pyramid with a wide base and narrow top. By 2000 it had come to look more like a church steeple, narrow and straight at the bottom with a bulge just above the middle (the "baby boom" generation) and a slow narrowing at the top (Figure 11.1).

For social workers, however, probably the most important change in the life cycle has been the definition and redefinition of different life stages. Although as second nature, social workers view individuals as passing through "ages and stages," in fact, this perspective is a relatively new phenomenon.

Growing Up: The Transition from Childhood to Adulthood

The structure and timing of the transition from childhood to adulthood has gone through two major changes over the past century. During the half century before 1970, growing up became more *standardized* as a larger share of the population went through

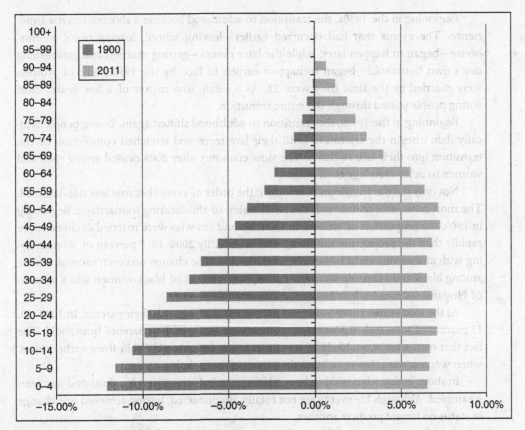

Figure 11.1
Age Pyramid, United States, 1900 and 2011
The classic age pyramid of 1900, with a wide base and a narrow peak, has given way to one with
an irregular shape.

Source: Author's calculations from Steven Ruggles, J. Trent Alexander, Katie Genadek, Ronald Goeken, Matthew B. Schroeder, and Matthew Sobek, *Integrated Public Use Microdata Series: Version 5.0* [Machine-readable database] (Minneapolis: University of Minnesota, 2010).

the transition at similar rates and similar times. Since 1970, the experience has become more diverse. The transition happens at different times and the proportion of a generation following the same path has declined.[3]

One way we can measure changes in the transition to adulthood is to use a set of life events as markers and then study when most of a generation goes through each transition. Here we focus on six life events: leaving school, leaving your parents' house, establishing your own residence, getting a job, getting married, and becoming a parent.

In the early years of the twentieth century, the transition took a long time. Some of the events—leaving school, getting a job—occurred early by contemporary standards. Typically, a large share of kids had left school by age 14. Other elements of the transition—getting married, becoming a parent—typically occurred in the late 20s or early 30s, not that different from contemporary averages. In addition, the sequencing of life events was fairly predictable. Typically, young people left school before they left their parents' house, and they got a job and established their own household before they married or had kids.

[3]For a more detailed discussion of the transition to adulthood, see Jordan Stanger-Ross, Christina Collins, and Mark J. Stern, "Falling Far from the Tree: Transitions to Adulthood and the Social History of the Twentieth Century," *Social Science History* 29, no. 4 (Winter 2005): 625–648.

Beginning in the 1930s, the transition to adulthood became a shorter, intense experience. The events that had occurred earlier—leaving school, leaving one's parents' house—began to happen later, while the later events—getting married and establishing one's own household—began to happen earlier. In fact, by the 1950s, half of women were married by the time they were 21. As a result, in a matter of a few years, most young people passed through the entire transition.

Beginning in the 1970s, the transition to adulthood shifted again. Young people typically didn't begin the transition until their late teens and stretched completion of the transition into their late twenties. The slow economy after 2008 caused young men and women to delay marriage even longer.

Not only did the transition take longer, the order of events became less standardized. The most noticeable feature was the relationship of childbearing to marriage. Beginning in 1960, the proportion of women in their 20s and 30s who were married declined more rapidly than the proportion not living with a child. By 2008–10, 7 percent of women living with at least one child had never been married. The change was even more dramatic among black and Hispanic women. Twenty-one percent of black women and 8 percent of Hispanic women in their 20s and 30s were single parents.

At the same time, more young adults were still living with their parents. In 2008–10, 13 percent of men and 10 percent of women were living in their parents' household. The fact that men were more likely to remain at home represented a shift from earlier times, when women were slower to leave their parents' household.

In short, today what used to be a relatively orderly transition to adulthood has been scrambled. Although life events are not totally disconnected, having achieved one change in status no longer predicts another.

Human Behavior

Practice Behavior Example: Know about human behavior across the life course, the range of social systems in which people live, and the ways social systems promote or deter people in maintaining or achieving health and well-being.

Critical Thinking Question: How might changes in the transition from childhood to adulthood influence our clients' well-being?

Three other changes in personal life have influenced the status of children: divorce, women working, and decline in fertility. First, divorce has become more common. In 1960 less than 5 percent of the population was divorced or separated (this doesn't count those who had remarried); in 2008–10, this figure had increased to 14 percent.

Second, the increase in women's labor force participation, noted in Chapter 8, had particular relevance for child welfare. As late as 1970, 70 percent of mothers with a child under the age of five in the household were out of the labor force. By 2010, 66 percent of women in this category were in the labor force. Mothers' labor force participation had several implications for child welfare policy. Child care shifted from a minor issue affecting relatively few women to a central topic of policy debates. In addition, the rise in working mothers raised concerns about how it would influence the social and psychological development of children (Figure 11.2).

The third major change affecting the welfare of children has been the decline in fertility. Many factors have contributed to the decline in fertility. Because of changes in women's access to higher education and better jobs, the roles of wife and mother must compete with continuing employment. Technologies for preventing unwanted pregnancies also have made a contribution. The biggest change, however, has been our expectations about child-rearing.[4]

---

[4]Richard Easterlin, *Birth and Fortune: The Impact of Numbers on Personal Welfare* (New York: Basic Books, 1980); Nathanael Lauster and Graham Allan, eds., *The End of Children: Changing Trends in Childbearing and Childhood* (Vancouver: University of British Columbia Press, 2012).

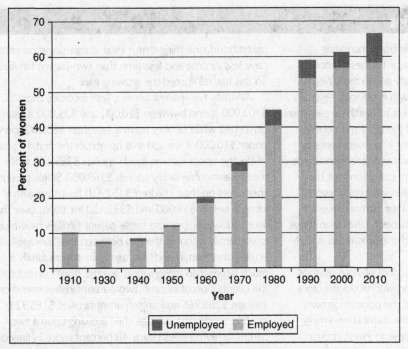

Figure 11.2

Employment Status of Women 18–49 with At Least One Child under the Age of 5 Present in the Household

Until the 1960s, it was relatively rare for women with young children to work outside the home. Now a majority of women do so.

Source: Author's calculations from Steven Ruggles, J. Trent Alexander, Katie Genadek, Ronald Goeken, Matthew B. Schroeder, and Matthew Sobek, *Integrated Public Use Microdata Series: Version 5.0* [Machine-readable database] (Minneapolis: University of Minnesota, 2010).

Before World War II, many parents expected that their children would support them longer than they would support their children. Kids entered the labor force earlier, pensions were rare, and Social Security did not exist. So the relatively few years that parents had to make a financial investment in their children seemed like a safe bet against the years that they could look to their children for financial support.[5]

Things have changed. Now, parents are expected to pay for college, SAT preparation courses, class trips, dance lessons, soccer equipment, braces, to say nothing of iPods, computers, or smart phones. Indeed, just since 1960, the cost of raising a child to age 17 has increased by 23 percent in real terms, primarily because of increases in the cost of housing, health care, and education/child care (although all of those iPods and smart phones must be in there somewhere). Overall, the US Department of Agriculture estimates that to raise a child born in 2011 to age 17, a lower-income family will spend about $212,000, while a higher-income family will spend about $491,000.[6]

Of course, the actual cost of raising children is also a product of social norms. Parents with the financial resources to avoid short-term crisis management could literally afford to think about the future and structure their strategies around family formation to reflect that planning. If a man and woman anticipated spending hundreds of thousands

---

[5]John Caldwell, *Theory of Fertility Decline* (New York: Academic Press, 1982).

[6]Mark Lino, "Expenditures on Children by Families, 2011," (US Department of Agriculture, Center for Nutrition Policy and Promotion, 2012), Miscellaneous Publication No. 1528-2011, p. 21, http://www.cnpp.usda.gov/Publications/CRC/crc2011.pdf.

Inequality and Child-Rearing

As discussed throughout this book, increasing inequality is one of the major themes in contemporary social welfare, both globally and in the United States. Some evidence of its growth is obvious—gaps in income, unemployment, and access to health care—while others are more hidden. One of the most momentous places the resource gap is growing is in investments in children. The child investment gap has special significance because it affects not only current conditions but has implications for the future. Children who enjoy investments of time and resources by their parents have a much better chance of leading successful lives than those who lack them. In short, the child investment gap is likely to be magnified over time.

Why has this gap grown? The most obvious reasons have to do with the economy and with family structure. As the gap between the rich and the poor has grown, those at the bottom of the income distribution simply don't have the discretionary income to invest in their children. The income squeeze is reinforced by a time squeeze, as low-income parents are more likely to lack the time to devote to their children.

But that is not all. Changing family structure, one of our themes in this chapter, also plays a role. Single-parent families are much more likely to sit near the bottom of the income pyramid. Although there has been a lively debate about the psychological impact of single parenthood, one thing that is clear is that single parents have less income and less time than two-parent families. So this has reinforced the growing gap.

Annually, two-parent families with incomes over $103,000 spend between $20,000 and $25,000 a year on a child, while families earning less than $60,000 spend under $10,000. If we add that up across the first 17 years of life, the upper-income family spends $389,670 while the lower-income family spends $169,080. Single parents spend less on their children: $157,410 for those with income below $59,000 and $333,420 for those over that figure. However, because single-parent families have much lower family incomes, the gap between the "average" single-parent family and "average" two-parent family is much larger than these figures suggest. If we correct for the distribution of income, two-parent families spend on average $258,966 and single-parent families $185,924. In other words, the average child growing up in a two-parent family receives nearly 40 percent more in financial resources from her parents than the average child in a one-parent family.

Of course, children growing up in higher-income, two-parent families are likely to enjoy other advantages. Their parents are less likely to be under stress or suffer from untreated health conditions, they have often had a better education, and they generally feel more satisfied with their lives.

---

of dollars on each child, they could plan to have fewer children. As a result, changes in the cost of children and social norms about the proper amount to devote to children led to a dramatic decline in fertility.

This "demographic transition" to lower fertility spanned the twentieth century with one sizable exception. In the years after World War II, between 1946 and 1964, American women gave birth to far more children than they did in the decades before or after. The "baby boom" is best explained as a result of the high level of economic opportunity brought about by an expanding economic and welfare state during those years.

In the 1970s, as the "baby bust" followed the boom, the timing of women's fertility also changed. Since the 1970s, the fertility rate of younger women has remained low. At the same time, the fertility rate of women in their mid to late 30s and in their 40s has increased.

Since 1990 the fertility rates for all age groups younger than 30 have fallen. Indeed, despite the loud public debate over teen pregnancy, no group has seen its fertility decline more than young women between the ages of 15 and 19. Among older women, however, fertility has continued to increase.[7]

---

[7]Brady E. Hamilton, "Births: Preliminary Data for 2009," *National Vital Statistics Reports* 59, no. 3 (December 21, 2010):3.

Changing Family Strategies and Household Structure

All of the factors we've reviewed—transition to adulthood, divorce, women in the labor force, fertility—come together in two ways. First, they express the *strategies* that families and individuals use in making decisions about their lives. Second, they influence the aggregate structure of households across American society.

Family strategies

As noted above, parents who are under stress because of financial and time constraints have little choice but to make decisions based on *short-term crisis management*. If you're facing a pile of bills you don't have the money to pay, you're less likely to think about where you want to be in 20 years. The more stress, the less likely one is to consider the long-term consequences of current actions.

We can think of these differences as a distinction between *protective* and *anticipatory* family strategies. Protective strategies took crisis management as the normal state of affairs. One had to make decisions assuming that, at any time, one might be overwhelmed by economic circumstances. Historically, protective family strategies included having many children (a hedge against old-age poverty), less schooling, and early movement into the labor force. Protective strategies frequently involved keeping housing costs in check either through overcrowding or by augmenting the household with relatives, boarders, or lodgers.[8]

Anticipatory family strategies assumed that the family would enjoy more economic freedom to make choices. Typically, these strategies included fewer children, increasing educational opportunity for kids, and later entry into the labor force. During its heyday, anticipatory strategies emphasized the importance of the nuclear family—mom, dad, and the kids—and sought to restrict the presence of other members in the household.

Overall, the shift from protective to anticipatory family strategies gained momentum during the past century. Originally, anticipatory strategies were more common among well-off families, but over time they became common as well among those with fewer financial resources.

Not all movement has been in one direction. During the Great Depression, for example, unemployed middle-class families that had used anticipatory strategies often began incorporating protective elements, like taking in boarders and reducing children's schooling. Overriding economic cycles, the increasing frequency of divorce has complicated family strategies.

The key is that family strategies are based on *expectations* about the future, and those expectations sometimes clash with reality. Indeed, like generals who are constantly preparing for the last war, family members often base their strategies on past expectations that don't fit with the conditions that they will actually face. In a famous study of children growing up during the Great Depression, sociologist Glen Elder found that they continued to harbor anxiety about their economic standing, even after the actual threat had passed.[9]

Finally, some parts of the shift from protective to anticipatory strategies seem reversible and others don't. Notably, families no longer seem to respond to hard times by increasing their fertility. In fact, during and after the 2007–09 recession, fertility declined sharply. At the same time, incorporating others into one's household continues to rise during

---

[8]Michael B. Katz and Mark J. Stern, *One Nation Divisible: What America Was and What It Is Becoming* (New York: Russell Sage Foundation, 2006), 156–158.

[9]Glen H. Elder, *Children of the Great Depression: Social Change in Life Experience* (Chicago: University of Chicago Press, 1974).

economic slow times. The Census Bureau reported in September 2010, for example, that the number of multifamily households jumped 12 percent between 2008 and 2010, the highest proportion since 1968.[10]

Household structure

Taken together, all of the changes discussed above have led to the eclipse of the two-parent family with children. Where in 1960 "mom, dad, and the kids" described more than 60 percent of all households, by 2008–2010 the number had fallen to 22 percent. In fact, 67 percent of children still lived in married-couple-with-children households, but only 36 percent of adults lived in a household with a child present.

Ethnicity matters. Three-fourths of non-Hispanic white children and 84 percent of Asian-Pacific Islander children live with two parents or stepparents (this includes remarried families). However, only 35 percent of black children, 62 percent of Hispanic children, and 60 percent of multiracial and indigenous children do so (Chart 11.1).

America's Changing Domestic Landscape

The lives of America's children are increasingly bifurcated. Children who grow up in high-income households with two parents enjoy ever-increasing resources and attention. Low-income children more often than not live with only one parent who has neither the time nor the financial resources to meet all of their needs.

Chart 11.1   Distribution of Households, Adults, and Children by Household Type and Presence of Children, 2008–10

	Percent of households			Percent of persons 18 and over			Percent of all children
	No children present	Children present	All households	No children present	Children present	All adults	All children
Married-couple family household	27.2%	22.0%	49.2%	31.3%	26.0%	57.3%	66.6%
Male householder, no wife present	1.9%	2.6%	4.6%	2.7%	2.7%	5.4%	7.1%
Female householder, no husband present	4.1%	8.7%	12.8%	5.7%	7.6%	13.3%	25.4%
Male householder, living alone	12.0%	0.0%	12.0%	5.9%		5.9%	0.0%
Male householder, not living alone	3.2%	0.2%	3.4%	3.8%	0.3%	4.1%	0.5%
Female householder, living alone	15.3%	0.0%	15.3%	7.5%		7.5%	0.0%
Female householder, not living alone	2.6%	0.1%	2.7%	3.0%	0.1%	3.1%	0.2%
All household types	66.4%	33.6%	100.0%	63.4%	36.6%	100.0%	100.0%

Note: 2.6 percent of the population does not live in households, of which children are 0.3 percent. These numbers are included in the column totals for individuals and children.

Source: Author's calculation from Steven Ruggles, J. Trent Alexander, Katie Genadek, Ronald Goeken, Matthew B. Schroeder, and Matthew Sobek, Integrated Public Use Microdata Series: Version 5.0 [Machine-readable database] (Minneapolis: University of Minnesota, 2010).

---

[10]Michael Luo, "'Doubling Up' in Recession-Strained Quarters," New York Times, December 26, 2010.

Yet these aren't the only barriers dividing "other people's children" from our own. Geography also plays an important role, first, because neighborhoods matter, and, second, because low-income kids are more likely to live in the neighborhoods that reinforce their disadvantage.

Historically, two-parent families dominated suburbs, while city neighborhoods were commonly composed of single-parent families and nonfamily households. The general decline of married-couple family households has hit both cities and suburbs. By the turn of the twenty-first century, married-couple families dominated few census tracts in American cities, while as the percent in the suburbs fell considerably.

New York City's Household Geography

In 2010, New York City was representative of the extreme concentration of different household types across the metropolitan landscape.

Married-couple families were concentrated in parts of Staten Island and Queens. Meanwhile in the city's surrounding suburbs, married couples were no longer the majority, but often represented 30 or 40 percent of all households (Figure 11.3).

Probably no city better captures the rise of nonfamily households than New York. The combination of single persons moving to the city in search of fame and fortune, cramped housing, and the explosion in cohabiting gay and straight couples made nonfamilies the predominant household form in much of Manhattan (New York County), as well as in sections of Brooklyn (Kings County) and Queens. Nonfamily households had become more common in the suburbs as well (Figure 11.4).

Meanwhile, neighborhoods with large numbers of low-income African Americans, Latinos, and immigrants—upper Manhattan, the Bronx, and large sections of Brooklyn and Queens—included large concentrations of single-parent families (Figure 11.5).

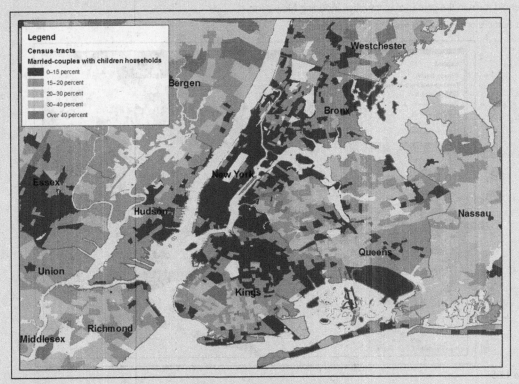

Figure 11.3
Concentration of Married-Couple Families with Children, New York City Metropolitan Area Census Tracts, 2005–09
"Traditional" families are now often a rarity in the center of major American cities.
Source: Author's original material based on US Census data.

Figure 11.4
Concentration of Nonfamily Households, New York City Metropolitan Area Census Tracts, 2005–09
Nonfamily households, often single-person households, roommates, or unmarried couples, are now the most common household form in the center of many cities, including New York.

Source: Author's original material based on US Census data.

Figure 11.5
Concentration of Female-Headed Households with Children, New York City Metropolitan Area Census Tracts, 2005–09
Female-headed households are more common in low-income neighborhoods but are now common in many parts of metropolitan America.

Source: Author's original material based on US Census data.

These patterns mean that low-income kids in single-parent families are more likely to live in neighborhoods with other single-parent families. This geographic concentration means that the kids' parents, neighbors, and friends face a common set of challenges to their family's welfare and well-being. Moreover, a host of neighborhood-based conditions—failing schools, insecurity and violence, and lack of civic resources—add to the already sizable disadvantages these families face.

These data lead us to a number of conclusions that influence social policy toward children:

1. The proportion of the adult population directly involved in the care of children is small and getting smaller.

2. Children are increasingly likely to live with one parent. This possibility is higher for black and Hispanic kids.

3. The increasing cost of raising children means that kids living in single-parent households face increased risk both during childhood and as they become adults.

Thus, low-income children find themselves in the perfect storm of social policy. They are among the most vulnerable members of our society, but increasingly the public sees them as their parents'—not our—responsibility. They are more likely to live in settings that magnify rather than mitigate their vulnerability. Meanwhile, with most Americans disengaged from child-rearing in general and the problems of low-income children in particular, they are socially invisible.

Assess your comprehension of "How Americans Raise Their Children" by completing this quiz.

THE RISKS OF CHILDHOOD

As a vulnerable population, children face a variety of risks. In this section, we consider three of them: mortality; poverty; and violence, abuse, and neglect.

Infant Mortality

The first risk any of us face is infant mortality. Birth has always been a dangerous process for mother and child both, although it is much less risky today than in the past. Still, as we've seen in Chapter 7, the United States has a poor record on this life transition, with an infant mortality rate similar to that of many poor nations.

Why is infant mortality so high? A large share of the infant mortality rate in the United States is the result of premature births. In these cases, the absence of prenatal care is a major contributor to infant death, because care increases the likelihood that problems can be identified and addressed early. Yet nearly 30 percent of pregnant women receive no care during the first trimester, and 7 percent receive no care before the third trimester.[11]

Two factors are associated with increased likelihood that a woman will not receive prenatal care. First, young pregnant women are much less likely to receive care. In 2008, for example, only 33 percent of mothers under the age of 15 giving birth received first-trimester care, while 54 percent of mothers between the ages of 15 and 19 had done so (Figure 11.6).

---

[11]US Department of Health and Human Services, Health Resources and Services Administration, Maternal and Child Health Bureau, *Child Health USA 2011* (Rockville, MD: US Department of Health and Human Services, 2011), http://mchb.hrsa.gov/chusa11/hsfu/pages/312pc.html.

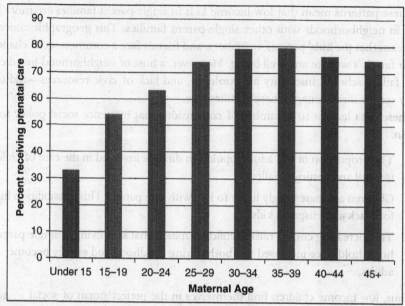

Figure 11.6
Receipt of First Trimester Prenatal Care by Maternal Age, 2008
Young mothers are much less likely to receive care early in their pregnancies, which poses a risk for both themselves and their babies.
Source: Based on US Department of Health and Human Services, Center for Health Statistics, National Vital Statistics System.

Second, some pregnant women belonging to some ethnic groups are much less likely to have received care. Two smaller groups—indigenous people and Hawaiians (53 percent) and Pacific Islanders (55 percent)—have the lowest rates of first-trimester care, but non-Hispanic blacks (60 percent) and Hispanics (65 percent) have much lower rates than the rest of the population.

One reason that the United States has such a poor record in providing prenatal care is because policy has often become entangled with the politics of abortion. Title X of the Public Health Service Act funds family planning and other preventive care services for women by distributing funds to states and a variety of organizations that provide reproductive health services, breast and cervical cancer screening, and education and counseling services. Although all grantees are prohibited from using the funding to perform abortions, antiabortion advocates have attacked Title X because one of the largest beneficiaries of the funding—Planned Parenthood and its affiliates—is also an abortion provider. Beginning in 2011, having gained control of the House of Representatives, Republicans sought to exclude funding for Planned Parenthood and reduce funding for Title X in general.[12]

Poverty

As noted in Chapter 4, American children have a much higher risk of living in poverty than young people in other developed nations. Even within the United States, children's risk of poverty is higher than that of other age groups. The likelihood that a child will be poor is strongly correlated with her race or ethnicity, family structure, and the type

---

[12]Jennifer Steinhauser, "House Republicans Seek to Remove Federal Funding for Planned Parenthood," *New York Times*, April 11, 2011, http://thecaucus.blogs.nytimes.com/2011/04/11/house-republicans-seek-to-remove-federal-funding-for-planned-parenthood/.

of neighborhood in which she lives. Here, we turn the question around and ask how poverty influences other elements of children's life. In particular, we draw on the increased understanding of how poverty among pregnant women and newborns influences the child's later development.

The interest in how early childhood poverty impacts later outcomes is associated with emerging scientific evidence on human development. It appears that "the astonishingly rapid development of young children's brains" leave them sensitive (and vulnerable) "to both environmental and family-level risks associated with poverty."[13]

The impact of early childhood poverty on school readiness has been documented in a variety of studies. Results from the US Early Childhood Longitudinal Survey, for example, discovered that poverty was associated with much lower rates of recognizing letters, counting, judging size, and understanding sequencing.

In addition to in utero and neonatal physiological causes, early childhood poverty is associated with a variety of psychological and sociological conditions. The quality of interactions between parents and children appear to suffer because of economic stress. Poor parents are more likely to use "punitive parenting styles and less likely to provide their children with stimulating learning experiences in the home." Poverty and economic insecurity also affect parents' mental health status. For example, "[d]epression and other forms of psychological distress can profoundly affect parents' interactions with their children." Finally, divorce generally leads to a decline of income among women, who are much more likely to be caretakers than men.[14]

Programs like the Carolina Abecedarian Project of the 1970s—a controlled experiment to study the benefits of early childhood education for poor children—demonstrated that intensive intervention from infancy to age five was associated with increased reading and math achievement, educational attainment, and employment and lower rates of teen pregnancy and criminal activity.[15] Head Start (see below), a less intensive intervention, has been shown to have more modest impacts later in life.

The short-term effects of poverty are clear enough. Poverty is associated with lower school readiness, lower reading and math achievement, and a higher rate of disciplinary and other behavioral problems in school. Again, relatively modest interventions appear to have sizable impacts on these problems. For example, welfare experiments that increased parents' income and employment were associated with preschool and elementary school children's improved academic performance, although employment increases without increased income did not. Likewise, the implementation of the earned income tax credit was associated with school achievement improvements among low-income children.

More recently, we have gained a better understanding of the relationship of early childhood poverty to longer-term outcomes. Poverty is associated with a decreased likelihood in finishing high school, as much as a $20,000 reduction in annual income, elevated rates of poor health, arrests (especially for men), and birth out of wedlock (among women). A closer examination of the data demonstrates that economic hardship early in life is particularly likely to be associated with these negative outcomes.[16]

---

[13]Greg J. Duncan et al., "The Importance of Early Childhood Poverty," *Social Indicators Research* 108 (2012): 87–98. Quote from p. 88.

[14]Duncan et al., "Importance of Early Childhood Poverty," 91.

[15]"Abecedarian Project," Coalition for Evidence-Based Policy, http://evidencebasedprograms.org/wordpress/?page_id=70.

[16]Greg J. Duncan, Kathleen M. Ziol-Guest, and Ariel Kalil, "Early Childhood Poverty and Adult Attainment, Behavior, and Health," *Child Development* 81, no. 1 (January/February 2010): 306–325.

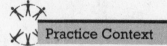

Practice Context

Practice Behavior Example: Continuously discover, appraise, and attend to changing locales, populations, scientific and technological developments, and emerging societal trends to provide relevant services.

Critical Thinking Question: How might the difference between a poor community with high collective efficacy and one with low collective efficacy influence one's practice with individuals, groups, or communities.

Environmental factors enhance the disadvantages of child poverty. As noted in Chapter 6, the neighborhood where a child grows up matters. Robert Sampson has demonstrated, using a detailed multilevel database, that two dimensions of neighborhood effects make a particular difference. First, to no one's surprise, neighborhoods with *concentrated disadvantage* (an index that includes welfare receipt, poverty, unemployment, female-headed households, racial segregation, and density of children) are associated with higher levels of violence, crime, and general social disorder. Second, more surprisingly, independent of concentrated disadvantage, Sampson and his collaborators found that local residents' belief that they can influence the quality of community life and their willingness to take action to do so—what he calls "collective efficacy"—has a significant influence on crime, violence, and disorder in Chicago's neighborhoods. These findings point to the fact that community-based interventions can have an impact on individual well-being.[17]

Violence, Abuse, and Neglect

Violence, abuse, and neglect are major risks to a child's chances of growing up to be a healthy adult. Children and youths face the risk of violence both in family settings and the wider community, with schools posing a particular hazard for young people.

Family violence involving children

Violence against children constitutes about 10 percent of all family violence. Using victimization data, just over 1 percent of all children experienced mistreatment in the early 2000s. Very young children, under the age of four, accounted for three-fourths of child mistreatment fatalities in 2002.[18]

We commonly distinguish *child abuse*—which involves physical assault, sexual abuse, and abusive treatment—from *child neglect*—which involves parents and caretakers' failure to take actions to protect their dependents, including abandonment, permitting delinquency, refusal to allow needed treatment, and other forms of inattention. When the public hears "abuse and neglect," they typically think of the most extreme cases: acts of violence and neglect that lead to death or near-death. Yet the vast majority of "abuse and neglect" cases involve less serious forms of neglect. Physical abuse, in fact, accounts for only 18 percent of all allegations.[19] The federal Administration on Children, Youth and Families estimated that in 2010 almost 1 percent of children (9.2 per 1,000) were the victim of a reported incident of abuse or neglect. Of the nearly two million reports of abuse and neglect in 2010, only 22 percent were substantiated. This still amounts to more than 400,000 substantiated cases. The vast majority of cases are reported by professionals, with teachers and police officers the most common source. Nonprofessionals reported only 28 percent of cases in 2010, with anonymous reports

---

[17]Robert Sampson, *Great American City: Chicago and the Enduring Neighborhood Effect* (Chicago: University of Chicago Press, 2012).

[18]Jennifer L. Truman, *Criminal Victimization, 2010* (Washington, DC: Bureau of Justice Statistics, 2011), http://www.bjs.gov/content/pub/pdf/cv10.pdf.

[19]US Department of Health and Human Services, Administration on Children, Youth and Families, "Child Maltreatment 2010," http://www.acf.hhs.gov/programs/cb/pubs/cm10/cm10.pdf.

being the most common nonprofessional type of report. Other relatives (7 percent) and friends and neighbors (4 percent) are much less common sources of reports.

Young children, under the age of four, made up about a third of all reports in 2010, while children 16 or 17 years of age made up only about 6 percent of cases. Children under the age of one had a victimization rate almost twice that of one- to three-year-olds. White families made up 45 percent of cases in that year, while African Americans and Hispanics composed 22 and 21 percent of all cases, respectively.

Community violence

Community violence refers to "acts of interpersonal violence that occur in community settings, including neighborhoods, streets, schools, shops, playgrounds, or other community locales."[20]

Although the data are open to interpretation, it appears that young people are at least twice as likely as adults to be victimized by severe violence and perhaps three times as likely to be victimized by less severe forms. Children living in low-income urban neighborhoods appear to be more at risk of violence than children living in other places. A 1997 study suggested that two-thirds of children in high-poverty neighborhoods had witnessed a shooting, and that one-fourth had personally been victimized.[21]

A large proportion of community violence affecting children occurs at school. School violence ranges from relatively minor fights between individual students to high-profile events like the Columbine High incident in 2005. Minor incidents are apparently quite common. In 2004, 14 percent of high school students reported involvement in a fight on school property. That year, over 100,000 students between 12 and 18 years of age reported being victims of more serious violent crimes.

In recent years, the topic of *bullying* has gained national attention. The Internet and social media have increased the avenues through which one or more students can target another. A significant proportion of bullying incidents are related to sexual orientation and specifically involve the targeting of gay or presumed gay students.

Exposure to violence, even in a secondary form, can have an adverse effect on a number of developmental issues, including the ability of children to develop trust and form and maintain social relationships. Community violence is associated as well with posttraumatic stress, increased aggression, and delinquency.

Assess your comprehension of "The Risks of Childhood" by completing this quiz.

POLICY RESPONSES TO THE PROBLEMS OF CHILDREN AND YOUTH

Given the vulnerability of children and youth and the variety of risks they face growing up, we would imagine that a rational society would mobilize its best resources and ideas to minimize these risks. Even the most hardheaded observer would grant that investments in children are likely to pay dividends and their neglect likely to yield losses that far outweigh the costs of prevention.

---

[20]Neil B. Guterman and Muhammad M. Haj-Yahia, "Community Violence," in *Encyclopedia of Social Work*, eds. Terry Mizrahi and Larry E. Davis, http://www.oxford-naswsocialwork.com/entry?entry=t203.375.
[21]E. J. Jenkins and C. C. Bell, "Exposure and Response to Community Violence among Children and Adolescents," in *Children in a Violent Society*, ed. J. D. Osofsky (New York: Guilford Press, 1997), 9–31.

The Urban Institute and Brookings Institution have collaborated in recent years to review spending on children across the entire federal budget. A number of federal programs that benefit children are discussed in different chapters because they benefit other populations as well. These include health programs (Medicaid/CHIP), income security programs (Social Security, TANF, Earned Income Tax Credit), nutrition programs (Food Stamps), and housing programs (Section 8, public housing). Together these programs accounted for 59 percent of the total federal budget spent on children in 2010 ($445.2 billion). Of the remaining 41 percent, the largest shares were represented by the tax system (21 percent) and the education system (15 percent). Two systems of particular importance from the standpoint of parents—child care and social services—together accounted for only 5 percent of all federal expenditures on children in 2010.[22]

In most advanced industrial nations, parents receive a payment from the government in support of their children. In a majority of countries surveyed by the Organization on Economic Cooperation and Development (OECD), these benefits were universal—that is, they are available equally to all citizens with no income test. Even in countries with an income test, the maximum eligible income is quite high. In Iceland, for example, the allowance of $3,153 is reduced by a percentage of income above $44,496, so that most middle-income families qualify. Other countries use a two-tier structure, with a smaller universal payment and a second, income-tested supplement. In Germany, for example, the universal, refundable payment (Kindergeld) is supplemented by an income-tested payment (Kinderzuschlag) if a parent is unemployed in order to care for a child (Chart 11.2).[23]

The United States has moved in fits and starts to incorporate universal payments through the income tax system:

Dependent exemptions—Individuals who have a tax liability are allowed to deduct a share of their income for each dependent child under the age of 18. In 2012 the amount was $3,800. This amount is deducted from one's income before taxes are calculated. However, because only 50 to 60 percent of households actually owe income tax, most low-income families do not benefit from this deduction.

Child Tax Credit—Individuals or couples are able to deduct from their tax liability up to $1,000 for each dependent child under the age of 18. This amount was doubled as a result of the 2009 stimulus bill and in 2010 extended through the end of 2013. Unless again extended, the amount will revert back to pre-2009 levels. The Child Tax Credit has included a *refundable* portion—with the inelegant name Additional Child Tax Credit—but the use of it was quite restricted until 2009, when it was expanded. Unless extended after 2013, it too will return to its restricted form.

Policies for Young Children (under 6 Years of Age)

Read "Ten Facts about the Child Tax Credit" to understand its benefits.

Until children go to school, there are few ways that social welfare policy affects them directly. However, interventions that benefit their caretakers—like parental leave and expanding high-quality child care options—can make a significant difference in a child's future prospects.

---

[22]Julia Isaacs, Heather Hahn, Stephanie Rennane, C. Eugene Steuerle, and Tracy Vericker, *Kids' Share 2011: Report on Federal Expenditures on Children Through 2010* (Washington, DC: Urban Institute and Brookings Institution, 2011), 23.
[23]Organisation for Economic Cooperation and Development, *OECD Family Database* (Paris: OECD, 2011), http://www.oecd.org/social/family/database.

Chart 11.2   Family Cash Benefits, OECD Nations, 2008

	Maximum benefit	Income-tested
Australia	$3,613	Yes
Austria	$2,150	No
Belgium	$1,739	No
Canada	$1,194	No
Czech Republic	$417	Yes
Denmark	$2,306	No
Estonia	$474	No
Finland	$1,643	No
France	$979	No
Germany	$2,530	No
Greece	$135	No
Hungary	$765	No
Iceland	$3,153	Yes
Ireland	$2,628	No
Italy	$1,495	Yes
Japan	$510	Yes
Latvia	$433	No
Lithuania	$331	No
Luxembourg	$3,846	No
Netherlands	$1,488	No
New Zealand	$3,133	Yes
Norway	$1,987	No
Poland	$278	Yes
Portugal	$536	Yes
Slovak Republic	$1,898	Yes
Slovenia	$263	Yes
Spain	$398	Yes
Sweden	$1,865	No
Switzerland (Zurich)	$1,950	No
United Kingdom	$1,883	No
United States	$1,056	Yes

Source: OECD Family Database, (Paris: OECD, 2011).

Parental leave

As noted earlier, research on early childhood suggests that the care of very young children has a significant impact on their later cognitive and social development. In recognition of these findings, most advanced social welfare systems grant parental leave for the care of children during their first year of life. It is common for leave to be paid for a period of time followed by another increment of leave that is not paid. For example, in the United Kingdom, mothers receive six months of paid leave and then are able to stay home for an additional six months with unpaid leave.[24]

Research-Based Practice

Practice Behavior Example: Comprehend quantitative and qualitative research and understand scientific and ethical approaches to building knowledge.

Critical Thinking Question: How might current knowledge on early childhood development and parental leave influence a social workers' practice with individual clients and in advocating for them?

Demand for parental leave in the United States mounted throughout the 1980s and led Congress to pass family and medical leave bills several times during the early 1990s. President George H. W. Bush vetoed these bills. However, during the first days of the Clinton administration in 1993, Congress passed and the president signed the Family and Medical Leave Act, which provides 12 weeks of unpaid leave. Generally speaking, employed women return to work earlier in the United States than in countries with paid leave. What is more, as noted in Chapter 8, the thrust of welfare reform policies require that poor women seek employment very early in their child's life. Thus, America's parental leave policies are in conflict with our understanding of early childhood development and patterns of public policy in the rest of the world.

Child care

During the 1970s, Congress passed legislation to expand the availability of child care for all Americans and to raise standards for centers and their workers. The Comprehensive Child Development Act of 1971 would have made it easier for poor mothers to seek employment, but it became an early target for Conservatives' attack on government meddling in the family. When President Nixon vetoed the bill, he suggested that it would cause the "Sovietization" of child-rearing in the United States.[25]

As a result, child care has remained a hodgepodge of programs and subsidies. Parents can use one of two possible tax benefits. Employers are allowed to establish dependent care accounts that allow employees to put aside pretax dollars for child care. If an employer does not offer this program, the family can use the *Child and Dependent Care Credit*. Individuals or couples who incur child care (or dependent care) expenses to enable them to work may claim up to $3,000 for one child or $6,000 for two or more children. In 2011 the percentage of expenses that an individual or couple were allowed to claim ranged from 35 percent for those with the lowest incomes to 20 percent for those with an adjusted gross income over $43,000. As a tax credit, the sum is deducted from the householder's tax liability, not from income; it is not refundable, so if the householder owes no taxes, they cannot benefit from a credit.

A variety of federal programs provide child care for low-income parents. The best known is Head Start, a product of the War on Poverty, which provides a broad school readiness program for children between the age of three and when they enter school. Over the years, Head Start has been the subject of a variety of evaluations, which have led to different conclusions about its effectiveness. The program appears to make modest contributions to a child's overall health and readiness for school when she leaves the program. However, these benefits do not seem to be sustained into the elementary school years.[26]

There is general agreement that Head Start has a greater impact on children who are enrolled in the program for two years (rather than one year only). In addition, the

[24]Jane Waldfogel, *What Children Need* (Cambridge: Harvard University Press, 2006), 64–65.
[25]Gilbert Steiner, *The Children's Cause* (Washington, DC: Brookings Institution, 1976).
[26]Westat, *Head Start Impact Study Final Report* (Washington, DC: HHS, 2010), http://www.acf.hhs.gov/programs/opre/hs/impact_study/reports/impact_study/executive_summary_final.pdf.

teachers' lack of training (only one quarter have a college degree) and their low pay (about a third that of elementary school teachers) clearly reduce the effectiveness of the program compared to early childhood education directed at nonpoor children. The relatively low proportion of Head Start spending devoted to the classroom also attracted attention.[27]

Several factors have made it difficult to enact reform. Obviously, improving the quality of teaching would require increasing the salaries of teachers. Congress is generally inclined to cut rather than expand Head Start, so increasing pay would require cutting the number of children served. As in many other aspects of child welfare, Head Start suffers from "penny wise, pound foolish" logic. High-quality early childhood programs demonstrate that intensive investments pay off over time, and low-quality interventions do not. Rather than reaping the benefits of increased investment, Head Start is stuck in a pattern of low investment generating mediocre results.

In addition to Head Start, child care centers for low-income families receive funds from the Child Care and Development Block Grant created as part of welfare reform in 1996. The largest share of the Social Service Block Grant spending is also devoted to child care.

It is plausible that at some point in the future Americans will recalibrate the age at which children start public school. School attendance for three- and four-year-olds has become nearly universal in some European countries, such as Belgium and Italy. Lowering the mandatory school age to enroll four-year-olds in *prekindergarten* would replace our current ragtag system of child care with a consistent higher quality system that equalizes rather than magnifies economic disparities.

However, although such a shift seems inevitable, it is clearly not on the immediate horizon. Indeed, in North Carolina, which has invested in public-school-based prekindergarten, the state legislature considered privatizing and cutting funding for the program in 2012.[28]

Public Education

Public education is universally available in the United States, but its extent, financing, and effectiveness vary greatly. Schools were originally conceptualized as a local responsibility. The idea of local schools supported through property taxes can be traced back to the Ordinance of 1785. The law's primary purpose was to allow the federal government to raise money through the sale of land on the American frontier. The law specified that land should be organized into 36-square-mile townships that would be subdivided into 36 one-square-mile sections. It further specified that the revenue from one of these sections would be reserved to fund a public school for the township.

Over the next two centuries, public education developed first as a local and then as a state responsibility. Most state constitutions include a requirement that the state assure the effective education of children, but until the twentieth century, state responsibility stopped with specifying the general outline of the school system and mandatory school attendance laws.

The federal government's role in elementary and secondary education was virtually nonexistent until the 1960s and 1970s when two important laws were enacted: the Elementary and Secondary Education Act of 1965 (ESEA, PL 89–10) and the Education for All Handicapped Children Act of 1974 (PL 94–142, discussed in the following section).

[27]Waldfogel, *What Children Need*, 112–113.

[28]WRAL.com, "Issue of NC Poverty, Need at Forefront of Pre-K Debate," March 1, 2012, http://www.wral.com/news/state/nccapitol/story/10799343/.

ESEA's primary focus was federal assistance to school districts serving low-income students (Title I). The act also included grants for library resources, education research and training, and for state departments of education. Title I was consistent with other elements of the War on Poverty because it focused on low-income populations and sought to bypass recalcitrant state governments perceived as unresponsive to the ethnically diverse populations that had settled in American cities over the previous generation. Title I revenue continues to be the major lever that the federal government possesses for changing educational policy. Still, in 2009–10, federal funding accounted for only a bit over 12 percent of the $594 billion that were spent on elementary and secondary education. The remaining funding is about equally divided between state and local spending.[29]

The primary source of local funding for public schools across the nation is the property tax. This link between local control and property taxes has been the defining feature of the American public school system, deeply embedding other forms of social and economic inequality. With a metropolitan area, one finds gigantic differences in the resources devoted to public education. The fact that the country has over 16,000 independent school districts adds to the fragmentation of public education.[30]

To some extent, state funding, which has increased over time, has played a compensatory role in reducing inequalities across districts. The state constitution in some states requires courts to take an aggressive role in reducing inequalities; while in other states, this has been left to the horse-trading of state legislators. Even in states that have a constitutional requirement, however, it has been difficult to translate the court decision into legislative action. Apparently, although there are many reasons why legislators representing affluent districts would resist efforts at equalization, opposition has often been "racial and ideological rather than simply driven by perceived economic self-interest."[31]

The federal government's changing role

The federal government's role in education has generally shifted with reauthorizations of the ESEA. The most notable recent reform was the No Child Left Behind Act (NCLB, PL 107–110) passed by Congress and signed by President George W. Bush in 2001. Given the current polarization of American politics, it is remarkable that the act was proposed by a Republican president, cosponsored by two Democrats (including Senator Edward Kennedy) and two Republicans (including the Speaker of the House during the 112th Congress), and passed with overwhelming bipartisan votes in both Houses of Congress.

What is even more remarkable is that a conservative president would propose a dramatic expansion of the federal government into policymaking at the local level. NCLB mandated all public schools (including public charter schools) to conduct standardized testing annually for all students. The results of these tests are used to determine a school's "annual yearly progress" (AYP). The AYP is used, in turn, to determine the amount of Title I funding that a school receives. In addition, school districts are required to provide alternative school choices to students in schools that fail to achieve their AYP standard.

No Child Left Behind has served to reinforce a variety of trends in public education at the state and local levels. First, there has been a widely held perception that existing educational systems—particularly large urban systems—were incapable of generating

[29]Mark Dixon, *Public Education Finances: 2010* (Washington, DC: Census Bureau, 2012), xi, http://www2.census.gov/govs/school/10f33pub.pdf.

[30]Dixon, *Public Education Finances.*

[31]Douglas S. Reed, "Court-Ordered School Finance Equalization: Judicial Activism and Democratic Opposition," in *Developments in School Finance, 1996,* ed. William J. Fowler, Jr. (National Center for Education Statistics, 1997), 97, http://nces.ed.gov/pubs97/97535g.pdf.

reform without external pressure. This incapacity is often attributed to the strength of school bureaucracies and of teachers unions. Second, the reliance on high-stakes standardized tests has become an increasingly popular education reform since at least the 1980s. Third, the NCLB has encouraged school districts to expand school choice.[32]

School choice is an elastic concept. In its narrowest formulation, it requires school districts not to restrict students to a single school, typically defined by district boundaries. At its broadest, advocates of *school vouchers* have argued that a larger share of school funding should be devoted to providing students and parents with a voucher that they can use at any public, private, or religious school. Although the use of public funding for religious schools raises a number of Constitutional questions, the Supreme Court has affirmed its constitutionality in several cases over the past decade.[33]

A less controversial direction of school choice policymaking has been the development of *public charter schools*. Public charters represent independent schools—organized as either nonprofit or for-profit entities—that receive public funding based on the number of students from a particular school district who attend them. Although critics worry that public charters ultimately have an adverse effect on public systems—by siphoning off funds and more highly motivated students and parents—they have remained generally popular.[34]

What is not open to dispute is that local geography continues to be the primary determinant of a student's chances of getting a decent education. Although school choice has proliferated and remains politically popular, there is little evidence to demonstrate that public charters consistently provide a better education for students.[35] Given the other barriers encountered by poor children, current debates over public school reform seem to be driven more by concerns about "who gets what" than by the effectiveness of one type of school or another in mitigating these barriers.

As charter and private schools have siphoned off more students, public districts have cut programs and closed schools. The students most affected by cuts and closures have often mobilized to resist these cuts.

---

[32]Mike Rose, "The Mismeasure of Teaching and Learning: How Contemporary School Reform Fails the Test," *Dissent* (Spring 2011), http://dissentmagazine.org/article/?article=3912.

[33]Linda Greenhouse, "The Supreme Court, 5-4, Upholds Voucher System That Pays Religious Schools' Tuition," *New York Times*, June 28, 2002, http://www.nytimes.com/2002/06/28/us/supreme-court-school-tuition-supreme-court-5-4-upholds-voucher-system-that-pays.html?pagewanted=all&src=pm.

[34]Sherman Dorn, "The Different Meanings of 'Public,'" http://shermandorn.com/wordpress/?p=4930.

[35]Ron Zimmer, Brian Gill, Kevin Booker, Stephane Lavertu, Tim R. Sass, and John Witte, *Charter Schools in Eight States: Effects on Achievement, Attainment, Integration, and Competition* (Santa Monica, CA: Rand Corporation, 2009).

Ultimately, public education is the perfect expression of the "other people's children" philosophy discussed earlier. Rather than serving as an instrument that compensates for the manifold inequities faced by poor children, public schools serve to reinforce those divisions by assuring that well-off children enjoy safe, supportive, and resource-rich educational experiences; while poor children must cope with dangerous school grounds, metal detectors, dilapidated infrastructure, and resource-strapped professionals. While the realities of public systems make it clear why many low-income parents are attracted to school choice, it is not clear that their increased satisfaction will translate into improved life chances for their children.

Special education

The other major involvement of the federal government in public school education relates to educational opportunities for children with disabilities. The history of treatment is filled with efforts to stigmatize and segregate children with disabilities. Some of the worst abuses—like the mass labeling of children as "feeble-minded"—subsided by the 1970s. Still, in 1975, when the Education of All Handicapped Children Act was passed, more than one million children were excluded from public schools because of a physical disability (including sight and hearing loss) or mental disability (most often, a developmental disability), and another 3.5 million were segregated in separate facilities with limited educational resources.[36] The act has been reauthorized several times, most recently in 2004, and is now known as the Individuals with Disabilities Education Improvement Act.[37]

The core of IDEA is straightforward:

(1) (A) to ensure that all children with disabilities have available to them a free appropriate public education that emphasizes special education and related services designed to meet their unique needs and prepare them for further education, employment, and independent living;

(B) to ensure that the rights of children with disabilities and parents of such children are protected; and

(C) to assist States, localities, educational service agencies, and Federal agencies to provide for the education of all children with disabilities;

(2) to assist States in the implementation of a statewide, comprehensive, coordinated, multidisciplinary, interagency system of early intervention services for infants and toddlers with disabilities and their families;

(3) to ensure that educators and parents have the necessary tools to improve educational results for children with disabilities by supporting system improvement activities; coordinated research and personnel preparation; coordinated technical assistance, dissemination, and support; and technology development and media services; and

(4) to assess, and ensure the effectiveness of, efforts to educate children with disabilities.[38]

---

[36]Jane West, *Back to School on Civil Rights: Advancing the Federal Commitment to Leave No Child Behind* (Washington, DC: National Council on Disability, 2000), 6.

[37]For a time, the act was called the Individuals with Disabilities Education Act. Although the most recent reauthorization has added the word "Improvement" to its title, it is still know as IDEA.

[38]PL108–446 (2004), http://www.copyright.gov/legislation/pl108-446.pdf.

IDEA requires all public school systems that accept funding under the act to create an Individualized Education Program (IEP) for each eligible student. The IEP must take into consideration the student's limitations and lay out educational goals in the "least restrictive environment." The IEP also identifies the special services that the student requires. The act also provides oversight of disciplinary actions involving a student with disabilities to assure that her disability is taken into consideration. It also specifies a set of parental rights, including the right to review all educational records; to be equal partners in developing the IEP; and to file complaints, seek mediation, or seek a due process hearing.

IDEA also mandates the establishment of *early intervention programs* for children with disabilities during their first three years of life. In contrast to the IEP, which focuses exclusively on the needs of the child, the Individualized Family Service Plan (IFSP) associated with early intervention is designed to consider the needs of both the child and her family.[39]

Although federal legislation has gone a long way toward assuring that children with disabilities are not excluded from the public education system, IDEA continues to generate controversy. Despite the $14 billion federal contribution to the funding of special education in 2009–(states contributed an additional $16.7 billion), the rights granted under the legislation are only a partially funded mandate that places potentially large burdens on state and local agencies. Particularly in low-income districts, which have a larger proportion of special education students and fewer financial resources, spending on special education is often seen as drawing funds away from the general public school population. As public charter schools are more likely to enroll non–special education students, this fiscal competition is likely to become more acute.

Although parents of children with disabilities have much greater say in their children's educational program than other parents, these legal rights are not always observed in practice. Parents who are more effective advocates for their children (or who have access to advocacy services) are likely to be more successful in gaining the services they desire than other parents. Again, particularly in large, low-income districts, many parents (especially low-income parents) are likely to be unsatisfied with the alternatives they are offered for their children.[40]

Social workers in public education

Historically, social workers have played a minor role in public education, but in recent decades this has begun to change. As districts have come to understand that many of the challenges faced by teachers and administrators have their origins outside of the school building, they have shown an increased willingness to employ social workers. Still, in 2008–10, only 4 percent of all social workers were employed in elementary and secondary education, where they made up only 0.4 percent of the labor force.[41] Indeed, social

[39]"Early Intervention Program for Infants and Toddlers With Disabilities" *Federal Register* 76, no. 188 (September 28, 2011), http://www.gpo.gov/fdsys/pkg/FR-2011-09-28/html/2011-22783.htm.

[40]This problem is exacerbated by the persistence of the disproportionate representation of African American children in special education populations, despite efforts to address it at the federal, state, and local level. Russell J. Skiba, Ada B. Simmons, Shana Ritter, Ashley C. Gibb, M. Karega Rausch, Jason Cuadrado, and Choong-Geun Chung, "Achieving Equity in Special Education: History, Status, and Current Challenges," *Exceptional Children* 74, no. 3 (2008): 264–288, http://www.indiana.edu/~equity/docs/exceptionalchildren.pdf.

[41]Author's calculation from Steven Ruggles, J. Trent Alexander, Katie Genadek, Ronald Goeken, Matthew B. Schroeder, and Matthew Sobek, *Integrated Public Use Microdata Series: Version 5.0* [Machine-readable database] (Minneapolis: University of Minnesota, 2010).

workers are more likely to interact with public education systems because of their work with particular populations—children with disabilities, children involved in the child welfare system—for which schools are one of many institutions with which they must interact.

Child Welfare and Child Protective Services

In a good society, *child welfare* (like the term *welfare* itself) would not carry a negative connotation. Yet in contemporary American society, the structure of services for children—including foster care, adoption, social services, and child protective services—does carry a negative connotation. On the one hand, child welfare and protective services bear sweeping responsibilities for assuring that America's children are safe and provided with the resources they need to develop and flourish. On the other hand, these services are delivered by systems that have such a low level of functionality that, over the past decade, a majority of states have entered into consent decrees in response to class action suits against the responsible agencies.[42]

The care of children who are not living with their parents is not a new phenomenon. In 1850, more than 6 percent of children under the age of 14 lived with neither parent. This percentage fell as low as 3.1 percent in 1970 before rising to 6 percent by the 2010 census. In the nineteenth century, most children not living with their parents lived with other relatives or nonrelatives, with only a few living in institutions. In 1850, for example, 19 percent lived with a grandparent, 15 percent with a sibling, and 24 percent with another relative. The 39 percent who lived with a nonrelative were typically boarders entering the "semiautonomous" state that many youths experienced in the nineteenth century. By 2010 the distribution had changed; a majority of young people not living with a parent were living with grandparents (53 percent) or other relatives (26 percent). The percent in institutions stood at 1.6 percent, considerably below the 1850 figure of 2.7 percent.[43]

Of course, the reasons for not living with one's parents have changed considerably over the past two centuries. Through the eighteenth and early nineteenth centuries, many of these children had been orphaned while others had been indentured or apprenticed. Indeed, in the eighteenth century, parents who had become dependent on the poor laws often were separated from their children who might be indentured as a way of compensating the town.

During the nineteenth century, two great changes influenced the treatment of children not in their parents' care. First, orphanages were among the many other institutions "invented" during the early and middle of the century. These institutions were the home to "half-orphans" whose surviving parent often did not have the means to support them. Indeed, the poor often turned to these institutions during periods of economic emergency or if a child were "incorrigible" and needed greater discipline or surveillance than the parent could provide.[44]

---

[42]Amy Kosanovich and Rachel Molly Joseph, "Child Welfare Consent Decrees: Analysis of Thirty-Five Court Actions from 1995–2005," Child Welfare League of America, http://www.cwla.org/advocacy/consentdecrees.pdf.

[43]Author's calculation from Steven Ruggles, J. Trent Alexander, Katie Genadek, Ronald Goeken, Matthew B. Schroeder, and Matthew Sobek, *Integrated Public Use Microdata Series: Version 5.0* [Machine-readable database] (Minneapolis: University of Minnesota, 2010).

[44]Timothy Hacsi, *Second Home: Orphan Asylums and Poor Families in America* (Cambridge: Harvard University Press, 1998).

Second, other forms of institutionalization proved more popular than the institutional confinement of children. By the middle of the century, Charles Loring Brace of the New York Children's Aid Society (CAS) developed an alternative approach to dependent children. Instead of institutionalization, Brace proposed that the children be taken to the countryside where they would be "adopted" by families. He reasoned that the labor needs of farmers would provide a strong economic reason for their participation. Between 1853 and 1929, the CAS relocated over 100,000 children.

The CAS experience with fostering young people anticipated many of the problems that would afflict the modern child welfare system. First, the CAS articulated a strong "child saving" philosophy, with a mission to rescue children from the bad influences of their parents and community. Second, although the CAS claimed to supervise its placements, it never had enough agents to do the job. As a result, abused and runaway children were not unknown.

The contemporary child welfare system was built on this nineteenth-century foundation as well as the Progressive Era's suspicions about "child rescue" and its preference for more family-like institutional settings. After the founding of the Children's Bureau in 1912, the federal government played several roles: first, by promoting policy and practice to states and localities; second, by administration of maternal and child health programs during the 1920s (Sheppard-Towner); and, finally, after the enactment of Social Security, by administration of both child welfare and health programs.[45]

The ambivalence noted by Brace has continued to influence swings in federal and state policy. During the past 20 years, it has influenced two major swings in child welfare policy. In 1993, Congress created the Family Preservation and Support Service Program to support state and local child welfare systems in expanding services to keep children with their parents. Four years later, it enacted the Adoption and Safe Families Act, which sought to give primacy to the "safety of the child" and increased the ability of child welfare agencies to terminate parental rights as a means of accelerating adoptions.[46]

Child protective services refer to programs designed to investigate and take necessary action in cases of child abuse and neglect; while the child welfare system addresses a wider range of issues including foster care, adoption, and supportive services for families and children. Although the two systems are separate, they have many connections, primarily because foster care is one of the most common outcomes of substantiated cases of child abuse and neglect.

The two systems were not clearly differentiated until the 1960s, when the issue of child abuse and neglect gained salience with the "discovery" of the *battered-child syndrome* by Murray Kempe in 1962. The medicalization of child abuse as a syndrome proved very attractive to state legislatures. Spurred to action by public outcry and the issuance of a model reporting law by the federal Children's Bureau in 1963, all 50 states passed *mandatory reporting* laws by 1968. These laws required health care providers, educators, social workers, and others in professional contact with children to report possible incidents of abuse or neglect to child welfare authorities.[47] These were followed in 1974 by the first national child protection legislation, the Child Abuse Prevention and Treatment Act (CAPTA). Barbara Nelson, in her study of the emergence of child abuse as a public

[45]Michael B. Katz, *In the Shadow of the Poorhouse: A Social History of Welfare In America*, 10th anniversary ed. (New York: Basic Books, 1996), 149–150.

[46]Jane Waldfogel, *The Future of Child Protection: How to Break the Cycle of Abuse and Neglect* (Cambridge: Harvard University Press, 1998).

[47]Waldfogel, *The Future of Child Protection*, 72.

problem, explains the rapid innovation in state and federal policy in three ways. First, the issue had *valence*, that is, there was general agreement that child abuse was a bad thing that something should be done about. Second, the issue was narrowly framed as a problem of battered children (rather than the much broader issue of all abuse and neglect). Finally, the idea of mandatory reporting offered a straightforward solution to the problem.[48]

Although child welfare and protective services have been driven by federal policy, the actual delivery of services is quite diverse. Some states provide services directly through state departments, while others serve only an oversight role, with actual services being provided by county or city departments. In some places, nonprofit organizations have an extensive role in providing services, while in others, most are provided by public employees. In the past decade, law enforcement has been drawn into the investigation of child abuse, sometimes independently and sometimes in collaboration with child welfare workers.

Funding for child welfare and protective services comes from diverse sources that often determine what services are available and for whom. Federal funding was originally provided under Title V of the Social Security Act. In 1958, for the first time, states were required to match federal contributions, which were subject to Congressional appropriations. In 1967, Title V was converted into IV-B—Child Welfare Services. States were required to provide 25 percent of the funding, and the total size of the program remained capped and subject to Congressional authorization.

Meanwhile, federal and state actions in two other areas greatly expanded federal funding for these services. Beginning in the 1960s, the federal government allowed states to seek compensation for dependent children in foster care as an entitlement—that is, as an open-ended percent of state costs. This foster care spending under Title IV-A was given its own program (Title IV-E) but remained an entitlement directed at children from AFDC recipient or eligible families.[49]

In the meantime, spending on general social services was undergoing a revolution. The 1962 Public Welfare Amendments included a commitment that the federal government would provide 75 percent of the cost of any approved services for welfare recipients or those "likely to become" welfare recipients, although they neglected to specify what social services were covered. Beginning with California in 1967, state officials discovered that the title provided an open-ended source of funding for a wide variety of services. After five years in which spending for social services had grown by less than $100 million, between 1967 and 1972, spending under these programs increased from $282 million to $1.69 billion.[50]

Eventually, this spending was converted to a single title—Title XX—of the Social Security Act. In 1981 the Omnibus Budget Reconciliation Act converted Title XX into the Social Services Block Grant (SSBG). The SSBG provides states with much more flexibility in allocating funding than the child welfare titles. However, this flexibility means that child welfare must compete with a variety of other potential uses of the funding. Of total SSBG spending in 2009, foster care and child protective services accounted for

---

[48]Barbara J. Nelson, *Making an Issue of Child Abuse: Political Agenda Setting for Social Problems* (Chicago: University of Chicago Press, 1984).

[49]Child Welfare League of America, "Overview of Title IV-E Foster Care Program," http://www.cwla.org/advocacy/overviewtitleIV-E.htm.

[50]Martha Derthick, *Uncontrollable Spending for Social Services Grants* (Washington, DC: Brookings Institution, 1975).

13 and 10 percent, respectively; while day care, services for people with disabilities, and case management accounted for 14, 11, and 8 percent of total spending.[51]

The fragmentation of child welfare spending certainly functions as a strain on the system. State and local officials face the daunting task of deciding what types of spending can be allocated to which federal programs and how most efficiently to use state dollars. The open-ended nature of foster care funding through Title IV-E may have distorted how states treated at-risk children.[52]

Certainly, the spending morass is emblematic of deeper problems within the child welfare system. As Jane Waldfogel pointed out, child protective services are built on the idea that parents are subject to virtually no oversight of their behavior until they "cross the line" by abusing or neglecting their children, at which point they lose a large amount of that autonomy.[53] Drawing a clear line between "good" and "bad" parents flies in the face of virtually all parents' experience. We all hope to be "good" parents but inevitably find ourselves challenged by limits on our knowledge, resources, and patience. I suspect nearly all parents can recall occasions when they felt that they had somehow not met their own definition of a "good" parent, yet would resist being labeled as a "bad" parent.

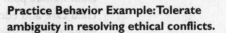

Ethical Practice

Practice Behavior Example: Tolerate ambiguity in resolving ethical conflicts.

Critical Thinking Question: Labeling parents as either "good" or "bad" rarely is a sound basis for intervention, yet, the child welfare system forces workers to act as if it is. What strategies can social workers use to operate ethically in this system?

The problem is compounded by exactly when and how one finds oneself labeled as a bad parent. When child abuse first became an issue, one of the features that invited public policy action was the clear and limited definition about what it is and how it should be addressed. Using mandatory reporting to address the battered-child syndrome promised the straightforward identification of problems and effective policy responses to them. Yet with only a minority of cases involving physical abuse, the promise of "clean" policy was a mirage. If anything, shifts in welfare policy (see Chapter 8) have made the definition of "neglect" even more difficult as states compel a larger share of poor parents to seek employment, regardless of the availability of adequate child care or subsidies.

In other words, a rational system of child welfare and protective services would incorporate a continuum of care that would fine-tune the services available and its intrusion into parent-child relationships to both the long- and short-term context within which people try to raise their children.

Assess your comprehension of "Policy Responses to the Problems of Children and Youth" **by completing this quiz.**

THE FUTURE OF CHILD WELFARE

Three strategies have dominated public policy around children over the past century: income, services, and asset-building.

Income strategies are based on the belief that many of the problems encountered by poor children are a product of the economic deprivation and "time poverty" of low-income parents who must balance work, family, and their personal life. Given what we know about the impact of poverty on children's development, there is reason to believe that if we reduce poverty, the magnitude of child welfare problems we now face would shrink accordingly.

[51]US Administration for Children and Families, Social Services Block Grant, Annual Report 2009, Chapter 2 (online), http://www.acf.hhs.gov/programs/ocs/ssbg/reports/2009/chapter_2.html.
[52]Howard Jacob Karger and David Stoesz, American Social Welfare Policy: A Pluralist Approach, 5th ed. (Boston: Pearson Allyn-Bacon, 2008), 403.
[53]Waldfogel, Future of Child Protection, 79.

Despite the compelling logic of this argument, there is little prospect of a new war on poverty on the horizon. As discussed earlier in the book, Americans are neither inclined to trust government, nor are they interested in the upfront costs of such a strategy. Perhaps more to the point, the fact is that we can't address child poverty without aiding the parents of poor children. The history of welfare reform since the 1980s suggests that this disconnect—our willingness to let "other people's children" suffer because we stigmatize their parents—will continue to shape welfare and child welfare policy.

Service strategies are based on the theory that if parents and their children were given more support they would function better. As this chapter makes clear, much of child welfare policy is focused on providing an array of services to children ranging from child care and educational services to foster care services, adoption services, and child protective services. Indeed, the large number of services and variety of funding streams appear to remain a severe constraint on the effectiveness of a service strategy. Karger and Stoesz have suggested that the bad interaction between fragmented programs and funding-driven policymaking should be a major focus of reform. Along with Lela Costin, they recommend that a *Children's Authority*—that is, "a local body that would provide a comprehensive array of services under performance-based management"—replace the existing fragmented system.[54]

Certainly, there is room for improvement across the board in the organization of services for children and youth. But it is hard to escape the conclusion that not only would comprehensive reform be a difficult goal to achieve, but that its actual benefits would fall short of its promises. Social services inevitably generate complex systems of interests. Those receiving the service, delivering the service, and funding the service—as well as the myriad intermediaries who sit between the funding and its recipients—all have particular interests in both the way things are and how they'd like to see things changed. Typically, what unites these disparate interests is a belief that expanding services would help fulfill their goals—a consensus that often puts them in conflict with legislators, taxpayers, and the general public. Decades and decades of education reform, for example, have not moved us closer to our presumed goals—unless the ultimate collapse of many urban public school systems is understood to be the unstated goal.

Indeed, if there is one approach to reform that cuts across all of these systems, it is *privatization*. The belief that market discipline can maximize the effective delivery of services, by spurring competition and using the profit motive, has animated many initiatives. Again, the cure is often worse than the disease. If the problem with service delivery is fragmentation and the diverse interests of those involved in a system, then expanding the number of entities and putting them in competition with one another is likely to exacerbate rather than ameliorate those conditions. Here, the expansion of charter schools seems instructive. Although *in theory* school choice would force public systems to innovate in order to compete with charters, the dynamics have not played out that way. Instead, public systems find themselves increasingly burdened with excess capacity, declining budgets, and a student body that has been effectively "creamed" by charter and private schools. Fighting fragmentation with competition promises more fragmentation.

Asset-building strategies are a seemingly new approach to the problems of children. As the name implies, asset-building strategies focus on expanding the capital people have that can be used to acquire other resources. For the past several decades, economists and other social scientists have broadened our ideas about capital. At the very least, we should differentiate financial capital (money and other goods convertible into money)

---

[54]Karger and Stoesz, *American Social Welfare Policy*, 411.

from human capital (skills and education that can be used to gain employment) and social capital (connections and access to social networks that can be used to obtain resources).[55]

The idea of financial asset building has been associated with the work of Michael Sherraden, who has been an energetic advocate of *individual development accounts* for several decades.[56] Originally, Sherraden contrasted asset-building strategies to income strategies, but more recently he has seen them as complementary. Still, in contrast to income programs that reinforce dependency, Sherraden suggests that savings accounts for the poor offer a variety of benefits including "increased orientation toward the future, increased self-efficacy, increased civic participation, and improved welfare of offspring."[57]

Asset-based strategies have manifested themselves in a variety of settings. The *microfinance* approach posits that small loans made to poor people to start a business can have a profound impact on their well-being. As founder of the Grameen Bank, Muhammad Yunus won a Nobel Prize for his advocacy of microfinance enterprise.[58] In a number of advanced welfare states, establishing savings accounts for the poor has attracted attention. For example, in 2002 the Labour government in the UK implemented long-term savings accounts for children called a Child Trust Fund. The idea was that the government would make a small initial payment and regular contributions so that when the child reached her 18th birthday she could use the savings for a variety of approved purposes. Unfortunately, when the Conservative-Liberal coalition gained power in 2010, it quickly announced that the government would terminate payments to the accounts.[59] In the United States, the efforts of the Clinton and Bush administrations to increase home ownership can also be seen as an asset-based strategy.

Advocates of asset-based strategies argue that one of their merits is the ability to attract conservative support not amenable to traditional approaches to increasing the resources of poor people. The UK experience suggests that this may not always be the case. Certainly, the financial services industry has often supported plans that hold the promise of increasing its business. In that sense, children's savings accounts might mirror the reception of individual retirement accounts (see Chapter 10). But whether the attractiveness of those commissions will convince conservatives to expand the resources available to the poor still awaits empirical verification.

Children, it is often said, are our future. Yet increasingly our young are growing up in settings that heighten their vulnerability. The institutions we've developed for their education and protection are experiencing tremendous strain, if not outright collapse. Moreover, the politics of age continue to work in favor of the old and against the young. Perhaps even more than the other areas of public policy addressed in this book, child welfare remains a field in which we find it easier to define the problems than to divine their solutions.

Test your understanding and analysis of this chapter by completing the Chapter Review.

---

[55]James S. Coleman, "Social Capital in the Creation of Human Capital," *American Journal of Sociology* 94 Supplement (1988): S95–S120.

[56]Michael W. Sherraden, *Assets and the Poor: A New American Welfare Policy* (Armonk, NY: M.E. Sharpe, 1991).

[57]Michael W. Sherraden, "Assets and Public Policy" in *Inclusion in the American Dream: Assets, Poverty, and Public Policy*, ed. Michael Sherraden (New York: Oxford University Press, 2005), Kindle ed.

[58]Ananya Roy, *Poverty Capital: Microfinance and the Making of Development* (New York and London: Routledge, 2010).

[59]"Child Trust Funds to Be Scrapped," BBC News, May 24, 2010, http://www.bbc.co.uk/news/10146734. In *The Third Lie: Why Government Programs Don't Work and a Blueprint for Change* (Walnut Creek, CA: Left Coast Press, 2011), 81–88, Richard Gelles has made a similar proposal, Futures Accounts, as the cornerstone of his approach to child welfare.

12

Social Workers' Role in Social Welfare Policy

INTRODUCTION

As a profession, social work is committed to "enhancing human well-being" with an emphasis on those who are "vulnerable, oppressed, and living in poverty."[1] Throughout this book, we've identified vulnerable populations in the United States, the role of policy in either reducing or exacerbating conditions of oppression, and alternative ways that policy could address these challenges. In this conclusion, we review the previous chapters and highlight opportunities for social workers to participate in the shaping of policy to address these issues.

As discussed in Chapter 1, we can understand social policy as divided into several different "worlds." The "little world" of policy consists of policymakers and those who seek to influence them. This little world contrasts with the wider policy force field in which thousands of people "make policy" in less formal ways. This "bigger world" ranges from micro-decisions—like an individual worker using discretion in deciding how rules about abuse and neglect apply to the case to which he is assigned—to more visible collective activities—like joining a march in favor of expanding immigrant rights. In this last chapter, we will look more closely at the different ways that social workers might engage in policy practice.

First, a word of caution. There is lots of injustice in the world. You could spend every waking hour addressing social issues and not get to a tenth of them. As we review ways for social workers to become involved in the world of policy, don't take them as a "to-do" list. One of the tricks of being an effective policy practitioner is to

[1]NASW Code of Ethics, http://www.socialworkers.org/pubs/code/code.asp.

reach the right balance of passion and consistency. To marshal the resources necessary to make a difference, you need to care deeply about the issue in question. At the same time, if you commit yourself to too many "causes," then it's unsustainable. You throw yourself into a cause, but even after a few weeks, other parts of your life start to fall apart. You don't get enough sleep and you let your work and personal life slide. Ultimately, you "burn out" and can't continue.

Over the next few pages, we'll lay out literally dozens of potential issues worthy of action. You won't have the ability (or even the desire) to get involved in all of them. Instead, identify a few for which you will be able to sustain a commitment. Some may come from your professional experience; if you work with kids or the elderly or immigrants, you may be moved to address their plight. Others may come from your personal life experience. For example, many women active in feminist causes got involved because of their own experience with sexism. Whatever the source of your issues, think about "right sizing" your passion so that you can sustain commitment over the long haul.

Professional Identity

Practice Behavior Example: Practice personal reflection and self-correction to assure continual professional development.

Critical Thinking Question: What skills might help prevent "burn out" in a social worker faced with multiple, conflicting demands?

SOCIAL WELFARE POLICY AND SOCIAL WORK COMPETENCIES

Since 2008, the curriculum standards for social work programs have stressed a set of core *competencies* that social workers should master by the end of their education. The *10 core competencies* are

- identify as a professional social worker and conduct oneself accordingly;
- apply social work ethical principles to guide professional practice;
- apply critical thinking to inform and communicate professional judgments;
- engage diversity and difference in practice;
- advance human rights and social and economic justice;
- engage in research-informed practice and practice-informed research;
- apply knowledge of human behavior and the social environment;
- engage in policy practice to advance social and economic well-being and to deliver effective social work service;
- respond to contexts that shape practice; and
- engage, assess, intervene, and evaluate with individuals, families, groups, organizations, and communities.[2]

Only one of these competencies explicitly discusses policy. It focuses on policy practice to advance well-being and deliver effective services. The policy statement goes on to focus on two skill areas in policy practice. First, social workers should be able to "analyze, formulate, and advocate" good policy. Second, they should be able to "collaborate with colleagues and clients" to advance this goal.

Yet if we look at all of the competencies as they are elaborated, we can see that many play a critical role in social workers' engagement with policy. For example, as part of identifying oneself as a social worker, the policy statement sees advocating for client

---

[2]"Education Policy and Accreditation Standards," Council of Social Work Education, http://www.cswe.org/File.aspx?id=13780.

access to services as a critical element, which is part of the "bigger world" of policy. Along similar lines, it is difficult to conform with the code of ethics of the profession without translating one's values into policy advocacy.

Critical Thinking

Critical thinking—the process of reflective reasoning about one's beliefs and actions—is clearly important in all aspects of social work practice. However, it's especially important in pursuing policy practice. Not only must we consider how a particular policy might affect our clients, we must consider the range of factors that could influence whether its implementation overall will have the desired effect. *Unintended consequences*—impacts that were not considered when a policy was adopted—are common. One could argue that unintended consequences are more the rule than the exception. Sometimes, as we advocate for a particular policy, our enthusiasm prevents us from considering the full range of possible consequences.

Take the example of rental housing policy for extremely low-income families (Chapter 6), which touches on competencies concerning *engaging difference* as well as *advancing social and economic justice*. If we consider policy only from the standpoint of social justice, we could argue that public housing models are obviously a good idea because the very poor are most in need of better housing. Yet, this shift in policy had the consequence of increasing racial and economic segregation, as the population of public housing projects became uniformly poor and African American or Latino. Since the 1990s, one could argue that housing policy has become less just because it has encouraged the construction of housing for families with moderate incomes. Yet, at the same time, these market-mix models have become more successful in creating livable neighborhoods. As in the case of clinical practice, critical thinking is crucial to assessing the intended and unintended consequences of policy.

Research and Evaluation

Hopefully, this text has made a strong case for the value of research. Systematic social investigation is critical during virtually all parts of the policy process. When one is trying to identify a social problem and get it onto the public agenda, research is a critical part of the process. More applied research is often needed to influence a change in policy. For example, one needs to know who is likely to support *and* who is likely to oppose a policy. Following Sun-Tzu's advice to "keep your friends close, and your enemies closer," one frequently must pay more attention to neutralizing opponents than to mobilizing supporters.[3] For those lucky enough to succeed in changing a policy, they must then undertake evaluation to make sure the policy is succeeding or, if not, to suggest modifications.

Policy evaluation has evolved into a highly technical field. Not many years ago, evaluation consisted simply of looking at a before-and-after comparison to see if the policy worked. Over time, evaluators have come to

Critical Thinking

Practice Behavior Example: Distinguish, appraise, and integrate multiple sources of knowledge, including research-based knowledge and practice wisdom.

Critical Thinking Question: Can you identify other examples from previous chapters where a policy was undermined by unanticipated factors?

[3]"Sun-Tzu," The Quotations Page, http://www.quotationspage.com/quotes/Sun-tzu/.

understand that the very act of studying the implementation of a policy influences its outcomes. As a result, policy analysts increasingly have focused on *social experiments* as the "gold standard" of policy evaluation. In these experiments, subjects (typically individuals) are *randomly assigned* either to the experimental or the control group, and the difference in outcomes between the two is determined to be the impact of the policy change. For example, before welfare reform was enacted, many experiments were conducted to test its new features. What combination of incentives and sanctions were most likely to increase the employment and income of recipients? Would reduced payments to parents whose children missed school result in increased school attendance?

Designing and implementing social experiments typically are the work of trained evaluators. However, social work practitioners are often the caseworkers charged with carrying out the research protocol, a fact that could raise ethical concerns. Should the worker try to "game" the system so that clients who, in the worker's professional judgment, would benefit from the experimental conditions get placed in that group? Or should the worker have faith that the experiment needs to remain truly random to determine if the experimental conditions are effective or not?

> **Research-Based Practice**
>
> **Practice Behavior Example: Comprehend quantitative and qualitative research and understand scientific and ethical approaches to building knowledge.**
>
> ---
>
> **Critical Thinking Question:** In the past, practitioners have sometimes worked to subvert the implementation of social experiments. How might a fuller understanding of research methods allow social workers to synthesize their practice knowledge with scientific inquiry?

Human Behavior and the Social Environment

Knowledge of human behavior and the social environment sometimes seems very distant from social policy. As noted in Chapter 4, many fields of social policy have been taken over by economists who impose a narrow idea about human motivations and behaviors. We've discussed concepts like "moral hazard" probably more than most readers would like. In reality, if people acted only to advance their own self-interest or increase their own pleasure—as many economic theories postulate—few people would care for a sick relative, contribute to charity, or risk taking a political position that might anger an employer or neighbor. The fact that all of these things actually happen suggests that, in order to make sense of policy, we need a broader understanding of what moves people to act and think in particular ways.

The final two core competencies relate to "responding to context" and the basic social work approach to "engage, assess, intervene, and evaluate." These might seem to be straightforward practice skills with little relevance for policy. Yet if we think through the "value added" by social workers to policy debates, it lies specifically in these areas of practice. As we noted in our discussion of poverty (Chapter 4), many years ago policymakers looked to social workers for advice on policy because of these practice skills and experience. Over the years, the flashy skills of policy analysts, economists, and others supplanted social work, to some extent because social workers did not keep up with these professions by honing their analytical skills. As a result, many policy discussions go forward with little real knowledge of the lives and people they affect. Social work has an imperative to use its practice skills to reenter policy debates on a wider range of social welfare issues. We need critical thinking and research, but if we are to pursue the enhanced human well-being that is our professional responsibility, we also need to develop an understanding of the causes and consequences of policy.

TYPES OF POLICY ENGAGEMENT

Policy Practice

Practice Behavior Example: Collaborate with colleagues and clients for effective policy action.

Critical Thinking Question: Each type of policy engagement requires a different set of skills and collaborations. What are the significant constituencies that are relevant for each type of policy engagement?

Before we turn to specific fields of policy where social workers could make a difference, we will discuss four different modes of policy engagement: conventional or mainstream policy practice, grassroots political engagement, social movements, and organizational policymaking.

Conventional or Mainstream Policy Practice

Conventional policy practice relates to a set of activities focused on the "little world" of policy. Using the *process model* discussed in Chapter 2, these activities usually relate to problem identification, the development of policy option, lobbying policymakers, monitoring policy implementation, or evaluating its impact.

Historically, social workers' role in mainstream policy practice has focused on *problem identification*. Because many social work jobs are on the front lines of fields, social workers often are among the first to perceive a new social situation that calls for action. In political terms, therefore, social workers can have a role in *agenda setting*, that is, identifying the social problems on which government and the voluntary sector need to focus.[4]

Many of us think of problem identification as a nonpolitical, objective process. It's as if the problem exists "out there" and the only job of the social worker is *discovering* it. Yet social problems are, in fact, socially constructed through interaction and conflict between different groups. Sometimes problems that are common and obvious go unnoticed. During the 1950s, for example, barely anyone paid attention to poverty, although 25 to 30 percent of the population had very low incomes.[5] At other points, a nonexistent problem becomes the basis for sweeping legislation. In 2011–12, in spite of the fact that in a handful of cases at best over the previous decade did someone try to impersonate a registered voter, a number of states passed "voter identification" laws that required registered voters to present photo IDs in order to vote. As a result, in the November 2012 election, several hundred thousand voters found themselves challenged at the polls because they didn't have a driver's license or passport. In this case, attacking a "social problem" that did not exist created a whole new one.[6]

Assess your comprehension of "Conventional or Mainstream Policy Practice" by completing this quiz.

Grassroots Political Engagement

Grassroots political engagement works at the boundary between the "big" and "little" worlds of policymaking. It might consist of working on a campaign around a particular issue—going door-to-door to talk with citizens, attending community meetings or, less formally, just talking about social welfare issues with your friends and family. For years I've told my fall-semester policy class that my indicator of "success" for the class is if the students can win arguments with their relatives about public assistance or Social Security

---

[4]John W. Kingdon, *Agendas, Alternatives, and Public Policies*, updated ed. (New York: Longman, 2003).

[5]Mark J. Stern, "Poverty and the Life-Cycle, 1940–1960," *Journal of Social History* 24, no. 3 (Spring 1991): 521–540.

[6]Nate Silver, "Measuring the Effects of Voter Identification Laws," *New York Times*, July 15, 2012, http://fivethirtyeight.blogs.nytimes.com/2012/07/15/measuring-the-effects-of-voter-identification-laws/.

at Thanksgiving. Honestly, I haven't ever evaluated my success by that standard, but it points to the importance of correcting myths and misinformation that often prevent good policy proposals from gaining support.

Social Movements

As noted in Chapter 3, social movements have been one of the moving forces in the history of social welfare. Social movements focus on changing both the dominant ideas that drive social policy and the institutions that result from those ideas. Involvement in a social movement can range from showing up for a big demonstration to organizing and leading a demonstration or other form of collective action. We often think about social movements as big and public, but plenty of planning and low-key activities are essential to building a successful movement.

Although demonstrations and high-profile stunts loom large in our historical memory of the early women's movement, in fact small groups that focused on "consciousness raising" were a critical part of the movement's origins. Activities whose purpose is to create a new way of thinking that challenges the conventional wisdom are critical to a social movement. Indeed, Manuel Castells has gone so far as to suggest that women's change in consciousness about their own power—even without their supporting of a specific political agenda—was an important dimension of feminism.[7]

Organizational Policymaking

Once a law is passed, a policy passes through many hands before it is implemented and actually affects people's lives. In Chapter 9, we examined the role of federal regulation writing on the disability rights movement. A similar process can happen at the state or local level as well. Government officials take the general idea of a law and translate it into rules governing behavior. Ultimately, a social agency will receive all of these regulations and be responsible for providing services that conform with the new set of rules and procedures. But even here, the agency may still have a fair amount of discretion in deciding how the policy will be implemented.[8]

As we've noted, social workers are in a position to play the role of frontline workers in addressing social problems. Often the policies that are supposed to guide our work are ambiguous and leave room for professional discretion. This ambiguity provides one way that all social workers are involved in "policymaking," often on a daily basis.

This is not always easy. Most social agencies operate in a state of chronic fiscal crisis, in which its responsibilities far outstrip its financial resources. Increasingly, social agency leadership tends to be drawn from business or public administration, so efficiency and conformity often take priority over advancement of human well-being.

Organizational policymaking can take a variety of forms. Staff meetings may provide an opportunity for clarifying the gap between an agency's mission, policy constraints,

---

[7]Manuel Castells, *The Power of Identity* vol. III of *The Information Age: Economy, Society, and Culture,* 2nd ed. (Malden, MA: Blackwell, 2004), 235–261.

[8]Jeffrey L. Pressman and Aaron Wildavsky, *Implementation: How Great Expectations in Washington Are Dashed in Oakland; or Why It's Amazing that Federal Programs Work At All, This Being a Saga of the Economic Development Administration as Told by Two Sympathetic Observers Who Seek to Build Morals on a Foundation of Ruined Hopes* (Berkeley: University of California, 1984) is the classic study of how the implementation process can shift the focus and effectiveness of a policy.

and actual procedures. Somewhat covert steps may sometimes allow a worker to advocate for particular clients. At the extreme, professional ethics might require a worker to
resist or refuse to follow orders.[9]

Organizational policymaking can be an effective approach, however, only if social
workers understand the broader policy environment in which their program operates.
Do budget decisions at the state or at the local level drive decision-making? Are the policies being challenged in court? Even though most of their day-to-day work may be clinical practice, knowing the broader landscape will allow social workers to become more
effective professionals.

POLICY PRACTICE OPPORTUNITIES

Throughout this book, we've focused on where social workers could enter into policy processes as part of their professional practice. They range from conventional
policy practice activities like lobbying to grassroots engagement, involvement in
social movements, and advocating within one's agency to change how policies are
implemented.

Food

The United States is an affluent country that is able to produce enough food to feed a
significant share of the world's population. Yet, as a nation, we face two social welfare
challenges associated with food.

Our first nutritional problem is that food insecurity remains a reality for many citizens. Although hunger and starvation are relatively rare in the United States, many citizens have days during the year when they aren't sure if they will have access to food.
Although some conservatives have attempted to trivialize this uncertainty, it can have
significant behavioral and psychological impacts on adults and children.

Among the behavioral effects of food insecurity is the other nutritional problem we
face: obesity. The proportion of the population that is significantly overweight continues
to rise, and members of low-income families are over-represented among the obese. Poor
people are subject to the same forces that are driving obesity in the general population—
increasing consumption of food outside the home, highly refined and engineered food
that hides its calorie content, and the lack of healthy choices. In addition, low-income
families face the need to maximize the number of calories they purchase for a dollar to
make their budgets stretch further.

The mainstream politics of nutrition policy are not easily accessible to social workers. The odd relationship between urban and rural legislators is likely to continue to
maintain support for SNAP/Food Stamps, WIC, and the school lunch program. At the
local level, many cities have moved to include more nutritional information on restaurant
menus. Increasing access to fresh food and reducing "food deserts" by promoting supermarket construction in low-income neighborhoods deserve social workers' support.

The two most prevalent grassroots approaches to food insecurity draw a sharp contrast. The expansion of food banks and feeding programs, on the one hand, and efforts to
expand "alternative food systems," on the other, appeal to different aspects of the social

---

[9]George Brager and Stephen Holloway, *Changing Human Service Organizations: Politics and Practice*
(New York: Free Press, 2002), 157–205.

worker's professional identity. Food banks provide social workers with the concrete experience of offering help to people in need, while alternative food systems appeal to a more abstract desire to shift our entire paradigm for thinking about nutrition.

Each approach has its drawbacks. Critics of food banks see them as reinforcing traditional notions of charity rather than empowering clients. Although alternative food systems promise a radical shift in our society's relationship to food, so far that message has been confined to a relatively affluent set of "foodies" who have enough time and money to afford the higher costs associated with organic and locally grown food.

Neither of these reservations is absolute. There is no reason why food banks and feeding programs can't be connected to change efforts that promote clients' empowerment and autonomy. Although community-supported agriculture faces barriers in enlisting low-income participants, the expanses of vacant land in many urban neighborhoods and the psychological rewards of growing food—along with the rather widespread practice of urban community gardening—may encourage broader participation in the future. Both of these sectors provide opportunities for social workers to engage in community practice that can have broader policy implications.

Housing and Community Development

The historical role of social work in the fields of housing and community development has declined in recent decades. Yet, given the centrality of shelter and social connectedness to social work's mission, it's a field that the profession should not ignore. As with food, opportunities for engagement are most clear at the local, grassroots level.

In 2013, the major challenge facing the nation is the hangover from the collapse of the housing market five years earlier. The proportion of homeowners with mortgages greater than the value of their homes remains high, and uncertainty about addressing the problem continues to act as a drag on housing markets, financial markets, and the construction industry. In the absence of federal action, many localities are proposing their own solutions. In 2012, San Bernardino County, California, considered a plan in which the county would seize houses that are "underwater" through the "right of eminent domain."[10] The proposal provoked strong opposition from the financial services industry, which feared that many companies and investors would lose money under the plan. As gridlock continues in Washington, we can expect to see more local efforts to address foreclosures, and these proposals are likely to be opposed by the deep pockets of the financial services industry. As these proposals emerge, we encourage social workers to stay informed about them and show your support through traditional political activities like letter writing, attending meetings, and voting for candidates that support reasonable ways of moving forward.

Social workers at work in low-income communities especially need to stay informed about the impact of housing strains on their clients. Individuals and families that are homeless or at risk of homelessness may represent only the tip of the iceberg. Many poor Americans lack adequate as well as affordable housing—"a decent home and suitable living environment," as promised by the Housing Act of 1949. Low- to moderate-income

---

[10]Jennifer Medina, "California County Weighs Drastic Plan to Aid Homeowners," *New York Times*, July 14, 2012, http://www.nytimes.com/2012/07/15/us/a-county-considers-rescue-of-underwater-homes.html?_r=1&pagewanted=all. "Eminent domain is an exercise of the power of government or quasi-government agencies (such as airport authorities, highway commissions, community development agencies, and utility companies) to take private property for public use," http://portal.hud.gov/hudportal/HUD?src=/program_offices/public_indian_housing/centers/sac/eminent/.

families struggle to maintain and stay in their homes, often exacerbating mental health problems. They may not *present* as a housing problem, but it is likely to be an important underlying strain.

At a more macro level, your agency should make a point of pulling housing and community development agencies into its institutional network. Doing so will provide referral possibilities for clients who need this help. In addition, these neighborhood-based organizations may sponsor a variety of community-building activities that would allow your agency to play a fuller role in the community.

Read the case study, "Chelsea Green Space and the Power Plant," on using community organizing around community development issues.

Social workers have developed some bad habits in terms of relating to the communities in which they work. They often drive in from a different neighborhood, park in a fenced parking lot, and spend their days in the office. Home visits—in which they reenact the role of "friendly visitor"—may be their only social interaction in the neighborhood. If social workers are to fulfill their professional aspirations, finding new ways to engage and become part of the communities where they work must have a high priority.

Community engagement is particularly important for those working in low-income migrant neighborhoods. Under the best of circumstances, migration is a traumatic experience, and most new immigrants and refugees face unfamiliar and formidable circumstances. Many legal immigrants cannot qualify for income and health programs, and undocumented immigrants have even less access to services. This does not reduce their need, of course. Migrant and immigrant rights advocacy has emerged in recent years as a significant social movement. At the same time, outreach to new Americans in your community can make a significant contribution to the process of social integration.

Social workers work with homeless services, and that presence gives them an opportunity for grassroots policy practice. As noted in Chapter 6, homeless services are shifting from an emphasis on providing temporary shelter to diverting at-risk and currently homeless individuals and families into permanent housing. This can pose an ethical dilemma for social workers because it means shifting money from addressing people's immediate needs to developing better opportunities in the future. Working at the local level to explain the implications of this policy shift to relevant constituencies could help reduce resistance and facilitate a more permanent response to the problem of homelessness.

Health Care

Social workers have a great stake in the health care system. Those working in hospitals know that negotiating with insurers and providers is a major focus of their work. Mental health services, too, are influenced by the availability and comprehensiveness of clients' insurance. Finally, many low-income populations find themselves trapped by their need to maintain coverage under Medicare and Medicaid. TANF recipients who can find only low-wage work risk losing their Medicaid coverage, while people with disabilities fear that pursuing economic independence may threaten their Medicare coverage.

For narrow professional reasons as well as broader ethical concerns, social workers have a great stake in supporting the implementation of the Affordable Care Act (ACA). When it goes into effect, health care reform will expand coverage for low- and moderate-income individuals and families and limit the ability of insurers to drop coverage because of preexisting conditions or to impose lifetime limits on coverage. The ACA also promises finally to achieve mental health parity so that mental health services enjoy the same coverage as physical health services.

Social workers need to be actively involved in assuring that health care reform moves forward. The scope of possible policy practice on health care is incredibly broad. The Supreme Court decision on Medicaid, which gives states the right to opt out of its expansion, means that lobbying, letter writing, rallying, and supporting pro-reform candidates will be of particular importance in states that refuse to expand their program.

The National Association of Social Workers (NASW) has taken a strong position in defense of the Affordable Care Act, filing *amicus curiae* (friend of the court) briefs in the Supreme Court cases on the individual mandate and Medicaid expansion.[11] With the Medicaid decision, NASW state chapters will now have to mobilize advocacy efforts as well.

Opportunities for policy practice around health care extend to one-to-one advocacy as well. Misinformation on the Affordable Care Act now seems to be more common than accurate information. It is likely that thousands of low- and moderate-income individuals who could benefit from the ACA are confused about whether it benefits them. Outreach efforts around using the state exchanges to obtain insurance and subsidies will be critical in accomplishing a central goal of reform—reducing the proportion of the population that is uninsured.

Even if the Affordable Care Act is fully implemented, there will be many health care policy issues on which social workers could focus. Whatever happens in health care over the next generation, social work practice will be influenced by efforts to reduce costs. On the positive side, when focused on making systems more effective, cost concerns can encourage reforms that benefit clients. The ACA includes significant incentives for preventive care, for example, which could encourage insurers and providers to create innovative outreach efforts to detect health conditions earlier. On the negative side, the large disparities that plague American health care will not disappear magically. Again, organization-level policy changes could help reduce these disparities.

Unemployment, Public Assistance, and Job Training

Unemployment, public assistance, and job training are not particularly promising policy fields for social work. Social workers have little "ownership" of these three areas of public policy. If the profession is to have any impact, it will have to happen on the ground—through social movements and professional discretion.

The bipartisan support for welfare reform has survived the breakdown of cooperation on almost every other social welfare issue. In 2012, the Obama administration had to defend itself against charges that it was "gutting welfare reform" because it offered states waivers to allow flexibility in administering TANF.[12]

Since 1996, as noted in Chapter 8, the public assistance system has become remarkably unresponsive to increased need. Although food stamp use skyrocketed after 2008, TANF barely moved up at all. Even those survival systems that emerged since the 1990s have come under attack. General Assistance—a state or county income-tested program for individuals who are not eligible for other public assistance programs—used to be available in almost every state. By the late 1990s, just over 30 states still had a program, most of which had severe restrictions on eligibility and time limits on benefits.

---

[11]"NASW Legal Briefs," National Association of Social Workers, http://www.naswdc.org/advocacy/healthcarereform/legalbriefs.asp.

[12]Trip Gabriel, "Romney Presses Obama on Work in Welfare Law," *New York Times*, August 7, 2012, http://www.nytimes.com/2012/08/08/us/politics/romney-accuses-obama-of-taking-work-out-of-welfare-law.html.

In Pennsylvania, General Assistance had been cut several times through the early 2000s, by which time recipients could receive aid for only three months a year. In very poor neighborhoods in Philadelphia, desperation gave birth to a *recovery house* movement, in which residents pooled their monthly General Assistance checks of $205 and food stamps to provide a roof over their heads, several meals a day, and the hope of a supportive environment for recovery from addiction. In 2012, however, as part of its effort to balance the state budget without raising taxes, the Pennsylvania General Assembly and governor eliminated General Assistance. As a result, the tenuous existence of the recovery houses has been threatened, and the prospect of homelessness among their former residents has increased.[13]

The lack of public outrage at the elimination of General Assistance is striking. We are no longer in an era in which one can gain a public hearing for expanding assistance in mainstream political debates. As discussed in Chapter 4, one role of social movements is to change the ideas and institutions that structure policymaking. It will take this type of mobilization, perhaps over decades, to change the ways that Americans think and act when it comes to public assistance.

The other opportunity for social workers in this policy area is relevant for professionals working in public assistance bureaucracies. As noted in Chapter 8, the new rules around behavioral and work requirements and the sanctions that enforce them have opened up a new area of professional discretion in the administration of TANF and job-training programs. Workers often use that discretion to reduce costs and caseloads while ignoring the needs of clients. In some localities, however, sanctioning has become a vehicle for identifying clients' barriers to independence. To the extent discretion is guided by professional values, rather than bureaucratic imperatives, it can contribute to meaningful policy practice.[14]

Mass Imprisonment

The growth of the American prison population is the nation's number one social justice issue. Whether one agrees with Michelle Alexander or not—that it represents the "new Jim Crow"—mass imprisonment today is damaging entire classes of Americans and absorbing resources that could be used to build, rather than destroy, opportunity and social well-being. Yet the criminal justice system is an institutional setting in which social workers are generally absent. The shift in Americans' ideas about criminal justice—from rehabilitation to punishment—has left little room for the skills and expertise of professional social workers.

The criminal justice system is linked to three separate fields of potential social work practice. Most obviously, prisoners need help coming to terms with their past, surviving in a penal institution, and thinking about their post-release lives. The group that social workers are most likely to encounter are the spouses, significant others, and children of prisoners who are likely to see their material standard of living decline from an already low level. Finally, even as incarceration rates begin to decline, the problems of reentry after incarceration are confronting a larger share of the population.[15]

---

[13]Allyn Gaestel, "Recovery Houses Facing Bleak Future," *Philadelphia Inquirer*, August 20, 2012.

[14]Richard C. Fording, Joe Soss, and Sanford F. Schram, "Devolution, Discretion, and the Effects of Local Political Values on TANF Sanctioning," *Social Service Review* 81, no. 2 (June 2007): 285–316.

[15]"Social Work Within the Correctional System," University of New England, http://socialwork.une.edu/social-work-within-the-correctional-system/.

On the level of conventional politics, we can expect some changes in the near future that will halt, if not reverse, the growth of the population under supervision. The same state budget crises that have led to cuts in health care, social services, and education are encouraging states to slow the expansion of the prison population. In various states, coalitions have mounted campaigns to change laws to restore ex-prisoners' citizenship rights.

If social workers are to have a role in prison reform, however, they will need to find a way back into the criminal justice system. A possible path for doing so is through voluntary services for prisoners. One impact of the rapid growth of prisons has been a decline in the range and quality of services available to prisoners. Between 1979 and 2005, in the average state, the number of professional services staff declined from 70 to 47 per thousand. Even before the decline in staff, only a minority of prisoners could access educational programs, counseling, or drug and alcohol treatment.[16] Now prisoners rarely have access to any of these services.

The expansion of volunteer services within prisons has been one response to the decline in institutional services. Many voluntary services are provided through faith-based programs.[17] Other programs seek to bring prisoners and college students together in classes. For the most part, these programs adopt an individual frame of reference in which the prisoner is asked to see his situation as a product of his bad decisions and behavior.[18]

Social workers are disadvantaged in working with prison populations because of their reduced presence within correctional facilities. Indeed, between 1980 and 2010, the proportion of social workers employed in justice, public order, and safety declined from 7.0 to 3.9 percent of all social workers.[19] Given this situation, it would appear that involvement in volunteer programs might be a starting point for increasing the role of social workers in corrections. Certainly, as "guests" in a setting largely antagonistic to their professional values, social workers cannot expect to be able to bring about sweeping change. However, increasing professional presence—even in a voluntary capacity—might provide a starting point for bringing those values to bear on an institution that has sweeping influence over low-income Americans.

Women and Interpersonal Violence

Interpersonal violence is a topic on which social workers can speak with authority. Addressing the concerns of abused women is central to many social work jobs. Moreover, the profession has sought to advance understanding of the phenomenon and to test the effectiveness of different ways of intervening to reduce abuse and mitigate its effects.

The recent controversy over the Violence Against Women Act (VAWA) provides an opportunity for social workers to use that knowledge to help frame the debate. After several decades in which addressing violence was a bipartisan concern, the 2013 congressional debate over reauthorization showed that the consensus has broken down.

[16]Michele S. Phelps, "The Place of Punishment: Variation in the Provision of Inmate Services Staff across the Punitive Turn," *Journal of Criminal Justice* 40 (2012): 348–357.

[17]Louis B. Cei, "Faith-Based Programs Are Low-Cost Ways to Reduce Recidivism," *Corrections Today* 72, no. 4 (August 2010): 48–51.

[18]Kerry Dunn, "Re-forming the Social: Neoliberal Voluntarism in the Warehouse Prison" (Ph.D. dissertation, University of Pennsylvania, 2009).

[19]Author's calculation from US Census and American Community Survey, Steven Ruggles, J. Trent Alexander, Katie Genadek, Ronald Goeken, Matthew B. Schroeder, and Matthew Sobek, *Integrated Public Use Microdata Series: Version 5.0* [Machine-readable database] (Minneapolis: University of Minnesota, 2010).

In Chapter 4, we discussed the decline in social workers' influence over the debate on poverty and used the idea of *ownership* to describe economists' role in policymaking. The idea of problem definition or policy ownership grows out of a belief that social problems are socially constructed. Rather than being "natural," they are the product of social processes that identify problems and frame solutions. Because society can't focus on all social ills, the emergence of a social problem is characterized by *selectivity*—only certain issues gain widespread recognition—and *competition*—different explanations of the causes and consequences of a social problem compete for attention and legitimation. Often the competition is associated with different groups' *ownership* of the problem, that is, recognition by the wider society that it possesses a unique expertise that provides insight into the problem. For example, if we view domestic violence as a psychological problem of men and women, then psychologists and other helping professions will be able to assert ownership; but if we view violence as essentially a criminal act, lawyers and law enforcement professionals will be able to assert ownership.[20]

The legal revolution around domestic violence has changed what abused women can expect from the law enforcement and criminal justice systems, but it has also underlined the limits of those strategies. Women who are subjected to violence need support to extricate themselves from abusive relationships as well as to cope with any police or court issues that arise from their escape. They also need safe houses, shelters, job and housing referrals, and an opportunity to process the experience.

Although law enforcement and criminal justice professionals now play an important role in defending policies around domestic violence, social work can also make a difference. Drawing on their professional experience in helping women rebuild their lives, social workers can speak with authority about the importance of the services funded by VAWA.

Disability Rights

The future of disability rights provides a similar set of opportunities for social work. Historically, social workers have been central to disability policy. During the expansion of services and programs for people with disabilities, social workers were the frontline workers providing those services. Many social workers were instrumental, as well, to the emergence of the disability rights movement during the 1970s. But as the movement grew, advocates were increasingly antagonistic to the definition of disability as an individual condition and to policies that focused on charity and social welfare instead of rights and independence. Thus, social workers and other helping professionals were often cast as opponents of disability rights because their "helping" had the effect—whether intended or not—of sustaining dependence.

Both the disability rights movement and social work have changed considerably since the 1970s. After winning important victories with Section 504 and the Americans with Disabilities Act, the movement has seen the effectiveness of those laws undermined by a series of court decisions that narrowed the definition of disability and limited the set of accommodations that employers were required to provide. Although the ADA has had an important impact on the ability of people with disabilities to operate independently, it has not achieved significant improvement in their employment opportunities. Meanwhile, social work has paid greater attention to understanding the nature of "helping" and its potential to reduce client autonomy and independence.

[20]Herbert Blumer, "Social Problems as Collective Behavior," *Social Problems* 18, no. 3 (Winter 1971): 298–306; Joseph R. Gusfield, *The Culture of Public Problems: Drinking-Driving and the Symbolic Order* (Chicago: University of Chicago Press, 1981), 10–13.

Now is a good moment for the movement and the profession to reengage. Laws may not be sufficient for people with disabilities to overcome the structural barriers (both physical and social) that prevent their independence. Social workers can support efforts to broaden the rights guaranteed under the ADA and to assure that people with disabilities have the services they need to realize those rights.

Same-Sex Marriage

Same-sex marriage has evolved from a fringe movement, from which liberal politicians and LGBT activists kept their distance, to a central element of mainstream political disputes. During the 1980s and 1990s, supporters of gay rights lost many political battles to those who claimed to defend "family values."[21] Yet in recent years, the counterargument—that banning same-sex marriage is a form of discrimination—has gained the upper hand. In 2004 the National Association of Social Workers (NASW) adopted a policy in support of same-sex marriage and based its position on its code of ethics' opposition to discrimination in any form.[22]

The issue is likely to remain a feature of mainstream political activity for the foreseeable future. With so many states passing constitutional amendments banning same-sex marriage and a smaller number legalizing it through judicial or legislative action, we are likely to remain "one nation, divisible" on the subject. Social workers need to be active participants in this debate, which will vary from state to state. In the few "swing" states that have neither affirmed nor banned same-sex marriage, it is important to support efforts to expand marriage rights. In states that have banned it, incremental efforts to broaden the rights of domestic partners in health care, employment benefits, and other areas can serve to educate the broader public about the costs of continuing discrimination.

The battle at the federal level is hard to predict. The Defense of Marriage Act (DOMA) had prevented spouses in same-sex couples who are legally married from gaining access to Social Security benefits. The Supreme Court ruled in 2013 that DOMA's ban on federal recognition of same-sex marriages was unconstitutional, but it refused to address whether state bans violated Americans' equal protection rights.

State-level policy will probably become more complex. In New Jersey, for example, the Supreme Court ruling may push state courts to recognize same-sex marriages.[23] In several states with bans, local officials have defied those laws by issuing marriage licenses.[24] Article 4, Section 1 of the US Constitution states that each state shall give "full faith and credit" to the "public Acts, Records, and judicial Proceedings of every other State." DOMA has provided states with an exemption from this clause for issues of same-sex marriage, which the Supreme Court let stand.[25] Unless the court rules on the fundamental constitutionality of same-sex marriage, we will continue to encounter a wide variety of conflicts at the state level.

---

[21]John Gallagher and Chris Bull, *Perfect Enemies: The Battle Between the Religious Right and the Gay Movement* (Lanham, MD: Madison Books, 2001), 197–228.

[22]NASW, "Same-Sex Marriage Position Statement," June 28, 2004, http://www.naswdc.org/diversity/lgb/062804.asp?print=1.

[23]Kate Zernike, "New Jersey Court to Hear Same-Sex Marriage Case," *New York Times*, August 13, 2013, http://www.nytimes.com/2013/08/15/nyregion/new-jersey-court-to-hear-same-sex-marriage-case.html?_r=0.

[24]Fernanda Santos and Heath Haussamen, "Marriage Licenses for Same-Sex Couples Force Issue to fore in New Mexico," *New York Times*, September 2, 2013, http://www.nytimes.com/2013/09/03/us/in-new-mexico-a-rush-to-the-altar.html?pagewanted=all.

[25]E. J. Graff, "Supporters of Marriage Equality Need to Quit Whining," *The American Prospect*, May 11, 2012, http://prospect.org/article/supporters-marriage-equality-need-quit-whining.

Older Americans

Over the past generation, compared to other social groups, older Americans have lived a charmed life with respect to social welfare. Thanks to Social Security and Medicare, they are the only social group in the United States that has seen its poverty rate drop significantly and that does not suffer from lack of health insurance. While public assistance has been decimated, Supplemental Security Income (SSI) has continued to grow. While most Americans have seen their health care protection become more restrictive, Republicans championed the expansion of Medicare Advantage and prescription drug coverage in the 2000s.

But storm clouds are gathering. Old Age, Survivors, and Disability Insurance (OASDI) can easily deal with its financial challenges if the two parties are willing to compromise, as they did in 1983. Medicare, however, faces more substantial financial problems that the Affordable Care Act only begins to address. For the past generation, conservatives have pursued a strategy of "starving the beast": push for larger and larger tax cuts and use the resulting deficits to justify spending cuts. The strategy has worked for many social programs. As a result, programs for older Americans and people with disabilities now stand out as the only ones that have survived intact.

The recession of 2007–09 and the continuing weakness of the economy that followed have exerted strong crosscurrents. On the one hand, increasing deficits have again increased calls to cut "entitlement spending." At the same time, the recession has hurt the financial status of people nearing retirement more than any other age group.[26] The private tilt in retirement income policy—away from Social Security and defined-benefit plans and toward defined-contribution plans—is only now bringing the revelation that middle-income couples cannot save enough money to assure a secure retirement.[27]

Social workers can contribute to the debate by using their practice experience to explain the status of older Americans to the broader public, particularly to younger adults who are susceptible to the "greedy geezer" argument. Social workers have direct experience with the great number of elderly who live near the poverty line, their service needs, and the potential of program cuts to increase the financial burden on their adult children. With their body of firsthand knowledge, social workers are well-positioned to inform the debate about the future of aid to older Americans.

Child Welfare

In contrast to programs for older Americans—where social workers will need to defend the status quo—social work must take initiative to reform child welfare systems that aren't working and to create new institutions and policies that address the new realities faced by America's children, especially children living in poor and low-income families.

The fortunate part of being a new professional is that you can look to the future in deciding what matters. In the field of child welfare, it will take a generation to build the institutions necessary to assure that all children reach adulthood with real opportunity to lead a rewarding life.

Let's begin with poverty. The poverty rate among children is currently above 20 percent. Although many children are raised out of poverty thanks to OASDI, no other

[26]Catherine Rampell, "Big Income Losses for Those Near Retirement," *New York Times*, August 23, 2012, http://economix.blogs.nytimes.com/2012/08/23/big-income-losses-for-those-near-retirement/?hp.

[27]Jacob Hacker, *The Great Risk Shift: The New Economic Insecurity and the Decline of the American Dream* (New York: Oxford University Press, 2008), 109–136.

program makes a significant contribution to reducing official poverty among children. Using a broader definition of poverty—like the Supplemental Poverty Measure discussed in Chapter 4—we know that several tax credits, such as the Earned Income Tax Credit and the Child Tax Credit, contribute to improving the economic circumstances of low-income families with children.

A variety of approaches have been suggested for expanding aid to these families. An assets-based approach, like that suggested by Richard Gelles, seeks to have government make annual contributions to individual accounts for every American child.[28] Others have advocated a basic children's allowance like that of other developed nations.

The breakdown of institutions that serve children poses risks, as well. Social workers can help develop an integrated system of services in support of parents and children— like that suggested by Jane Waldfogel—to replace a system that intervenes only when a parent "crosses the line" into abuse or neglect;[29] support the expansion of parental leave, child care for working parents, and preschool opportunities; advocate to improve the educational opportunities available to low-income urban residents; and reform our systems for financing public education to reduce geographical disparities.

Given the current political and fiscal climate, it is hard to imagine any of these approaches getting much of a hearing, but that doesn't reduce their need. More than any other field discussed in this book, social workers must contribute to changing the conversation about the well-being of children, youth, and families through civic engagement at all levels from the local community to the nation. Promoting public discourse on these issues will take persistence and patience. It will require facts and data and stories that illustrate the realities faced by children growing up in today's America.

At the same time, social workers must be willing to *not* do something: defend failed systems. We know that many social workers in the child welfare system are now asked to undertake impossible jobs—essentially, to give full attention to every case they're responsible for but also to take on two or three times the number of cases they can adequately supervise.

Assess your comprehension of "Policy Practice Opportunities" by completing this quiz.

BRIAN BRAINERD / DENVER POST / GETTY IMAGES

Nola Miguel, a social worker at Bruce Randolph School and 7-year-old Lorissa Rios attending a meeting to discuss Denver Public Schools and weigh in on how to improve them.

---

[28]Richard Gelles, *The Third Lie: Why Government Programs Don't Work and A Blueprint for Change* (Walnut Creek, CA: Left Coast Press, 2011), 79–88.

[29]Jane Waldfogel, *The Future of Child Protection: How to Break the Cycle of Abuse and Neglect* (Cambridge: Harvard University Press, 2001).

In some situations, reform will require caseworkers to blow the whistle on failures in the child welfare system.

CONCLUSION: THE NEXT SOCIAL WELFARE SYSTEM

The publication of this book coincides with a very discouraging time in the history of social welfare. Many programs that have historically supported low-income people have been eliminated. Many rights of marginalized groups are being challenged and undermined by state legislators and federal courts. Even our bedrock social welfare programs—Social Security and Medicare—have become fair game. And the major social welfare policy success of the past generation, health care reform, faces an uncertain future.

It's at times like this that I return to history. American history has unfolded in long waves. Certain ideas inspired a past generation, which used them to construct and bequeath institutions. Over time, as that generation has faded, its ideas and institutions—which once seemed so fresh and exciting—have become the "conventional wisdom" that the next generation has sought to challenge and undermine.

It is my belief (or should I say, it is my hope) that we are in the final years of a long swing that began with the rise of Conservative America during the 1970s. The traumas and turmoil of the 1960s set America on a cultural trajectory dominated by distrust in government and fear of economic decline and racial conflict. A cultural narrative of "taking the country back" from alien forces merged with an economic agenda focused on shifting economic and political power back to a small elite.

This Conservative ideology has appealed to a generation of Americans worried about racial strife and economic decline, but these ideas have now become stale. The most fervent supporters today are the so-called Tea Party movement, a movement dominated by aging older white Americans who, ironically, are as worried about protecting their government-run pensions and health care as they are about the federal deficit.[30]

As new professionals, you and your classmates are entering the field of social work at a promising time in American history. Over your careers, we are likely to see a revival of Americans' concern for truly equal opportunity and social equity. This shift won't happen automatically. As the next generation, you will have to build the movements, the ideas, and the institutions that challenge what has gone before. In so doing, you will make your contribution to a long legacy. As you pursue your practice, you will need as well to engage social welfare policy.

Assess your analysis and evaluation of the chapter's content by completing the Chapter Review.

---

[30]Theda Skocpol and Vanessa Williamson, *The Tea Party and the Remaking of Republican Conservatism* (New York: Oxford University Press, 2012).

Index

US Department of Education, 43, 116, 225
US Department of Health and Human Services, 43, 48, 191, 192, 195, 197, 200, 223, 224, 251, 267, 270
US Department of Housing and Urban Development, 43, 85, 86, 129, 139, 145
US Department of Labor, 29, 198, 248
US Department of Veterans' Affairs, 172
US Equal Employment Opportunity Commission, 251
US General Accounting Office, 15
US Medicare Payment Advisory Commission, 163
US National Institute of Justice, 219
US President's New Freedom Commission on Mental Health, 173, 175
US Social Security Administration, 43, 85, 87, 236, 237, 240, 241, 246, 247
US Substance Abuse and Mental Health Services Administration, 176
US v. Morrison (2000), 50
Utility theories, 76

V
VA. *See* Veterans Administration (VA)
VAWA. *See* Violence Against Women Act (VAWA) of 1994
Venkatesh, S., 146
Vericker, T., 272
Vertical adequacy, 13, 186
Vertical integration, 30–31
Veterans Administration (VA), 172
Veterans health care system, 172
and Medical Benefits Package, 172
Vidal, A., 146
Violence, 215–221
and gender, 215–221
Violence Against Women Act (VAWA) of 1994, 50, 217, 221, 297
Violence Against Women Survey, 219
Vitiello, D., 114
Vladeck, B., 162
Voluntary charity, 63, 64

von Drehle, D., 67
Voter ID laws, 215
Voting Rights Act, 1965, 127
Vouchers, 11

W
Wacquant, L., 206, 207, 214
Wages for housework campaign, 253
Wagner-Murray-Dingell proposals of 1940s, 157
Waldfogel, J., 16, 274, 275, 281, 283, 301
Walking-around money (WAMs), 42
Waller, M., 199, 200
Walmsley, R., 213
WAMs. *See* Walking-around money (WAMs)
"War on crime" of 1968, 214
War on drugs in 1971, 214
Wealth, 80–81
Wealth creation, 119
Weavers Way Community Programs, 114
Webb, A., 248
Webster, C., 158
Weil, L. A., 156
Weil, M., 142
Weinberg, D. H, 197, 225
Weir, M., 36, 37, 39
Welfare, 69
Welfare capitalism, 25–27, 156–157
Esping-Andersen's analysis, 25–27
"hard" services, 157
"softer" services, 157
Welfare capitalism movement, 247
Welfare reform, 178, 191
Welfare reform law of 1996, 16, 47
Welfare regimes, 25–27
conservative, 25
liberal, 25–26
social democratic, 25–26
Wenocur, S., 143
West, J., 196, 278
Westat, 274
Western, B., 213
Wheeler, J., 36
WIA. *See* Workforce Investment Act (WIA), 1998
WIC. *See* Women, Infants, and Children (WIC)
Wildavsky, A., 291
Wilensky, H. L., 23

Williamson, V., 302
Wilson, W. J., 92
Window of opportunity, for reforms, 154
Winne, M., 113
Witte, J., 277
Wolff, E. N., 81, 119
Women, Infants, and Children (WIC), 95, 110–111
administration, 111
benefits, 110–111
eligibility, 110
categorical, 110
income, 110
nutritional risk, 110
residential, 110
financing, 111
Women's oppression, 215–221
discrimination, in hiring and promotion, 215–216
domestic violence, 220
marriage equality, 228–229
unequal treatment, in education, 216
Women's work, 179
Women violence, 297–298
Woodward, C. V., 68, 126
Woolley, J. T., 98
Workforce Investment Act (WIA), 1998, 198–200
Work Incentive Improvement Act of 1999, 226
World Health Organization, 81, 154
Wrigley, E. A., 100
Wyatt v. Stickney, 175

Y
Yates Report (1824), 63
Yunus, M., 285

Z
Zelizer, V. A., 64, 66
Zernike, K., 299
Zerubavel, E., 54
Zhao, Z., 113
Zimmer, R., 277
Ziol-Guest, K. M., 269
Zuckerman, S., 167